ALL OUR FUTURES

Principles and Resources
for Social Work Practice
in a Global Era

CHATHAPURAM S. RAMANATHAN

Chathapuram S. Ramanathan, PhD, ACSW, LMFT, is president and chief executive officer of Human Service Enterprises. He has been a social work educator for 15 years and has taught in graduate schools of social work for over ten years. During the summer of 1992, on behalf of Michigan State University, Dr. Ramanathan and a colleague initiated and implemented a social work theory and practicum in the context of India. His research and publications include international social welfare, cross-cultural social work, occupational social work and substance abuse. He has published twenty refereed articles and has contributed to several books and monographs. Dr. Ramanathan has presented over fifty papers and workshops in the United States, Canada, India, Sri Lanka, and Portugal. He serves on the editorial boards of three journals. For two years he served on the Michigan Department of Mental Health's committee on multicultural mental health education and training. He is a current member of the Council on Social Work Education's International Commission since 1992. He has also served the Council as a trained site visitor.

ROSEMARY J. LINK

Rosemary J. Link, PhD, LISW, CQSW, is professor of social work and chair, Professional Studies Division, Augsburg College, Minneapolis, Minnesota USA. Dr. Link chaired the Augsburg College Department of Social Work through the initial accreditation of their MSW program and is teaching in both social work and the Augsburg Graduate Program in Leadership. Dr. Link is a current commissioner for the Council on Social Work Education (U.S.) and is an external examiner for the University of the West Indies at Mona, Jamaica. As a former school and family social worker in North London, England, Dr. Link has a special interest in children's rights and family participation in social service planning. Dr. Link has published several articles relating to children, poverty, and family centers, and her next book is an analysis of the impact of U.S. welfare reform on children in poverty. Dr. Link is also co-chair of the NASW, Minnesota Chapter International Committee. She has co-taught student courses in Mexico, the United Kingdom, and Slovenia with colleagues in those countries and has presented papers on international issues in social work in Slovenia, Mexico, the United Kingdom, and, in the summer of 1998, in Israel and India.

ALL OUR FUTURES

Principles and Resources for Social Work Practice in a Global Era

CHATHAPURAM S. RAMANATHAN AND ROSEMARY J. LINK
with a foreword by
SHANTI KHINDUKA

BROOKS/COLE • WADSWORTH
I(T)P® An International Thomson Publishing Company

Belmont • Albany • Bonn • Boston • Cincinnati • Johannesburg • London • Madrid • Melbourne
Mexico City • New York • Pacific Grove • Scottsdale • Singapore • Tokyo • Toronto

Sponsoring Editor: *Lisa I. Gebo*
Marketing Team: *Steve Catalano, Aaron Eden*
Editorial Assistant: *Susan Wilson*
Advertising Communications: *Margaret Parks*
Production Coordinator: *Kelsey McGee*
Production Service: *Matrix Productions/*
  Merrill Peterson

Manuscript Editor: *Victoria Nelson*
Interior Design: *Adriane Bosworth*
Cover Design: *Laurie Albrecht*
Photography: *Donna DeCesare*
Typesetting: *R&S Book Composition/Susan Gerber*
Cover Printing/Printing and Binding:
  WebCom, Limited

For more information, contact:

WADSWORTH PUBLISHING COMPANY
10 Davis Drive
Belmont, CA 94002
USA

International Thomson Publishing Europe
Berkshire House 168-173
High Holborn
London WC1V 7AA
England

Thomas Nelson Australia
102 Dodds Street
South Melbourne, 3205
Victoria, Australia

Nelson Canada
1120 Birchmount Road
Scarborough, Ontario
Canada M1K 5G4

International Thomson Editores
Seneca 53
Col. Polanco
11560 México, D. F., México

International Thomson Publishing GmbH
Königswinterer Strasse 418
53227 Bonn
Germany

International Thomson Publishing Asia
60 Albert Street
#15-01 Albert Complex
Singapore 189969

International Thomson Publishing Japan
Hirakawacho Kyowa Building, 3F
2-2-1 Hirakawacho
Chiyoda-ku, Tokyo 102
Japan

Printed in Canada

10 9 8 7 6 5 4 3 2 1

Library of Congress Cataloging-in-Publication Data
Ramanathan, Chathapuram S.
    All our futures: principles and resources for social work practice
in a global era/Chathapuram S. Ramanathan & Rosemary J. Link;
with a foreword by Shanti Khinduka.
        p. cm.
    Includes bibliographical references and index.
    ISBN 0-534-35587-0
    1. Social service—Methodology. 2. Social service—International cooperation.
  I. Link, Rosemary J. II. Title.
HV40.R284 1998
361.3—dc21   98-24882
                                                                  CIP

This book is dedicated to our children, whose love, joyful expectation and creativity is our inspiration:

Vinay Swami Ramanathan
Sophie Doris Link
Amy Gwendoline Link
Alexander Mitchell Link

and all the children of the world, who are our future

Contents

CHAPTER FIVE

Infusing Global Perspectives into Social Work Values and Ethics   69
Rosemary J. Link

CHAPTER SIX

Global Approaches to Learning Social Welfare Policy   94
Anthony Bibus and Rosemary J. Link

CHAPTER SEVEN

Informational Tools for Social Workers: Research in the Global Age   121
Richard Estes

CHAPTER TWELVE

. . . .

Professional Growth in the Global Context   206

John F. Jones and Asfaw Kumssa

CHAPTER THIRTEEN

. . . .

Future Visions for Global Studies in Social Work   219

Chathapuram S. Ramanathan and Rosemary J. Link

Foreword

Despite its lofty rhetoric that exalts human interdependence and international cooperation, social work in the United States has largely remained an America-centered profession. Social work education, too, has failed to make serious strides to learn or teach about the rest of the world. The Curriculum Policy Statement of the Council on Social Work Education includes no more than an innocuous and fleeting pronouncement about the interdependence of nations and the need for worldwide professional cooperation. Only a handful of programs offer even a single course on international social work. In most institutions library resources on international social welfare and social development are pitifully inadequate. The situation is no better with regard to financial support for foreign students to study social work in the U.S. or for U.S. students and faculty to study social work in other countries. Faculty exchange programs between U.S. schools of social work and educational institutions abroad are few and feeble. Fewer than 600 international students at the baccalaureate, masters, and doctoral levels were enrolled in U.S. social work educational programs last year out of a total that approached 50,000. Although data on American students studying social work in other nations do not exist, one can surmise their number is smaller still. Both U.S. students and faculty remain indifferent to learning foreign languages. No wonder that social work faculty and students in general have little consciousness and less involvement in international social work. This ignorance and insularity feed the unspoken but widespread notion that U.S. social work offers a model of social work practice worth emulating by other nations.

Fortunately, even in America there exist a band of active scholars who forcefully challenge this conclusion and its underlying assumptions and premises. In *All Our Futures*, Drs. Chatapuram S. Ramanathan and Rosemary J. Link, co-editors and authors or co-authors of seven of the thirteen chapters, show that countries in the Global North as well as the Global South can fruitfully learn from each other's experience with regard to framing social problems, formulating social policies, crafting culturally relevant methods of practice interventions, organizing local communities, and mobilizing indigenous resources. They warn against considering the United States as the fount of all social work wisdom or innovation. And they make a passionate plea, instead, for mutuality and reciprocity among nations and among professionals across national boundaries.

The contributors to this volume include prominent social work educators with a deep and abiding commitment to international collaboration in social work. They argue that many problems of the contemporary world can neither be analyzed intelligently nor combated effectively without a transnational perspective. They demonstrate, for example, that migration, structural unemployment, violence, hunger, and refugee rehabilitation are international issues, that the challenge to help a growing elderly population is not confined to one country or continent, that the hopes, fears and dreams of children are a concern for all who care for the well being of humanity, that the problems of drugs, AIDS, child labor, ethnic discord, poverty and social exclusion must be addressed as global challenges.

Social work educators and students will find the various chapters of the book instructive in their discussion of such required content as social work values and ethics, human diversity, promotion of social and economic justice, populations at risk, human behavior and social environment, social welfare policies and services, social work practice, social research, and field work. The imaginative assignments at the end of each chapter should help the student synthesize the material covered in the chapter.

But the book goes beyond discussing the CSWE-prescribed areas in a social work curriculum. By including an informative chapter on computer and internet resources on international social work, it encourages students to explore this area further on their own. The discussion of structural readjustments required by the World Bank and the International Monetary Fund introduces material frequently ignored by social work educational programs. Several chapters cite important United Nations conventions, some of which have been ratified by a vast majority of other countries but not yet by the United States. The promising concept of social development, inexplicably neglected in much of American social work education, is explained in a lucid chapter. Similarly, practical tips are offered for faculty development programs for international social work as well as for developing field practica abroad.

One does not have to agree with every assertion, every claim, every criticism, and every proposal advanced by the learned editors and authors of this exceedingly useful volume to be grateful for their contribution to the profession of social work by this gift of a sorely needed source that is unique, timely, and reader-friendly. If part of the reason for the insularity of American social work can be attributed to the relative paucity of usable teaching material on international social work, the publication of this book should help us transcend our provincial interpretation of a profession whose value base of universal human rights makes it an inherently international and global enterprise.

Shanti K. Khinduka
Dean, George Warren Brown School of Social Work
Washington University, St. Louis

Preface

This book grew out of the authors' philosophical framework, which affirms the interdependence of nations and a commitment to sustainable human development globally. These beliefs are in line with the United Nations development reports and the Convention on the Rights of the Child and are shared by the team of contributors. Furthermore, the themes of connection and interaction among social workers worldwide along with the emphasis on reciprocity of professional technology and practice rather than the export of expertise from Western nations to the Global South are consistent throughout the book and are reflected in the orientation of all the writers. Similarly, the commitment to use of language that does not stereotype nations as "Third" or "First World," developing or developed, as well as language that is gender neutral, is woven throughout the text. This philosophical approach serves both as the foundation for the book and as the framework for the lively debate and presentation of a variety of perspectives on the exhilarating and timely topic of reaching out for more global content in social work practice. The material gathered here reflects the social work profession's attempt to facilitate a more humane and multidimensional approach to social and economic development. Throughout the book there is also both a commitment and a sensitivity to "marginalized" citizens of the globe.

This volume's team of writers has worked closely together at a number of levels, including the International Commission of the Council on Social Work Education (U.S.) and the International Association of Schools of Social Work (global). The principal authors, who are cowriters in equal collaboration for seven of the thirteen chapters, have appreciated the close working relationships, support, and encouragement for this book from the team of prestigious contributors who have shared our vision. The vivid, poignant images of Donna De Cesare's lens have added a further powerful dimension to the narrative.

In accomplishing the work of this book, the authors wish to acknowledge C. V. Swaminathan, Mark A. Peterson, and Subbiah Kannappan for their helpful feedback; Lavanya Krishnan for her inspiring poem in Chapter 13; Amy Brallier for her secretarial support; and Andrew Link, Pravina Ramanathan, and writers' group colleagues Anthony Bibus, Ron Rooney, Kim Strom-Gottfried, and Maura Sullivan for their constant encouragement. We are also grateful for the detailed and constructive feedback of our reviewers: Sonia Jackson, University of Swansea, Wales; Howard Karger, University of Houston; Shanti Khinduka, Washington University; Margaret Martin, East Connecticut State University; Gary May, University of Southern Indiana; and David F. Metzger, Indiana University.

The writers also wish to acknowledge the continuing inspiration of Katherine Kendall, Nanavatty Meher, and the memory of Daniel Sanders, Constance Fabumni, and Dame Eileen Younghusband, whose vision this century has been unwavering in helping us to seek a peaceful and more just world.

About the Contributors

Yvonne Asamoah, PhD, is a professor at the Hunter College School of Social Work. She is currently chair of the Human Behavior and Social Environment sequence and chair of the Council on Social Work Education's International Commission. Her professional interests include consulting on multicultural issues, multicultural training, aging, homeless women with children, and international issues in the social work curriculum. She presents often at national and international conferences and was in charge of the social work program in Ghana for a number of years.

Anthony Bibus, PhD, is the BSW program director and teaches social work at Augsburg College in Minneapolis, Minnesota, U.S.A. He has been a social worker for over 25 years. Since receiving his doctorate in social work from the University of Minnesota in 1992, he has been focusing on how much social workers can learn from each other worldwide. He is consulting editor for the *Journal of Baccalaureate Social Work and Community Alternatives International Journal of Family Care.*

Doreen Elliott, PhD, is professor of social work and director of the doctoral program at the University of Texas at Arlington. For many years she was on the faculty of the School of Social Work at the University of Wales (Cardiff). Her recent books include *The World of Social Welfare: Social Welfare and Services in an International Context; The International Handbook on Social Work Education;* and *The International Handbook on Social Work Theory and Practice,* coedited with Nazneen Mayadas and Thomas Watts. Other international activities include research and presentation of papers in New Zealand, Russia, and India. Other published work, consisting of numerous articles, book chapters, and three books, has focused on social work in the residential setting; juvenile delinquency; field practice in social work education; comparative international approaches to policy and social work education; and, most recently, theory building and the search for an international approach in social work through social development.

Richard J. Estes, PhD, is professor of social work at the University of Pennsylvania. Dr. Estes's international activities have been extensive. He has held visiting professorships in Iran, Norway, the People's Republic of China, Morocco, Korea, Hawaii, St. Louis, Japan, Mongolia, the Russian Federation, Belgium, and elsewhere. Dr. Estes currently is a special consultant in social development to the United Nation's Economic and Social Commission for Asia and the Pacific (Bangkok). He also serves as senior advisor to the Preparatory Group of China United Foundations, China's national organizing committee of emerging private foundations. In the United States, Dr. Estes is the founding president of the Philadelphia Area Chapter of the Society for International Development (SID). In 1997 he was awarded the "Distinguished Recent Contribution to Social Work Education Award" by the Council on Social Work Education, the International Rhoda G. Sarnat Prize of the National Association of Social Workers (NASW), and the Best Article in *Social Indicators Research*

Award of the International Society of Quality of Life Studies. Dr. Estes has written numerous articles; his books include: *At the Crossroads: Dilemmas in Social Development Toward the Year 2000 and Beyond* (New York: Praeger, in press); *Internationalizing Social Work Education: A Guide to Resources for a New Century* (Philadelphia: University of Pennsylvania School of Social Work, 1992).

Lynne M. Healy, MSW, PhD, is professor and director, Center for International Social Work Studies at the University of Connecticut School of Social Work. She is a member of the boards of CSWE and IASSW, past chair of CSWE's International Commission, and has been a visiting professor/lecturer in Jamaica and Mauritius. Her publications focus on administration, women and leadership, and international social work education. Dr. Healy is a member of the editorial board of *Administration in Social Work* and the *Asia Pacific Journal of Social Work.*

John F. Jones is professor at the University of Denver Graduate School of Social Work and previously dean. Prior to serving at UD, he was chair professor of social work at the Chinese University of Hong Kong. He was also founding dean of the School of Social Development at the University of Minnesota–Duluth. He has written numerous books on social development, international social work, and social work education.

Asfaw Kumssa, PhD, is the coordinator of the United Nations Center for Regional Development (UNCRD) Africa Office in Nairobi, Kenya. He earned his MS in national economic planning from Odessa National Economic Planning Institute, Ukraine, and his MA and PhD from the University of Denver, where he was subsequently adjunct professor of economics and global political economy. Dr. Kumssa has published in the *International Review of Administrative Sciences, Journal of African Studies, Social Development Issues, Regional Development Studies,* and *Regional Development Dialogue.* He recently coedited a book with Carolyn L. Gates, *Transition of Asian, African and European Economies to the Market, and Socioeconomic Dislocations* (UNCRD, 1998).

Karen Lyons, PhD, CQSW, is reader in social work at the University of East London. She has substantial experience in the field of European exchange schemes and has run a degree program in international social work studies since 1994. Her research interests include education and career patterns of social workers as well as comparative and international social work. The last area is reflected in a forthcoming text, "International Social Work: Themes and Perspectives."

Nazneen S. Mayadas, PhD, is professor of social work at the University of Texas in Arlington. She has taught as an exchange professor in Wales, the United Kingdom, and as a visiting professor at Washington University, St. Louis. Her practice experience has been in India, Canada, and the United States. She has served as chief of social services in the office of the United Nations High Commissioner for Refugees (UNHCR), where she acquired familiarity with social services in Africa, Asia, Europe, and Central and South America. She has published numerous articles and book chapters in the areas of clinical practice and international social work. With Paul Glasser she coedited *Group Workers at Work.* She is the coeditor with Thomas Watts and Doreen Elliott of three *International Handbook* volumes on social welfare, social work education, and social work practice.

James Midgley, PhD, is Harry and Riva Specht Professor and Dean of the School of Social Welfare at the University of California at Berkeley. He was previously at Louisiana State University, where he served as dean of the School of Social Work and as associate vice chancellor. Prior to serving at LSU, he taught at the London School of Economics and the University of Cape Town. He has published 17 books on social work, social policy, and development; some 40 book chapters; and 70 journal articles. He serves on the editorial boards of eight major journals. He has given the Daniel Sanders Memorial Lecture at the University of Illinois, the Peter Hodge Memorial Lecture at the University of Hong Kong, the Kenneth L. Pray Lecture at the University of Pennsylvania and the Allen T. Burns Lecture at the University of Chicago. In 1996, he received the International Rhoda Sarnat Prize from NASW for his efforts to enhance public recognition of social work.

Arline Prigoff, PhD, is a professor in the Division of Social Work at California State University, Sacramento and a current member of the International Commission of the Council on Social Work Education. Her group seminar on international social work focuses on the social consequences of economic globalization and on community economic development.

Introduction

ROSEMARY J. LINK
CHATHAPURAM S. RAMANATHAN

The world was my university.

—INDIRA GANDHI

There is a world of learning in social work that has yet to be fully explored. Everywhere we see evidence of the shrinking of the globe through enhanced information technology, travel opportunities, and economic development, but it seems that social work educators and practitioners have been slow to recognize the interdependence of national, continental, and cultural systems and thereby slow to encourage international awareness in their students. This book addresses the current expectation and implementation process for social work students and faculty to become more global in their professional endeavors. It defines the realities of our contemporary interdependence and identifies strategies to bring 21st-century social workers naturally to a global attitude.

Continually expanding international trade is the reality for national economies throughout the world, including the United States (Yandrick, 1986). Few students in the Global North are unfamiliar with the Gap clothing company, and some participated in the Gap Project protest, which alerted consumers to the exploitation of child and women's labor. The global nature of the contemporary economy is a reality and because of this the transfer of social and instrumental technology is inevitable and has tended to flow from countries of the Global North to the Global South (Ramanathan, 1991). In the past the transfer of social work knowledge has also been unidirectional. However, Midgley (1997) argues that social workers in the north have much to learn from social workers in the south. Our book is based on this belief—that social workers across the globe can always learn from each other in an atmosphere of reciprocity where social and economic injustice is challenged. Scholars have argued that as economically powerful countries such as the united states of the European Union and the United States of America move into the 21st century, they need to forge a new relationship that shifts "from the old ideas of aid, to the new idea of mutual gain through cooperation" (Smuckler, Berg, Gordon, 1988, vi).

There are signs that this shift is happening—for example, in the increasing numbers of papers on global topics discussing mutual gain through cooperation that are delivered at national and international conferences. However, the daily routines of social workers have still to incorporate global resources (Prigoff, 1995; Healy, 1996). In February 1996, the U.S. National Association of Social Workers national teleconference presented vignettes of communities organizing creatively across the globe, providing reminders of the universal themes of poverty, violence, and social and economic injustice that are the core causes to which social work is devoted (NASW, 1996). In this video conference, the narrator Charles Kuralt commented on the unique leadership that social workers can bring to global understanding. Therefore, the millennium brings a task ahead for social workers to articulate the universal themes of the profession while acknowledging and respecting local differences (Midgley, 1997; Guzzetta, 1996).

To facilitate professional standards of practice and integrity, a general practice in social work education worldwide is to try to guarantee a knowledge base for the profession. Sometimes accrediting bodies and professional associations serve to establish what this knowledge base consists of and what the curriculum should be. It is the premise of this text that sharing learning with others globally is a fundamental task that still needs further implementation in social work curriculum. For instance, the International Federation of Social Workers' Ethics Committee is working on an international code of ethics, and the U.S. Council on Social Work Education Standards states that "effective social work education programs recognize the interdependence of nations and the need for worldwide professional cooperation" (CSWE Standards, USA, 1994).

This book has the following goals:

- To capture the imagination of students and educators in developing the conceptual base of global interdependence in social work.

- To provide resources and foster innovation in coursework and field internship experiences.

- To identify technology and strategies for participatory learning that help to narrow the gap in the ways students learn about global innovations in practice; to increase attention to practice innovations originating in southern nations that are applicable to northern nations.

- To review global experience and to identify comparative case studies that illustrate creativity in one part of the world that is relevant to another.

- To identify elements of social work that are core elements for international practice.

- To contribute to the development of general principles in the social work profession worldwide while simultaneously respecting the uniqueness of local history and culture.

This book's framework draws on Bloom's (1956) taxonomy of learning, which identifies steps in processing new ideas ranging from description of knowledge and comparison to analysis, practical application, evaluation, and synthesis. Cross's (1986) work on "cultural competence" has also been drawn upon in a parallel process to prompt awareness of the stage that practitioners, educators or social work agencies may have reached. These stages range from historically destructive attitudes, such as colonialism or insular attitudes toward the rest of the world, to neutral ideas based on geocentrism, to precompetence, competence, and advanced competence in cultural interaction—which in this context means continually reaching to participate in globally oriented work. The standards of the U.S. accrediting body, the Council on Social Work Education, have been utilized as a guide in organizing the chapters. These standards may be geocentric in part, but they are open to innovation and are the basis for the accreditation of widely varying professional programs within the United States, from Howard and Atlanta universities in the African-American tradition, to the traditional top ten universities, to church- and culturally related smaller programs. This encouragement of innovation provides opportunities in the classroom for reviewing the relevance of global experience and case studies from a range of countries, but it also leads into the wider arena of global issues and general principles in the profession worldwide.

Schools of social work in Asia and Africa have similar centralized accrediting standards and are often connected to the international professional associations. Europe is gathering data for the equivalency of social work qualifications that is organized from the European Commission in Brussels, and Britain's National Institute of Social Work has oversight for all British programs. An integrative framework for this global approach has been developed and is portrayed in Table 1.1, and this framework will be developed in each chapter. Column heads represent the broad topic areas of social work programs in many countries; vertical columns represent variables relating to global social work.

Despite the increasing attention to curriculum standards, the inconsistency in the ways students learn about global innovations in practice is well documented. For instance, in their research outlining social work in a variety of countries, Hokenstad, Khinduka, and Midgley (1992) state that "relatively few [U.S.] social workers have studied social welfare programs or social work practice in other countries during their professional education; fewer still have had practice experience in another nation or with an international organization." In 1992, Jackson spoke of British social work education as just beginning to look beyond its borders, given the impetus of the European Community initiatives in transfer qualifications and professional equivalency (Jackson, 1992). Since then, the European Social Charter has been drafted in order to promote mobility of labor and to examine the economic and social needs and opportunities of families and children and to review the equity of women's wages (Santer, 1995). Diffusion of Western social service/social work technology to the southern nations is also well documented in the literature (Gangarde, 1970; Nagpaul, 1972). Practitioners in India, for example, are concerned that there is a hierarchy of methodology; they believe that European-American models hold too much influence to the exclusion of creativity throughout the world, resulting in cultural borrowing that does not fit or benefit indigenous communities (Khinduka, 1971; Peters & Link, 1990).

Students are invited to reflect and to formulate their own interpretation to the current combination of resistance and uneven interest in global issues. Questions frequently raised

TABLE 1.1

Framework to Assess Engagement in Global Social Work Learning

Elements of global social work	Practice and Field
Personal review of global awareness	interested in other countries and world regions
Knowledge of mutual learning country to country	comparing work philosophy, social role, choices across countries
Understanding of cultural competence and respectful language	proactive in exploring culture, aware of own bias and prejudice
Analysis of human rights	applying UN documents to practice
Historical analysis	knowing impact of past on current resources, socioeconomic status
Review of values and ethics	identifying implications of different approaches, country codes
Evaluation of local variations	exploring theories in different nations
Synthesis of professional activity	seeking alternatives, links with other places, building with global awareness

by those who resist this content will be addressed and replaced with proactive responses framed as questions such as the following:

1. Why study global concerns when there are so many domestic issues to cope with?
2. How can we fit in more areas of study on top of so much curriculum?
3. Does a global approach promote uniformity over cultural uniqueness?

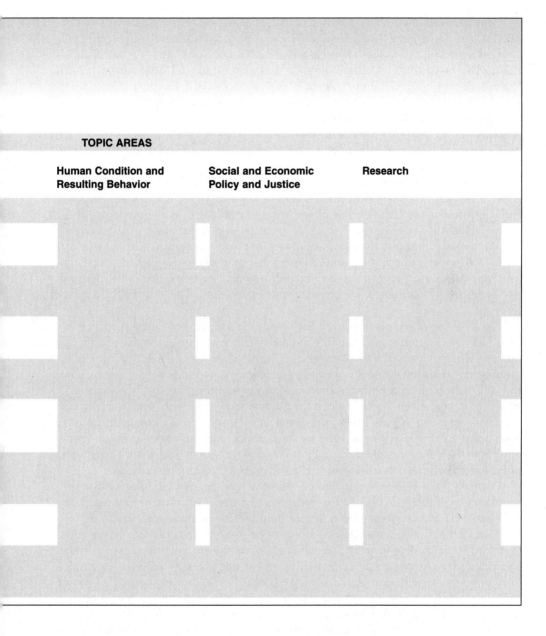

TOPIC AREAS

Human Condition and Resulting Behavior	Social and Economic Policy and Justice	Research

4. What do we mean by "cultural borrowing," anyway?

5. How does a global perspective promote enhancement of the quality of life of people served through the social work profession?

This process of questioning and responding is carried out through all the chapters, thus facilitating the integration of the learning experience. Students who actively reflect will also feel confident about taking responsibility in promoting the efficacy of a global view.

Consistent with the authors' philosophical premise, we will be moving beyond the "developed" and "developing" categories and referring to nations collectively in geographically oriented terms. For this text we are using the terms "Global North" and "Global South," as classified by the UNCTAD (United Nations Committee on Trade and Development). Global North designates northern Europe, eastern European economies in transition, North America, and the southern exceptions Japan, Singapore, Australia, and New Zealand. We hope this terminology will soon become obsolete as we move toward global recognition of the common human condition. We cite the exceptions to point out the existing indicators that define the globe in economic terms alone; when we include social and political constructs, we redefine these labels and simply use geographic locations.

Economically we will examine examples from the Global South, such as the Grameen Bank or the Self-Employed Women's Association (SEWA), which have incorporated and challenged traditional classifications of workers and producers. As the producers of the women's film, *A People's Alternative,* state: "Never underestimate the power of a woman with a video camera. . . . the tape shows women who do not have electricity in their homes learning how to produce, direct, shoot and edit video. For most of these women 'rewind,' 'stop,' 'play' and 'pause' are their first words of English" (Media Network Guide, 1994). Technology is not evenly distributed, but capacity and initiative are. This fact will be a theme throughout the book.

The gathering of authors in this text demonstrates a wide range of international experience, social work expertise, and humility about how far we have yet to travel in reaching for universal elements in social work education. In Chapter 13 we revisit the tension between respecting indigenization of social work while reaching for universal principles that reinforce the work of the profession. From an interdisciplinary perspective, Ramsey Clark, former U.S. Attorney General, states: "Social justice is the end that social work seeks, and social justice is the chance for peace" (Clark, 1988). Furthermore, the assumption of all contributors to the book is that learning is a two-way street for all countries, simultaneously sharing and benefiting from the innovations of others, and that no one set of nations, such as the United States or European countries, has more answers than others based on historical context.

Currently, there is increasing awareness that structural poverty and injustice have universal features in urban and rural areas throughout the world. Relevant here are definitions of "sustainable human development," drawn from the United Nations statement on contemporary human conditions (United Nations, 1995)—conditions that encompass countries where human development is jeopardized by ambivalent political support, meager social budgets, underresourced communities, and stressed, heavily indebted economies. Even in relatively well-resourced areas of the Global North, human service budgets are shrinking, urban communities are under severe strain, and social workers must constantly defend themselves. B. Jordan, writing from a European perspective, refers to social work everywhere as "a political act," thus raising the universal issue of how far commitment goes in reducing poverty and injustice (Jordan, 1988; Clark, 1988). The political, economic, and social nature of social work are constantly interlinked, and these realities are the foundation of this book.

It is therefore another goal of this text to further understanding of those core elements of social work across the globe that can strengthen the profession when recognized collectively. The text anticipates that this dialogue will simultaneously respect local differences. At a 1996 conference in the United States, Guzzetta (1996) reminded colleagues that economists and information technologists have long realized the importance of common language to further their networks and that social work has a challenge ahead to establish global principles. Guzzetta asked his colleagues to promote an academic environment that expects to learn from country to country well beyond the traditional European-American tradition of exporting "Western consulting skills to southern nations . . . In the act of seeking a common language for social work, of understanding economic, physical, social aspects of the human condition, we will find more universals than differences and many unexpected sources of learning" (Guzzetta, 1996).

BUILDING CURRICULAR INITIATIVES

With the power of language as an integral part of the book, curricular initiatives and written commitments are explored in a number of regions, including the development of social work programs in India, the U.S. Council on Social Work Education's development of standards, and the collaboratives currently being built in the European Union to build credential exchange (for example, through the Maastricht Program and the Slovenia/Spain/United Kingdom curriculum cooperative).

U.S. international educators (Kendall, 1969; Sanders, 1986) have espoused global approaches to curriculum over the last decades, and they have explicitly acknowledged the value and utility of contributions of social work practitioners and educators globally. However, it is striking that for the first time in its history, the U.S. CSWE revised its standards in 1995 explicitly to make the commitment quoted earlier—that in order "to be effective," curriculum must "recognize the interdependence of nations and the need for worldwide professional cooperation." Although this wording is written into the accreditation document, it has yet to appear in the Interpretative Guidelines that help to operationalize compliance for U.S. schools of social work. Thus, infusing global issues into curriculum in the U.S. is still a slow process that is perhaps indicative of the uneven path in many parts of the globe. This text offers social work programs worldwide a model that may have relevance for their integration of global content. The authors acknowledge the need for incremental steps in bringing about innovations and furthering global dialogue on universal principles for social work education.

OVERVIEW OF THE BOOK AND CHAPTER FLOW

In general, both undergraduate and graduate social work students report that they are able to see the relevance of the various courses in social work curriculum only when they are about to graduate. To help students to obtain this overall understanding, it is our goal to model integration of global issues by laying out the linkages of the various knowledge, value, and skill areas in social work. The framework used in each chapter is one way to facilitate this conceptual task, and the flow and common references among chapters is another.

The book comprises thirteen chapters: Chapter 1 explains the infusion of international perspectives throughout the curriculum and introduces a framework for engaging students in scrutiny of the extent of their knowledge in global issues. Chapter 2 examines the history of international perspectives referring to a number of countries and using the case study of U.S. curriculum. Chapters 3 to 10 review typical social work education content areas, introducing case studies for comparison and identifying universal principles while acknowledging global curricular variations. Chapter 11 clarifies the meaning of social development for the new century and Chapter 12 identifies practical steps in professional growth opportunities in a global context. Chapter 13 provides a capstone for the book and includes a complete version of the framework introduced in this first chapter.

It is important that students be familiar with the historical development of social welfare and the social work profession worldwide, and this overview of chapters begins with Chapter 2. Initiatives in taking a more global approach to social work are not new, and the historical framework provided in this chapter sheds light on some of the complexity and context of the development of global curriculum. An example of reciprocity is the tradition in Indian and Bangladesh social work education of utilizing U.S. educational models while simultaneously developing their own innovations, which are now utilized in the United States (Desai, 1987). The Grameen Bank stands out for its originality: initially a social development project, it has been picked up by community organizers in Pine Bluff, Arkansas. As reported in the UNICEF report *State of the World's Children* (1997), "The Grameen Bank in Bangladesh has achieved widespread international recognition for its success in providing credit to the poorest members of society—over 90 percent of them women—who would never receive it from mainstream financial institutions . . . today the Bank employs 14,000 staff and works in more than half of Bangladesh's 68,000 villages."

Another example is the U.S. and European tradition, in which international perspectives and collaboration have been developing in phases throughout the 20th century. Settlement house movements and charity organization societies in the United States were based on English models (Leiby, 1978; Trattner, 1990). Similarly, British psychiatric social work training was based on the American experience in clinical social work, while community organization was based on the social pedagogue model from the Netherlands (Irvine, 1978).

This historical view of reciprocity also includes the extensive kinship networking of African Americans to survive the slave trade. The role of kinship networking has only recently gained visibility in the mainstream social work literature as a significant strength in community building (Billingsley, 1993; Solomon, 1976; Pinderhughes, 1989; Beverly, 1989; Chestang, 1972).

Chapter 3 refers to the Human Condition and Behavior and assesses both the strengths and areas of changes needed at the person, group, and environmental levels. The ability to undertake interactive and multilevel assessments facilitates appropriate intervention strategies. Consequently, case examples are offered with an emphasis on one level of assessment, such as the individual's self-esteem described in the Project 1993 research project and accompanied by analysis at all three system levels adopted in this text. Both the assessment process and implementation or measurement of effectiveness of practice interventions are governed by our value and ethical base. Chapter 3 emphasizes the power of language in relation to self-esteem of service users, and the theme is picked up in Chapter 4 in relation to practice.

The power of language, so central to social work assessment and practice, is not systematically explored in social work education at the macro level. At the micro level of practice, however, the work of Burgest (1986) and Pinderhughes (1989) enables students to increase their conscious use of nonracist or judgmental vocabulary. At the macro level specifically, in the nomenclature of nation states we have used terminology such as "Third World" and "developing" to refer and to categorize people and simultaneously expect them to refer to themselves in the same way. This is not only disempowering but also gives an inflated sense of the technology that is being transferred and is oblivious of cultural norms, as stated by Kondrat (1994): "We tend to judge ourselves by our intention and others by their behavior." In this context Kondrat prompts the insight that judgment according to intention can be a justification for colonization or oppressive behavior.

In Chapter 4, it is recognized that no society has a unique set of problems with no global relevance, and no society has a monopoly on the solutions. The chapter identifies practice as a contribution to social development and offers examples to illustrate micro, mezzo, and macro approaches. An example of reciprocal exchange of practice ideas at the micro and mezzo levels is the English "patch system" instituted with the Seebohm report in the 1970s. In this system social work teams were located in neighborhoods that the social workers studied and came to know well, mapping resources, meeting the local police and leaders, getting to know the family groups, and working to empower communities as well as working with the individual "case" focus. This patch concept has been adopted in Australia and the U.S. state of Iowa (Adams & Nelson, 1992).

Another common element is community organizing as a key aspect of social development. Although their mutual relevance has not been sufficiently acknowledged, community organization and social development have been discussed separately in the social work literature. We view social development as a broader intervention tool that integrates practice skills of community organization. While community organization brings people together to find their power to act toward solutions to community challenges in macro and mezzo systems, historically it has been less concerned with economic development and has not addressed the personal or human condition at the micro, individual, or family (mezzo) levels. Because the social development approach embraces these system dimensions interchangeably, we view social development as the umbrella framework and community organization as a crucial element. We hypothesize that some current confusion in this area may have been reinforced by the fact that in the process of knowledge development thus far, social development has been viewed as relevent to interventions in the Global South; meanwhile, social development knowledge generated in the Global South has not been regarded by practitioners and educators in the Global North as germane to community organization. As an illustration, in the Media Network social development presentation, *In Her Own Image,* a community worker engages a group of women in asserting land claims. The steps of organizing are universal ones and can be witnessed in the work of the Trabajadora Domestica, the women's rights organization in Cuernavaca, Mexico, discussed in Chapter 3; in the literacy projects in Kerala, India; and in the family centers in England. In many countries, social work focuses on the local environment, starting from scratch on innovations rather than picking up threads begun elsewhere (Link, 1995). Thus limited by false geographical boundaries and terminology, the social work profession is caught up in the place, time, agency, and culture that local practice communities know best. This text challenges a narrow frame of reference for practice and emphasizes the need for a more expansive perspective in the comparative case studies offered in Chapter 4.

The discussion of awareness of the power of language also relates to social work ethics in Chapter 5. The approach to ethical decision making in practice decisions and professional behavior varies from country to country. For some practitioners there are detailed "codes" of practice to guide actions, while for others ethics is a broad arena of principles that embody the profession of social work itself. To review these various approaches enriches our awareness of all the ways we can be alert to prejudgment, cultural bias, and potential dilemmas; it also leads us to a deeper recognition of the many layers involved in consciously ethical decisions. In this context, the International Federation of Social Workers (IFSW) is actively seeking to identify common ethical principles that social workers worldwide can relate to and use, and the participation of all in this process is invited by IFSW President Elis Envall (Envall, 1997).

Chapter 6 explores and relates to practice global approaches to social policy and identifies global policy instruments that undergird all our work. For students, frameworks for assessing social policy in a global context are particularly useful and the frameworks of colleagues from the United Nations and the United States are reviewed and applied. Case studies of current policy design and implementation are brought together in ways that facilitate our understanding of common global social work processes.

Chapter 7 demonstrates that the rapid pace of social change as a result of technology is also of critical relevance in the uneven pattern of global social work education. Technology leads to both opportunity and power imbalance, especially since resources vary from country to country; social workers can be both alert to opportunity and to falsely assumed limitations. The consequences of power imbalance have been discussed at multiple levels such as conceptual, economic, and relational in previous chapters; this chapter identifies educational opportunities that address access to resources and redress power imbalance. There are detailed assignments to assist students and colleagues in achieving access to research tools such as search engines and recognizing both the potential and limits of this technology.

Chapter 8 both returns to the discussion of language and expands our awareness of the many layers of communication involved in culturally competent social work with populations at risk. Use of disempowering language adversely affects people without resources or power. Yet such language has been frequently used to legitimize subjugation by oppressors during ethnic diversity conflicts (for example, ethnic "cleansing" in Croatia, collective labeling of Middle Easterners as "terrorists" or reference to the Hmong people as "illiterate").

Postmodernists believe that words reflect and shape our world and that we know our world through languages and the symbols we have created to define, describe, and interpret it. The words, interpretations, languages, and conversations of people in power tend to be accepted as truth and fact-based knowledge; in contrast, the language, symbols, interpretations, and conversations of the disempowered become marginalized. Thus, the voices of the disempowered become subjugated and silenced and their stories are not told (Foucault, 1980; Hartman, 1991). Naming and assigning names of marginalized people can inflict irreparable harm. Historically, individuals and groups of people have been referred to as inferior, subversive, or evil; references like these have been used to justify everything from social isolation to genocide. Thus, in the postmodernist view, speech is action, not merely a reflection of innocuous ideas (Hartman, 1991).

In this context, some political leaders' vision reflect consistency with the postmodernist views while others are in contradiction. For instance, the 15 million people of Roma who are spread the world over have imbibed and absorbed features of many lands and peoples as well as retaining memories of elements of Indian civilization, which they regard as their original home. This internationalism has a particular value in our times. The history of the Roma people is one of sorrow and suffering. It is also the story of the triumph of the human spirit over adversity. The persecution that the Roma have faced for nearly a thousand years, marked in our own days by Hitler's genocide, makes them an example of courage and endurance. Inaugurating the second International Romani Festival in Chandigarh, India, the former Prime Minister of India, Mrs. Indira Gandhi, declared: "I feel a kinship with the Roma People. I have always admired their love of adventure, their closeness to nature and above all, their fortitude and resilience" (Gandhi, 1960). In the contemporary world, ethnic hatred and violence directed against gypsies in Romania has escalated dramatically since the 1989 revolution.

Another consequence of power imbalance and a constant integrative theme throughout this book relates to economics and is discussed in Chapter 9, which identifies key power brokers, such as the World Bank and the International Monetary Fund (IMF), and describes their work and their impact on communities, especially in the Global South. Social workers have certain indicators as yardsticks, such as classification systems of countries by gross national product that exclude women and children's labor, to justify the placing of countries in hierarchies implying power differential. Further, we may say that intentions are good, but there is a lack of open acknowledgment of this differential, the gaps in economic assessment, the prejudicial images invoked, and the impact on communities in which social workers practice. According to the International Labor Organization, more than 88 million children are working in conditions that threaten their health and place their welfare in jeopardy (Nurske & Castello, 1991). For many students, social practice and policy comes alive in their field practicum, and Chapter 10 builds on the insights of Chapter 6 to identify a variety of ways students can be involved in field experience beyond their familiar environments.

Chapter 11 addresses models of sustainable social development. Social workers are expressing a renewed interest in social development, as James Midgley points out: "Although social workers played a key role in conceptualizing social development in the 1970s and early 1980s, interest in the field waned. It is only in the last few years that social workers are again embracing social development" (Midgley, 1997). The chapter reviews current resources and networks and discusses their implications for building dialogue among social work practitioners and educators in countries of the Global North and South.

Chapter 12 identifies opportunities for professional growth in the global context. Central to these opportunities are exchanges of faculty, practitioners, students, and consultants. Case studies trace steps in setting up exchange programs and student opportunities for global coursework, along with faculty linkage among schools north and south, east and west.

Chapter 13 reviews the preceding chapters and discusses futuristic considerations in global social work education and social welfare of world citizens. It will include recommendations for future education, practice, and research. Also, as introduced here in Chapter 1, common principles for the profession of social work are identified in their global context and the cells of the framework introduced in Table 1.1 are completed.

In summary, the key assumptions for this text are as follows:

- The social work profession is strengthened by the recognition of global interdependence among social workers and their countries.

- The "melting pot" philosophy has evolved to one of cultural pluralism.

- Universal principles are possible while recognizing and respecting local uniqueness.

- Reciprocity and inclusiveness lead to empowerment.

- Conscious choice of language is central to power relationships that foster distributive justice; hence the term "global" leads us to a sense of *we*, whereas "international" maintains nation-to-nation *us* and *them.*

- Adopting an international perspective promotes appreciation and sensitivity to issues of diversity within national boundaries.

Outcomes of the book, we hope, will be:

- Confident awareness of the interdependence of people of the world

- Increased dialogue in order to recognize core elements of social work across the globe that can strengthen the profession when recognized collectively while also respecting local differences

- An innovative learning environment for social work students through use of practical case studies that assume interdepedence between countries

- A gathering together of practice, policy, and research case studies that can be applied to classrooms globally

- The identification of the power of language by redefining and reviewing use of common terms such as "developing"

- An exploration, with a review of demographics, of the realities of cultural pluralism in communities worldwide and their implications for social work education

- A contribution to the development of global principles for the social work profession

The tension between addressing social work issues from the at times unconscious geocentric position of most literature to the conscious global reach of our goals is a key theme in this text and one the authors have been trying to implement with scrutiny even though we all have a tendency to place our country of origin and particularly the U.S. first in lists of nations. It both a humbling and enriching task that we recognize will always be with us as we become more aware of the ways certain countries are elevated at the risk of demeaning others. Identifying educational tools and outcomes is helpful in this process, and these tools will be reviewed throughout the text and especially in Chapter 13. As a result of reading and using a book that integrates ideas across social work practice and curriculum, we hope that students, social workers, and educators will review their own geocentric perspectives, expand their reach for sources of learning beyond familiar boundaries, and challenge their creativity to include knowledge and expertise gathered from colleagues globally.

. . . .

STUDENT ACTIVITIES

1. Know the world: Examine the listing of countries in the UNICEF report, *The State of the World's Children* (1997), and check the location of any country unfamiliar to you. In what ways do countries such as Surinam, Somalia, and Slovenia play a role in your life?

Know the World from a Different Perspective

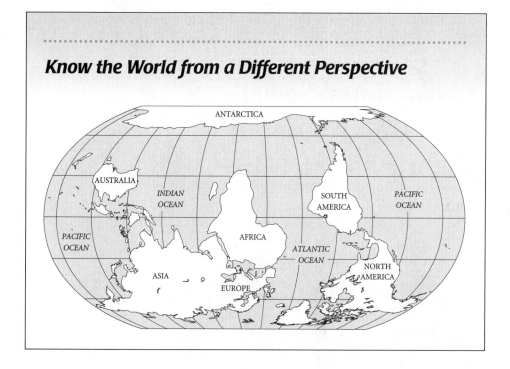

2. Take the framework in Table 1.1 and draft ideas for its completion; review your ideas as you read further chapters in the book.

3. Identify the changing patterns of family purchasing power in the Global North and Global South discussed in the UNICEF report, *The State of the World's Children,* and suggest ways to influence these patterns.

International Social Work Curriculum in Historical Perspective

LYNNE HEALY

Effective social work education programs recognize the interdependence of nations and the need for worldwide professional co-operation.

—U.S. CSWE STANDARDS, 1995

Global interdependence has increased recent social work attention to international content in social work education in many countries. Yet international content in social work curricula is not a new phenomenon. This chapter will discuss key themes in the historical development of international social work learning and curricula and their interrelationship with events in the profession and wider sociopolitical environment. Examples will be drawn from several countries, but the primary focus of this chapter will be the historical experience of social work in the United States. In studying this history, students will see the interconnections among global events, world wars, economic and political shifts, and the progress of social work in the world arena.

Social work education, a 20th-century phenomenon, has been shaped by the major events of the era. These events include the two world wars, the Cold War and its end; independence movements and the creation of new nations in Asia, Africa, and the Caribbean; the creation of the United Nations; the civil rights movements in the United States; immigration waves; the Vietnam War; and more. Intervening forces affecting the development of international curriculum include national and professional attitudes of worldmindedness versus isolationism, public and academic interest in general foreign language and international education, and the availability of funding streams for international programs.

As social work education has developed over the past century, international contacts among social work educators and opportunities for international work and other exchanges have experienced ebbs and flows, often mirroring trends in the larger environment. Along with the fluctuations in opportunities and contacts have gone fluctuations in attention to, and interest in, international curriculum in social work. Recurring issues in international curriculum include debates over its importance, its relevance to practice, its purposes, and the appropriate focus or emphasis within the broad scope of potential international content. In addition, strategic issues persist concerning the appropriate methodologies for designing and structuring international curricula. After a brief examination of key periods in the history of social work education's interface with global opportunities, the discussion will focus on a survey and assessment of international aspects of social work curriculum.

TWENTIETH-CENTURY HISTORY: IMPACT ON INTERNATIONAL CONTENT

While the history of the 20th century can be interpreted in many ways, international social work education can be seen as having been affected by four main periods: early international linkages and the search for a common professional agenda (pre–World War I through the mid-1930s); relief and development involvements, including international expansionism (1945 through the late 1960s); isolationism (1970s through the mid-1980s); and revitalization (1990s onward). These periods will be briefly discussed, with comments on the interrelationship between international and domestic political events, supports available to social work education, and the development of international curriculum.

Early History: Seeking International Contact and Affiliations

Formal social work education began at the turn of the century almost simultaneously in Europe and the United States, and by the 1920s it was developing in South America, India, and South Africa. The first fully developed school of social work was founded in Amsterdam in 1899. This school was followed in Europe by a two-year course organized by the London Charity Organization Society in 1903 and a school of social work in Germany in 1908. In the United States, meanwhile, the New York Charity Organization began a six-week summer school of philanthropic work in 1898, a course that grew into a one-year program at the new New York School of Philanthropy in 1904 (eventually, Columbia University School of Social Work). Schools in Boston (1904) and Chicago (1908) followed (Kendall, 1967b). There was rapid development throughout the first third of the 20th century in the United States and Europe; simultaneously South Africa opened a School of Social Work in 1924, the first school of social work in Latin America was founded in Santiago, Chile in 1925 and, with finance from the Tata Trust, the first school in India, known as the Sir Dorabji Tata School of Social Work, was founded in 1936 (see Case Study 2.2 in the Student Activities section at the end of this chapter for a discussion of social welfare and social work education history in India).

Social workers and educators were working internationally on causes before World War I, most notably that of world peace. While social work emerged independently in Europe and the United States, educators on both sides of the Atlantic felt the need to consult with each other and to share issues and perspectives and to search for common purposes. The first International Conference of Social Work was held in 1928 in Paris, drawing 2481 delegates from 42 countries, including 279 from the United States (First International Conference of Social Work, 1929). A section on social work education was held as part of the official conference. From this start, the International Committee of Schools of Social Work was formed in 1929 with 46 member schools in ten countries (Kendall, 1978); today, it is the International Association of Schools of Social Work, with representation in most countries of the world.

The early formation of an International Association of Schools of Social Work is significant and has implications for international curriculum. It signifies that almost from the beginning social work educators have seen sufficient commonalities to link social work education worldwide and that international collaboration and interchange have been viewed as a valuable and productive venture. Beginning with Sophonisba Breckenridge and Porter Lee in 1928, U.S. educators have participated in international congresses and have brought new ideas back to their own schools. International contact among educators is one factor that continues to influence the development of international curriculum and to shape the attitudes and knowledge of those educators involved. As expressed by a speaker at the first conference, "International social work, to be practical and efficient, demands . . . constant contact between social workers on an international intellectual basis" (Jebb, 1929, p. 651). During this period, the emphasis was on sharing information about content and searching for commonalities in definitions and standards.

The Aftermath of World War II: Opportunities in Relief and Development

Opportunities for international contact are continually reshaped by larger events. The outbreak of World War II suspended all significant international contacts among social work educators. Then the end of the war created new and expanded opportunities for involvement in relief and development work, first in Europe and China, and later in countries in Africa and Asia, bringing an influx of international students into U.S. social work programs. After the war, there was an "intense interest in many countries in an exchange of scientific methods and experience in social welfare" (Friedlander, 1949, p. 207). U.S. social work educators became involved through the United Nations Relief and Rehabilitation Agency (UNRRA) in a systematic program that sent experts to liberated nations to begin training of social workers so that health and welfare services could be developed or reestablished. The program was deemed so important that it was continued under the auspices of the newly established United Nations.

Responding to the movements toward independence and national development in the former colonies in Asia, Africa, and the Caribbean and believing that modern social services would be a key element of successful new societies, the United Nations continued and expanded programs to establish social work education around the world. A two-pronged approach was used: deploying experts from the United States and Europe to provide technical assistance and providing scholarships to U.S. graduate schools to personnel from Africa, Asia, and Latin America. As Stein noted in 1957, the "presence in American and Canadian schools during the past ten years, particularly, of social work students from all parts of the world has heightened the awareness by all schools of the complex issues inherent in such training . . . and has helped quicken both school and general social work interest in the 'international'" (Stein, 1957, p. 2). Similarly, Stein commented on the "profound impression on social work" created by World War II and the opportunities for international service which arose in its aftermath (1957, p. 1).

By the 1960s, social work education in the United States had identified two clear purposes for internationally related education: to train experts for overseas service in "Global South" nations, and to provide social work education for students from Asia, Africa, and Latin America. As will be discussed later in the chapter, numerous professional activities were initiated to support these two goals. A confluence of factors unraveled the international programs established in the postwar period and severely reduced U.S. influence and interest in international social work. Case Study 2.1 describes this process as it pertains to the United States.

Turmoil in the Sixties; Isolationism in the Seventies

The late 1960s initially promised to bring funding to continue and expand international curriculum efforts. Funds for curriculum and other programs in international social work education were expected to flow from the passage of the International Education Act of 1966 by Congress. In a speech to the U.S. Council on Social Work Education's 1968 annual program meeting, an official from the U.S. Department of Health, Education, and Welfare (DHEW) predicted that money would be available for education of competent graduate-level specialists in international social work (Miller, 1968). In fact, the act was never funded. Both federal and foundation funds allotted to international education dropped dramatically in the period between 1969 and 1979; while federal expenditures dropped from $20.3 million in 1969 to $8.5 million in 1979, Ford Foundation funds for training in international affairs dropped from $27 million annually to less than $3 million in 1978 (National Council on Foreign Language and International Studies, n.d.) The decline in interest in international issues and careers was felt in many fields, including social work.

A number of events in foreign and domestic affairs converged to cause this turn to isolationism, a turn experienced acutely in social work. The Vietnam War brought on a watershed of disillusionment with the U.S. role in international affairs and fueled intense anti-imperialist sentiments among the newly independent nations of the world. There was a movement to reject curriculum models borrowed from the U.S. and Europe and to indigenize the teaching of social work. American influences on social work in the Global South were attacked as irrelevant or damaging (Khinduka, 1971). So intense was the scholarly outcry that *International Social Work* took the unusual step of publishing an editorial declaring that the subject was "threadbare" and saying that no further articles on the topic would be published (1972). To be an American social worker interested in international work was suddenly suspect and carried the risk of being labeled an imperialist.

At the same time, the civil rights movement, urban unrest and renewal, and the war on poverty emerged to capture the attention of American social workers. Domestic issues became the priority and, by the mid-1970s, the only agenda of U.S. social work. "We have enough problems at home" was the new rationale for ignoring international curriculum, now seen as an exotic extra at best, and imperialistic at worst.

Revitalization in the 1990s?

Although recent history is difficult to assess, the 1990s appear to be a time of revitalization of international interest, both generally and in social work. Again, dramatic changes in the political environment have had an impact. The end of the Cold War has created opportunities somewhat similar to those in the postwar period, as countries in eastern Europe have scrambled for technical assistance in social work education. Social work educators have developed projects and have been engaged to provide consultation to help Romania, Bulgaria, Hungary, the Baltic nations, and the republics of the former Soviet Union to establish social work education and related service programs. Emergence of a global economy and large waves of immigration in the early 1990s have convinced most observers that global interdependence is a reality. Thus, international issues are once again defined as important in social work education.

Throughout each period, the impact of these international events was heightened by supporting events and policies in the organized profession. While a number of organizations have been important, this chapter will focus on the impact of the Council on Social Work Education's (CSWE) efforts in supporting or discouraging international curriculum. While the International Association of Schools of Social Work is also an important organization, its primary contribution to international content has been in providing opportunities for contact and exchange of ideas. Although they are nation specific, the lessons of the U.S. Council on Social Work Education experience can be applied more universally.

··

ORGANIZED PROFESSIONAL ACTIVITIES AND SUPPORTS FOR INTERNATIONAL SOCIAL WORK

Through inclusion of international issues in its regular conferences and publications, collaboration with other organizations, and sponsorship of a series of curriculum conferences, the Council on Social Work Education historically provided encouragement and support for internationalizing social work education, especially in response to developments in the 1950s and 1960s. In terms of impact on curriculum, a series of collaborative conferences held in the United States between 1959 and 1969 were particularly significant. These were the Interprofessional Conference on Training of Personnel for Overseas Service, held at Cornell University in 1959; the Interprofessional Conference on Professional Training for Students from Other Countries, held in Boston in 1961; the Conference on International Social Welfare Manpower, held in Washington, D.C., in 1964; and the Workshop on Teaching Comparative Social Welfare in 1969. Through cosponsorships, the conferences demonstrate the existence of significant collaborative relationships with key agencies in international work. For example, the 1964 conference was sponsored by CSWE with the United States Agency for International Development (USAID) and the U.S. Department of Health, Education, and Welfare, and participants were sent by the United Nations, the Organization of American States, and the Department of State (Conference on International Social Welfare Manpower, 1965).

As their titles demonstrate, the earlier conferences focused on the two key roles identified for U.S. social work education in the international arena during the 1950s: educating international students and preparing U.S. experts for overseas consultancies. The 1969 conference, however, shifted attention to the importance of cross-cultural learning and comparative social welfare content for all students in U.S. schools of social work. In the introductory paper for the conference, Konopka suggested two broad new goals for international curriculum content: (1) to improve the practice of social work in one's own country, and (2) "to prepare for intelligent international cooperation in social work practice, theory and research" (1969, pp. 1–3). Because of unfortunate timing, instead of launching a new era in international curriculum development, her ideas languished for several decades.

The Council on Social Work Education had identified international cooperation as one of its key functions in a bylaws amendment adopted in 1964 (Kendall, 1967a). Structurally, the Council implemented this function and supported international projects through an International Committee, upgraded to become the Commission on International Social Welfare Education in 1967. The board also created a Division of International Education and adopted a program of international cooperation for social work education in 1967 (Kendall, 1967a). Through contracts with the U.S. Agency for International Development, CSWE was engaged directly in the development of social work education in Central America, Zambia (then Northern Rhodesia), and India (Hilliard, 1965; Gangrade, 1962).

Review of issues of the *Social Work Education Reporter* published during the late 1950s and 1960s reveals the extent of international activities at the Council during this period through the publication of many relevant news articles, often 25 to 50 percent of each issue (Healy, 1985).

In contrast, review of the issues of the *Reporter* from the years 1977–1982 reveals that international issues are rarely mentioned—perhaps a few brief notices per year (Healy, 1985). In 1971, the staff member who had given leadership to international efforts at the Council left to become Secretary General of the International Association of Schools of Social Work. The loss of leadership combined with the negative impact of the events of the 1960s to spark a major decline in international focus at the CSWE. The International Commission was abolished, as was the International Division and its programs.

In fact, total disappearance of international structures lasted only a few years. In 1978, a Committee on International Social Work Education was reestablished at the request of interested members, although without staff and without official recognition in the Council bylaws. Throughout the 1980s and 1990s, the committee worked to strengthen international curriculum by publishing a bibliography, a newsletter for educators, a resource book of course outlines, establishing an annual International Issues Symposium, and advocating the addition of international content to the Curriculum Policy Statement. The designation of the group was changed to International Commission in the early 1990s. In spite of this recognition and the projects undertaken, international programming and emphasis at the Council in 1997 remains far below the 1967 level.

Official Curriculum Policy

It is through the standards-setting and accreditation processes that the Council on Social Work Education has the greatest potential to influence curriculum in any area, including international. Social work programs in the U.S. are accredited by the CSWE based both on meeting guidelines for curriculum content and organization and on various structural requirements for adequacy of faculty, funding, and other resources. Curriculum standards are based on an official Curriculum Policy Statement (CPS) issued and periodically updated by the Council. Compliance with this statement provides legitimation for a program's curriculum; therefore, the inclusion or absence of mention of content areas in the policy statement serves as an important incentive or disincentive to curriculum development.

Throughout most of the history of social work education in the United States, curriculum policy has been sporadic at best in attention to international content. Of the five Curriculum Policy Statements adopted since the formation of the Council on Social Work Education in 1952, two have contained no reference to international matters (1952 and 1984); one includes a single reference (1971); the most recent contains an ambiguous phrase (1994), and only one explicitly encouraged programs to include international perspectives (1962).

It is not surprising that the CPS adopted in 1962 is the most supportive of international perspectives, as its formulation occurred during the years of considerable international activity outlined previously. Eight goals for social work education are delineated, including the following: "[the student] perceives and is able to interpret social work as a profession dedicated to the promotion of individual and social welfare in his own and other societies" (CSWE, 1962, p. 2). The standards for the Social Welfare Policy and Services component of the curriculum specify that the student is to be helped to "develop a historical, philosophical, and comparative perspective on social welfare systems in his own and other societies and a capacity for critical appraisal of current social welfare programs" (CSWE, 1962, p. 3). Further, the outcomes to be achieved should enable the student "to identify, analyze, and appraise . . . the movements and forces that have given expression and form to social welfare goals, nationally and internationally, with attention to contributions from the profession and leaders in political and social reform" (p. 3).

Redrafted in 1969, the next CPS retained a single educational goal related to international knowledge in stating that the student should be able to "recognize the political, economic, social, and cultural influences on the social services both in his own country and in other countries" (CSWE, 1971, p. 1). This is a weaker statement than the goal in the 1962 version, which conveyed the idea of a global profession. The 1971 standards for Social Welfare Policy and Services curriculum are related implicitly to U.S. policies, with no references to other systems. No references to international attitudes, knowledge, or outcomes can be found in the 1984 statement. The impact of the omission was compounded by the specificity of this CPS, the first to explicitly require content on women, ethnic minorities of color, and oppression. Coupled with demanding requirements for specializations at the master's level, this CPS left many program directors and faculty feeling burdened and resistant to additional content requirements.

The statement adopted in 1992 takes a timid step back toward recognizing the importance of international perspectives. Included in a section of the CPS called "Premises Underlying Social Work Education" is the following statement: "Effective social work programs recognize the interdependence of nations and the importance of worldwide cooperation." The choice of words is puzzling. Was there an intentional avoidance of the words "international" or "global," the more widely recognized terms to refer to interdependence? The 1962 Curriculum Policy Statement therefore remains the only one in which the words "international" and "comparative" appear in curriculum policy in the U.S.

Furthermore, during the months of data gathering that preceded the adoption of the new CPS, the International Commission of the Council had recommended language for inclusion, using the word "international" explicitly, and making numerous suggestions for ways to encourage international content without requiring it. Instead, the new statement included the statement on interdependence only as a Premise, a section of the CPS that is not reflected in the evaluative standards that guide schools toward their accreditation. Programs are therefore not held accountable for addressing the concepts expressed in the Premises. Although drafted using open-ended language that leaves opportunities for including international content open, the present official curriculum standard, is considerably less supportive of international content than the 1962 statement.

Having reviewed the context of world events, social work opportunities, and the overarching supports from professional structures, activities, and official curriculum policy, it is time to examine what international curriculum has actually been developed and taught to social work students.

International Content Around the World

Treatment of international content in various countries follows several patterns. In Canada, Europe, the United States, and Japan, the debates over whether to include international content and what content to include have similarities. In countries where social work lacks a significant indigenous literature, the situation is somewhat different.

EUROPE/UNITED KINGDOM. European schools have been encouraged to increase international content by the move toward economic and political unity among European nations. Professional mobility within the European Union has been adopted; therefore, social workers trained in one country in the Union can work in any other member country if their course meets the agreed-upon multinational standard. Suddenly, it became important for social workers in Europe to know something about their counterparts in neighboring countries. Various grant programs of the European Union, such as the current SOCRATES project, preceded by ERASMUS, provided funding for professional exchanges. Lyons (1996) reported that modules on European comparative welfare became available to some social work students in Britain and several programs offering more extensive work on comparative social welfare have been developed. A one-year course leading to a degree in European Social Work is a collaborative effort between a university in the United Kingdom and a school in Denmark; this program requires both academic work and a practicum in the other country for all enrolled students. Comparative European welfare systems is also the focus of a one-year master's degree in Comparative European Social Studies established in 1994 at the Maastricht Hogeskool in the Netherlands.

Lyons believes that these programs are too narrow to meet the needs of students for international content. As she wrote: "By the early 1990's it seemed clear that a course based on a comparative European model would not maximize the opportunities for students to participate and give meaning to their own aspirations to work cross-culturally and internationally" (1996, p. 190). An alternative model, developed at the University of East London, emphasizes global problems such as poverty, migration and disaster intervention. While students do a project abroad, the course also emphasizes intercultural work at home.

Nagy and Falk, in their 1995–96 survey of international aspects of curriculum in Europe, Australia and North America, also labeled efforts in Europe as "Euro-Centric" (1996). While 24 among the 60 responding European schools offered an internationally focused course and 19 offered content on cross-cultural knowledge, the content showed little evidence of interest in issues of the Global South and emphasized internal multicultural populations.

JAPAN. Since its inception, social work education in Japan has been largely focused on domestic issues. The first course in international social welfare was introduced by Ashikaga in 1978 (Mori, 1996). Recent growing interest in international education can be linked to the increased role of Japan in world affairs and to an increase in "international social welfare problems" that arise from migration into Japan and from Japan's increasing number of international contacts (Mori, 1996, p. 217). In 1986, Japan hosted the international social work conferences; in 1988, the Japanese Society for the Study of Social Welfare added an international social welfare section to its congress. Over the past decade, increases in coverage of international issues in Japanese social work education have been tracked through a series of surveys, beginning with one in 1985 that showed 4 out of the 31 schools offering an international course (Miwa, reported in Mori, 1996). In 1988, 11 out of 48, or 22.9 percent of schools of social work offered a course on international or comparative social welfare, and about 50 percent had at least some international content (Kojima, 1988). Most of the courses focused on comparative social welfare policy, with some emphasis on the function of social work in other countries and on basic concepts of social and economic development. Kojima's second survey in 1992 found an increased percentage of schools offering international courses: 14 out of 39, or 35.9 percent (Mori, 1996). In 1996, Mori's survey revealed a more substantial increase, with 29 out of 51 responding schools (56.9%) reporting courses on international aspects of social welfare. The predominant focus remains comparative social welfare, but there are also courses on Asian sociology, war and peace, human life and death, and some multicultural social work content (Mori, 1996). Mori concluded that although the number of courses has grown markedly, international social work is not a well-developed subject area in Japanese social work curricula. The courses are mostly optional and often use part-time lecturers. Noting that the contents vary widely, she concludes: "This may be because of a healthy plurality of ideas about international social welfare, but it is more likely to be due to international social welfare being still a fragmented and not established mainstream course of study" (1996, p. 219).

INTERNATIONAL CONTENT IN THE SOUTH. Although not labeled international content, social work in many countries in the Global South is taught using foreign materials and at least an implicit comparative approach. Students in Africa and Asia are exposed to social work writings from the United States and the United Kingdom and learn about social legislation and social services in other countries. In addition, social work programs in the South often make use of United Nations materials on issues such as sustainable development, children's rights, women's development and other issues. Thus, students are exposed to global social problems and to efforts of world organizations to address them. The value of cross-national work has been recognized in some programs. In Jamaica, the social welfare training course initiated in 1962 at the Social Welfare Training Center of the University of the West Indies required students from Jamaica to complete a brief practicum in Puerto Rico while students from other Caribbean islands did their practicum in Jamaica (Francis, 1997). All students were guaranteed the opportunity to experience working in a different culture and system as part of their social work training.

GLOBAL TRENDS. Globally, at least minimal inclusion of international content is reported by 73 percent of social work programs, according to a survey of member schools of the International Association of Schools of Social Work (Healy, 1990). Almost 44 percent of schools have placed students in other countries for fieldwork. The responses showed interesting regional differences as well as considerable worldwide agreement. A sense of what international content is taught around the world was revealed by responses to a question asking respondents to indicate whether various content areas were covered by all or most students in their courses. In descending order, the results were: social and economic development concepts (53% of responding schools report that all or most students cover); regional social policy issues (45.5%); cross-cultural information (42%); global social policy issues (34%); comparative social welfare policy (29%); global interdependence (23%); functions of relevant United Nations organizations (22%); social work in other countries (19%); international social work organizations (13%); and cross-national research methods (9%).

Some regional differences were evident. For example, while no Latin American school reported offering a discrete course on international topics, all said that their students receive content on concepts of social and economic development and on regional social policy issues. In North America and Europe, fewer than half the respondents said that these areas are covered for the majority of students. Among North American respondent schools, 52 percent offer special courses on international issues, the highest percentage among the regions, yet North America reports the lowest percentage—5.8 percent—when asked what percentage of the average student's course work is devoted to international content. Other regions ranged from a high of 18.8 percent among programs in Africa, to 14 percent in Asia, 8.8 percent in Latin America, and 7.3 percent in Europe (Healy, 1990). This suggests that international curriculum in the U.S. and Canada has focused on students with special interests while neglecting global education for the average student.

International Content in U.S. Social Work Curricula

Examination of international content in U.S. curricula can begin with a simple counting of the number of programs that include some international content and proceed to analysis of how it is included (degree of comprehensiveness and curriculum model used); what purposes international content serves in the curricula; and the types or foci of the international content selected.

As suggested in the preceding discussion of curriculum policy, international content is not currently defined as an essential component in the education of professional social workers in the United States. It is up to individual programs to decide whether to include international content in their curricula, a decision often made in the context of competition among many content areas for time in a crowded curriculum and shaped by interests and expertise of faculty members and administrators at any point in time. There remain many social work curricula with no planned inclusion of international content.

When included, international content can be required or elective and can vary along a continuum from extensive to sparse. In addition, the content can be organized into separate courses, or it can be infused into one or more existing components of the curriculum. The most common choices are to offer one or perhaps two separate, usually elective, courses on international topics, and/or to add modules or readings to foundation or specialization courses broadening topics to include international perspectives (infusion). Two additional models are specialization and internationalization, although these are rarely implemented. To establish a specialization, a graduate program organizes a cluster of courses and field experiences in international social work to prepare students for specialized practice. The term "internationalization" is used to refer to comprehensive infusion of international content

TABLE 2.1   *International Content in U.S. Curricula, 1956–1996*

Year of Survey	N or (%) Responding Programs	Percent Offering Course on ISW	Percent with Some International Content	Percent Programs with Foreign Students Enrolled	Percent Faculty Recent Overseas Assignment
1956 [a]	32(—)	22%	66%	NA	NA
1967 [b]	(44%)	35%	NA	91%	41%
1982 [c]	75 (86%)	36%	43%	90%	33%
1989 [d]	34 (77%)	38%	79%	NA	NA
1992 [e]	167 (44%)	20%	NA	33+%	NA
1996 [f]	136 (34%)	19%	90%	NA	NA

Publication Information/Population Surveyed

[a]Stein, 1957: CSWE member schools (included both U.S. and Canada at that time).
[b]Prigmore, 1968: CSWE member schools (U.S.).
[c]Healy, 1986: CSWE-accredited graduate schools.
[d]Healy & Kojima, 1991: International Assocation of Schools of Social Work Member Programs. Results are for U.S. member programs.
[e]Johnson, 1996: CSWE-accredited baccalaureate programs.
[f]Healy, 1997: CSWE-accredited baccalaureate programs.

into all major required aspects of a social work educational program. In addition to these approaches, many schools claim to use "informal infusion," through which faculty and/or students enrich the educational program by sharing international experiences in an unplanned fashion.

Inclusion of international content in the curriculum in the United States has been documented over the past four decades through periodic surveys. Quantitative results are summarized in Table 2.1. Some caution must be exercised in interpreting the results; while survey findings fairly accurately report the number of special courses offered, it is more difficult to document infusion of content. The table shows slow but steady growth in the number of international courses taught in U.S graduate schools (it should be noted that only the later studies report on baccalaureate education). More interesting are shifts in the focus of international offerings. In 1957, 81 percent of schools reported that their international content emphasized comparative social welfare (Stein, 1957). A decade later, finding high enrollments of foreign students and many faculty on overseas assignments in Latin American and East Asia, Prigmore concluded that responding schools were engaged in largely one-way relationships with other countries, emphasizing the dual goals of developing opportunities for faculty to engage in overseas technical assistance and of educating foreign students. The 1982 survey showed continued emphasis on comparative social welfare, but with an emphasis on Western industrialized nations rather than Latin America and Asia. Content evident during the 1980s emphasized knowledge outcomes, with much less attention to student attitudes or skill development.

The inclusion of a reference to global interdependence and worldwide cooperation in the 1994 Curriculum Policy Statement has encouraged programs to improve international content. The 1996 survey revealed that 28 percent of baccalaureate programs had already made some modifications in response to the new CPS. Others (38%) judged their own programs inadequate to address the spirit of the statement on interdependence. The emphasis on global interdependence is also reflected in a shift in the focus of international content. The majority of the 69 outlines of specialized courses in international social work collected for a recent curriculum volume emphasized social development policy and practice and/or examined global social problems, with an emphasis on interdependence (Healy and Asamoah, 1997). More course objectives specify attitude and skill outcomes in addition to international knowledge.

Field practicum provides an important potential area for substantial international learning. Surveys have shown that while many schools have placed small numbers of students in other countries, there have been few efforts to establish comprehensive and ongoing international placement programs (Healy, 1986). Obstacles to international placements have limited their development, including comparability of courses and expectations between countries, difficulties in securing field supervision, language expertise needed, and the time and effort required to identify and arrange placements and housing. When successful, however, educators tend to agree that an international placement can be a profoundly beneficial experience for the student, and this discussion is taken up in Chapter 10.

Summary of Current State of International Curriculum

Review of the history and current status of international aspects of social work curriculum reveals a still underdeveloped area in a variety of countries. Stein's 1957 characterization of the state of international content as "uneven, varied in direction and purposes" (p. 1) and not institutionalized as an important element of social work remains accurate as an assessment of the present. The literature strongly suggests that interest and activity in the general arena of international education in social work were highest in the 1950s and 1960s. Yet there has been recent progress. The most important gain made in North America over the past four decades is the shift in attention to global interdependence and the needs of American students for international education. Other gains include steady growth in resource materials for educators, including four guides to curriculum development (Estes, 1992; Healy, 1991; Van Soest, 1992; Van Soest & Crosby, 1997) and a number of books on international social work and social welfare. Despite these positive trends, international curriculum in North America has not yet addressed the new learning goals in a systematic and integrated way.

Globally, international curriculum also appears to be in the beginning stages of development. Concerns over ensuring that curriculum meets appropriate learning goals and is practice relevant are being expressed in Europe, Japan, and elsewhere.

•••

IMPLICATIONS OF THE LESSONS OF HISTORY

Historical analysis should assist in understanding the present and in preparing for the future. This history strongly suggests that progress in the development of international curriculum is most likely when a number of factors converge to provide a supportive environment. As discussed earlier, social work education occurs within a larger context and will continue to be affected by national and international events. A national climate of openness and world-mindedness will encourage the same in the academic sector; such a climate also makes funding for international projects and education more likely. Within the profession, a curriculum policy that explicitly includes international content is likely to help, as would expanded opportunities for international contact for faculty and students. When these supports exist in the larger environment, individual faculties are more likely to identify international content as a priority and to devote the resources of funding, time, and legitimation to ensure that faculty competence is developed and that work proceeds on curriculum.

Awareness of the history of international activities in social work education in the post–World War II period may expand the vision of what is possible for the future. It is clear that social work was viewed as a first-line activity in early international assistance efforts, including the first technical assistance projects of the U.S. government and the international relief programs following the liberation of Europe and China. The United Nations saw social work education as an essential ingredient in national development, providing the expertise necessary for developing social service systems. The official organizations representing social work education, including the IASSW and national organizations such as the CSWE, may reexamine their potentials for international roles in the future, building on the knowledge of what was possible in the past.

Curriculum development may also benefit from collaborative international work to discern what areas are most important within the vast potential content arena known as "international." The findings of the global survey discussed briefly earlier did show some world consensus on optimal attitudes, knowledge, and skills to be transmitted through international curriculum. There was general agreement among respondents from all regions that students should develop sensitivity to cultural differences; a concern for nations with severe rates of poverty; a general world view; and an appreciation of global interdependence. Knowledge outcomes favored include knowledge of the role of culture in understanding behavior; basic concepts of social development; an overview of world social problems; a world perspective on social work issues; cross-cultural practice principles; and knowledge of social welfare policy in other countries. Global attitudes and knowledge should enable social work graduates to act as informed citizens; to practice effectively with different ethnic groups; to improve their own practice through knowledge of alternative social welfare systems; and to give leadership domestically to addressing practice problems generated by international events (Healy, 1990). While testing of the degree of consensus is in order, these findings may provide an agenda for beginning collaborative work on international curriculum.

Although it is rated low in importance by the survey respondents, the author believes that students must also gain an understanding of the profession in its international context. History suggests that this is a "lost goal," previously highly valued by educators but now seen as important by few. Without an appreciation of social work as an international profession, new practitioners will not be able to lead the profession toward collaborative efforts or toward a vision of new international roles for social work. There may be value, therefore, in resurrecting the goal expressed in the 1962 CSWE Curriculum Policy Statement that students should be able to "interpret social work as a profession dedicated to the promotion of individual and social welfare in [his] own and other societies" (p. 2).

Finally, for the United States, the 1994 Curriculum Policy Statement, in spite of its seemingly tentative endorsement of an international perspective, was written with the flexibility to encourage development of curriculum truly responsive to global interdependence. First, according to the words and spirit of its Preamble, a curriculum responsive to global interdependence and capable of preparing professionals for international collaboration is a requirement for achieving effectiveness. In addition, the individual sections of the statement are written in inclusive and open-ended language that can accommodate and even encourage comprehensive infusion of international content on social policy, human behavior and social environment, and human diversity of the kind we are proposing in this book.

Prospects for international curriculum seem promising as we approach the 21st century and the end of the first century of social work education. The 1990s have brought revitalization of interest in the field along with expanded opportunities for international contact. While the world events that lie ahead cannot be predicted with certainty, the profession can learn from the past and strengthen its own structures and policies to encourage and support the further development of an international perspective in social work education worldwide.

STUDENT ACTIVITIES

1. Why has official curriculum policy on international content been slow to develop in the United States? Has this delay been beneficial or detrimental for social work education?

2. How similar or different is the development of social welfare in the Global North and the Global South, using the example of India in Case Study 2.2 compared with the example of the United States in Case Study 2.1? *Note:* In the Indian context, social work is considered to be one element in delivering social welfare. Therefore, it is important to recognize efforts beyond the realm of social work.

3. Define your understanding of indigenous and identify the role colonialization played in influencing indigenous social work learning and coursework.

CASE STUDY 2.2

Social Welfare and Social Work Education History: An Indian Experience

CHATHAPURAM S. RAMANATHAN

As in all the nations of the Global South, development planners in India view the provision of social services as an integral part in the efforts to enhance the quality of life and functioning of its population. Although improvement in quality of life is the ultimate goal of development planning, efforts not only aim at increasing economic growth, but also focus on the distribution of the benefits of economic prosperity (Bose, 1987; Krishnamurthy, 1987). Prior to independence, the approach to social welfare was more oriented toward social problems and social reform, with a focus on structural institutional reforms and bringing about changes in public opinions and attitudes. The Chinese traveler Hsuan-Tsang observed in the seventh century that the Indian people were always in the habit of planting trees to provide shade to travelers and voluntarily dug wells for drinking water for the community. Thus, community had its own indigenous organizations for providing services on a collective basis. For a long time, communities based on caste had welfare programs for their own benefit. Members of the caste were expected to contribute to caste fund either in cash, kind, or labor, and help other members in need. During times of crisis or calamities, the village community pooled its resources (Gangrade, 1987).

Social welfare programs were primarily indigenous in their conceptualization, objectives, content and implementation. There were a few welfare organizations started by Christian missionaries or social defense[1] legislation influenced by the British enactments, but these were exceptions. National leaders, despite their involvement in the freedom struggle, were actively involved in welfare work. The role of the state in the execution of welfare programs was negligible. Historically, unlike in many other countries, development of social welfare services in India has taken place mostly outside the statutory framework, except in the case of social defense and social reforms (Bose, 1987). Although, social welfare was not unknown in India, social work education is not indigenous in origin but was to a large extent influenced by the development of social work education in the United States. In 1925, Clifford Manshardt, an American Protestant missionary who graduated from the University of Chicago in theology, came to India and in 1926 founded the Nagpada Neighborhood House, similar to a settlement house in its objectives and activities. With financing from the Sir Dorabji Tata (an Indian industrialist) Trust, the first school, known as the Sir Dorabji Tata Graduate School of Social Work, was founded in 1936. The faculty consisted of one German Jewish refugee, one Indian with a background in education and theology, an Indian graduate in sociology from the University of Bombay, and an American visiting professor. The school was later renamed the Tata Institute of Social Sciences in 1944 (Desai, 1987).

Fifty years after the founding of the first school, by the mid-1980s there were 43 schools of social work in India. The first year curriculum offers core or foundation content, including social work methods; in the second year, courses are organized more from fields of practice. The highest percentage of students are enrolled in labor welfare and industrial relations specializations. Other specializations include community development, correctional administration, medical and psychiatric social work, and family and child welfare (Desai, 1987; Brigham, 1984). Besides undertaking micro intervention, Indian social work educators emphasize an orientation toward social development, social action, and social change. Innovations in fieldwork placements stress placements in communities around the problem in the institution in which the student is placed—for example, a focus on community health for students placed in hospitals. Another innovation is to place students around a problem focus rather than agency focus. The "floating" placement deemphasizes agency structural constraints. In India, the schools of social work, the University Grants Commission (a national body governing all educators), the Association of

---

[1] *The Encyclopaedia of Social Work in India* defines social defense as protection of society (against crime) over and above expiatory punishment. Amelioration of the offender, not mere penalty. Promotion of human treatment to humans.

Schools of Social Work in India, the Department of Social Welfare at the center (federal) and in the states, and the Planning Commission are crucially involved in the organization and delivery of education for the profession (Desai, 1987).

••

4. The chapter argues that events in the political environment affect the degree of interest in and support for international curriculum. Identify and discuss events in the current environment that may affect international education.

5. Learn more about recent consultation efforts in social work education in eastern Europe. Compare and contrast these with earlier efforts. Is there evidence that models of consultation have changed?

6. According to the Joint Working Group on Development Education, U.S. citizens need to accept global interdependence as "an irrefutable fact of life on which action must be based" (1984). What are the implications of this statement for social work curriculum development? Assess your own curriculum in terms of preparation for global interdependence.

Understanding the Human Condition and Human Behavior in a Global Era

ROSEMARY J. LINK, CHATHAPURAM S. RAMANATHAN, AND YVONNE ASAMOAH

I speak to the black experience, but I am always talking about the human condition—about what we can endure, dream, fail at, and still survive.

—MAYA ANGELOU

There are many dimensions to the understanding of human behavior, including the bio-psycho-socio-cultural-spiritual, economic, and political realities of the people studied. Despite changing demographics that make global understanding of these issues critical, topics of human behavior are still often treated from a narrow domestic perspective. However, if we view the world as a system of interdependent parts, it is impossible to study the behavior of people who are affected by major disruption—such as migration, structural unemployment, violence, hunger, or refugee status—without going beyond national borders. In the same way, reaching for a global approach to human behavior leads to scrutiny of terms that may be culture bound—for example, concepts such as "independence," "self-esteem," and "motivation." To study human behavior from a global perspective is to reach for constructs that can relate to many differing cultures, such as *interdependence* of self (with family, village, and community life), *social well-being, empowerment, resilience, reverence for nature, artistic expression,* and *peace.* Similarly, the premise of this chapter is that human behavior is more a result of surrounding conditions than individual characteristics and personality.

Furthermore, when we view human behavior as a consequence of the human condition, then the separation between what is domestic and what is international becomes moot. Use of the human condition as an overarching framework is consistent with broader issues of social justice and human rights. Viewing worldwide social systems and United Nations policy instruments as based on consensus among countries also gives students and social workers the opportunity and parameters to assess and intervene in communities in new ways. From the 1950s, when concepts of "developing" and "developed" countries were gaining currency, it was believed that economic development would be the key to "development" of social well-being. However, as discussed in Chapters 2 and 9 of this book, the United Nations has more recently emphasized issues of social development as a crucial component to economic change if a more universal state of human well-being is to be attained. While social development in its widest form means guaranteeing the right to peaceful pursuit of life to all ages, it is also an approach to human service. In Chapter 10, Midgley defines social development as "a process of planned social change designed to promote the well-being of the population as a whole in conjunction with the process of economic development." Understanding the human condition is a prerequisite to this approach.

Thus, through building a global perspective, students can add insights about the human condition and more adequately understand, analyze, and predict human behavior. For example, the U.S. Public Broadcasting System series *Childhood* traces families in Russia, Brazil, Japan, and the United States, vividly documenting the universal hopes, fears, dreams, and hurdles of childhood while recognizing the many different patterns of nurturing. The film is one way of drawing out this expectation that we grasp for the widest and most inclusive context in understanding the human condition. This approach also helps us to be cognizant of the role of nation state policy in the ways humans are shaped by their environments (for instance, in their access to clean water or employment across a border). Policies directed to social conditions of health and well-being invoke opportunities that can maximize life transitions and facilitate critical stages of human growth.

Another example of the way a global reach helps us to recognize how artificial it is to see national borders as separations between micro or macro systems is the 18th Street Gang members in Los Angeles. These disenfranchised young people are frequently rounded up and deported to El Salvador, where they pick up with another branch of their gang so that their interactions are seamless despite the structural efforts of immigration and law enforcement to disband or break them (De Cesare, 1993). Thus, while we see the levels of micro, mezzo, and macro interaction as helpful reminders of the different ways in which we interact with our environment, we are searching for ways to *maintain the focus constantly on all three.* We use the concept of different lenses in a parallel process to Bibus and Rooney's discussion in their work on cultural competence (Rooney & Bibus, 1996). Even though we may describe and analyze a case study from a micro view in the lensfinder as we focus on the individuals, we will constantly keep the mezzo and macro lenses available.

System levels of the environment are defined in the following ways and illustrated in Figure 3.1.

1. *Micro levels* include individual behavior and individual responsibility.

2. *Mezzo levels* include group, family behavior, and community; family will be defined in the widest context and is viewed from a strengths perspective as always resourceful rather than "broken" or "dysfunctional."

3. *Macro levels* include the impact on human behavior of economic and social structural conditions, mobility of labor, and socioeconomic investment.

It is important to keep remembering that many aspects of human behavior interweave at all levels; for example, the concept of violence in relation to child and family poverty in a

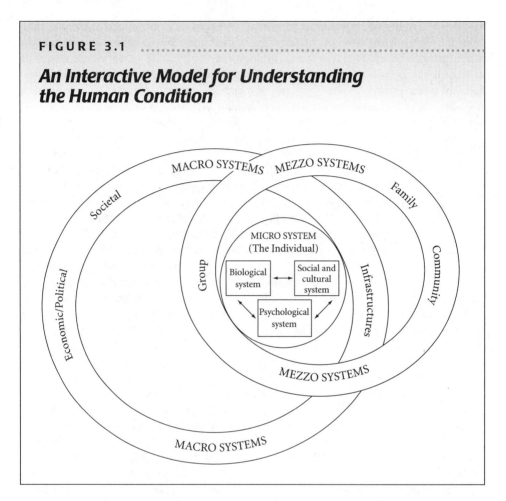

FIGURE 3.1

An Interactive Model for Understanding the Human Condition

systems framework recognizes that poverty is another form of violence—in Mahatma Gandhi's words, the "worst form of violence."

In this chapter, case studies from a variety of countries will demonstrate approaches that help in understanding the diversity and common elements of the human condition and development through the various systems and cycles of the life span. One chapter cannot address all phases of human behavior; rather, showing the way a global approach can identify universal elements in understanding the human condition and human behavior is the goal. While each theme will be illustrated with a case study that will emphasize one level of interpretation, be it micro, mezzo, or macro, implications for the other dimensions will also be reviewed (See Figure 3.1). Connections also will be made between human development and the discussion of diversity conflict in Chapter 8 and social justice in Chapter 9. The key themes of this chapter include:

1. *Issues of culture:* with an emphasis on micro levels and questions identified for exploring mezzo and macro behaviors.

2. *Environmental and ecological factors of human development* over the life span, with an emphasis on mezzo levels and questions identified for exploring micro and macro levels.

3. *Paradigms of empowerment and uses of power with an emphasis on macro questions,* and indicators for study concerning micro and mezzo levels of interaction.

4. Summary of the human condition as the key to human behavior.

SYSTEMS AND ECOLOGICAL TERMINOLOGY

While addressing these various dimensions this chapter identifies interactions between individuals (*micro*), communities (*mezzo*), and nations (*macro*) systems within an ecological framework. Philosophically, social work has distinguished itself from other helping professions by acknowledging that social policy and practice must build on and inform each other as evidence of the person-in-environment focus (Davis & Hagan, 1992). In the past, social work practice in North America and western Europe has been criticized for focusing too much on micro or individual interactions and "blaming the victim" (Courtney, 1993; Ryan, 1976). Similarly, problems in practice and research are frequently identified at the "person level" (Kagle & Cowger, 1984). With increasing utilization of systems theory during the 1970s and 1980s, social work educators in many countries consciously reviewed courses for a more even mix of attention to mezzo or community interventions and to macro or institutional and structural work. Courses were identified as micro or macro, a practice that ironically may have perpetuated an unhelpful separation of issues; the result is that elements of structural policy that drastically affect people's lives get left out of individual practice conversations, as discussed in Chapter 9.

Despite the emphasis in the social work literature that social workers intervene at the interface of person and environment to bring about change, limited attention is paid to the operationalization of this perspective (Meyer, 1987; Coulton, 1995). A focus on the human condition globally helps us to assess the interface of person and environment and thus serves as a guide in developing appropriate intervention strategies. Van Soest (1997) addressed this tension in her discussion of conceptual definitions of levels of violence. In Van Soest's approach and that of the Violence and Development Project Centers of the U.S. National Association of Social Workers, often inspired by Gandhi, violence inflicted on individuals is seen as the tip of the iceberg in a world that constantly perpetuates conflict. Examples of violence at the structural level include oppressive policing and corrections policies alongside inadequate funding for education, and punitive "welfare" legislation or sanctioning of violence when it is murder by the state (defined as "capital punishment").

Germain (1993) has similarly made a helpful distinction between systems theory and an ecological framework: the former is an umbrella theory of how units are organized, and can be related to technology or formal organizations as well as to human relationships in the organization of social life. Ecological theory, however, always reflects cycles of human interdependence and healthy and dynamic biological and psychosocial growth. In this book, ecological theory both belongs to and expands the more general systems approach; ecological theory emphasizes the social work theme of always considering the whole "person in environment" and the multiple interconnections that promote optimum growth and behavior.

Issues of Culture: Micro Levels of Interpretation and Assessment

The first example illustrating micro and macro levels of interpretation of human behavior relating to culture is the Detroit (U.S.A.) Project 1993.

The success of African-American people may depend upon their ability to function effectively in two worlds, one black and one white in the context of the contemporary United States (Beverly, 1989). Where there is a lack of individual and group self-esteem, African-American youth may be hindered in their efforts to effectively compete with other groups in a pluralistic society. Negotiating and effectively functioning in both the majority and the minority culture is a critical ingredient that may influence success. Navigating through two distinctly different cultures requires individuals of African descent to deal constantly with uncertainties, as identified in the project summary in Case Study 3.1.

The Project 1993 research identified self- and group esteem as critical components in development and behavior. It is a universal feature of human behavior, as demonstrated in the PBS film *Childhood*, that children and youth in different countries of the world will smile and relax when they are either praised or feel positively recognized and safe. Similarly, fear, shock, and tension are apparent in new situations such as earthquake drills, swimming lessons, or separation from caregivers, whether the young people are in Brazil, the United States, or Russia. Following worldwide filming, the psychologist Jerome Kagan states in *Childhood* that "the foundations of development are universal, while the forms and structures of nurture may differ." Project 1993 describes research on young African Americans who were dropping out of school because they did not feel recognized by their teachers or their larger community. The group was taken from their U.S. urban environment to Ghana, where they were suddenly in the majority culture across the nation, with positive effects relating to their group and self-esteem. Previous research has assessed black and white participants' communication patterns and found that self-disclosure and confidence were higher within the cultural peer group (intraethnic) than in encounters between cultural peer groups (interethnic) (Gudykunst & Hammer, 1987). Cross-national experiences that reduce uncertainties in ways young people feel about themselves may be useful in increasing positive interactions across multicultural groups in the United States, thereby reducing the prejudice that leads to exclusion and racism. Simultaneously, education that expands interethnic understanding of heritage and culture also expands feelings of recognition and participation.

CASE STUDY 3.1

Project 1993: Detroit

CHATHAPURAM S. RAMANATHAN
CREIGS BEVERLY

This project researched the role of cross-cultural experience as it relates to self-esteem. A unique feature of the research was the combination of observations of a group that traveled from the United States to Ghana. Cross-cultural experience that is removed from the current majority and minority transactions may provide opportunities that are devoid of the internalized consequences of racism. The project's mission was to provide each participant with an enriched school experience for four years.

The sample for the Detroit study was drawn from a participant pool of 89 high school students who were involved in a school dropout prevention program called "Project 1993." The high school is located in the city of Detroit's eastern part and has an enrollment of approximately 1,400 students. Over 96 percent of the student body is African American, and a substantial percent of the students come from one-parent families. The high school is located in one of the most economically disadvantaged communities of southeastern Michigan. It has a population of 16,000 and an unemployment rate of about 25 percent. Nearly 96 percent of the population is African American; nearly three-fourths have incomes under $15,000 and over two thirds of the population have incomes less than $5,000. Participants in Project 1993 were identified by teachers and counselors from feeder middle schools entering the high school. Project participation was based on poor attendance, poor academic performance, high disciplinary problems, or involvement with the juvenile justice system.

Once students were enrolled in the project, they participated in a six-week intensive summer program prior to entry into high school. Besides receiving instruction in mathematics, science, and English, the students were also involved in special efficacy seminars in drug abuse prevention, nonviolent resolution of interpersonal conflict, and life goal planning. Other experiences included peer counseling, conversational French, cultural events, and career exposure. During the academic years the students participated in academic and nonacademic program activities. Project staff served as counselors and advocates for the students and also worked collaboratively with families of participants.

Participants who had high school grade point averages (average of the first three years after enrollment in the project) of 3.0 or better were taken on a trip to Ghana for two weeks as a reinforcer for their academic achievements. This travel provided an opportunity to experience a sense of cultural relativity and formation of an identity antithetical to their experience in America. The hypothesis was that the participants would show improvements in their overall self-esteem as well as in the dimensions of peer self-esteem, home self-esteem, and school self-esteem. Reentry group work services were based on a self-help/support group format.

Students' overall self-esteem and various dimensions of self-esteem, such as peer, self, school, and home esteem, improved at statistically significant levels as a result of Project 1993. While there was no statistically significant relationship between self-esteem and school performance, this outcome could result from the fact that the self-esteem measures and school performance were measured at different time frames and there was a shortage of time for changes in self-esteem prior to graduation.

• •

Simply vocalizing and discussing African American history with youth may not in and of itself establish a solid foundation for self-identity, a critical component in determining our behavior toward others. While this type of exposure and orientation is important, particularly for students of all cultures, the key may be to establish a scenario in which reference group identity is tested in the crucible of another culture for reinforcement. In other words, the strength of one's identity cannot be tested against itself but must be tested against another culture to determine its strength and efficacy. Certainly, in terms of this project, the students' self-esteem benefitted both from the work in their Detroit schools and through their experience in Ghana.

Taking a Systems Perspective: The Micro, Mezzo, and Macro Perspectives

Although the main focus in the Project 1993 case study is the micro level of human behavior in relation to the self-esteem of individual students, it is important to assess all levels of a system's interactions before deciding on a locus of social work action. Let us turn briefly to the mezzo impact and the macro implications. While Project 1993 focused on self-esteem, it expanded the culture-bound emphasis in the United States on self and individual by referring to peer and group esteem. The essence of self-esteem relates to the human condition in terms of our needs to be nurtured, honored, and connected to our immediate caregivers and community. Thus a *global concept may be social well-being,* where the interdependence of the esteem of self in relation to others is understood.

Cross-cultural experiences could also be utilized as part of community leadership training. At the micro and mezzo levels, synthesis may be possible in dialogue and discussion between social workers and their clients around instrumental and noninstrumental behaviors depending upon the setting. It does not become a question of which values are better, reference group values and behaviors or outer-group values and behaviors. Rather, for social workers and clients alike, it becomes a question of what is functional. The process of respectful communication may also lead to a review of one's traditional values—as is the case in our expectations of children to experience childhood rather than be laborers or victims of violence (U.N. Convention on the Rights of the Child, 1994). While micro knowledge helps us to undertake individual levels of assessment of human behavior, mezzo knowledge assists us in assessing human behavior in a small group, family, and community context. Thus from a mezzo focus, the questions relating to the social groups surrounding the individual are asked: How are the school, community, family, peer group functioning in enhancing or reducing esteem and promoting social well-being? Can specific positive encounters, as demonstrated in this case study, be introduced?

THE MACRO LEVEL OF ASSESSMENT. Resources will probably prohibit the strategy of cross-cultural immersion from country to country; from a *macro perspective,* however, considerable attention has been provided recently to issues of cultural relevancy, cultural sensitivity, respect, and competency in all domains of education for children. While this discussion is particularly heated in U.S. schools, it also relates to countries formerly colonized and in the process of revising educational systems that relied on Anglo or Spanish language and tradition. In Mexico, for instance, there are over fifty indigenous languages and community workers with the Trust for the Health of the Indian Children of Mexico have published the art of Indian children as an affirmation of their history and creativity. As the Trust emphasizes, "Many must work to honor the lives of these children of luminous words and brilliant ideas" (Trust for the Health of Indian Children, 1994). Guillermo Espinosa Velasco, director of the National Indian Institute, speaks for all indigenous peoples: "These murals were painted by Indian children, living repositories of complex cultures which have survived through the sheer will of Indian people, in spite of terrible adversity" (Trust for the Health of Indian Children, 1994). Similarly, African-American youth in the United States flourish when their ideas are given voice and recognition in the educational system, as demonstrated in Project 1993.

In El Salvador the Jorge family can only afford to send one child to school

Generally, the 20th century has seen a gradual realization of the impact of former colonialization and the repercussions of using Western forms of education and curriculum content over local culture and traditions. For example, North American stereotypes of Asians date back to the late 19th and early 20th centuries, when they were considered an inferior race. The Japanese were stereotyped as intelligent and sly; the Chinese first as exotic curiosities and later as "inassimilable, immoral and treacherous heathens." This early stereotyping influenced perceptions of Asian Indians as superstitious, backward, and spineless, with filthy and immodest habits (Balgopal, 1995). Despite the negative stereotypes, Asian Americans are also viewed as being successful, intelligent, hardworking. Consequently, they are stereotyped as a model minority. Implicit in this perspective is the misleading notion that they do not face many problems, and even if they do, the close-knit Asian American families and ethnic communities prevent psychosocial stressors (Uba, 1994).

Such macro-level stereotyping has had profound consequences historically in terms of social work practice and teaching. It has maintained concepts of the culturally neutral "professional role" over the realities of local culture and traditions and the need for expanded "cultural competence" in working among different cultural experiences and traditions. For example, as California seeks to recognize the new majority of Spanish speakers, other states are still reacting hastily to the needs for bilingual staff, culturally competent human service professionals, and police. The town of Wilmar, Minnesota provides a microcosm of this process as longer-term residents meet the new migrants, and local media emphasize difference rather than the common human condition in articles such as "Migrant Workers Changing the Face of Rural Minnesota" (Sommers & Ruiz, 1995). During this process, some of the earlier wave of Scandinavian immigrants may forget that they, too, were migrants. Community tensions rather than cooperation result when there is reaction to the "differences" of "not like us" features of the incoming workers, rather than welcoming people who help to maintain a rural population and who are willing to work in an unpopular and low-paid labor market (including harvesting beet fields and chicken processing). Figure 3.1 illustrates the interactions between the micro, mezzo, and macro levels of self-esteem and social well-being discussed in this case study.

• •

ENVIRONMENTAL AND ECOLOGICAL FACTORS IN THE HUMAN CONDITION, WITH AN EMPHASIS ON THE MEZZO LEVELS

"Taking charge of our own lives" is a universal element in social work throughout the world, even though the various approaches, concepts and cultural context of the "helping" profession changes, so that "own lives" will be viewed as a collective in some regions and more individually in others. In the Silent Valley project, for example (see Case Study 3.2), groups of concerned citizens were protesting construction of a large dam to be funded by the World Bank in Kerala, India. Although the central and state government had authorized implementation of the plan, the people's movement, including community organizers and activists, challenged this project on the basis of negative consequences for the environment and social displacement of individuals and families. This case study illustrates how individual people take charge of their lives both within (that is, in micro terms of individual accomplishment) and without (in their external mezzo and macro relationships with communities, institutions, and governments).

CASE STUDY 3.2

The Silent Valley National Park

CHATHAPURAM S. RAMANATHAN

Silent Valley, a national park in Kerala, India, is situated in the Kundali Hills of the Western Ghats, at the southwestern corner of the Nilgiri Hills in Palghat District. The nearest town and location of park headquarters, is 40 kilometers by road to the south. Originally declared a national park, in 1980 this park was supposed to be excluded as the site of a proposed hydroelectric project. The same area was originally constituted reserved land under Section 26 of the Forest Act in 1888. The park is bounded by Attappadi Reserved Forest to the east and the vested forests of Palghat Division and Nilambur Division to the south and the west, respectively. Silent Valley is an integral part of the ecosystem of the region. Although the specific area where the dam was to have been constructed is believed never to have been settled, there are indigenous tribal people (Rahmani, 1989). There are settlements 2 kilometers southeast of the area and 5 kilometers southwest.

The Silent Valley forests, locally known as "Sairandhrivanam" and considered by many to be one of the last representative tracts of virgin tropical evergreen forest in India, became the focus of India's perhaps fiercest and most widely publicized environmental debate in the late 1970s, when the Kerala State Electricity Board decided to go ahead with a hydroelectric project in the valley (Agarwal et al., 1985). The project was expected to generate 240 megawatts of electricity and to irrigate some 100,000 hectares of land in the relatively less developed Palghat and Malappuram districts.

Four main types of vegetation are recognized: tropical evergreen forest, which forms extensive dense stands along hills and valleys; subtropical hill forest between; temperate forest, popularly referred to as *sholas* and characterized by unrelated evergreen species with a dense closed canopy; and grasslands (Unnikrishnan, 1989). Faunal diversity is very high and includes a number of endemic and threatened species (Zoological Survey of India, 1986). Regarding the flora in the area, 966 species belonging to 134 families and 559 genera are thriving. Also, 110 plant species of importance to Ayurvedic medicine (indigenous medicine), a part resistant strain of rice, and other economically valuable plant species contribute to the area vegetation (Nair & Balasubramanyan, 1984). Twenty-six species of mammals excluding bats, rodents and insectivores, such as Asian elephants, tigers, leopards, 120 species of birds, and 19 species of amphibians have been recorded (Balakrishnan, 1984; Jayson, 1990; Mathen, 1990).

A task force of the National Committee on Environmental Planning and Coordination, under M. S. Swaminathan, the then Secretary of Agriculture of the Government of India, and several nongovernmental conservational organizations, including the Bombay Natural History Society, Kerala Sastra Sahitya Parishad (Kerala Science and Literature Society), and the Indian Science Congress, urged the government of Kerala to abandon the scheme, but to no avail. Further, the government of Kerala refused to endorse the Joint Committee's findings (Agarwal & Narain, 1985). The dispute became highly politicized and innumerable state and national organizations, as well as international organizations such as World Wildlife Fund, became involved in the "Save Silent Valley" campaign. To appease conservationists, the government of Kerala created a national park in December 1980 that excluded the proposed project site from the area. In November 1983, the hydroelectric project was finally shelved and the present national park declared a year later, in deference to the weight of public opinion and to the sentiments of the then prime minister, Indira Gandhi.

A significant amount of research has been conducted in Silent Valley, such as environmental impact assessments, generated by the controversy over the hydroelectric project (Vijayan and Balakrishnan, 1977; Ramakrishnan & Singh, 1981; Nair & Balasubramanyan, 1984), vegetation studies (Basha, 1987). The flora has been examined by the Botanical Survey of India (Manilal, 1988) and the fauna by the Zoological Survey of India (1986). Additionally, several ecological studies have been conducted by the Kerala Forest Research Institute (1990).

••

This case study may be viewed at the mezzo level in terms of family, group, and community action. At the group level of human behavior, people are mobilizing their natural family networks. Although family members are not all living together, they still encourage, reinforce, and support the cause of Silent Valley. However, there are numerous examples of similar actions in communities worldwide. For example, the Texas protest against nuclear waste dumping (see Student Activity 1 at the end of this chapter). At the mezzo level, not only is the individual's job at stake, but the group of people as a whole is also affected when the community has to be uprooted or is deprived of its natural resources, habitat, and continuity of the familiar.

At the family level, children witness that their parents and relatives, through active participation in the life of the community, are able to stand up for principles they believe in and against powers that may seem overwhelming. Thus, the children have a good role model for their own struggles. The metameaning that is communicated at the family, group, and community level is a sense of empowerment over their destiny. This sense of empowerment has implications historically in terms of ancestral and heritage issues; in the present in terms of livelihood and continued feelings of being connected with their community; and in the future in terms of the positive impact on coming generations' feeling of power and knowledge that people can take charge of their destiny.

Additionally, this sense of connectedness with community reflects what Powell (1988) considers spiritual intimacy: "Spiritual intimacy is created through the shared revelations of faith, beliefs and insights into spiritual matters" that can help "to create a common bond, a context of belief in which understanding and trust can be fostered."

The Micro Level of Assessment

In their personal lives, self-esteem for people fighting the Silent Valley hydroelectric project was a key element; in the process of organizing, individuals came to believe that they had a powerful voice. It has been well documented in globally recognized literature that there is a direct relationship between control over one's life and consequent self-esteem. In the Silent Valley protest, individuals came together with their neighbors and families and eventually made a major impact on the larger macro environment. This process included responding to their initial fears of loss of livelihood by mobilizing their internal resources, including belief in self, ability to speak out, the power of positive thinking—all despite massive structural challenges that they encountered from powerful institutions.

Also at the micro level is the impact of a sense of spirituality and connectedness with surroundings when people are expected to leave the place of their ancestors. Native American history is a poignant reminder and echo of this process, as illustrated in Chief Seattle's message written in 1854. This speech was made to mark the transfer of ancestral lands to the U.S. Government.

Chief Seattle's Message*

1854

The great Chief in Washington sends word that he wishes to buy our land. The Great Chief also sends us words of friendship and good will. This is kind of him, since we know he has little need of our friendship in return. But we will consider your offer. For we know that if we do not sell, the white man may come with guns and take our land.

How can you buy or sell the sky, the warmth of the land? The idea is strange to us.

If we do not own the freshness of the air and the sparkle of the water, how can you buy them?

Every part of this earth is sacred to my people. Every shining pine needle, every sandy shore, every mist in the dark woods, every clearing and humming insect is holy in the memory and experience of my people. The sap which courses through the trees carries the memories of the red man.

The white man's dead forget the country of their birth when they go to walk among the stars. Our dead never forget this beautiful earth, for it is the mother of the red man. We are part of the earth and it is part of us . . .

So, when the Great Chief in Washington sends word that he wishes to buy our land, he asks much of us. . . . So we will consider your offer to buy our land. But it will not be easy. For this land is sacred to us.

This shining water that moves in the streams and rivers is not just water but the blood of our ancestors. If we sell you land, you must remember that it is sacred, and you must teach your children that it is sacred, and that each ghostly reflection in the clear water of the lake tells of events and memories in the life of my people. The water's murmur is the voice of my father's father.

The rivers are our brothers, they quench our thirst. The rivers carry our canoes, and feed our children. If we sell you our land, you must remember, and teach your children, that the rivers are our brothers, and yours, and you must henceforth give the rivers the kindness you would give any brother . . .

This we know. The earth does not belong to man; man belongs to the earth. This we know. All things are connected like the blood which unites one family. All things are connected.

Whatever befalls the earth befalls the sons of the earth. Man did not weave the web of life, he is merely a strand in it. Whatever he does to the web, he does to himself . . .

One thing we know. Our God is the same God. This earth is precious to him. Even the white man cannot be exempt from the common destiny. We may be brothers after all. We shall see.

These adult behaviors and responses in taking away or trying to preserve ancestral land do not arise in a vacuum. Individuals are constantly interacting in the context of their cultural environment at all ages and stages of the family, group, and village life to protect their future well-being. Thus, individual self-esteem, cultural identity, and structural change are crucial at all ages and in all circumstances result in cooperative or conflictual human behavior. The parallels of the Silent Valley and Chief Seattle's experience are a powerful reminder of the constant cycles of human behavior in common conditions of challenge or deprivation.

The Macro Level of Assessment

The Silent Valley protest has policy ramifications in terms of how international banking industries need to work in synchronization with nongovernmental organizations in planning, designing, and implementing the project. Also, it is very telling that policies formulated from a Western perspective, without adequate sensitivity to local issues, can ensure that the project fails. These local issues include a tradition of farmers' rights to land ownership according to the Indian Land Reform Act and the connection and sensitivity of people to their environment; children also learn at an early age the importance of revering the nature that

*Excerpted with permission from Robert Cooney & Helen Michalowski (eds.), *The Power of the People*. Philadelphia: New Society, 1987.

surrounds them. In direct contrast to such feelings of respect, the people who planned this dam were far removed from the spiritual and meaningful connections of the habitat of these people.

Both the lack of connection to local people's reality and the promise of economic gain facilitated the World Bank project, which primarily operated from a Western economic perspective without adequate attention to sustainability of the "developmental initiative." In the context of macro issues, there are also policy ramifications in terms of the connection between international policies that might favor the Global North and their negative consequences in the Global South. A parallel example to the Silent Valley protest that students may want to study is the controversy of U.S.-owned companies along the Mexican border with the United States that the Mexicans call *maquedores*. These businesses are criticized for benefitting from cheap labor without due attention to improving working conditions or providing clean water supplies to communities. Water is the key to healthy communities in preventing infant mortality; maintaining sanitation and personal cleanliness, irrigation, and adult health; and avoiding famine. The structural goals of a project may be driven by the rationale of Western approaches to increase access to energy or sources of labor while the local needs of people who have traditionally been considered powerless are trampled. Furthermore, there is a connection between poverty in economically advanced countries and poverty in economically challenged countries: the faces of undernourished children without access to immunization or clean water are the same the world over.

Recognizing a sense of place and resilience were human behaviors displayed in the Silent Valley protest. It has been suggested that the difference between an immigrant and a refugee is that immigrants send their spirit ahead to a new place and the body follows; refugees send their bodies and their spirits remain at home. In the Silent Valley conflict, people fought and overcame their imposed displaced person or refugee status.

······································

PARADIGMS OF EMPOWERMENT AND USES OF POWER

Let us turn here to the macro level of human behavior in terms of economic and social conditions and the power of people to overcome policies and traditions that exclude, exploit, or ignore. Our example is labor rights: macro issues such as the value of women's work, child labor, and labor rights are the umbrella, and case studies draw out connections and universal elements.

The Macro Level of Assessment

Case studies provide a macro perspective of labor worldwide, with examples within the issue of domestic workers in Mexico seeking recognition of women's rights, child labor in Bangladesh and the search to free children, labor organizing in the United States and the right to a fair wage. The first case study for illustration of macro issues is based on the Centro de Apoyo de la Trabajadora Domestica, in Cuernavaca, Morelos, Mexico. Although this material is reviewed in the context of human behavior focusing on the empowerment and self-esteem of women, it could also be used in policy or practice study.

Center for Domestic Workers, Cuernavaca

ROSEMARY J. LINK

The Center for Domestic Workers is an employment rights and child care resource for women who have traditionally been undocumented and poorly paid in an informal employment sector. The Center began in 1985 as an advocacy group for women, and it vividly portrays behavior at the individual level of cooperation leading to structural intervention in terms of women's rights and family well-being.

Domestic service makes up a vast section of the workforce for women in Mexico, especially in Cuernavaca, site of many weekend homes for wealthy Mexican families. These workers are among the most exploited, and they have few advocates in the community to challenge this exploitation: they often work without basic labor rights, adequate wages, provision for free or national holiday time, health support, and protection from unfair dismissal or abuse. The Center drew together social workers, community workers, and a sociologist to address these issues. They obtained premises and concentrated on establishing advocacy and outreach. Educational information was also given to domestic workers' employers. Their original focus on workers' rights expanded into recognition of family needs, including daycare provision, parenting support, women's groups, and literacy.

The director of CATDA, Dinora Morales, explained to one of the authors that when her social workers and volunteers go into the *colonias* (neighborhoods), they generate much interest and response to the dialogue they offer. In assessing resources, there is a capacities focus: "We wait to deal with literacy . . . we do not want to lose the energy or self-esteem, literacy comes later." The presumption is that workers and families will rely on oral and pictorial communications. The capacities, dignity, and worth of individuals are emphasized, separate from their educational attainment.

The Center's annual report confirms that this agency is actively involved in achieving adequate home conditions for children and their mothers, with support from the daycare center and network of friendship and skills groups. All women and children using these services do so voluntarily. The director referred to tension for social workers who put themselves at risk as leaders because of disapproval from some social groups. They recognize their work as a "political act"; in Morales's view, this is a society that is accustomed to poverty, and those who are wealthy are ambivalent about this level of social action (Link, 1997).

On the macro level, the traditional Partido Revolucionario Independiente (PRI) is being constantly challenged for its laissez-faire attitudes after decades in power, and as the opposition parties organize, including the People's Democratic Party (PRD), to bring about change, social workers are often at the forefront of community action. We find this structural role for social workers in many countries where social workers hold high office, such as in India, where a social worker chairs the policy body of higher education at the national level; or in Norway, where there is a national ombudsman for children's rights; or in the United Kingdom, where the new (1997) Labour Administration has 50 seats in Parliament held by social workers. There are some distinctions here between countries of the Global North and South that cannot be underestimated, such as the realities in areas where stark poverty stands in the shade of extremes of wealth and oppressive control and where social workers' lives are threatened for their collective courage and action.

• •

This case study can prompt discussion at many levels. For example, in a U.S. human behavior class the question keeps arising: How far can social workers expect to make an impact on national policies in relation to workers' or parents' rights? One way to frame this issue includes reference to the Swedish and Norwegian policy that makes physical punishment of children illegal (Germain, 1995). This startles U.S. students brought up in a culture with a history of physical discipline and adult control into a contemporary debate over the merits of corporal punishment.

Taking further this reference to the human right to be free from molestation, the U.N. film *The Rights of the Child* demonstrates the plight of children pressed into labor, and a recent U.N. study discovered 250 million children working globally (*Minneapolis Star Tribune,* 1996). The film expands the debate on the rights of the adult to harm or exploit, expanding it beyond the micro level of direct experience and discipline to the macro debate of how we allow child labor to continue. People reinforce child labor by purchasing from companies such as clothing or rug retailers who have a history of exploiting young people in sweatshops in South American countries and often closer to home (UNICEF, 1997). These issues are crucial to a discussion of optimal conditions for child development and opportunity along with adult responsibility in a global context. Furthermore, the Convention on the Rights of the Child provides a framework for the steps that can be taken to end child labor. These are outlined by the United Nations Children's Fund:

1. Immediate elimination of hazardous and exploitative child labor

2. Provision of free and compulsory education

3. Wider legal protection

4. Birth registration of all children

5. Data collection and monitoring

6. Codes of conduct and procurement policies

The commitment to the rights and special needs of children passed into international law in 1990 with the adoption of the Convention on the Rights of the Child by the United Nations Assembly. The majority of countries have accepted the convention and ratified the principles through their own political processes (with the exception, as of 1996, of the Cook Islands, Oman, Somalia, Switzerland, the United States, and the United Arab Emirates). The convention is discussed further in Chapter 5 in terms of social work ethics in work with children.

The Micro Level of Assessment

At the micro level, women's labor projects across the world, whether they be the workers' organization in Cuernavaca or the cooperatives in Bolivia or the Self-Employed Women's Organization (SEWA) in India, give women a belief in themselves and their worth (Media

Network, 1995; Gross, 1992). In many cultures, women have historically been ascribed roles of subservience. Particularly with industrialization in the countries of the Global North men have benefitted from a male-oriented economic, social, and political system, while in agricultural areas women often complete the work but without the compensation (Gilligan, 1982). As women's creativity in the world of work becomes recognized, there is an accompanying sense of accomplishment and power (Link, 1995).

The Mezzo Level of Assessment

In terms of the mezzo level, we see immediate positive consequences for communities where individuals feel that they are contributing to their environment, where they feel heard and valued. The women involved in labor action are displaying characteristics of resilience in times of economic crisis and change. Their creativity and challenges to traditional perceptions (for example, challenging the European-American emphasis on literacy over community networking) lead to innovations in the ways they tackle issues which affect their children's well-being. In the Charles Kuralt–NASW video *Violence and Development,* there is a memorable and poignant sequence on a mill in Northern India entirely run by women: "Our story tells the world there is a place, a place where women own and run a rice mill" (NASW, 1996).

• •

THE HUMAN CONDITION AND HUMAN BEHAVIOR IN A GLOBAL CONTEXT: CONCLUSIONS

As students study topics relating to the human condition through a variety of case studies in the global environment, the realization dawns that we are more universal in our common human needs than different. As Charlotte Towle urged U.S. social workers in the 1930s to appreciate their similarities with "clients" more than the distance between them, so now we realize our mutuality in this broadest of contexts (Towle, 1945). The ecological systems perspective reinforces the recognition that just as systems are interdependent, so too are nations, and borders are less relevant. Certainly, borders are more than relevant to those who cross them secretly, but so too are the realizations that we use social, political, and geographic constructs in different ways, sometimes toward social justice and sometimes to reinforce oppression. For example the concept of opening borders in the European Union is seeking more justice for mobility of labor. Meanwhile the border between the United States and Mexico is aggressively policed in contrast to the much traversed "boundary waters" between the United States and Canada.

A more global approach to understanding human behavior includes at least five assumptions:

1. That human behavior is a result of the common human condition (rather than, for example, individual failure or deficit).

2. That most social workers, in both the Global North and South, have been part of a historical tradition in their education that included cultural borrowing, stereotyping, prejudice, and deepseated vestiges of colonialism.

3. That we have still to reach effectively for constructs that relate to many different cultures across borders.

4. That the study of behavior in a global context needs the widest ecological and systems perspectives.

This chapter has offered illustrations of our reach toward terminology and global constructs that are culturally viable. Some of the constructs offered are *social well-being* as an extension of self-esteem; *interdependence* of all people; *heritage* as sense of place; *empowerment* as group action to take charge of destiny; freedom to *play in childhood* as a part of human development; *cultural relevancy* in education; *spiritual intimacy* and observation of the *human condition* before interpretation of behavior.

A focus on the human condition in the global environment alerts us both to the possibilities for cooperation that recognition that a sense of "us" brings, and to a sense of urgency that without this perspective we risk continued and irreversible damage to our eco and social systems. A recent U.S. headline read "Logging split . . . in Surinam." The forests of Surinam have been relentlessly pillaged by transnational corporations and the timber exported to countries of the Global North. Recently it has been discovered that a rare periwinkle flowers there: this precious flower contains drugs that have been discovered to be helpful in the fight against many cancers, and suddenly the ravaging of these forests takes on a more common human meaning.

....

STUDENT ACTIVITIES

1. Discuss the following case study to identify the micro, mezzo, and macro levels of human behavior and the consequences and impact of this behavior on the environment.

CASE STUDY 3.4

Impact of Nuclear Waste on the Social Environment

K. R. RAMAKRISHNAN

This case study illustrates the impact of a proposed nuclear waste dump project on the people of Deaf Smith County, Texas, at the micro, mezzo, and macro levels and how the largely farming and agricultural community organized itself in thwarting the efforts of the U.S. Department of Energy (DOE) and other business interest groups in constructing the site. The factors that probably influenced the Department of Energy when choosing the site included the fact that all requirements of site characterization, such as geological acumen, had been met. The site was considered to be located in a sparsely populated, remote area and was assumed to be lacking social, economic, and political influence. There was support for DOE from a group of people who were interested in the jobs and dollars that the project would bring to the community.

Under the leadership of local ranchers, farmers, and community organizers, STAND (Serious Texans Against Nuclear Dump) was organized. STAND, networking with groups like POWER (People Opposed to Wasted Energy Repository), STHOP (Stay the Hell Out of Panhandle), and others formed a cohesive unit to challenge the DOE and business interest groups on the basis of negative consequences to the environment and disruption of family life. People's building opposition to the site stemmed from their awareness of disruption to their environment and areas of their livelihood.

At the micro level, individuals became knowledgeable about the threats to their land, water, and air. People became anxious about their own safety and that of future generations. Their sense of spirituality and connection with their surroundings was quite evident when questions regarding one generation's legacy of unearned risks for generations of unborn were raised. Individuals responded to their initial fear of health consequences and degradation of their environment by mobilizing their internal resources. The community members, organized into various groups, were made to believe in their ability to stand up and speak out against powerful special business interest groups. Community members met the challenge from the DOE and especially the out-of-state company that had been contracted to do the construction. Individuals voiced their fears and opinions in community talk sessions and radio talk shows. Women thrust themselves into the fray through the formation of WIFE (Women Involved in Farm Economics). Hispanics voiced their opposition through their church groups. Students participated through discussions and debates in their schools. Socials, dances, and dinners were organized to raise funds and to heighten community consciousness and solidarity. Individuals from all walks of life—rich and poor, old and young, male and female—were involved in the community wide movement.

At the mezzo level, the focus was on the individual's transactions with other individuals and small groups within the social environment. This is the interface that involves interpersonal relationships among families, peer groups, and immediate work groups. In our case example, the community was faced with the issue of selecting between economic considerations and health and environmental safety. In some instances, the issue split families; in others, the nuclear dump issue brought families and groups together. STAND mobilized the community by establishing an ongoing network of persons and organizations. Groups like STHOP and WIFE and youth in schools provided people with a sense of empowerment over their destiny. It is interesting to note that instead of one group called HAND (Hereford Against Nuclear Dump) carrying on the fight, a wide variety of groups was involved in the confrontation. Subdivisions of the larger community enabled leaderships to develop in each group. This effect also enabled each group to gain recognition and importance. Instead of getting lost in a big crowd, individuals participating in the smaller groups of their interest and choice found themselves wanted and felt proud of their contribution. People felt connected with their community. Their participation in the affairs of their land and water not only provided them with an opportunity to take charge of their destiny but also had a positive impact for future generations' feeling of power.

• •

2. The following case study about a person with Hansen's disease appears to illustrate a micro level of human behavior; however, many issues interact in this situation. Identify the levels of interaction and compare them with a field experience of your own.

TABLE 3.1

Framework to Assess Engagement in Global Social Work Learning

	Practice and Field
Elements of global social work	
Personal review of global awareness	interested in other countries and world regions
Knowledge of mutual learning country to country	comparing work philosophy, social role, choices across countries
Understanding of cultural competence and respectful language	proactive in exploring culture, aware of own bias and prejudice
Analysis of human rights	applying UN documents to practice
Historical analysis	knowing impact of past on current resources, socioeconomic status
Review of values and ethics	identifying implications of different approaches, country codes
Evaluation of local variations	exploring theories in different nations
Synthesis of professional activity	seeking alternatives, links with other places, building with global awareness

CASE STUDY 3.5

A Hansen's Disease Patient in Madras

CHATHAPURAM S. RAMANATHAN

As a practicum student in a graduate social work program in South Asia, I was placed in a Hansen's disease treatment and education center in the city of Madras, India.

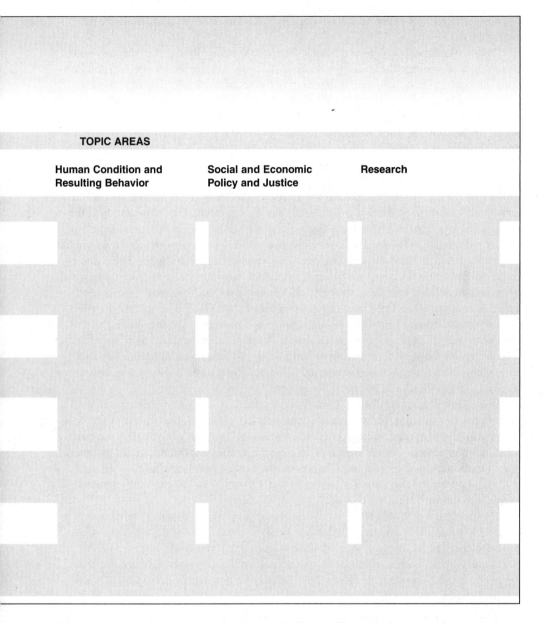

TOPIC AREAS

Human Condition and Resulting Behavior	Social and Economic Policy and Justice	Research

Given the social stigma attached to Hansen's disease (formerly known as leprosy), I prepared myself emotionally for the placement. During the orientation week I realized the impact of the illness and the manner in which the disease spreads. One assignment was in the "advanced ward," where clients had severe physical deformities. The client was a 20-year-old-Muslim man, "Kasim," whose extremities were affected to the extent that two-thirds of the length of his fingers had been surgically removed. Kasim had been in the facility for three months, and through the use of social work interviewing skills it was gathered that Kasim's own family had shunned him. This rejection had had a profound negative impact on his esteem. The following is an excerpt from the student's journal.

"Next to Kasim's bed, there was a book shelf, and the client had placed the holy book Quran there. Given that the student was Hindu, in order to establish an effective and functional rapport through the operationalization of the social work principle of acceptance and a nonjudgmental attitude, I asked if Kasim would read a few verses from the Quran and reflect and share the meaning it had for him. I had processed this intervention with my faculty liaison, who indicated to me it was a good idea, and it would also aid in mobilizing Kasim's inner strength, i.e., his spiritual self. The rationale was, ultimately the will to change has to come from within, and given the very low self-esteem of Kasim, mobilizing his inner strength became critical.

"To my dismay, when I asked Kasim to read a few verses from the Quran, he became very upset. With tears gushing through his cheeks, he responded that he is so unholy [because of being inflicted with Hansen's disease] that he was unworthy of touching the Quran. As Jacobi (1951) suggests, '. . . the diseased person or the person, too, for whom life has lost its meaning stands before problems with which he vainly struggles. The greatest and most important problems are basically insoluble; they must be so because they express the necessary polarity imminent in every self-regulating system.' I helped Kasim to deal with this emotionally charged predicament that society had placed him in, and the effect of its internalization on him. With Kasim's approval, I accessed a Muslim student volunteer to help read the Quran on a few occasions. Through this process, I was able to demonstrate to Kasim the continuum of Spirituality and Religion, and Spirituality and Humanness. This internal mobilization did help strengthen Kasim's self-esteem, and he then did pick up the Quran in one of the sessions."

These adult behaviors, albeit responses to the human condition of Hansen's disease, do not arise in a vacuum. Individuals are constantly interacting in the context of their cultural environment at the family, group, and community levels, all which reflect societal values and prejudices—that is, mezzo level. Here it becomes important that we pay attention to the educational component—educating the general public and families on the myths and misinformation that contribute to social stigma—in this case, the stigma of people inflicted with Hansen's disease.

The baccillus that causes Hansen's disease thrives in tropical climates. The disease is completely controllable and treatable. If this disease is viewed as a global problem, there will be the needed momentum to enlist the commitment of nations in both the Global North and Global South to eradicate this totally controllable disease. However, because of the resource and technology limits of tropical nations, many people in the Global South still suffer from Hansen's disease.

• •

3. Questions for students following the discussion of Case Study 3.3 (see pp. 43–44) can represent a general framework for review.
   a. What values appear different and the same for this Mexican center as compared to students' personal values or those of their country's approach to social welfare and social work? Prompts could include: How do people in the community view illiteracy? How are people at minimum wage and in poverty viewed? What are some risks and opportunities for workers and participants?

    b. What knowledge of human behavior and community organizing is being used here? How is the approach different or the same from one country to another? When are community members viewed as partners, clients, actors, or dysfunctional people?

    c. What approach to human behavior by workers seem uppermost at the Center? How might a "needs assessment" be carried out from a strengths perspective?

    d. How would you draw an ecomap to demonstrate the networks that transformed the center's work?

4. Complete the framework for human behavior in Table 3.1 (developed from the original matrix in Table 1.1 in Chapter 1).

Infusing Global Perspectives into Social Work Practice

DOREEN ELLIOTT
NAZNEEN MAYADAS

There can be no security or real peace if vast numbers of
people in various parts of the world live in poverty and
misery. Nor indeed, can there be a balanced economy for
the world as a whole if the undeveloped parts continue
to upset that balance and to drag down even the more
prosperous nations.

—JAWAHARLAL NEHRU

It is by now a conventional truism that we live in a global age: we see international influences in almost every walk of life, and our daily lives are influenced by a global economy and political world view. The practice of social work has a long-established tradition of internationalism. With European origins, the profession came to the United States and subsequently was exported again to different parts of the globe. Schools of social work for the professional education and training of social workers were set up in many countries, as discussed in Chapter 2. Schools all over the world have been influenced by the Western model of social work education, especially the American model since it produced the literature that influenced practice.

Increasingly, however, this approach was questioned as countries all over the globe sought to establish independent models for practice that more closely suited the culture and history of the country. Healy (1995) describes the "retreat from internationalism" as the result both of reduced federal and institutional funding and of the Vietnam War, which led Americans to reassess their global role. Mayadas and Elliott (1997) describe this phase as the third in the development of internationalism in social work, characterized by regionalization, polarization, separation, and localization. Movements such as indigenization in the Middle East and India and the reconceptualization of social work in Central and South America led to the growth of indigenous models that were more appropriate and specific to the needs of the country (Cornely & Bruno, 1997; El Nasr, 1997; Nanavatty, 1997; Queiro-Tajalli, 1997). In this postindigenization phase in international social work, what is now the role of a global perspective? Does this mean a return to the "professional imperialism" of the past, or is there a new perspective (Midgley, 1981)?

BENEFITS OF A GLOBAL PERSPECTIVE

A global approach contributes to recognition of the universals in human experience. Without diminishing the importance of differences, it is possible to focus on commonalties and thereby facilitate appreciation of different interpretations of similar human experiences. Recognition of commonalties and increased knowledge of, and respect for, differences helps to dissipate fear and mistrust and ultimately promotes world peace through improved international understanding. A global perspective offers multiple dimensions of analysis and provides new ways of analyzing problems from a multicultural and pluralistic viewpoint. Globalization is interdependence, where the philosophical base undergirding action is cooperation and not competition. A global perspective, as the term is used for this chapter, suggests an open and analytic approach; a systematic ability to accept as well as to reject practice models; and a willingness to share ideas, technology, and personnel and to work collaboratively toward the mutual benefit of all countries concerned.

Where, in this increasingly global world in which we live, stands the profession of social work? From a U.S. perspective, international social work may seem to be limited to a few international nongovernmental organizations such as Save the Children, UNICEF, and the International Committee of the Red Cross. Work with military families in American bases across the world is recognized as having a global perspective, as is work with immigrants and refugees, for which there are centers in most major cities. International adoptions and working with employees of multinational corporations are newer arrivals on the global social work scene. Widespread public awareness of the changing demographics of the United States challenges ethnocentric attitudes. How can social work benefit from this new globalism? What benefits are there to be found in a global approach?

A common global experience in social work relates to the lack of an easily identifiable professional role. If one asks passers-by in the street in many cities of the world what a social worker does, the responses would be very similar in their confusion of role definition. Social work, unlike many other professions, does not have a strong professional identity. To incorporate a stronger worldwide perspective and a greater shared professional identity into the profession would be to strengthen the professional identity of social work from a regional and national perspective as well. Because the benefits of a global perspective seem so obvious yet have not been applied consistently in social work practice, it is necessary to look at some of the barriers to achieving this perspective.

THE GLOBAL PERSPECTIVE: BARRIERS AND OPPORTUNITIES FOR PRACTICE

A global perspective requires the ability to live with diversity, pluralism, and value differences. The question that arises is: How can a global perspective be translated into practice principles and operations? Harris (1997), in his analysis of international social work practice, points out the difficulties of exchange. While values and knowledge at the abstract level of globalization may find considerable agreement among international social workers, a number of unforeseen difficulties arise at the operational level. In the European Community, for example, movement across national boundaries is no longer restricted but is impeded by professional issues such as salary, differential professional qualifications, licensure requirements, language, and communication.

Another obstacle to a global perspective is the degree to which problems are encountered across countries and the manner in which these problems are manifested. Since the impact of problems is experienced differently, reactions to it vary. There may be an absence of concerted action by the very group whose members are victimized by the problem within their respective regions. An example is genital mutilation of the female child in Africa. While social workers in the West are extremely sensitive to child abuse, nothing is done on a global level against this violent and health-hazardous practice. The 1995 Beijing Conference on Women addressed the issue, but it has continued to remain at the academic level (United Nations, 1996). If this ritualistic practice were viewed from a global perspective, it is more likely that Western feminist organizations would have taken a proactive stand and acted against it as a human rights issue.

Another barrier to globalization is the value differences among members of the same gender group from different religions and cultures. Women from a traditional Islamic background are conditioned to regard women's rights issues strictly from a Quranic law perspective. For example, inheritance rights were a heated issue of debate at the Beijing Conference for Women. The traditionalists opposed equal inheritance rights and supported the religious laws that give the woman half the assets inherited by her male sibling (United Nations, 1996). Issues such as these point to the influence of socialization and culture as a barrier to globalization. Recognizing the role of diversity in values, cultures, religion, and socialization, the Beijing Platform for Action states that "no true social transformation can occur until every society learns to adopt new values, forging relationships between women and men based on equality, equal responsibility, and mutual respect" (United Nations, 1996, p. 73).

That cultures are localized in regions and in nationalism is another barrier facing attempts at globalization. Harris (1997) questions the efficacy of a Western trained social worker from Germany serving a migrant family from Algiers in France. The point is well taken that regional perspectives strongly influence social work practice, as discussed in Chapter 10; theories utilized in one geographical area are selected specifically to meet the needs of that region. One example in the United States is the emphasis in social work on psychodynamic, individualistic models of pathology. Yet another example is the use of the Diagnostic and Statistical Manual 4th Edition (DSM IV), which reinforces the individualistic models of pathology; and the proliferation of private practice supported by financial investment in the insurance industry, and meets the current managed care needs.

When regional and national interests take precedence over global concerns, it is difficult to advocate interest in a global perspective of practice, which may go counter to regional advantages and prove costly to the well-established complacency of the profession in that area. It would be a considerable economic loss for service providers in the United States to abandon use of the U.S. DSM–IV taxonomy comparable to the International Classification of Diseases (I.C.D.9) and thus forego third-party payment benefits from high-powered insurance agencies. Hence it is to the advantage of all U.S. service providers involved to play by the rules of the insurance industry that controls the economic gains of social work practice. Such sectarian interests, however, are antithetical to a global perspective and strive hard to preserve their special interest.

A further barrier to globalization is the role played by media in publicizing social problems. In today's society, the media control information and exert tremendous influence in shaping attitudes and reactions; they can create or destroy a global perspective. But because the media are also interactive with the demands of the public, each shapes the other's behavior. Harris (1997) states that public attitudes in the West are extremely vulnerable to distress close to home but can seldom relate to the problems of the Global South countries; it is as if the former is reality and the latter fiction (Hokenstad, Khinduka, & Midgley, 1992). The media, which have the capability to both make or mar perceptions of incidents, select to perpetuate this myth, bombarding news coverage with localized information while making only cursory allusions to worldwide social problems, political situations, and human-made and natural disasters overseas.

Operationalization of concepts is another difficulty that lies in the path of globalization (Midgley, 1997). While no social work practitioner will question the profession's dedication to social justice, human rights, equality, and the well-being of humankind and the social order, these goals are interpreted in various parts of the globe through the unique cultural lens of each specific society. For example, the well-being of humankind in the West is measured through psychosocial and economic independence. In many other parts of the globe, this concept is operationalized through interdependence and the assumption of greater responsibility for others in the family, community or society (Gambrill, 1990). Similarly, Midgley (1997) discusses the difficulty of having a common definition of the term "social security." Interpretations range from the U.S. model of social insurance to the much wider and inclusive health care models in Latin America. With such polarized positions at the concrete level of social work practice and comparative research, can globalization move from an idealized level of abstraction to the concrete dimension of service delivery (Harris, 1997)?

While impediments may slow the globalization of practice operations, the preparation of social workers at the educational level has taken steps toward internationalization (Hokenstad, 1984; Healy, 1986, 1988; Asamoah, Healy, & Mayadas, 1997; Healy & Asamoah, 1997). International conferences, despite language barriers, attract professionals from all parts of the globe to share ideas and disseminate information. Papers, research studies, books, and journal articles reference a wealth of reading touching on global conditions. Despite the number of existing comparative studies of policy analysis, however, the emphasis remains unidirectional from the Global North to the Global South (Midgley, 1997). Here again economics plays a significant role. The monetary value of legal tenders in the international market prohibits the Global South from participating at international conferences and taking advantage of exchange programs at the same rate as their more opulent peers. Funding sources for research are also more limited in the Global South. Consequently, information disseminated through journals leans heavily towards materials from industrialized countries. In short, the economic balance is disproportionately distributed between the Global South and the Global North and acts as a deterrent to globalization.

Efforts are currently underway globally, including in the United States, to incorporate international perspectives into social work curricula at the baccalaureate and graduate levels (Asamoah, Healy, & Mayadas, 1997). As discussed in Chapter 2, isolated attempts at short international courses, field placement, doctoral dissertations, and joint degree programs are occasionally reported, but these efforts are to be credited to the interest of individual faculty and their schools rather than representing an attempt at globalization on nationwide bases. Some examples are the Maastrich Institute joint program between Holland and England; the Bristol, U.K. collaborative with universities in the United States; a University of Texas (Arlington) collaborative doctorate with Monterrey, Mexico; a master's program with the University of Texas (El Paso) with Mexico; and a North London University clearing house arrangement for doctoral dissertations in international subjects.

Furthermore, organizations such as the International Federation of Social Workers (IFSW), the International Association of Schools of Social Work (IASSW), and the International Congress on Social Work (ICSW) have existed through the second half of the twentieth century. However, the membership of these organizations does not represent world nations. Midgley's (1997) position on the economic imbalance among countries explains the restriction of membership to the industrialized world. In situations where the economic barrier is surmounted, country-specific credentials for practice and education come into play. There are no universally acknowledged standards for equivalency determination, and professionals from outside the borders of a region cannot automatically pass through the invisible professional boundaries. This situation may be attributed to the position that social problems have cultural nuances and may only be studied and dealt with inside that cultural context by those who are immersed in that society (Becerra, 1997; Brown & Oliveri, 1997).

Another opportunity for globalization may be via the various schemes of distance learning and modern technology. Certainly, the computer age has brought the world much closer together. With opportunities for interface mushrooming, globalization of practice perspectives should not be such a Herculean task. It would appear that while there is recognition for a global perspective, no overarching framework has thus far been developed to draw parallels between this abstract concept and its operational referents at varying levels of social work practice.

In the following section, some examples of a global perspective relating to social exclusion, micro-enterprise, and social development are discussed to illustrate the issues discussed in the preceding section.

SOCIAL EXCLUSION: A MACRO EXAMPLE AND A MICRO CASE STUDY

> Recently adopted into everyday language, the term [social exclusion] embraces the sinister reality of a world of have-not: the homeless, jobless, powerless, penniless.
> —M. Gaudier (1993, p. 64.)

Social exclusion is a European social and political concept that was used by the International Labor Organization (ILO) and the United Nations' Development Program (UNDP) and applied to a series of studies in ten countries to determine its global applicability and to explore what kinds of reciprocal learning might take place.

The concept of social exclusion had its origins in politics and policy studies in France. The 1974 coining of the term is credited to René Lenoir, then Secretary of State for Social Action. Influenced by the ideas of Jean-Paul Sartre and Catholic social action theology, the term gained widespread use in the 1980s with increased awareness of the "new poverty," a consequence of economic restructuring, transitional economies, and retrenchment in the welfare provisions of the so-called welfare states. Social exclusion has been adopted by the European Union as a central plank of social policy planning (Gore, 1995a) and may be defined as economic, social, political, and cultural exclusion. From an economic point of view, in an industrial economy it may be defined as exclusion from or within the labor market. The experience of long-term unemployment or employment within the labor market that is restricted by skill level to part-time employment or gender-related restrictions within the labor market (such as the concentration of women in low-paid service-related jobs) all constitute forms of social exclusion—of being barred from making an adequate livelihood (Rodgers, 1995). In an agrarian economy, exclusion can take the form of exclusion from ownership of land or other property. Exclusion from credit is another manifestation of economic exclusion, as is exclusion from education, transportation, housing, welfare, and other social services. Restriction of state responsibility for welfare has grown as political new right movements have questioned the very basis of the welfare state, leading to exclusion from social services (Glennister & Midgley, 1991).

In cultural terms, social exclusion may mean the disadvantage experienced because of difference caused by race, ethnicity, sexual orientation, age, or disability; it may take the form of discrimination against the person labeled deviant, the immigrant, or a person belonging to an ethnic or racial minority. Wolfe (1995) argues that it may mean exclusion from consumer culture. Political exclusion may mean disenfranchisement through lack of transport in rural areas or inability to negotiate the bureaucracy, exclusion may also be demonstrated by a more subtle lack of representation in the political process of the interests of members of peripheral groups in society. Wolfe argues that even within a democratic structure with a multiparty system, exclusion from political choice may take the form of "arbitrary rule by local bosses, landowners, military forces and police" (1995, p. 92). The point here is that exclusion occurs because of lack of participation and influence in the political process and the inability to influence one's own treatment and environment. Exclusion from political choices implies powerlessness and injustice.

Social exclusion is therefore an umbrella concept that covers poverty and related issues arising from poverty: lack of power and influence, lack of access to labor markets and social networks, marginalization, alienation, stigmatization, underclass status, lack of assets, dependency, injustice, lack of rights: "Social exclusion . . . is a practice of the more powerful which structures the possible field of action of the less powerful" (Gore, 1995b, p. 113).

The study from which much of the foregoing summary is drawn applied this concept to ten countries in a study supported by two organizations within the United Nations, the International Labor Organization (ILO), and the United Nations Development Program (UNDP). The countries involved in the study were Russia, Kazakhstan, Thailand, Tunisia, the Republic of Yemen, Tanzania, Peru, Mexico, Cameroon, and India. These ten countries were selected from three groups: former communist countries in economic transition, recently industrializing countries, and least developed countries (Rodgers, Gore, & Figueiredo, 1995).

In each country an excluded group was studied. Although these groups differed considerably, they had in common exclusion through race, gender, or class (caste). The study found that in general, although the authors were well aware of the pitfalls of exporting ideas from the North to the South, "social exclusion" is not a purely Eurocentric concept and that it led to new applications and insights into policies in various countries. In turn, understanding of the concept itself was expanded and broadened so that there was reciprocal benefit (Gore, 1995a).

In Yemen, for example, the concept was applied to the *akhdam,* a group of marginalized people of unknown origin who live in slum conditions; are mostly illiterate; and, like the harijans in India with whom they may be compared, were formerly relegated to the lowest jobs in society such as sewage workers and waste collectors. Government policies in the 1980s led to greater integration of this group through affirmative action into higher-status employment and increased education options, thus leading to improved social integration. The term *akhdam* was forbidden as a stigmatizing label (Hashem, 1995). One of the study's recommendations was that social integration be incorporated in future planning as well as job market integration.

In Tunisia, the concept was first used by the Social Studies Center in Tunis in 1992. The Tunisian U.N. study identified five policy measures that aimed to combat exclusion. These included measures to address poverty; the promotion of micro-enterprises; increased job creation; reform of employment services; and measures to integrate the unemployed (Bédoui & Gouia, 1995).

In Tanzania, a similar five-pronged approach to policy planning was recommended, but this plan focused on rural populations. The Tanzania study highlighted the position of rural women as landowners and included a recommendation that women should have full rights to ownership and inheritance of land (Tibaijuka & Kaijage, 1995).

In Peru, the study led to a reinterpretation of the causes of poverty, especially within indigenous populations in the Andean and Amazon regions. The reinterpretation involved recognition that the market economy excluded these poorest groups and recommended policies to address this lack (Figuera et al., 1995).

Implications of the Social Exclusion Model for Social Work Practice

These examples illustrate the global perspective in action in a planned concerted effort involving two international agencies and ten countries to demonstrate the effectiveness of reciprocal learning and new insights gained by exchange of professional ideas. While social exclusion has been included as a macro practice example for the purposes of this chapter, its true strength lies in the fact that it may be regarded as a "pivotal concept which aims less to identify the contours of empirically observed reality than to highlight the relationships between processes, between micro and macro mechanisms, between individual and collective dimensions" (Yépez, 1994, p. 15).

Social exclusion is a concept that may be applied at the international, national, regional, and individual levels. At the international level, the Global North has made the rules for international loans through the International Monetary Fund. Countries whose economies are not based on postindustrial technologies cannot compete on the same terms and therefore become excluded from the development process, amassing huge debts through loan interest payments to wealthy nations. At the national level, we see differential treatment of regions within individual countries. In 1997, Scotland voted in a national referendum to have its own Parliament separate from the British Parliament in Westminster. This change was initiated largely because of the sense of injustice Scots have experienced in not receiving their fair share of economic benefits and other resources. Within a nation, groups may be excluded on the basis of race or ethnicity, and individuals may be excluded from the labor market through changes resulting from the transition from an industrial economy with many less skilled jobs to a technological base for the economy with a reduced number of less skilled jobs. Individuals may also be excluded for reasons specific to them, such as physical or mental incapacity to work.

In social work assessment, whether it is the clinical assessment of an individual or a needs assessment of a community, this broader perspective will impact the way in which we relate to and work with clients. While recognizing the importance of individual responsibility, we are much more likely to be able to take an empowerment and strengths perspective and at the same time avoid pathologizing the individual whose exclusion may be heavily influenced by external factors.

. . . .

SOCIAL WORK PRACTICE AND MICRO-ENTERPRISE: MICRO AND MEZZO EXAMPLES

Micro-enterprise is illustrated through Case Study 4.1, which presents an example of technology transfer from the Grameen Bank in Bangladesh to the Full Circle Fund (FCF) project in Chicago.

CASE STUDY 4.1

The Grameen Bank and Its U.S. Adaptation

The Grameen (rural) Bank was created by Mohammed Yunus in Bangladesh in the 1970s. Then a young professor appalled by moneylenders extorting exorbitant interest rates from small loans to the poor, he decided to extend individual loans from his own pocket to the poor so that they could set up their businesses. Banks require collateral, credit, and character—the three C's of banking; Yunus ignored these precepts and gave out small independent loans to groups of women. Each group had five women who were not related by blood or by marriage. His words summarize the thinking behind this remarkable project: "Credit is a fundamental human right . . . collateral is merely a device to deceive the poor" (Counts, 1996, xv). Each member of the group was held responsible for the others' project integrity and loan repayment. If any person defaulted, the entire group was debarred from further loans until the debt was settled. By 1996, the project had grown to include 2 million borrowers in 34,000 villages and a daily disbursement of US $1.5 million; the simple interest charged on loans generated an income sufficient to pay a staff of 11,000 Grameen Bank employees across Bangladesh. Today, the project has been repeated around the world in inner cities in the industrial nations, and the chief beneficiaries have been women.

Yunus's ideas were adapted in the United States in a Chicago project initiated by two young women, Connie Evans, an African American, and Susan Matteucci, an Anglo American. Their clients were low-income women, many of whom were on public assistance. The theme remained the same as that of the Grameen Bank, but the process was modified to fit American conditions. For instance, the factor of time was introduced in structuring center meetings, a concept of low priority in Bangladesh. Since then, other similar, micro-enterprise projects have been adopted in many areas of the United States with equal success. As of 1995, the Grameen Bank model has operated in France, Scandinavia, Canada, and the United States as well as in many Asian countries (Counts, 1996).

• •

Other instances of micro enterprise are built on the principle of asset accumulation, such as individual development accounts (IDAs), which serve as anti-poverty initiatives and provide access to credit and savings for the poor (Sherraden, 1991). The Women's Self-Employment project (WSEP) of Chicago, which took its initiative from the Grameen Bank, developed an IDA program in December 1995. By August 1996, a total of 39 IDAs were active and twenty-one more were under consideration, with total net assets amounting to $8,500 (Edwards, 1997). Similarly, a Wisconsin IDA community action project established in 1996 matched monies at the rate of four to one to help individuals set up private enterprises. IDA programs are reported as operating expanded programs in public, nonprofit, and private organizations all over the United States with expansions and variations in projects (Edwards, 1997). A total of twenty-five studies of IDAs in the United States were evaluated to determine the effect of asset accumulation on personal and family well-being, economic security, and civic participation. Asset accumulation showed a positive association with economic security, a reduction of violence against women in the home, and a greater stability for children through parental home ownership (Page-Adams & Sherraden, 1996).

The philosophy underlying these initiatives is that economic well-being impacts all aspects of human well-being and that given the appropriate access to asset accumulation, the poor move from impoverished dependency to self-sustaining interdependency. This philosophy is finding consistent support through empirical data and rigorous evaluations of these rapidly spreading programs (Page-Adams & Sherraden, 1996). Programs such as these reinforce the concept of micro-enterprise as a globally relevant practice intervention and address clinical practice issues such as stress management, family violence, self-esteem, and family preservation in an economic framework consistent with the social development model.

Implications of Micro-Enterprise Initiatives for Social Work Practice

The establishment and growth of the Grameen Bank is built on principles consistent with social work practice. The primary beneficiaries are women who, previously excluded from the labor market and from participating in the economy, become empowered both economically and personally, with far-reaching implications for individual families and for the role of women in society. When women become economically independent in a family, they have more options in avoiding abuse and violence and are in a better position to protect children. In families where violence is not an issue, family members live healthier lives through better diet and the ability to afford health care. The entry of large numbers of women into the economy through micro-enterprise projects such as those in Bangladesh and India contributes to, and accelerates, the changing role of women out of conditions of social and economic dependency. Empowerment is thus a goal and a consequence of asset-building policies and practices. Along with empowerment comes increased self-esteem and the ability of people to improve their quality of life. The principles of this project are also consistent with the concept of the actualizing tendency. Both Rogers (1965) and Maslow

Women in El Salvador rebuilding their village destroyed in war

(1968) viewed all human beings as capable of achieving their goals of self-fulfillment. They believed that given the right conditions, people have the capacity to self-actualize and better themselves. Today this approach may be reframed as the strengths perspective in social work. The Grameen Bank projects avoided the old individual pathology model in favor of an empowering, strengths-building, and developmental model (Saleeby, 1993). Their difference from the Rogerian model lies also in the connection with economics as an integral part of social development.

The methods and strategies of intervention in this model are similar to those of social group work. Group pressure and group support, minimizing coalitions by placing unrelated persons in a group, interdependence of members for goal achievement, mutual reliance for loan procurement, peer approval for business expansion, and collaborative effort in program management are all cooperative, developmental goals. Principles from behavioral social work can also be identified in the implementation of the Grameen Bank concept—for example, in the progressive increase in loans contingent on satisfactory repayment serves as a reinforcer of responsibility and discipline in borrowers. Cognitive-behavioral methods are used through the medium of training groups in preparation for loan management. Thus, learning the task before undertaking it is seen as a prerequisite for borrowers before they are deemed ready to manage business cooperatives. Community spirit is fostered by arranging small groups of six to eight units of borrowers who join together in a self-governing community for the continuing development of their center. Self-determination is discharged through village centers that require simultaneous development of infrastructure and human resources by participants, resulting in economic expansion and leadership roles for the community. The concurrent economic and civic developments illustrate the institution-building function of the social development model.

The Grameen Bank project highlights social development principles by demonstrating that access to investment capital transformed living conditions for many in an impoverished country from destitution to self-sufficiency. Consistent with traditional approaches in social work of working with the poor, people who were excluded from the labor market and from participation in the economy and who would not have been considered for loans by traditional banks were the targets for this project. The new developmental element is that instead of charity, the model is based on trust and belief in people's ability to better themselves on one hand and on integration into the labor market on the other.

We may learn one other important lesson from the Grameen Bank projects. Faced with long-term unemployment, multiproblem families, and violence to and abuse of women and children, as social workers we may often become too easily cynical or overwhelmed and settle for the bandaid or quick fix for the short term. The despondency that we cannot change the system gradually creeps in and ideals are compromised. The Grameen Bank is an inspiration to social workers worldwide because it demonstrates that from small beginnings large systems can be changed and institutional development can take place, that people in poverty do have surprising resources along with the inevitable problems, and that given the right conditions they can remove themselves from poverty.

SOCIAL DEVELOPMENT: A GLOBAL MODEL

A third example of how social work practice can benefit from a global perspective is the social development model. The illustrations given from social exclusion ideas and from micro-enterprise developments illustrate that the rigid distinction between micro and macro is not borne out in practice. If we use an exclusively micro or clinical practice perspective, there is a danger that important avenues for change will not be used. For example, if a clinical practice approach to empowerment for women had been used in the Grameen Bank project, it would have been much less effective than it would combined with an economic approach. However, social work in the industrialized nations and especially in the United States uses individual approaches to a greater extent than interventions combined with a structural model such as the micro-enterprise programs. The advantage of a global perspective is that it puts the situation in a new light.

Applied to social work practice, the social development model offers new options for integrating both micro and macro approaches to the best advantage. As cited in Chapters 3 and 11, Midgley defines social development as "a process of planned social change designed to promote the well-being of the population as a whole in conjunction with a dynamic process of economic development." What distinguishes social development from other approaches, Midgley proposes, is that it links economic development with social issues and, conversely, that social change is designed to serve economic goals. The term "sustainable development" is thus derived from this interaction of social and economic imperatives for change.

Economic development principles have been widely used by agencies of the United Nations in projects around the world at the policy and planning level as well as in community-based initiatives. In the past few years the United Nations has made a strong recommitment to linking economic and social development and, as part of this agenda, to address the issue of the oppressed role of women across the world. In the words of former U.N. chief Boutros Boutros-Ghali:

> Investment in human resources must, therefore be seen not merely as a by-product of economic growth, but rather as a powerful and necessary driving force for all aspects of development. . . . A major goal in this regard is the empowerment of women. With the emerging consensus on the priority and dimensions of development has come a deeper understanding that in virtually every dimension of development—whether political, social, economic, environmental or security related— the role of women is central. (1995, pp. 40, 98)

The 1995 World Summit for Social Development (WSSD) held in Copenhagen, Denmark, is another example of a global recognition of the need for sustainable development. Known as the "Social Summit," the conference addressed three principle themes: eradication of poverty; expansion of productive employment and reduction of unemployment; and social integration (United Nations, 1997). These themes are considered to be equally applicable to the developing and the developed world. The Summit declaration, which is set out in Box 4.1 on p. 66, summarizes the principles of Social Development: justice, participation, recognition of the dignity and worth of the individual, nondiscrimination, tolerance and respect for human rights, universal access to health care and education, empowerment, gender equity, and international cooperation.

CASE STUDY 4.2

Social Exclusion and Child Abuse*

Terri Johnson, a 32-year-old Caucasian female, was one of three siblings born to Mary and George Brown. They lived in a low-income, deteriorating suburban area just outside a major U.S. city. George, who was just starting up a yard-servicing business with two friends, died suddenly after a heart attack when Terri was 6 years old, her sister Janice was 8, and her brother Jim 5. Mary Brown became depressed and got into financial difficulty when her husband's partners dissolved the business, leaving numerous debts. The family had to live with Mary's parents for a time. The relationship with Mary's parents was terminated abruptly when she and the children moved in with Bill Green, who had numerous convictions for driving under the influence of alcohol and had served a short prison sentence for burglary. Mary Brown was hospitalized for three short periods during Terri's childhood. The care of the children at those times was in the hands of Bill Green, whom Mary had married after three years of living together.

Terri Johnson's childhood was unhappy, and she later told a Child Protective Services worker that she was physically and sexually abused by her stepfather. She did not get on well with her sister and brother and sees them very rarely because both moved to different parts of the country. Terri did reasonably well in school, and after a period of changing clerical jobs frequently and problems with anorexia, at age 20 she began what turned out

---

*This is a fictitious case adapted from composite case material provided by Jorge Medina Gutierrez, MSSW, a Child Protective Services social worker.

to be a steady job as a bookkeeper in a small local company where, it seems, she functioned adequately for about six years. After relationships with several boyfriends, two abortions, and marginal involvement with drugs and prostitution, she became involved with her supervisor and married him. At age 26, she gave birth to her son David, who is now 6 years old. After their divorce, Terri developed depression and once again turned to drugs and prostitution. She was laid off from her job and appeared several times in court for prostitution. Three years ago, she gave birth to twin girls who were "crack" babies.

Terri attributed her bad luck to the birth of her children and said that she just wanted to have a good time for once. She was angry that she felt unable to provide for them economically and declared that she never wanted to be a mother anyway. Terri's drug habit got worse, and after several incidents of abuse and neglect the children were placed in foster care. The policy of the Child Protective Services agency was family preservation, and they tried to work with Terri to return the custody of the children to her. She entered a drug treatment program but did not complete it. The case continued for three years, with parental rights finally being terminated and the children freed for adoption. Just prior to signing the release forms, Terri was imprisoned for a violent attack on a neighbor and for unlawful possession of drugs. She is serving a sentence of eighteen months.

· ·

The social development model may be said to represent the response to social exclusion at all levels of organization—local, national, and international—whereas the social exclusion model identifies the deficits and is a useful assessment tool. Social development offers a comprehensive and constructive approach to social problems and issues. Case Study 4.2 is an illustration of the ways the concept of social exclusion influences practice strategies of assessment and intervention. Questions for students include the following: In what ways would social work interventions that included micro-enterprise or asset-based programs assist this client? How would a social development approach to this case differ from a traditional social work approach? The worldwide renewal of interest in development and the focus on social development by the United Nations offers a global example from which we may take note for social work practice at the regional and local level.

Social Work Practice in Social Development

> The battle for people-centered and sustainable development will be won or lost not in the corridors of Governments, but in every hamlet and home, in every village and town, in the daily enterprise of every member of the global community and every institution of civil society.
> —Boutros Boutros-Ghali (1995)

The goals of social development are consistent with those of social work: to create planned social, economic, and institutional change with a view to improving the lives of individuals. The values are also consistent: participatory democracy (client self-determination), social justice, gender equity, cooperation, investment in human resources, empowerment, and fulfillment of individual potential (strengths perspective). Much of the literature on social development has focused on a macro approach to social policy, planning, and administration. Less attention has been focused on the potential offered by social development as an integrative model for direct social work practice. Meinert and Kohn (1987), suggest a process model, Elliott (1993) suggests a model linking social development and systems theory as an integrative model of social work practice. Billups (1994) suggests an integrative framework linking micro and macro practice; Mayadas and Elliott (1995) link social groupwork and social development. Elliott and Mayadas (1996) link social development with clinical practice in social work, arguing that one of the reasons that social development has not been incorporated into social work practice in North America, as it has in other countries, is the predominant role of the medical or clinical model in American social work. This, they suggest, should not be such an inhibiting factor to the inclusion of social development ideas, and they demonstrate links through discussions of empowerment practice, the role of economics in clinical practice, multicultural practice, and psychotherapy as liberation. Social development has the potential to shift the paradigm in American social work from one in which, as Seidman (1983) has said, it is "trapped within the premise of individualism" to a model that would facilitate a global approach; greater international exchange; sustainable development; empowerment of individuals, families, and communities; and social and economic integration. The paradigm shift would be akin to the reconceptualization and indigenization of social work that has taken place in countries across the world. Social development offers the possibility of a new social work perspective and dynamic for the 21st century.

THE WAY FORWARD

This chapter has reviewed some examples of global initiatives and has examined the global transferability of the concepts. Social exclusion, a European concept, is reviewed from the point of view of macro practice and its applicability in ten nations with different economic systems; the example also gives us insight into assessment at the individual level. Micro-enterprise projects are reviewed from the point of view of micro and mezzo practice, with illustrations of how projects similar to the Grameen Bank can be transferred to the United States. Social development is discussed as a framework that integrates micro, mezzo, and macro practice with each other and with a global perspective.

The way forward for social work in the 21st century is through a strengths perspective in assessment; empowerment practice and social, economic, cultural, and political inclusion in interventions; the adoption of multicultural models of practice; the recognition of the importance of economics in the lives of individuals and the influence it has on social systems and in social problems; and the adoption of economic interventions such as micro-enterprise initiatives to achieve individual and group empowerment. Social development is a framework that can enable social work to achieve this end. It is hard to make this transition without a global perspective. We need to see conditions such as absolute poverty writ large to help us address relative poverty; we need to see situations through the outsider's eyes to understand social exclusion; we need to see micro-enterprises operating in Bangladesh to understand their potential for rural and urban America.

STUDENT ACTIVITIES

1. Review the United Nations' Social Summit Declaration in Box 4.1. How far do you think these commitments apply to social problems, policies, and social work practice in the country in which you live?

BOX 4.1

U.N. Social Summit Declaration

The (Social) Summit Declaration cited 10 commitments, each followed by specific recommendations for action at the national and international levels. They include in part:

1. Creating an economic, political, social, cultural and legal environment that will enable people to achieve social development.

2. Eradicating poverty in the world, through decisive national actions and international cooperation, as an ethical, social, political and economic imperative of humankind; focusing policies to address the root causes of poverty, giving special priority to the rights and needs of women and children and other vulnerable and disadvantaged groups.

3. Promoting the goal of full development as a basic priority and enabling all men and women to attain secure and sustainable livelihoods through freely chosen productive employment and work;

4. Promoting social integration by fostering social stability and justice, based on non-discrimination, tolerance and the protection of all human rights, as well as respect for cultural, ethnic and religious diversity, equality of opportunity, solidarity, security and the participation of all people in these efforts;

5. Achieving equality and equity between women and men, and promoting their equal partnership in family and community life;

6. Promoting universal and equitable access to quality education and health care, rectifying inequities affecting women, children and vulnerable social groups;

7. Accelerating the economic, social and human resource development of Africa and the least developed countries by promoting the development of democratic institutions and finding effective solutions to such problems as external debt, economic reform, food security and commodity diversification;

8. Increasing and/or utilizing more efficiently the resources allocated to social development to achieve the goals of the Summit through national action and regional and national cooperation;

9. Ensuring that structural adjustment programs (internationally sanctioned economic and fiscal reforms designed to stabilize and streamline national economies) include social development goals that promote basic social programmes while increasing the quality and efficiency of social expenditures;

10. Improving and strengthening the framework for international, regional and subregional cooperation for social development in a spirit of partnership through the United Nations and other multilateral organizations. (United Nations, 1997, pp. 49–50)

2. Compare and contrast social work practice in two countries with that in the country in which you live.

3. Review Case Study 4.3 and answer the following questions:
   a. How do you see micro, macro, and mezzo perspectives linked in issues relating to social exclusion?
   b. How does the concept of social exclusion apply to home ownership?
   c. How do the policy initiatives suggested by Scanlon relate to a social development perspective in social work?
   d. Imagine yourself as a community worker in an inner city housing area who has been asked to work with Scanlon's (1996) second policy implication in Case Study 4.3. How would you work with the community to help stabilize the neighborhood and increase home ownership? What social work intervention model would be best suited for this task, and why?

CASE STUDY 4.3

Home Ownership

The "American Dream" has long considered home ownership a key to personal happiness and fulfillment. As a goal of public policy, it has been fostered in many industrialized nations. It is argued that home ownership "increases financial stability, improves self-esteem, enhances autonomy, stabilizes communities and promotes social and political involvement."
—Scanlon (1996, p. 3).

Home Ownership for People Everywhere (HOPE) is a program designed for low-income families to purchase homes through U.S. federal government subsidies. This program, initiated by Jack Kemp, Secretary of Housing and Urban Development in the Bush administration, operated through increasing access of low-income workers to home ownership through financial assistance policies which reduce the cost of home ownership (Scanlon, 1996). Justification for projects such as this stems from psychosocial and economic theoretical positions that home ownership has positive effects on people's well-being because it is a source of asset accumulation, personal stability, security, control over space, and empowerment (Sherraden, 1991).

However, some empirical studies on home ownership have shown findings that asset accumulation from home ownership is not effective in neighborhoods with deteriorating property values. Segregated neighborhoods are particularly vulnerable, and research shows that significant differences in equity accumulation between white and black home owners. (Oliver and Shapiro, 1995; Long and Caudill; 1992; Parcel, 1982). A HUD study (1995) reinforces the data showing that lower-cost homes could be a liability with negative equity (Scanlon, 1996). A study carried out in Coventry, England, supports the finding that poor neighborhoods have a negative association with homeowner benefits (Doling & Stafford, 1989). Conversely, in a study of auto workers Page-Adams and Vosler (1995) found less depression and alcohol abuse and greater accumulation of wealth among homeowners than their renter counterparts. Other positive outcomes of home ownership were a negative correlation with domestic violence and school dropout of children (Page-Adams, 1995; Green & White, 1994).

Scanlon's (1996) review suggests three policy implications:

- "Federal Tax Policy that promotes home ownership for the middle and upper class is generating not only economic, but also social and psychological inequalities. Tax policy should be altered to equalize class and racial disparities in housing tenure." (p. 22)

- "Homeownership benefits may be attenuated by overwhelming neighborhood conditions such as crime, poverty, infrastructure deterioration, unemployment and violence. Therefore, promotion of homeownership should be pursued in tandem with community stabilization efforts." (p. 23)

- "The income instabilities of poor and working class families suggests potential for loan default due to income fluctuations or sudden financial stresses related to home owning such as property tax increases or home repair. Therefore, low income homeownership programs must be structured to decrease the risk of income shocks in causing loan default." (p. 24)

Infusing Global Perspectives into Social Work Values and Ethics

ROSEMARY J. LINK

Philosophers have thought for centuries about the justification, derivation, and application of principles of ethics—what is right and wrong ...

—F. G. REAMER (1991)

The study of ethics means turning of a searchlight on our behavior and how our actions fit with the well-being of others. The bright light that causes us to constantly pause and consider the impact, moral and social, of our actions lies at the core of social work. Some countries have an Ethical Code that guides social work practitioners in the most beneficial or right course. Others provide a set of assumptions that accompanies identification with, and qualification into, the profession. This chapter will discuss some of the tensions in the use of concepts such as "beneficial" or "right and wrong" and will identify various approaches to ethics in social work in different countries. Common threads will be identified and a comparative analysis will highlight the way that a variety of teaching and learning approaches can help us to be more self-aware and to assess our own steps in ethical behavior and decision making. A review of differing approaches to ethical reflection in various parts of the world is especially illuminating for the teaching of this difficult and at times agonizing topic. This discussion will be supported by case studies from Mexico, the United States, England, and Slovenia. The chapter includes the following:

1. A definition of social work ethics and the range of study implied.

2. An identification of different approaches to ethics in social work from one country to another.

3. Common elements and divergent views, a framework from Seedhouse in the health setting.

4. A synthesis of streams in ethical professional social work thought and universal elements.

••

DEFINITIONS OF ETHICS AND THE RANGE OF STUDY IMPLIED

As our social world becomes increasingly complex, the expectation that "professional" education and training adequately prepares individuals to behave ethically toward the clients, colleagues, and communities they serve needs constant questioning. There are no easy solutions to the values-based study of ethics, and a primary challenge is to recognize our ethnocentric and geocentric approach. Reflective of the discussions in Cross's (1986) work on cultural competence, our ethical competence depends on our ability to understand our own perspectives both culturally and ethically. In Mexico, colleagues speak of working ethically and expect responsible and moral behavior by social workers but do not have a specific code (Bibus & Link, 1997). Recently Indian social workers have questioned the relevance of clinically orientated Western codes for Indian community development and prefer the term "declaration" of ethics for people-centered work (Desai, 1998). The International Federation of Social Workers has an international code (see Box 5.l), but it is under constant scrutiny and is currently being reviewed by a committee of international social workers (Envall, 1997). Some countries have specific codes that are updated and revised according to developments in health, human service, and technology. Such developments include questions of the right to die and the complex family involvement in planning for terminally ill young people suffering from the epidemics of AIDS and cancer. In their cross-cultural study of social work with the dying, Parry and Shen Ryan discuss the ethical dilemma for a social worker acting as "cultural broker" for a family where the son is dying of AIDS and the father is homophobic. They suggest that implementing the self-aware social work role of "cultural broker" is crucial in ethical decision making in such circumstances. The role of culture broker recognizes the complexity of negotiating between formal systems, such as hospitals and churches, and family and cultural beliefs in a society which can be rejecting: "There are differences among groups and differences within groups, and the uniqueness of each family and person with whom we work must always be considered paramount" (Parry & Shen Ryan, 1995, p. 224).

In addition to understanding differing cultural beliefs about human rights, Cacinovic Vogrincic (1997) speaks of the importance of studying philosophy as a part of social work's preparation for professional behavior. She describes the basic elements of practice in Slovenia and how discourse among social workers on their professional role is ethically and morally based:

> The social work relationship—every project with working points and concrete steps, is based on the definition of the problem: the agreement, the understanding, the consense cocreated, investigated, interpreted together with the client(s). . . . If we take the paradigmatic "together with the clients" seriously, then we need to add the special constructionist contribution: knowledge for what Lynn Hoffman calls "the ethics of participation." In my understanding that means to replace the objective observer (social worker) with the idea of collaboration, where no one has the final word, no one needs the final word, what we need is a conversation that can be continued. Consensus, understanding, definitions, enable us to name the next step . . . the social worker becomes the *participant-facilitator.* (Cacinovic Vogrincic, 1997, p. 2)

Building on this dialogue with colleagues, social work ethics from the relativist perspective of this book refer to the self-aware scrutiny of behavior in the search to achieve the most good and the least harm in a social situation. However, as philosophers have noted through the ages, the definition of "good" and "harm" are elusive. Social work itself is both a political and ethical act. To study ethics is to recognize how dynamic these concepts are, to learn from steps in reasoning that others have applied, and to constantly engage in furthering our insight and recognition of responsibility by sharing case studies and the approaches of international colleagues.

In his study of ethics and healthcare in Europe, David Seedhouse suggests that "both ethics and health (human service) work are beset by the problem that people in complex societies have different values and beliefs amongst each other . . . there are no clear-cut solutions" (1989, p. 9). Recently in Minneapolis a kidney transplant was reported in the local newspaper between a 22-year-old European-American man and a young Hmong woman, the friend of his family (*Minneapolis Star Tribune,* 30 August, 1997). The young woman would have died without the transplant, but her family had long opposed it for cultural reasons as well as objections to the intrusive nature of Western medicine. Eventually the woman went ahead without her mother's support, although her extended family was very important to her. At times the Western doctors expressed frustration that she kept going back to her family to discuss decisions and, from their view, delayed needed action. Basing their beliefs on hundreds of years of cultural tradition, the family preferred herbal remedies, without the cutting into the body of surgery. Similarly, a young woman in the writer's extended family in the Shetland Islands underwent mastectomy, three cycles of chemotherapy, and much pain in the Western treatment of breast cancer, only to die within twelve months, which was the life expectancy without treatment.

Within the study of ethics there is an historic tension relating to the absolutist (or cognitivist) position that actions are either morally right or wrong in themselves and the relativist (noncognitivist) position that actions are inextricably linked to their consequences. In many countries there is the added and often unconscious contradiction that individuals may be clear in themselves that an act is morally wrong—for example, killing another human—but at a societal level they participate in a system that permits "death by legal intervention" (*Accident Facts,* 1996). The cognitivist schools of thought hold that it is feasible to "reach conclusions about right and wrong and that ethical principles are true or false," and the noncognitivists think it is impossible to find absolute moral principles, "that we can only have an opinion or preference" (Reamer, 1991). Realizing that this book would be written differently in other parts of the world, the authors of this text are working from a noncognitivist, relativist framework.

Philosophers who, in the layperson's language, adopt absolutist views belong to the *deontologist* school. As stated by Loewenberg and Dolgoff (1985), this position "stresses the overriding importance of fixed moral rules . . . an action is inherently right or wrong, apart from any consequences that might result . . . ethical rules can be formulated and these should hold under all circumstances." For example, they will argue that the rule, "A social worker shall tell the truth to her client" is always correct and applies in every situation, no matter how much damage such a stance may cause. The relativists in philosophy belong to the *teleologist* school, for which ethical decisions are made "on the basis of the context in which they are made or on the basis of the consequences which they create" (Loewenberg & Dolgoff, 1985). In a society where deontologist thought prevails, ethical decision making may appear more clear-cut and for some enclosed societies, such as the Amish of Dutch origin in the United States, it may be so. However, both schools are relevant to social work thinking, since our profession is always conscious of the influences of the larger environment in which we act and the need for guiding principles, based on collective experience and critical thinking, upon which to act.

From a Western perspective, the study of ethics seems to be one of relativity and degree, according to time, place, culture, and circumstance, and yet social workers in some parts of the world work under regimes that are absolutist in their beliefs. The social work profession recognizes that we learn from each other, from one country to another, and in this arena of ethical behavior it is critical to stay open to a variety of approaches. Professionals may tackle the need for consistency in professional ethical behavior in a number of ways such as:

1. Search for the "objectively good." One might pursue some ultimate value or ordering of values.

2. Search for a set of rules, or code of practice to provide "a firm uncontroversial basis."

3. Appeal to law.

4. Adopt a relativist position. (Seedhouse, 1989, p. 9)

For Reamer, the expanding dialogue and drawing up of codes of ethical behavior represents the "maturation of the profession." He adds: "Although good practice by itself ordinarily translates into good ethics, there are times when practice principles do not illuminate or resolve troublesome ethical dilemmas and in these cases, we must draw on sound, conceptually based reasoning" (Reamer, 1995, pp. ix–x). The reasoning or critical reflection that is part of social work education is the core of ethical behavior. In this book, however, the writers are cautious in suggesting that a code of ethics in itself reflects maturity in the profession. In one country, the focus of studying and applying ethical behavior may be through a code. In another, it will be through the study of philosophy and client self- or collective determination that moral behavior is discussed and implemented. In some countries, including Mexico, Norway, and the United Kingdom, there is more reliance on the professional discretion and judgment of workers and less emphasis on legislating ethical practice than, for example, in the United States.

The International Code in Box 5.1, which refers to standards of ethical conduct in general ways concerning clients, agencies, organizations, colleagues, and the profession, offers unifying principles for social workers worldwide. By implication, the code in its international reach is leading us to conceptualize ourselves as a global society that respects the distinct cultural pieces of its makeup. The International Code also respects relative difference among cultures and therefore implies a relativist approach.

IDENTIFICATION OF INTRACOUNTRY APPROACHES TO ETHICS IN SOCIAL WORK

As the countries of eastern Europe struggle in transition from a variety of forms of communism and socialism to more western style democracy, questions of ethics abound. Colleagues in the former Yugoslavia explained to the writer that social workers have always been freer thinkers than their political colleagues within the socialist regime. The shifting economies have not meant such a drastic philosophical change for social work, except in the concern that communism placed a burden of "sameness" and strict "codes of labor practice" upon people, that now are opening up. Ironically, as the West seeks to increase its specification of

BOX 5.1

International Code of Ethics for the Professional Social Worker

INTERNATIONAL FEDERATION OF SOCIAL WORKERS
P.O. BOX 4649, SOFIENBERG, N–0506 OSLO, NORWAY
E MAIL: SECR.GEN@IFSW.ORG

Social work originates variously from humanitarian, religious and democratic ideals and philosophies and has universal application to meet human needs arising from personal-societal interactions and to develop human potential. Professional social workers are dedicated to service for the welfare and self-fulfilment of human beings; to the development and disciplined use of scientific knowledge regarding human and societal behavior; to the development of resources to meet individual, group, national and international needs and aspirations; and to the achievement of social justice.

1. BACKGROUND

Ethical awareness is a necessary part of the professional practice of any social worker. His or her ability to act ethically is an essential aspect of the quality of the service offered to clients.

The purpose of IFSW's work on ethics is to promote ethical debate and reflection in the member associations and among the providers of social work in member countries.

The basis for the further development of IFSW's work on ethics is to be found in "*Ethics of Social Work—Principles and Standards*" which consists of two documents, "*International Declaration of Ethical Principles of Social Work*," and "*International Ethical Standards for Social Workers*." These documents present the basic ethical principles of the social work profession, recommend procedure when the work presents ethical dilemmas, and deal with the profession's and the individual social worker's relation to clients, colleagues, and others in the field. The documents are components in a continuing process of use, review and revision.

2. INTERNATIONAL DECLARATION OF ETHICAL PRINCIPLES OF SOCIAL WORK

2.1 Introduction

The IFSW recognises the need for a declaration of ethical principles for guidance in dealing with ethical problems in social work.

(continued)

International Code of Ethics
for the Professional Social Worker *(continued)*

The purposes of the International Declaration of Ethical Principles *are:*

1. to formulate a set of basic principles for social work, which can be adapted to cultural and social settings.

2. to identify ethical problem areas in the practice of social work (below referred to as 'problem areas'), and

3. to provide guidance as to the choice of methods for dealing with ethical issues/problems (below referred to as 'methods for addressing ethical issues/problems').

Compliance

The *International Declaration of Ethical Principles* assumes that both member associations of the IFSW and their constituent members adhere to the principles formulated therein. The IFSW expects each member association to assist its members in identifying and dealing with ethical issues/problems in the practice of their profession.

Member associations of the IFSW and individual members of these can report any member association to the Executive Committee of the IFSW should it neglect to adhere to these principles. National Associations who experience difficulties adopting these principles should notify the Executive Committee of IFSW. The Executive Committee may impose the stipulations and intentions of the Declaration of Ethical Principles on an association which neglects to comply. Should this not be sufficient the Executive Committee can, as a following measure, suggest suspension or exclusion of the association.

The *International Declaration of Ethical Principles* should be made publicly known. This would enable clients, employers, professionals from other disciplines, and the general public to have expectations in accordance with the ethical foundations of social work.

We acknowledge that a detailed set of ethical standards for the member associations would be unrealistic due to legal, cultural and governmental differences among the member countries.

2.2 The Principles

Social workers serve the development of human beings through adherence to the following basic principles:

2.2.1. Every human being has a unique value, which justifies moral consideration for that person.

2.2.2. Each individual has the right to self-fulfilment to the extent that it does not encroach upon the same right of others, and has an obligation to contribute to the well-being of society.

2.2.3. Each society, regardless of its form, should function to provide the maximum benefits for all of its members.

2.2.4. Social workers have a commitment to principles of social justice.

2.2.5. Social workers have the responsibility to devote objective and disciplined knowledge and skill to aid individuals, groups, communities, and societies in their development and resolution of personal-societal conflicts and their consequences.

2.2.6. Social workers are expected to provide the best possible assistance to any-body seeking their help and advice, without unfair discrimination on the basis of gender, age, disability, colour, social class, race, religion, language, political beliefs, or sexual orientation.

2.2.7. Social workers respect the basic human rights of individuals and groups as expressed in the *United Nations Universal Declaration of Human Rights* and other international conventions derived from that Declaration.

2.2.8. Social workers pay regard to the principles of privacy, confidentiality, and responsible use of information in their professional work. Social workers respect justified confidentiality even when their country's legislation is in conflict with this demand.

2.2.9. Social workers are expected to work in full collaboration with their clients, working for the best interests of the clients but paying due regard to the interests of others involved. Clients are encouraged to participate as much as possible, and should be informed of the risks and likely benefits of pro-posed courses of action.

2.2.10. Social workers generally expect clients to take responsibility, in collabora-tion with them, for determining courses of action affecting their lives. Compulsion which might be necessary to solve one party's problems at the expense of the interests of others involved should only take place after careful explicit evaluation of the claims of the conflicting parties. Social workers should minimise the use of legal compulsion.

2.2.11. Social work is inconsistent with direct or indirect support of individuals, groups, political forces or power-structures suppressing their fellow human beings by employing terrorism, torture or similar brutal means.

2.2.12. Social workers make ethically justified decisions, and stand by them, pay-ing due regard to the *IFSW International Declaration of Ethical Principles,* and to the *"International Ethical Standards for Social Workers"* adopted by their national professional association.

2.3 Problem Areas

2.3.1. The problem areas raising ethical issues directly are not necessarily univer-sal due to cultural and governmental differences. Each national association is encouraged to promote discussion and clarification of important issues and problems particularly relevant to its country. The following problem areas are, however, widely recognized:

(continued)

International Code of Ethics for the Professional Social Worker (continued)

1) *when the loyalty of the social worker is in the middle of conflicting interests*
   - between those of the social workers own and the clients
   - between conflicting interests of individual clients and other individuals
   - between the conflicting interests of groups of clients
   - between groups of clients and the rest of the population
   - between systems/institution and groups of clients
   - between system/institution/employer and social workers
   - between different groups of professionals

2) *the fact that the social worker functions both as a helper and controller*
   The relation between these two opposite aspects of social work demands a clarification based on an explicit choice of values in order to avoid a mixing-up of motives or the lack of clarity in motives, actions and consequences of actions. When social workers are expected to play a role in the state control of citizens they are obliged to clarify the ethical implications of this role and to what extent this role is acceptable in relation to the basic ethical principles of social work.

3) *the duty of the social worker to protect the interests of the client will easily come into conflict with demands for efficiency and utility*
   This problem is becoming important with the introduction and use of information technology within the fields of social work.

2.3.2 The principles declared in section 2.2 should always be at the base of any consideration given or choice made by social workers in dealing with issues/problems within these areas.

2.4 Methods for the Solution of Issues/Problems

2.4.1. The various national associations of social workers are obliged to treat matters in such a way that ethical issues/problems may be considered and tried to be solved in collective forums within the organization. Such forums should enable the individual social worker to discuss, analyse and consider ethical issues/problems in collaboration with colleagues, other expert groups and parties affected by the matter under discussion. In addition such forums should give the social worker opportunity to receive advice from colleagues and others. Ethical analysis and discussion should always seek to create possibilities and options.

2.4.2. The member associations are required to produce and/or adapt ethical standards for the different fields of work, especially for those fields where there are complicated ethical issues/problems as well as areas where the ethical principles of social work may come into conflict with the respective country's legal system or the policy of the authorities.

2..4.3. When ethical foundations are laid down as guidelines for actions within the practice of social work, it is the duty of the associations to aid the individual social worker in analysing and considering ethical issues/problems on the basis of:

1) The basic *principles* of the Declaration (section 2.2)
2) The ethical/moral and political *context* of the actions, i.e. an analysis of the values and forces constituting the framing conditions of the action.
3) The *motives* of the action, i.e. to advocate a higher level of consciousness of the aims and intentions the individual social worker might have regarding a course of action.
4) The *nature* of the action, i.e. help in providing an analysis of the moral content of the action, e.g. the use of compulsion as opposed to voluntary co-operation, guardianship vs participation, etc.
5) The *consequences* the action might have for different groups, i.e. an analysis of the consequences of different ways of action for all involved parties in both the short and long term.

2.4.4. The member associations are responsible for promoting debate, education and research regarding ethical questions.

3. INTERNATIONAL ETHICAL STANDARDS FOR SOCIAL WORKERS

(This section is based on the "*International Code of Ethics for the Professional Social Worker*" adopted by the IFSW in 1976, but does not include ethical principles since these are now contained in the new separate International Declaration of Ethical Principles of Social Work in section 2.2 of the present document.)

3.1 Preamble

Social work originates variously from humanitarian, religious and democratic ideals and philosophies and has universal application to meet human needs arising from personal-societal interactions and to develop human potential. Professional social workers are dedicated to service for the welfare and self-fulfilment of human beings; to the development and disciplined use of validated knowledge regarding human and societal behaviour; to the development of resources to meet individual, group, national and international needs and aspirations; and to the achievement of social justice. On the basis of the *International Declaration of Ethical Principles of Social Work*, the social worker is obliged to recognise these standards of ethical conduct.

3.2 General Standards of Ethical Conduct

3.2.1. Seek to understand each individual client and the client system, and the elements which affect behaviour and the service required.

3.2.2. Uphold and advance the values, knowledge and methodology of the profession, refraining from any behaviour which damages the functioning of the profession.

3.2.3. Recognise professional and personal limitations.

(continued)

International Code of Ethics
for the Professional Social Worker (continued)

3.2.4. Encourage the utilisation of all relevant knowledge and skills.

3.2.5. Apply relevant methods in the development and validation of knowledge.

3.2.6. Contribute professional expertise to the development of policies and programs which improve the quality of life in society.

3.2.7. Identify and interpret social needs.

3.2.8 Identify and interpret the basis and nature of individual, group, community, national, and international social problems.

3.2.9. Identify and interpret the work of the social work profession.

3.2.10. Clarify whether public statements are made or actions performed on an individual basis or as representative of a professional association, agency or organisation, or other group.

3.3 Social Work Standards Relative to Clients

3.3.1. Accept primary responsibility to identified clients, but within limitations set by the ethical claims of others.

3.3.2. Maintain the client's right to a relationship of trust, to privacy and confidentiality, and to responsible use of information. The collection and sharing of information or data is related to the professional service function with the client informed as to its necessity and use. No information is released without prior knowledge and informed consent of the client, except where the client cannot be responsible or others may be seriously jeopardized. A client has access to social work records concerning them.

3.3.3. Recognise and respect the individual goals, responsibilities, and differences of clients. Within the scope of the agency and the client's social milieu, the professional service shall assist clients to take responsibility for personal actions and help all clients with equal willingness. Where the professional service cannot be provided under such conditions the clients shall be so informed in such a way as to leave the clients free to act.

3.3.4. Help the client—individual, group, community, or society—to achieve self-fulfilment and maximum potential within the limits of the respective rights of others. The service shall be based upon helping the client to understand and use the professional relationship, in furtherance of the clients legitimate desires and interests.

3.4 Social Work Standards Relative to Agencies and Organizations

3.4.1. Work and/or cooperate with those agencies and organizations whose policies, procedures, and operations are directed toward adequate service delivery and encouragement of professional practice consistent with the ethical principles of the IFSW.

3.4.2. Responsibly execute the stated aims and functions of the agency or organizations, contributing to the development of sound policies, procedures, and practice in order to obtain the best possible standards or practice.

3.4.3. Sustain ultimate responsibility to the client, initiating desirable alterations of policies, procedures, and practice, through appropriate agency and organization channels. If necessary remedies are not achieved after channels have been exhausted, initiate appropriate appeals to higher authorities or the wider community of interest.

3.4.4. Ensure professional accountability to client and community for efficiency and effectiveness through periodic review of the process of service provisions.

3.4.5. Use all possible ethical means to bring unethical practice to an end when policies, procedures and practices are in direct conflict with the ethical principles of social work.

3.5 Social Work Standards Relative to Colleagues

3.5.1. Acknowledge the education, training and performance of social work colleagues and professionals from other disciplines, extending all necessary cooperation that will enhance effective services.

3.5.2. Recognise differences of opinion and practice of social work colleagues and other professionals, expressing criticism through channels in a responsible manner.

3.5.3. Promote and share opportunities for knowledge, experience, and ideas with all social work colleagues, professionals from other disciplines and volunteers for the purpose of mutual improvement.

3.5.4. Bring any violations of professional ethics and standards to the attention of the appropriate bodies inside and outside the profession, and ensure that relevant clients are properly involved.

3.5.5. Defend colleagues against unjust actions.

3.6 Standards Relative to the Profession

3.6.1. Maintain the values, ethical principles, knowledge and methodology of the profession and contribute to their clarification and improvement.

3.6.2. Uphold the professional standards of practice and work for their advancement.

3.6.3. Defend the profession against unjust criticism and work to increase confidence in the necessity for professional practice.

3.6.4. Present constructive criticism of the profession, its theories, methods and practices.

3.6.5. Encourage new approaches and methodologies needed to meet new and existing needs.

codes and uniformity in professional behavior, colleagues in eastern Europe are debating the client's "right to reality" and the client's empowerment and right to decision making in collaboration and dialogue with, not under the power of, the critical thinking of social workers (Cacinovic Vogrincic, 1996; Zavirsek, 1997). Socialism was about the collective action of all in expectation of the best consequences for society as a whole. The practice went awry—as indeed capitalism has in terms of distribution of wealth, as discussed in Chapter 9. Prior to Slovenian independence in 1991, housing, health care, and education were universally available in Yugoslavia in a way that is now being questioned in the Slovenian legislature. Under the newly Westernized, democratic, and freer market system, services have become commodities in the marketplace. Even as changes in human services are appearing so rapidly, Cacinovic Vogrincic (1997) reminds her colleagues that ethical practice means the reality of service users' lives must be heard.

In Mexico, "conscientization" lies central to the question of ethics and is very close to the concept of the "right to reality" in eastern Europe. Mexican social workers are involved in traditional Western roles of practice in prisons, schools, and hospitals, but many are also involved in radical political struggle, working with communities to achieve human rights. Community work is frequently central in Mexican social work because workers help in the organization of large groups of people—for example, for land use reform, for clean water, for women's labor rights (Bibus & Link, 1997; Frederico & Whitaker, 1996). There is constant debate between the political messages and media "truths"—for example, over trade with the United States, inflation, the extent of the poverty of indigenous peoples, and the reality of their lives. This tension is encapsulated in the term "conscientization," which refers to the process of understanding the gap between what we are told and what is; what is and what can be.

The process of conscientization combined with observation and action, identified as the dynamic "praxis" by Paulo Freire (1980), is one of the keys to ethical behavior. Social workers engaged in community action in Central America often place themselves at risk for their lives in the interests of freeing people from poverty. In the film *In Her Own Image* (Media Network, 1991), women in Bolivia talk of their cooperative marketing and the resistance, discouragement, and lack of social support from powerful people who run the banking community. They have overcome these obstacles through their own actions and in concert with community activists. In Bangladesh, as discussed in Chapter 4, the Grameen Bank has expanded its loan policy in a way that has fundamentally changed women's lives. These are large issues of change that have come about through reflection, conscientization, and courageous action.

In the United Kingdom, the social workers' code of ethics has been expanding over the years. As in other western European nations, discussions about the profession early in the 20th century saw direct splits between the settlement and community work followers of Toynbee Hall (the first settlement house established in 1887) and the medically linked stream of the profession that took up the psychotherapies of Sigmund Freud and Melanie Klein. For those working in the community, judgment on individuals in poverty was suspended in favor of political analysis on the distribution of wealth. For those connected to the medical stream of thought, individuals were readily judged as sick and less responsible than professionals in decision making. These widely differing approaches meant that ethics attached to the medical domain focused more on the individual "patient," while ethics for social workers working in the community focused more on dialogue and power sharing between service users and those in authority. As Karen Lyons indicates in Case Study 5.1, these aspirations are elusive.

Ethical Decision Making in the United Kingdom

KAREN LYONS

Mrs. K. is a 43-year-old woman who came to the United Kingdom from eastern Europe to study when she was 18. She had married an Englishman soon after and had two children. The marriage ended acrimoniously when the children were young and she has had no contact with them since. Recently, Mrs. K. was referred to the Disability Team of a Midlands social services department by the social workers from the neurological department of a local hospital diagnosed as suffering from multiple sclerosis. It was thought that her condition would deteriorate, raising the need for care in the community.

Until her hospital admission, Mrs. K. had been receiving sick pay from her employers, but this had ceased. On making contact, the social worker found Mrs. K. to be independent and reluctant to accept any intervention, saying that she intended to return to work. When she finally accepted that she was physically unfit to do so, she agreed that the social worker should help her sort out her finances, which now seemed parlous. Assuming that she had no other source of income, the social worker advised her about income support, disability allowances, and housing benefits, which she duly obtained.

Some weeks later, after complaints from neighbors about Mrs. K.'s behavior, the social worker visited and found Mrs. K. in a poor state and overwhelmed. Among the muddle were several official-looking unopened letters and, with Mrs. K.'s agreement, the social worker began looking through these. On opening a letter from a bank, the social worker found a statement indicating savings in excess of the amount disregarded in benefit claims. The social worker urged Mrs. K. to notify the appropriate benefit agencies about this herself. However, Mrs. K. became very angry, accused the social worker of prying into her affairs, and refused further contact. Some weeks later, neighbors and police contacted the Department, concerned for Mrs. K.'s safety. The social worker was ambivalent to become involved again due to the client's recent rejection of her help and the ethical issues discussed in the narrative of this chapter.

• •

In discussing the ethical issues involved in the case of Mrs. K., students may review their own cultural expectations concerning dependence and independence; the role of the social worker; pressures from other "professionals" and police; the power of the social services and subtle dilemmas of professional power and judgments relative to ethical decisions about confidentiality; responsibility to taxpayers; and community care. While the time and place of the case study bring relative issues—for example, in relation to the concept of "benefits," social worker "supervision" and "community care"—there are universals in terms of individual rights to privacy as well as choice and collective responsibility concerning income distribution and care of the disabled.

It is evident that as "codes of ethics" develop around the world and as professional social workers subscribe to the international code, the work of agreeing on one code will never be complete. However, although the task continues to change and to become more complex, there are many common themes. For example, the study of ethics in western Europe has embraced at least four levels of behavior: the client, the professional, the community, and the structural environment. These form the structure for the International Code in Box 5.1. The U.S. Code of Ethics is similarly divided; by adding attention to agency and profession, they have six sections: responsibilities to clients, to colleagues, to practice settings, to professionals, to the profession, and to the broader society (NASW, 1996).

One striking area of rapid change with concurrent implications for social work ethics is technology. Technology in the Global North has raced away at such a pace in the 1980s and 1990s that it is hard to become "conscientized" about its real implications. The technological breakthroughs of the World Wide Web and the Internet mean that individual data are accessible in a way that challenges many of the former expectations of confidentiality and protection of privacy (NASW, 1997). George Orwell, in his chilling and prescient work *1984,* foresaw a world where "Big Brother" would be in charge and there would be very little privacy for the individual. Schools of social work education in the Global North and Australasia are joining in the scramble to ensure protection of student data although the protection of client data is clearly at risk. This dilemma stands in stark contrast to the uneven access to technology in other parts of the world. As outlined in Chapter 7, there is a fabulous range of resources for those who have the technology, the source of energy, and the maintenance services available, and currently this advantage is widening the gap between colleagues and nations.

At the time of writing, a caravan is leaving the U.S. Midwest with supplies for URAC-CAN (University of the Autonomous Regions of the Caribbean Coast of Nicaragua) through the Pastors for Peace initiative. It is an ethical dilemma that we send supplies to be supportive when the infrastructure of the receiving country does not always have the means to update or influence the nature of these supplies. Our parallel action must be to question our conscientization about differential access to technology, which maintains a sense of false superiority between nations. The Pastors for Peace initiative is a welcome role model for social workers because it combines action in sending supplies with personal contact through the journey, dialogue with the receiving community, and eventually expanded education and conscientization of the senders.

The development of technology overrides discussions of ethics, however, because it often outpaces human interaction. To say it overrides discussion does not imply that it takes the place of ethics—it means simply that ethical behavior is at risk in the Global North more than ever before. Thus our place on the earth's surface determines the extent we are engaged in ethical analysis and simultaneously the extent we can expect to be in charge of the outcome of our analysis. For social workers there is a dire need for questioning and concern about the sharing of data and access to previously private and confidential information. Thus, in the unfolding story of the study of ethics, the question for now and the 21st century is: How can we come more closely together in identifying core elements of ethical behavior without intervening in the rights to determination of approach from one country to another?

COMMON ELEMENTS AND A FRAMEWORK FROM SEEDHOUSE

One of the common elements of the study of social work ethics across the globe is the core intent to be responsible in professional actions. The notion to act in a way that enhances people's lives is also central to social work, but it is difficult from an ethical perspective in view of the way one person may judge what is enhanced against another. The social work activity of focusing on the process as well as the task is a notably practical and common theme, as is the expectation that social workers act with cultural understanding and competence. As noted earlier, the philosophical approach of a social worker determines the extent to which every concept needs to be examined. In an absolutist context, an action that is right or wrong is claimed to be clear; in the relativist context, the majority of our concepts, such as that of "enhanced functioning," are open to scrutiny. However, it is crucial to maintain the tension of ethical analysis as we seek common elements in order to advance our awareness of the impact of our actions, to further our conscientization, and to avoid reacting at a personal rather than professional level to behavior as discussed in the following example.

As social workers analyze the steps in their thinking, they can more easily understand the behavior of others. In a crucial learning process for this writer as a young school social worker in North London, England, in the 1970s, there was a case of conflict that became personalized where more sophisticated thought in an ethical framework might have prevented both professional and client pain. Dawn was a 15-year-old "truant" and her school wanted "court action" as soon as possible. To the social worker, Dawn was coping with the suicide of her mother, the alcoholism of her father, and the needs of younger siblings. Dawn was parenting before her time in her cultural setting and missing out on education in a period of transition while other extended family supports were sought (for example, arrangements were being made for a grandmother to move in temporarily). To the school, it was inherently clear that Dawn had missed too much classtime and needed court-ordered protection, with possible removal from home. To the social worker, the young woman was working to maintain some continuity in her rapidly disintegrating family and was behaving with great resilience and tenacity. The social worker thought at that time that the consequences of forcing a court-ordered return to school, even separation, would be harmful for Dawn, for the younger siblings, and for the family's process of grief work.

Ultimately the school principal complained to the social worker's supervisors, and the social worker and the school were called into a confrontation. In retrospect, the school was acting from a deontological ethical perspective; it saw itself as protecting Dawn and was not challenging the social worker in a personalized way. The social worker, working from a teleological perspective, was thinking through social consequences of actions while reacting to the pressure of the educational institution. The situation may have been less explosive between the professionals and in the client's best interests if this analysis had been made immediately.

Urgent practical jobs the world over provide insufficient time for reflection and learning from prior ethical challenges. Sometimes efforts to delineate and to streamline a process of action do not help. In the United Kingdom, an attempt to make decisions on health care services has led to much controversy. Known by the acronym QALYS (Quality Adjusted Life Years), it is "a means intended to produce efficient calculation of health service priorities" (Seedhouse, 1989). The process of applying a QALYS analysis in patient care arose from debates in the *British Medical Journal* over the "economics of coronary artery bypass grafting" (Williams, 1985). According to M. Williams, "The essence of a QALY is that it takes a year of healthy life expectancy to be worth a score of one, but regards a year of unhealthy life expectancy as worth less than one. Its precise value is lower the worse the quality of life of the unhealthy person. If being dead is worth zero, it is in principle, possible for a QALY to be negative, i.e. for the quality of a person's life to be judged worse than being dead" (quoted in Seedhouse, 1989, p. 119).

For medical social workers, this reasoning may seem shocking. It is in complete opposition to the valuing of individual life and the uniqueness of people, their experience of health, pain, and length of life (Barash et al., 1996). Indeed, QALYS has met with much controversy but is a product of the emphasis on consumer commodity over service, economic reasoning over humanity, pressures of fiscal responsibility and profit over human needs. Social workers involved in health, medical, and hospice settings often find themselves at the most difficult place in terms of ethical decision making and this sort of analysis. A parallel example relating to whose life is worthy of service is discussed by Dr. Skarnulis in relation to developmental disabilities in Case Study 5.2.

Who Shall Survive?
Ethical Decision Making with People
Who Have Disabilities

ED SKARNULIS

The ethical challenge to social workers at every level of practice is found in bold relief in the treatment of children and adults with disabilities, arguably society's most vulnerable members. Children and adults with disabilities have historically been more at physical and emotional risk than almost any other societal group when decisions about their welfare have been put in the hands of others.

Exposés of "snake pit" dehumanizing institutional conditions in the United States are well documented and such conditions were not unique to this country. In an attempt to increase Rumania's population, Nicolai Ceausescu's regime imposed a "celibacy tax" on families with fewer than five children, banned all contraceptive devices, and banned all abortions. The result, documented on ABC-TV's *20/20* (5 October 1990), was the abandonment of more than 125,000 Rumanian children, many with severe disabilities, to a life of misery in large institutions hidden in rural areas around the country. Germany's extermination in the 1930s and 1940s of over 100,000 people with disabilities is also well documented.

Other challenges to the well-being—indeed, the very existence—of children and adults with disabilities have been raised. Often the threat comes from the very professions charged with helping them. In 1979, at the opening of the Kennedy Center in Washington, D.C., a film entitled *Who Shall Survive* was shown. Narrated by Eunice Shriver-Kennedy, this painful documentary followed the decision of parents (with permission by Johns Hopkins Hospital officials) to withhold food and water from their newborn baby who had Down syndrome. The child needed a relatively minor surgical procedure performed, and the parents were given the choice of allowing the procedure to be performed or letting the child die. Visibly shaken hospital medical staff express the ethical conflict and feelings of helplessness they experienced in listening to the child's cries and watching the child die. Key themes in the film relate to ethical decision making when professionals are confronted with differing views of the right to survive. As a direct result of this experience, new ethics review protocols were put into place for doctors, social workers, and nurses.

A five-year experiment was conducted at the University of Oklahoma Health Sciences Center in the 1970s in which a formula was used to determine when infants born with spina bifida would be given "active treatment" (Shaw, 1977). The creator of this formula, Dr. Anthony Shaw, authorized a team of physicians, nurses, physical and occupational therapists, a *social worker* (emphasis added), and a psychologist to make the decision to give or withhold all medically indicated treatment, including an operation to close the spinal lesion and the implanting of a shunt to drain spinal fluid from the brain. Twenty-four babies did not get active treatment. All died. All infants who received active treatment survived. The formula was as follows:

QL (quality of life) =
NE (the child's natural physical and intellectual endowment) × H + S
(the contribution the child can expect from his family and society).

Obviously, since the potential of a child is nearly impossible to predict with any degree of accuracy at this stage of development, as is a "societal contribution," the parents' wealth was a powerful determinant in the team's deliberations. Not surprisingly, "the quality-of-life formula was neither discussed with nor revealed to the parents" (Hentoff, 1985).

This use of economic justification for service decision making reflects what might be called a "return on investment" measure of the value of a human being. The more likely one is to become self-supporting, or at the very least to have caretakers who will prevent dependency on the larger society, the greater is the likelihood a person with disabilities will not be threatened by others. Even media exposés of horrible conditions in settings that house people with developmental disabilities are made more wrenching for the viewer when people with normal intelligence are found in such settings. The Rumania television special was peppered with disbelieving phrases like "children who are otherwise perfectly normal." "Normal intelligence" (read "potential for productivity") becomes a code for the belief that lifelong dependency is not to be tolerated. Even within different disability communities, this form of social stratification has taken hold. People with physical disabilities, for example, are quick to distance themselves from children and adults with mental retardation with protestations like "I'm not retarded!" Intelligence is often a metaphor for one's claim to membership in the human race.

How can we move toward a world which values the essential humanity of all people, including those of us who have disabilities? Some answers have become more evident, particularly in the past decade with the closure of institutions and the successful return of people with developmental disabilities to their home communities, as well as the inclusion of children with disabilities in schools.

First, people have to be *present*. In the past we have been so preoccupied with the specialized needs of people with disabilities that we forgot those needs which we all share. Children need loving, nurturing homes. They need contact with other children. Families of children with disabilities need to be given support to meet their child's needs. Children need to be together in preschools and schools, with whatever supports are necessary. Education isn't just the 3Rs. Educational settings educate by giving kids an opportunity to imitate each other, to interact with one another. "Out of sight, out of mind." Adults with disabilities need to live in ordinary homes in their home communities, rather than in large, isolated congregate settings. They need to work in real work settings, side by side with the rest of us. The increased integration of this population into the mainstream of society has increased the opportunity for contact with, and awareness of, who people with disabilities are. Thus, even starting in early childhood, nondisabled people become familiar with the fact that people are just people.

Another way in which barriers have been reduced is through the use of *respectful, people-first language.* This seemingly insignificant choice of words has increasingly been adopted by professionals working in the field of disabilities. Why? It is a recognition that the first words we hear are the ones we remember. If we hear reference to the disability first—e.g., "the mentally retarded man"—we remember mentally retarded, but if the first words are "child with" or "woman who has," we frame our perceptions accordingly.

The media, often through collaboration with professionals in the field of disabilities, has helped make this particular civil rights movement one of the most successful. Internationally acclaimed films like *Mask, My Left Foot, Rain Man,* and *Elephant Man* have had an enormous impact on building positive public perception of people with disabilities.

A basic element in assuring that ethical service and the rights of people with disabilities are not abridged is recognizing the importance of their presence and *participation in all decisions which affect them.* They must be at the table and be empowered to direct the way in which resources will be made available to them. This requires that there be a clear understanding of the choices which exist.

In summary, social workers in schools, in medical settings, in family service agencies, and elsewhere have innumerable opportunities to put forward an agenda that includes ethical treatment of people with disabilities. Personal proof . . . serving as role models for others, advocating for the full civil rights of people, and taking a stand in favor of the full inclusion of people with disabilities in every aspect of life . . . are all ways social workers can make this group of citizens a part of everyone's community.

• •

The prime minister of Slovenia has described his country as "a Land of Blossoms and Thorns." Blossoms are seen in terms of the new democratic constitution, the opening of trade with the West, and the opportunities for growth and new ideas. Thorns are the tension in maintaining the strengths of the previous regime; scrutinizing its failings, such as the outdated emphasis on institutions for the mentally ill; and the commitment to collective action for health, transport, education, housing. So it is with the study of ethical behavior in social work as we reach for more global understanding. There are blossoms in coming together to appreciate and to learn from the unfolding stories and human realities from one country experience to another and thorns in the tension of not claiming one process as the only way. However, it is also chilling that even as we see progress blossoming, we participate in creating new thorns—for example, by indirectly funding medical "advances" that include ethically questioned breakthroughs concerning use of animal organs in humans and cloning of animals and potentially human beings.

One framework for ethical decision making that has captured the imagination, comes from the health field and could be adapted to the systems thinking and ecological approach of social workers; it is the Seedhouse grid laid out in Figure 5.1.

In summary, the grid for ethical decision making identifies a central place to begin in expecting "respect for persons equally," "respect for autonomy," "create autonomy," and "serve

FIGURE 5.1

Seedhouse Grid

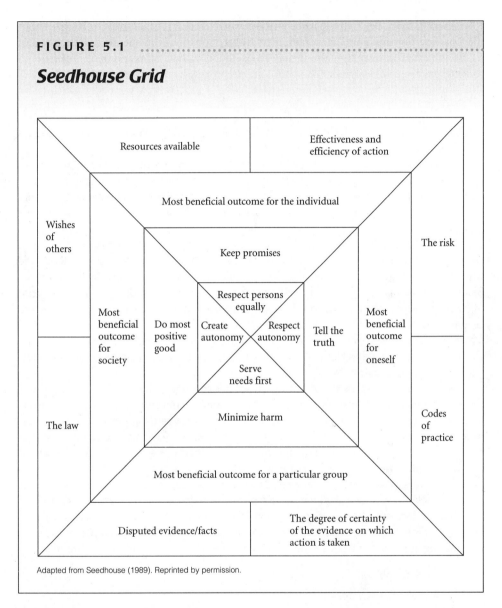

Adapted from Seedhouse (1989). Reprinted by permission.

needs before wants." This last goal, identifying needs before wants, has sometimes been the domain of the professional; in this ethical context it is the social worker's task to ensure that the client and community identify their needs, with the social worker as an ally rather than the professional who is taking charge. Moving outwards from the center of the grid, the additional layers of ethical considerations become increasingly complex. For example, "truth telling" is a key stressor in terms of the individual's right to know a medical diagnosis. The attempts of doctors to estimate length of life have been much criticized, while attitudes to telling the truth about a diagnosis vary widely from culture to culture (Lewis, 1986; Hirshberg & Barasch,

1995; Parry & Ryan, 1995). It is particularly noteworthy that this grid includes dialogue about the "increase of social good" and reminders to keep looking from the micro to the widest macro context. The outer layer also includes recognition of legal rights and makes reference to codes of practice as one segment of a very complex process.

• •

A SYNTHESIS OF STREAMS IN ETHICAL SOCIAL WORK THOUGHT

National boundaries have always been artificial in terms of environmental health, the spread of disease, and the flow of clean air and water. In the domain of professional ethics it is similarly artificial for any one country to rely on its code as discrete or adequate by itself. Currently, practitioners and agencies that have access to sophisticated technology have increased tools to fight injustice, poverty and oppression. However, simultaneously there is the tension that people without these contemporary trappings are less than or lacking in creativity. As Mother Teresa has taught us, we learn by the humility of being with people who survive without basics rather than by our information systems. Also in India, Emma Bhatt founded and organized the largest women's organization in India, perhaps the world, the Self-Employed Women's Union (Gross, 1992). Without personal computers, she managed to engage a mass movement in social justice. Is it ethical for social workers to become technology bound in a way that distances them from clients and client reality? Are we carried on the tide or making choices? How often do we pause and reflect on these processes? One such pause is portrayed in Box 5.2.

Thus the tension for the social work profession is constantly to seek to define the implications of ethical questions, their context, reality, and relationship to the larger environment, before taking action. Codes of practice often miss the wider context of ethical issues in terms of human rights—for example, to health, clean water, and sustainable development of communities now and in the future. The most helpful elements of codes of practice are the way they prompt questions for detailed facets of a decision and for the various groups of actors as well as the way they lead us to frameworks for decision making. Loewenberg and Dolgoff have identified a nine-step sequence for thinking through an ethical decision that connects readily to the International Code in Box 5.1. The early focus on clarifying the society's values is a key reminder of the complexity of an absolute or relativist social context and the implications of this context for the worker, the client, and the community:

1. Identify the problem.

2. Clarify the society's values.

3. Establish goals.

4. Identify alternate targets.

5. Assess and weigh possible outcomes.

6. Identify and rank-order the ethical principles involved.

7. Select the most appropriate option.

8. Implement the option.

9. Evaluate the results for subsequent intervention. (Loewenberg & Dolgoff, 1992)

BOX 5.2

Personal Professional Journey, Mexico 1991

ROSEMARY J. LINK

A day in the foothills near Tepotzlan stays with me forever. We had driven into the *campo* to visit families who may be willing to receive students for homestays. I am invited to spend a day to be part of a family's activities. The journey takes us along dusty roads; we stop at a vegetable and fruit market. Neat pyramids of every color of bean are set out on mats beneath tarpaulins, strung with baskets, flowers, beads, herbs. Many fruits and foods are new to me as I look in wonder at the colors and absorb the vibrant life—so many new discoveries to feast my senses. We travel on slowly, behind carts and donkeys laden with sugarcane. Our destination is a mile or so uphill, beyond the track's end. I am hot and aware of my heart rate as I notice my Mexican colleague striding up this spectacular terrain.

My Spanish is halting at best but I am welcomed warmly and offered frescoes and a seat in a white-walled courtyard with bare earth, jasmine, and much activity. My colleague settles in for a few hours' conversation over recent events. Government officials have been visiting to talk about putting up a football pitch for the local youth, despite the villagers' urgent call for roadways and water. The talk is of the people's priorities and the economic choices and ethics of the current government, who try to buy people's votes with football pitches instead of water supplies. As I gather confidence to try my ideas in my newly acquired vocabulary, I am drawn in and my colleague leaves.

Two sons arrive on horseback; a daughter lights a fire in the wall, striking sticks for a spark. I watch her, mesmerized as she pats and flips a tortilla so expertly, chatting and laughing with a grandparent who is smoking and swaying watchfully from his hammock (no word for nursing homes here). I am aware of his inquisitive gaze and I feel gawky, out of place. Heaven's sake, don't expect me to show my firelighting, horse-tending, hog catching, or culinary skills! I have a brace on my front teeth; it suddenly feels like an emblem of strange priorities. It also makes it very difficult to bite hard food. I am offered a corn cake and struggle politely, not wanting to offend; it tastes wonderful after my too early breakfast but is like iron. Quietly I slip it into my sundress pocket. Foolish city person. A piglet speeds out of the house, scuffles for a moment with a sibling, then shoots her nose in the air, corn cake: quick as a flash she is diving in my pocket and my hosts are laughing as I struggle away, the cake still concealed. Their mirth and relaxation as they prepare for *comida* are infectious. How often do I miss lunch in my usual pelting routines? What more am I missing?

I am invited to eat and follow the daughter's example of washing her hands in a stone bowl to the side of the yard. We pour water on our hands; it flows through the central outlet into a spiral groove round the stone stem. Chicks cluster to drink at the base, the remainder flows through onto a wild profusion of herbs in a garden patch. Why did it take me forty years to appreciate water; to think about how every drop is used and the ethical consequences of denying our right to turn on a tap?

As we seek to identify steps on the journey to increased critical thinking in ethical decisions, we recognize that it will always be an unfolding process of great complexity. Dialogue with colleagues in a variety of countries confirms that ethical considerations are a universal component in social work. The particular form or emphasis that ethical review takes reflects the history and socioeconomic and cultural context in which social work has developed. For example, the recent emergence of countries from eastern Europe from strict socialist regimes has led to a concern for individuality and the focus on a person's "right to reality" to be "listened to, to be heard and to be taken seriously" (Cacinovic Vogrincic, 1996). In Latin America and India, the tension between people in poverty and wealth has prompted a broad-scale political interpretation of ethical considerations in the language of conscientization and people-centered development (Desai, 1990). In countries such as the United States, the detailed codes of ethics may be reflective of a more legal tradition reflected in the current wave of "diagnostic regulations" and the form of service delivery known as "managed care."

When the approach to ethics is explored in a world context beyond our usual national frame of reference, a number of universal principles are identified. Some of these are outlined in the code in Box 5.1 and others represent the universal challenges and principles for social workers who seek social and economic justice. To this writer, these principles fall into three categories:

1. Widest perspective for assessment
   - Before acting, review personal value, history, and cultural bias; ask the question, "How am I influenced personally and professionally by this question or problem?"
   - Review the value base, history, and culture of the other(s) concerned with the ethical question.
   - Question geocentrism and the impact of the location of people involved; what would be different if this dialogue were happening elsewhere in the world and why?
2. Inclusion of the service user in dialogue and decisions
   - Discuss the "right to reality" of the service user and their family or community; spend time defining this reality.
   - Acknowledge the "power" of the professional.
   - Attend to the use of clear language.
   - Consider the question of "conscientization": To what extent is the immediate ethical tension reflective and part of wider societal and global issues?
3. Joint evaluation
   - Was the outcome lasting in its resolution of the ethical questions in the workers', service users', and community view?
   - Which actions by the workers worked best?
   - Which actions by the service user(s) worked best?
   - Did all members feel included and respected?
   - What would be different in a future instance of this ethical decision?

It is clearly a considerable task for the International Federation of Social Workers to gather these varying perspectives for us all. However, to synthesize these streams and to learn from one another across the globe is a key to helping the profession toward deeper understanding and effective action in this ever more complex domain.

STUDENT ACTIVITIES

1. When are we acting in a way that reflects the deontologist school of philosophy, and when are we acting in a way that reflects the teleologist school? How separate are these streams of thought? Give examples of your thinking. How adequate are these two streams of theory in characterizing ethical issues globally?

2. Discuss Case Study 5.3, relating to public use of data gathered in an ethics based disciplinary hearing. What are the arguments for and against use of secondary data?

CASE STUDY 5.3

Privacy of Ethics Procedures Upheld

Reviews by NASW of ethics complaints against member social workers are confidential and may not be introduced as evidence in lawsuits, the Massachusetts Court of Appeals has ruled.

The November decision in *Swatch v. Treat* said that documents from the Massachusetts Chapter's investigation of a client's complaint against a member could not be used in the client's subsequent civil suit. The appeals court ordered a lower court to remove all references to the NASW report from documents about the case.

"This is really important for our members," said NASW General Counsel Carolyn Polowy. "A lot of NASW members wonder whether the documents and information presented in an adjudication hearing can be used against them in a subsequent court case. This decision supports the proposition that they can't be sued on the basis of an NASW Committee on Inquiry finding."

While the *Swatch v. Treat* decision is principally applicable in Massachusetts, it can be cited as support for confidentiality of peer review procedures in other states which have statutes protecting that confidentiality, Polowy added.

"The court decision is significant in its support of NASW's right to conduct peer reviews and to protect our process from misuse for some secondary gain," said NASW Adjudication Manager Elizabeth DuMez. She pointed out that the decision also identified NASW's peer review process as one that emphasizes education and improvement rather than punishment.

The NASW member's client filed suit in superior court after the Massachusetts Chapter Committee on Inquiry (COI) established that the respondent social worker had not met her ethical duties. The client then used the COI report and recommendations as the basis for a civil damage lawsuit.

To protect their interests in keeping the adjudication process confidential, NASW and the Massachusetts Chapter filed a motion to remove the NASW documents from the court case. The superior court rejected the claim.

But the appeals court decision, which upheld all of NASW's claims, determined that COI proceedings are peer review processes under the Massachusetts statute protecting such processes. Generally, that law keeps peer review documents confidential and bars them from private judicial proceedings.

"The objective of peer review is rigorous and candid evaluation of professional performance by a provider's peers," the court wrote. "The ability of peer review committees to speak with candor and the willingness of persons called before them to be equally forthright would be seriously hampered by public release of proceedings or reports of the peer review body."

Additionally, the decision affirms NASW's right to enforce the contract, signed by all complainants, that pledges confidentiality for all materials related to their COI proceedings.

The court also ruled that NASW may intervene in a court proceeding in which its COI documents are mistakenly in use—even if NASW is not a party in the underlying lawsuit—and intervention is the only way to seek protection and removal of the documents.

Polowy noted that the intermediate appellate court showed sensitivity to the need for confidentiality in ethics adjudication by clearing the courtroom of spectators while the case was argued on appeal.

The court also protected the identities of the parties involved in the suit by using fictitious names on case documents.

The time limit on an appeal to the Massachusetts Supreme Court has expired, so the intermediate appellate decision is the final ruling in Massachusetts, Polowy said.

NASW News, 42, 2, Feb. 1997.

• •

3. In his book *Developed to Death,* Trainer (1994) states that the hunger of millions of the world's children is a question of ethics. What does he mean? Outline the current situation for children in relation to world hunger (a place to start would be the UNICEF Document *The State of the World's Children 1997*); identify the ethical questions raised; discuss your own approach and identify the theoretical base you are using.

4. How does a professional's respect for the client's "right to reality" become evident in our practice? Give an example of an application at an individual or community level.

5. Does your country of practice have a code of ethics? How can we relate the International Code of Ethics with a country code? What are the universal principles? In what ways does a country code differ? How would you add to the International Code, bearing in mind that it is under constant scrutiny?

6. Review Case Study 5.4 and apply this approach to ethics to the country where you practice.

CASE STUDY 5.4

Ethical Issues and Value Dilemmas in a Global Economy: An Example of Occupational Social Work

CHATHAPURAM S. RAMANATHAN

Occupational injury rates are generally alarming in nations of the Global South. In a global economy, expansion of multinational corporations in developing nations, particularly Asia, is inevitable. Unfortunately there is an inverse relationship between increased economic activity as a result of multinational investment and the health and safety of workers in these countries. In order to ensure similar safe and healthy work environments, occupational social workers in multinational corporations in Asia can benefit workers by advocating for standards similar to those mandated in legislation in the United States through the Occupational Safety and Health Act and Federal Coal Mine Health and Safety Act legislation. Given that workers in the Asian countries are more vulnerable in their health, safety, and wellness, social workers have an ethical obligation to raise social justice issues and actively advocate on behalf of these workers in multinational subsidiaries (Ramanathan, 1994).

Roles for occupational social workers may arise in response to legislative requirements. For instance, in Indian industries where there are more than fifty women employees, employers are mandated to provide and to maintain child care assistance "creche" for children 6 years and under. These centers are to be staffed by child care workers (Srivastava, 1967). The 1976 amendment of the Factories Act of 1948 mandated employers to provide child care assistance if they employ 30 women. This is stipulated by the Indian Factories Act of 1948 as amended in 1976 (Srivastava, 1988):

> (1) In every factory wherein more than thirty women workers are ordinarily employed there shall be provided and maintained a suitable room or rooms for the use of children under age of six years of such women. (2) Such rooms shall provide adequate accommodation, shall be adequately lighted and ventilated, shall be maintained in a clean and sanitary condition and shall be under the charge of women trained in the care of children and infants. (3) The Provincial Government may make rules—(a) prescribing the location and the standards in respect of construction, accommodation, furniture and other equipment rooms to be provided, under this section; (b) requiring the provision in any factory of free milk or refreshment or both for such children; (c) requiring that facilities shall be given in any factory for the mothers of such children to feed them at necessary intervals.

Further, the report of the royal commission on labor explicates that the employer provide short periods of absence from work at necessary intervals to nursing mothers. The existence of these kinds of legislation in the host countries affect the role of occupational social workers. Occupational social workers also have an ethical role to help industries to increase their corporate social responsibility regarding both health and safety of their workers and the communities in which these industries are located. The absence of the latter is still very clear in our minds regarding the Union Carbide incident in Bhopal, India, where thousands of people died and several thousand were permanently affected because of the poisonous gas leak from the Union Carbide factory, triggered by acceptance of lower levels of safety standards than those of Union Carbide factories in the Global North (Ramanathan, 1992). Also, the extent of compensation provided to the families of the dead and injured were very minimal, thus implicitly conveying that the value of human life varies in different parts of the globe.

•••

Global Approaches to Learning Social Welfare Policy

Anthony Bibus
Rosemary J. Link

I can never be what I ought to be until you are what you ought to be. This is the way our world is made. No individual or nation can stand out boasting of being independent. We are interdependent.

—Martin Luther King, Jr.

This chapter is a resource for making our learning about social welfare policy and services global in scope. In many respects social work is social policy in action (Jordan, 1984). To paraphrase one social work educator (Sharon Keigher, personal communication, 1997), social workers can bring policies to life in the same way musicians turn sheet music into melodies. There are examples of social workers taking a lead role in policy making, such as contributing to the Children Act of 1989 in England, setting up the Ombudsman for Children in Norway, and serving in the legislature in India and the United States of America in increasing numbers. In the form of legislative mandates requiring new services, social policies reverberate in local communities and individual family life. However, not all effects of policies are beneficial for the "vulnerable and oppressed individuals and groups" whom social workers are ethically committed to serve (NASW, 1997, p. 5). For example, cuts in human service budgets in the United States have reduced funding of shelters for people who are homeless, and public subsidies supporting affordable housing have also been cut back. Social workers are often in a position to buffer as well as amplify the effects of social policies, but their capacity to practice effectively for the benefit of people they are serving is contingent on their competence in social welfare policy and services (Iatridis, 1995). Using a global perspective helps social work students analyze, influence, develop, implement, and evaluate social welfare policies in a way that enriches their understanding of policy making, expands policy options, and grounds social policy in the vital global connections that drive contemporary life.

As this book emphasizes, we cannot rely solely on a domestic focus in any aspect of social work practice, and the need for a broader view and set of knowledge and skills is particularly apparent in the area of social welfare policy (Asamoah, Healy, & Mayadas, 1997). This chapter uses examples from a number of countries, including Mexico, the United Kingdom, India, Europe, and the United States, to highlight global connections for learning social welfare policy and services. The multifaceted impact of social policies on communities is traced; also highlighted are skills social workers need to influence social welfare policies so that they protect, sustain, and nurture people.

Beginning with a definition of social welfare policy that assumes a global perspective, the chapter moves to examples of using international ties for learning about and synthesizing social welfare history, practice, and field practicum experiences. We continue with considerations of how global approaches to analysis of social welfare policy can serve to integrate the aspects of social work study, including research, human condition, special populations, diversity, and social and economic justice into a complete picture. During these discussions, we consider global social policy instruments such as United Nations documents. For child welfare, the Convention on the Rights of the Child (United Nations, 1989) is a key guide for interventions; for women's issues, the Report on the Beijing Conference (discussed in Chapter 9 of this volume) provides a common voice for poverty, employment, and status concerns; and the Declaration on Human Rights, despite representing after fifty years more vision than reality, remains a beacon for social workers (United Nations, 1994). In conclusion, we explore the implications of global approaches to the customary frameworks of analysis used by social workers in policy work, assisted by the crossnational policy analysis of Tracy (1992). To be effective, analysis of social welfare policies must be an interactive process involving the global community of social workers, other professional colleagues, and service users in generating new ways to meet human needs on a global basis.

GLOBAL APPROACHES

As interest in more global approaches to social work has been increasing, there are isolated examples of classes or workshops similar to the one imagined by Bibus in Box 6.1. Mary reports on a graduate seminar in the United States that explored interconnections between global threats of violence and poverty and immigration; one of her students wrote: "I came to realize that the services I provide on a daily basis are influenced by the global crises we confront" (1997, p. 595). What would social work education be like for students if a truly international perspective were integrated into learning social welfare policy and services? Imagine what might happen in a typical classroom in an introductory social work course or workshop in a social work agency retreat as a session is about to begin . . .

Another example of a program with the objective of understanding a wide regional context is the Maastricht–North London collaboration. In this joint effort, students from all over Europe and now expanding to Africa and the United States come together for short intensive study of social policy development (Maastricht, 1997). Students compare their own

BOX 6.1

Imagine Globally Oriented Learning

ANTHONY BIBUS

Participants are in clusters. One cluster surrounds the instructor planning an up-coming field trip to the general assistance office downtown. There will be an op-portunity for the participants and a group of social work students visiting from Japan to meet with people who had slept on the floor of the general assistance office last night because they were homeless and the shelters were full. (This arrangement is referred to as "safe waiting," a euphemism that will need careful interpretation from English into Japanese.)

A trio of participants is concentrating on a computer screen with an E-mail message from a social worker in France explaining the system of children's al-lowances there. One participant proclaims: "Wait until I tell my uncle! He thinks that increasing welfare payments based on the number of kids causes parents to have more kids because they get more money!" The group moves on to contact the home page of social workers in Prague to learn about economic readjustment.

Another group is at a table paging through UNICEF reports on *The State of the World's Children* (1997), taking notes on indicators of health, nutrition, education, social welfare, resources, and economic and population trends. Also on the table are issues of *International Social Work,* the *Indian Journal of Social Work,* the *British Journal of Social Work,* and the *Journal of Social Development in Africa* along with other UN reports and atlases. There's a globe in the middle of the table that features the southern hemisphere on top, and over on the wall prominently framed and hung, is NASW's poster *Global Family Ties,* with the caption: "Families are the strength of every nation. . . . Everywhere, families are the first providers of social services." We notice other posters and sayings around the room, such as "Partners in Global Exploration" and "Social Welfare Policy = LIFE."

Another group of participants is nervously sorting through a set of overhead transparencies and cueing a videotape for the first item on the agenda for the class: their presentation on their recent study tour in Cuernavaca, Mexico. With a Diego Rivera mural and Mexican music in the background, the narrator on the video in-troduces themes of national sovereignty and migration. There are several mentions of the North American Free Trade Agreement (NAFTA) and discussion of which seg-ments of the Mexican, Canadian, and U.S. populations seem to be benefiting the most.

Other participants are just arriving and settling into a circle in the middle of the room. One of the books they carry compares social welfare systems in a variety of countries while another describes the "patch" approach to community-based ser-vices in England and Iowa (Adams & Nelson, 1995). The clusters finish their work, and participants and instructor come together to begin the session. The instructor and participants brief each other on progress that work groups are making in ad-dressing the questions they have been reflecting upon in earlier sessions.

experiences and come to realize how service context, history, and geographic location all influence the design and implementation of policy. Questions students can use in analyzing policies from a variety of countries include:

- What is the definition of "social welfare policies"? What do they do? Give an example.
- Who develops social welfare policies?
- What services do social welfare policies govern? Give an example.
- Who provides these services?
- Who benefits? Who suffers?
- Are people who use social welfare services part of deciding which social welfare policies are implemented and how? Are they part of planning for services, choosing what needs services are to address, and seeing if the services are working as intended?
- How is the example of a social welfare policy interrelated with global distribution of wealth and other social and economic justice issues?

Social work scholars, educators, and practitioners are increasingly calling the attention of the profession to the critical importance of understanding the global nature of social welfare policy issues today. Asamoah and colleagues (1997) list several ways that global interdependence creates avenues for reshaping the profession, including the unique focus of social work on human rights and social justice. In Chapter 11 of this book, Midgley discusses the reverberations of world events and their effect on, for example, social work with refugees and migrant workers, developing themes introduced in his earlier work:

> In the past, social policy makers in the industrial countries often formulated policies for new social programs without paying any attention to the experiences of their colleagues in other countries. By ignoring these experiences, domestic policy makers often made costly mistakes. Today, it is much more common for policy makers to obtain information about innovations in other countries. (1997, xiii–xiv)

If they are attuned to the global nature of social welfare policy and services, social workers can be a fruitful source for this international information and a valuable link to the wisdom and experiences of both practitioners and people who use social welfare services worldwide. The remaining sections of this chapter provide guidelines for preparing social work students for this critical work.

••

DEFINITION OF SOCIAL WELFARE POLICY
FROM A GLOBAL PERSPECTIVE

A key step in a global approach to learning about social welfare policy is defining this policy in a way that reveals how social forces, needs, and problems are not confined within national boundaries. For example, public health and population movements such as immigration are intricately and dynamically related with changes in culture and commerce. Social welfare issues such as violence, hunger, poverty or social exclusion (Walker & Walker, 1997), homelessness, substance abuse, human rights, infectious disease, infant mortality, racism, care of aged and disabled, can only be fully understood and addressed "transnationally" (Healy, 1992; Hokenstad, Khinduku, & Midgley, 1992; Iatradis, 1995; Link & Bibus, 1998; Midgley, 1995, 1997; Van Soest, 1997). "Social welfare policy" must then be defined in a way that makes these global interconnections explicit even as the immediate human needs that particular policies address appear local in scope. For example, local initiatives to prevent abuse of children by prohibiting corporal punishment in schools, teaching peaceful conflict resolution, and helping parents learn more nurturing and effective discipline techniques are obliterated if the children face gunshots in the playground or land mines on their walks home: "The greatest and most important challenge for social workers is to become global professionals who understand the deeply embedded and submerged structural foundation of violence, which feeds violence at the institutional and individual levels in an increasingly interdependent world" (Van Soest, 1997, p. 345).

Policies are essentially plans for collective action; *social welfare policies* are plans to meet particular human needs related to people's well-being; they are courses of actions that people choose through their governments (in democracies) and through international unions (such as the European Union), intending to weave or strengthen the social fabric. These actions can take the form of services, benefits, and income supports (Gilbert & Specht, 1974). Recalling Titmuss's (1962, 1968, 1974) pioneering conceptual leadership in the fields of social policy and social work education, Midgley defines *social welfare* as "a state or condition of human well-being that exists when *social problems are managed,* when *human needs are met,* and when *social opportunities are maximized*" (1997, p. 5). Thus, social welfare policies are intended to support this condition of well-being for people. Jansson (1994), also building on Titmuss, refers to social policy as "a collective strategy to address social problems" (p. 4) and further identifies skills needed by social workers in the social policy area as those that help "change the environment that shaped clients' lives" (p. 11). In contrast to some other social policy scholars, as we will see, Jansson does not restrict the definition of policy to formal governmental documents but broadens understanding of social policy to include informal as well as formal policies, unwritten and implicit as well as written and explicit, personal orientation and action as well as agency procedures. DiNitto broadens this definition still further, stating that social welfare policies are "anything government chooses to do, or not to do, that affects the quality of life for its people" (1991, p. 2). For this book, *social policy* is defined as the plan and action taken by governments, unions of nations, and community organizations that affect the distribution of resources and services to promote people's well-being.

· ·

THE INFLUENCE OF VALUES ON POLICIES AND SERVICES

With an international perspective, it becomes clear that the well-being, income distribution, and social security of people in one region are intimately related to worldwide economic, environmental, political, health, and other forces. No one government can enact social policies effectively without the cooperation of other governments. For example, both the United States and the United Kingdom have embarked on strategies for welfare reform, moving from reliance on cash assistance and other benefits to reliance on employment and accompanying market forces to meet the needs of citizens; both countries use the phrase "welfare to work" to describe this programmatic shift. However, neither country, despite their status as economically developed and recently prospering, can assure their citizens that jobs with living wages and decent benefits for health care, retirement, or disability compensation will be available. Job markets in both countries are predominantly dependent on global market forces such as the prevailing wages for skilled or unskilled labor, the availability of energy and fuel, and the movements of multinational corporations. We must develop a global welfare state to match, negotiate with, and mediate the demands of global corporations and to address the paradox of growing national wealth for some people and simultaneous structural inequality and increasing poverty for many others (Peter Townsend, personal communication, 1997; Stoesz & Karger, 1993; see also Chapter 9 of this volume). It is instructive to note that in India social policy is more closely aligned with the workplace and government's role in assuring that the needs of workers are met than in many countries of the Global North. For example, for every factory employing more than 150 people, a social worker must be employed. Where there are more than 50 women employed, day care must be provided and staffed by child care workers. Employers must allow short periods of absence from work at necessary intervals for mothers to nurse their infants (Ramanathan, 1991; Srivastava, 1988).

Actions called for in policies entail choosing one set of services over another or transferring resources from one group to another or requiring them to be shared. Thus, what is adequate welfare to one country might result in suffering for another. Each country's social welfare policies should identify the threshold of need—or "consensus about the tolerable rate of a problem" (Iatridis, 1995, p. 1862)—below which residents will not be allowed to fall. However, decisions about which services are best and about what level of human needs can affordably or feasibly be met cannot be made in isolation: "No nation can solve its social problems unilaterally" (Healy, 1995, p. 1509). Those decisions and choices of action that each country makes, though, are fundamentally based on priorities given to particular values in that country. "At bottom, all questions of social policy are ideological and questions of value" (Hoshino, 1985, p. 14; see also Chapter 5 of this volume). Or as Iatridis puts it: "Social policy is planned from the perspective of a set of values and ideology" (1995, p. 1856). And if social welfare policy is living and breathing in social work practice, then values are its life blood.

Countries will vary on which values are given precedence over others in forming public social welfare policy, and countries will vary on the degree of consensus with which those primary values are shared. While the European Union is trying to reframe the market value of women's work, the video *In Her Own Image* (Media Network, 1991) reveals the lack of recognition given to the economic contribution of women's work in the economies of Africa, South and Central America, and India. The United States is an example of a nation founded on complex and often competing values (Marmor, 1990; Whitaker & Federico, 1997). Karger and Stoesz explain that in the United States, as in most countries, the policies that shape social welfare services often "reflect the preferences of those in decision-making capacities. According to veteran policy analyst David Gil, 'choices in social welfare policy are heavily influenced by the dominant beliefs, values, ideologies, customs, and traditions of cultural and political elites and privileged strata'" (1994, p. 7). Recounting the ancient English law that prohibited giving alms to able-bodied people, Suppes and Wells add: "Such a law clearly reflected the interests of the ruling class. Since the time of the plague, many secular laws related to the poor have been designed to control the labor supply at least as much as to relieve the suffering of the destitute" (1996, p. 71). These are dominant values of the

Global North and might not coincide with the "crucial social policy values in social work practice," globally, which Iatridis lists as "social justice, equality, democratic processes, and empowerment of disadvantaged and powerless people" (1995, p. 1856).

Therefore, a global approach to teaching social welfare policy will call for rethinking of both the value base of the profession and what should be the value base of welfare policies. Asamoah and colleagues suggest that one new globally oriented value should be:

> based on "universality of life claims," defined in a recent *Human Development Report* (United Nations Development Program, 1994, p. 13) as a belief that no child "should be doomed to a short life or a miserable one merely because that child happens to be born in the 'wrong class' or in the 'wrong country' or to be of the 'wrong sex.'" . . . Extending social work's strong affiliation of equity, justice, and individual worth to include the "universalism of life claims" is an important step in promoting the global perspective. (1997, p. 394)

They recommend identifying social work as an "International Human Rights Profession" as one of three possible unifying frameworks for the profession in the coming century (the other two are social development and cross cultural competence). The Universal Declaration of Human Rights and other U.N. documents such as the International Convention on the Rights of the Child then govern social workers in a global approach to defining social welfare policy. In addition to grounding our policy understanding and practice in globally oriented social work values, we must remember the historical heritage that guides practice at its best. Reflections on the heritage of the profession reveal how social workers have used their practice as a window to human needs (Chambers, 1967, 1971) showing society where social welfare policies should be refocused.

•••••••••••••••••••••••••••••••••••

USING INTERNATIONAL SOCIAL WORK TIES TO TEACH SOCIAL WELFARE HISTORY

International comparisons can serve to highlight the rich and mixed history of social workers' role in social welfare history (see Student Activity 1 at the end of this chapter). For example, the dynamic exchange between Toynbee Hall in London and Hull House in Chicago (Trattner, 1994) illustrates the benefits of cross-national contacts. Social workers' early role in the international peace and justice movements is a model for contemporary students and practitioners (Sullivan, 1993). Useful connections can be made to the growth of family centers in England that have reached back to the heritage of university settlements (Stone, 1994). Just as the women of Hull House built a playground for immigrant children to use in Chicago one hundred years ago, recently Barnardo's Fulford Family Centre in the Hartcliffe neighborhood of Bristol, England, surveyed the needs of a housing estate, discovered that there was an absence of safe play areas, and with community residents successfully advocated for these areas to be developed. The growth of family centers in England and the simultaneous growth of family-based services and family-centered collaboratives in the United States during the 1980s offer another example of how fruitful historical analysis can be (Adams & Nelson, 1995; Link, 1995; NASW, 1995; Pecora, Whittaker, & Maluccio, 1992; Stone, 1994). Table 6.1 shows how one policy—the U.K. Children Act of 1989—was implemented in strikingly different forms. Some family centers focused on people's deficits while others focused on empowering, even radical strategies involving service users.

TABLE 6.1 *Analysis of Policy Implementation: Family Centers in Britain**

Philosophy/Conceptual Base	Characteristics of Agency	Atmosphere
Deficit Model: Social Work Profession Directed		
1. Statutory controlling: protective	involuntary	investigative
	closed limited access	surveillance
	status-hierarchy	control
	noninvolvement-users	
	professional "expertise" emphasized	dysfunctional parent
	regulations, standards emphasized	labeling
	formal referral	assessment
	therapy/structured intervention	
2. Caring preventive	mix closed and open access, voluntary clients	protective
	anticipation in cooperative organization	parental encouraging skills where lacking
	noncourt ordered	silent on resource deprivation
	status quo	abuse focused
Opportunity Model: Social Work Partnerships: Service User Influence		
3. Networking– (neighborhood) and community support	positive view of family	open communication
	voluntary	negotiation
	informal settings: drop ins	positive language
	professionals as facilitators vs. experts	voids labeling
	empowering	strengths
4. Radical self-help	user control	cooperation
	mutual aid	empowerment through action
	mutual respect	self-generating
	participatory management valued	

*"Deficit and opportunity" concepts drawn from Cannan (1992).

As discussed in Chapter 2, the history of the profession of social work raises similarly useful comparisons and contrasts. For instance, a parallel and interactive movement, emphasizing both individually focused casework and community centered practice, emerged in Mexico and in the United States (Bonilla, 1993). However, a significant difference stands out in making this comparison as one notes how community-based practice grounded in radical analysis of social policy and grassroots mobilizing waned (at least temporarily) in the United States (Specht & Courtney, 1994; Teare & Sheafor, 1995) while it is still strong in Mexico (Bibus, 1995). Social work educators and practitioners in Mexico assert that while models of social work from the United States influenced the early development of social work in Mexico, Mexican social workers have turned away from what they perceived as a predominant focus in the United States on individual adjustment to a broader focus: helping students in Mexico learn to work with communities to produce structural change to meet people's needs. For example, social work students working with a field instructor in a village near Cuernavaca, Mexico, met with community members and negotiated a task documenting the history of how the village had risen from the sugarcane fields; one of the streets of the village was named for the date that construction materials, lobbied for by villagers with the organizing help of the social worker (who was the field instructor), were finally delivered by the government. Recent history of the profession in North and South America reveals the profound influence the model of shared learning and consciousness raising articulated by Paulo Freire (1983) has for so many social workers and social work educators in U.S. and Latin American contexts (see Chapter 5 in this volume).

One of the benefits of social workers' involvement in the global community of social workers is learning the parallels and contrasts as the history of the profession in one country is compared with another's. Membership in associations such as the International Federation of Social Workers, the Inter-University Consortium for International Social Development, or the International Association of Schools of Social Work (Healy, 1995) can provide contacts for educators and students and connections to practitioners in other lands. Study tours and semesters abroad offered by such organizations as the Center for Global Education (Augsburg College, Minneapolis, MN) and the Bristol International Credit Earning Program (University of Bristol, England) bring participants into contact with social workers in other countries who are aware of their professional heritage and its relationship to social welfare policy. Students can share with each other the fruits of these contacts through formal and informal sharing in class and out. Exposure to the benefits of immersing students in the community with practitioners and opportunities to meet and even live with people in other countries can also influence the manner in which social work classes are conducted. After teaching in Mexico, for example, we are much more likely to integrate community members and clients in teaching social work (Bibus, 1997).

••••••••••••••••••••••••••••••••••

USING INTERNATIONAL TIES TO LEARN ABOUT THE INTERCONNECTIONS OF POLICY WITH PRACTICE

These opportunities for contact between social work educators and students with practitioners in other countries also provide glimpses of what social workers do on the job. The principles of effective practice and interconnections between practice and policy come into clearer focus. In addition, the assumptions we have made but not fully examined about what is effective and about the nature of those interconnections are also challenged as we witness how social workers in other countries do their jobs.

For example, in Mexico social worker Josefina Vázquez Pérez focuses much of her practice on actively joining with communities in advocating for improved utilities, water, housing, services and schools (Bibus, 1995; Link & Bibus, 1998); villagers refer to their social worker as helping open their eyes to their social welfare needs and how to influence their government to meet those needs. Similarly, social workers in family centers in England carry out their commitment and directives of their agency and national policy (see the Children Act of 1989; Social Services Inspectorate, 1995) to involve people who use the services of the family center in shaping the center's policies (Stone, 1994, p. 123). At the Fulford Centre, service users meet fortnightly in a Parents' Council (Christine Stones, personal communication, June 30, 1997) and significantly influence the agency's agenda and services. At the Cornmarket Family Centre in Bath, (which in contrast to the non-profit Fulford Centre is operated by the local public child welfare authority), parents and staff join as partners in establishing a nurturing environment at the center for parents as well as children: "In order to meet the needs of kids, we must meet the needs of parents" (Val Bean, personal communication, July 1, 1997). In the 1997 national elections in England, over 50 social workers were elected Members of Parliament as part of the new Labour government, placing themselves in position to affect national social welfare policies directly (Bull, 1997). They will be working on implementing England's version of "welfare to work" and "devolution," or sharing of responsibility and resources for social welfare between national and local governments. Future exchanges of learning with U.S. colleagues hold much promise as each country compares seemingly similar policy initiatives. In the United States, a newly initiated National Committee for Educating Students to Influence State Policy and Legislation is gathering and disseminating tips for social work educators on how to teach students skills in policy making.

In studying policy, we must recognize how intricately policy and practice are entwined. Policies of course affect the lives of those whom practitioners are serving as well as of the practitioners themselves, their role, what they're allowed to do or restricted from doing to help: "Social policies both create and constrain the possibilities of any social practice" (Chambers, 1986, p. 30). Moreover, skills useful or essential in direct helping are also essential in developing or influencing policies. Without such skills as listening, identifying the other person's goals and priorities, clarifying objectives, problem solving, negotiating, mediating, leading meetings, and mobilizing interest or pressure groups, all also useful in practice, social workers would not be equipped to influence policies.

International comparisons (such as those made earlier between Mexico and England) accentuate the potential unity of practice and policy. Social workers in developing countries such as Mexico, Slovenia, Taiwan, Guam, and India work from a community development model, concentrating on mobilizing communities to influence policies so that the needs of the population most often suffering are better met. Using a dual focus on person-in-environment, practitioners in developing countries tend to lean toward interventions that affect change in the environment at the macro level to meet human needs more universally. This activism on behalf of social and economic justice, community organization, and political advocacy on public issues—that is, on behalf of structural change—is as much or more a part of daily practice as individual adjustment, direct services, and helping with individual troubles. Social workers use counseling and education to assist individuals and families and groups in becoming aware of how social policies support or inhibit achievement of their goals and develop skills needed to improve social policy and services and make them more responsive. Case Study 6.1 describes how a social work educator and practitioner in Mexico brought this kind of policy practice integration to life.

CASE STUDY 6.1

Josefina Vázquez Pérez Helps Students Make Connections Between Policy, Practice, and Professional Values*

In a social work class in Cuernavaca, Mexico (under the auspices of the Center for Global Education based at Augsburg College in Minneapolis, MN) students from the United States had opportunities to compare their experiences visiting agencies such as institutions for children and day activity centers for older adults in Mexico and the United States. In one of the centers for children, infants were housed in cinder-block barracks, alone in metal cribs, with no adults in attendance. As some students left the facility sobbing, social worker and educator Josefina Vázquez Pérez noted that students may have witnessed how people are first abandoned by their families, then by society. Pérez realized, she said, that we in the United States focus on trying to solve the problem of the moment. But, she added, we must also remember that the problems of the moment have their origins in past events, past historical periods, and a complex array of national and global forces beyond the particular situation our clients are facing. So we must take a short-term, mid-term and long-term perspective on possible solutions. The short-term problem might be the disintegration of the family and potential harm and danger to the children. Our approach and services may be limited by what the state offers, she said, but we must allow those affected to participate in the solution of the problems and this effort must be interdisciplinary. It is the social worker's job to bring the other professions together and to challenge all with a wider view.

Later Pérez brought the class on field trips to two small villages of *jornaleros,* day workers who cut cane with machetes and are paid by the weight of what they cut. She told the class that the workers are often cheated. It is exhausting and dirty work and only available during harvest season four months out of the year. The cane is scorched just before harvest to burn off the thorns, so the workers are covered with soot when they come back to their homes after a day in the fields. The work is also dangerous, and workers often begin when they are too young to be employed legally; recently a 13-year-old accidentally had his fingers chopped off. In the past the laborers were given clean water and food while they worked, but not any longer. Their boss reportedly said that if workers survive on the poisoned and polluted water in their village, dirty water while they're working won't hurt them.

*Adapted from Bibus (1995).

Many of the families are indigenous and all are poor. But they are organizing with the social worker's support. One of the villages is three years old and more organized now than the other newer and smaller village. There are about 80 families, and with social workers' help they have formed committees to be recognized by the government. At the time of the visit in 1994, they had managed to obtain materials (though not construction expertise) from the government program Solidaridad for roads, houses, and a water tower. They still did not have a school building, though. Villagers told the visitors that they have hope and know that they have accomplished some things but must still fight for their public services. They indicated that they view the social worker as an equal, a *compañera,* not as an expert or official who has given them charity. We asked one of the men what social workers did with the people of the village. He replied: "*Abrir los ojos*"—open our eyes.

Afterwards students generated the following themes in reflecting on the visit:

- Social work can be a bridge between people and resources and can undo some of the damage done by judgmental "we versus they" attitudes.

- The help people received from the government did not diminish their motivation but in fact seems to have strengthened their resolve, determination, aspirations, and hope that other needs might be met.

- Some of the difficulties faced by poor people in Mexico are overwhelming and beyond the reach of what any one of us could do to relieve them; there is an enormous gap between what we in the United States have and what is available for the people of the village we visited.

- Therefore, the public in the form of government responsibility (internationally) must intervene.

- Exposure to unhealthy living conditions is a good example of a private trouble that is a public issue.

- We wonder how to sustain courage and keep going as the *jornaleros* have done.

During another class session in Cuernavaca, we applied NASW's Code of Ethics to a case situation presenting an ethical dilemma. Pérez explained that Mexican social workers have no formal code, but one is needed since so many practitioners have little education and training and can easily slip into pushing people around to meet job expectations. For example, she related how her colleagues at a public social service agency would order families to sweep their streets and pick up trash so the workers could report to their superiors that the number of families who had swept and cleaned was at the expected count. Workers spent less time and energy on understanding how the families were living, their struggles, goals, and dreams. She said colleagues often expressed disgust for the lifestyle of some families, whom they saw as fleabitten, dirty, with strange and primitive customs that the workers felt obliged to change. In practice there is much emphasis on reports and not much on actual support for families. She told us how one client refused to sweep her street even when the worker threatened to withhold benefits. The client said that she resented being ordered around. She planned to sweep her street, but not when the worker wanted her to.

The fact that the macro and environment side of the dual focus is so much more manifest in the practice of social workers in developing countries is in part the result of the influence of their national policies in some cases ignoring environmental or systemic responses to human needs (Whitaker & Federico, 1997). Policies have profound effects on social workers' and other helping professionals' practice, constraining and even forbidding social workers from serving. During the 1980s, social workers and health workers practicing in the Quiché region of Guatemala were threatened, tortured, and even killed or exiled for trying to help villages seen by government or rebels as sympathizers to the other side (Alfonso and Vilma Morales, personal communications, 1994–1996; Swensen, 1994). Social policies that favor rich and ruling classes over the rest of the population—neoliberalist economic policies (Fisher & Karger, 1997; Whitaker & Federico, 1997) favoring the merchant class, for example—lead to imbalance in meeting basic needs for many residents of the Americas. Practitioners in the United States may soon witness similar deterioration in the social fabric as a result of the recent withdrawal of federal responsibility for entitlement programs serving the poor; the effects of the Personal Responsibility and Work Opportunity Reconciliation Act of 1996 may challenge the myopic focus on individual direct services and result in social workers recommitting to their settlement house roots. Thus policy cannot be studied as discrete or abstracted from practice, either as general frameworks, obscure regulations, and dry procedures with little relevance to actual practice or as complicated legalistic legislative documents and processes. Social welfare policy must be studied and experienced as it is lived each day and affects daily lives.

We are emphasizing the connections between practice and policy because practitioners in the Global North often believe that their daily practice has little to do with social policy; it is seen as part of administrators' responsibility, not line staff's. Students must continuously keep attention on the interaction between practice and policy (Pecora et al., 1992). Policy and practice are not conceptually identical. The former is the plan, the intent or goals, and procedures to accomplish them; the latter is the implementation, acts carrying out and adjusting procedures to accomplish intended goals *in vivo*. Still, skills needed for making helpful "good" policies are also needed for good practice, and vice versa. Partnership and collaboration among community members; service users; and professionals in health, education, business, religion, and human services in addition to social workers are the keys to effective social welfare policy and service. Once again, international comparisons can provide models for the damage that can be done without this partnership: in England a massive breakdown in professional collaboration contributed to neglect of children in the Cleveland area and subsequently to national legislation that requires interdisciplinary cooperation to protect children and serve families (Her Majesty's Stationery Office, 1995). This same comparison demonstrates to other countries the kind of policy making that responds to mistakes by setting up a much more coordinated and integrated helping system.

· ·

SOCIAL WELFARE POLICY AND FIELD PRACTICUM EXPERIENCES

The wider context of field practicum experiences is set in Chapter 10; however, the connections with social policy are crucial and help us see what gets included and left out from country to country, another reminder that only through full view of the patchwork can we begin to understand all the components of social work policy practice. "Compared to the U.S. curriculum, social work programs in Mexico, Poland, and Sweden include more time in agency-based field practice and more classroom emphasis on the impact of political and economic systems on social welfare" (Whitaker & Federico, 1997, p. 307). In the United States it is difficult to find field practicum settings that focus on the kind of community organization and advocacy for more just social welfare policies that is common in Mexico. Ideally, field practicum experiences should provide opportunities to unwrap a superficial veneer that imagines policies are someone else's purview, to show the extensive nature of policies' influence on everything an agency does and every practicum activity and client situation. In reality, practicums, field trips, and study tours in other countries might be the richest resource for such experiences.

A useful ingredient, then, in the recipe for studying social policy from a global perspective is the opportunity for students or instructor or both together to participate in a short study tour or longer semester abroad (see Chapter 10 of this volume). The often life-changing and inspiring experiences of exchanging ideas and observations with social workers in other lands add flavor and enrich domestic classroom discussions. In addition, the most profound insights are often those we have when gazing back on our own social welfare policies and practice habits from the fresh perspective of another country's varying and many times more effective responses to similar human needs. As emphasized throughout this text, we have much to learn from other countries, not least from those in the Global South.

••

POLICY AND INTERNATIONAL RESEARCH

Social research must be the foundation for understanding and influencing social welfare policy, starting first with scholarship about one's own country in a context of policy instruments that are based on global consensus, such as the United Nations' Declaration on the Rights of the Child, which became international law as the Convention on the Rights of the Child in 1990. Ninety-six percent of the world's children live in countries that have ratified the Convention (exceptions as of 1996 include Oman, Somalia, Switzerland, United Arab Emirates, and the U.S.). UNICEF states that "the Convention has produced a profound change that is already beginning to have substantive effects on the world's attitude towards its children. Once a country ratifies, it is obliged in law to undertake all appropriate measures to assist parents and other responsible parties in fulfilling their obligations to children" (UNICEF, 1997). This document is therefore a crucial starting place for social workers concerned with child welfare research, since its ten principles (summarized in Agostinelli, 1979) form the basis of our work and beliefs:

United Nations Declaration on the Rights of the Child
Every child in the world has rights.
Every child has the right to have a name and a country.
Every child has the right to have enough food to eat, a place to live, and a doctor's care.
Every child who is handicapped has the right to special treatment and care.
Every child has the right to grow up in a family feeling safe, loved, and understood.
Every child has the right to go to school and to play.
Every child has the right to be watched over and taken care of in times of danger.
Every child has the right to be protected from cruelty or unfair treatment.
Every child has the right to grow up without fear and hatred, and with love, peace
and friendship all around.

Recently, in a North American school for at-risk youth, student interns, social workers, educators, and pupils have embarked on a journey to understand the impact of macro policies on their world and their own environment. As a consequence, they have learned about realities of hunger and fundamental needs in a range of countries and reviewed their own circumstances and power to change, as outlined in Case Study 6.2.

CASE STUDY 6.2

Students Discover the World and Their Own Power: The "Face-to-Face" Program

In the summer of 1997, students at an alternate school for at risk youth organized a symposium with the help but not the direction of their supporting adults. The symposium invited educators, parents, social workers, and policy makers from the legislature of the area to come and hear their story and view their poster gallery of research on issues of concern to them.

During the symposium the students role-played their experience of reality on the streets and in their social groups in their schools. For many, issues of violence, discrimination, and victimization had been a key theme. The students also showed a film of their current lives, their poetry, and their music. During the symposium, guests were invited to view posters on world hunger, children's rights, and poverty. Pictures also demonstrated artwork in their alternative school, murals that depict them recognizing themselves as citizens of the world, ready to tackle their future and to be a part of it.

In closing, a panel of students explained what they ask:

- of themselves: for example, to spend more time with their families, to volunteer, not to play "he says/she says" games, to use their heads for more than coat racks; to honor and respect others.

- of adults: to teach us our heritage; to role-model to show us how to get on with others; parents spend time with us; to be listeners, not always think you're right; we act like we can do everything ourselves but we still need you, we need healthy places to hang out.

- of policy makers: to take a chance to talk to us; if you don't understand us, ask us questions, talk about us in positive ways, involve young people in planning, don't blame us for poverty.

They echoed their learning about the Convention on the Rights of the Child and asked that they not be labeled as "dropouts"—that they be seen for their potential, their creativity, and their abilities.

••

Similarly, a group of gang members in Honduras has come together to change their lives with the help of a local police officer and community organizers. Donna DeCesare has documented their lives and their experiences as "*trece* wetbacks," crossing three borders to enter the United States illegally, only to be returned to their poverty-stricken homes (DeCesare,

1997). DeCesare's research has identified a group of young people who demonstrate resilience in the extreme; who are denied "enough food to eat, a doctor's care, the right to grow up feeling safe" but cooperate together to survive, as shown in her illustrations in this book. The elements of their resilience, where they build on opportunity rather than deficit, are striking features of their future hopefulness and that of the community workers who are encouraging them. Too often in the past they have been arrested and labeled as deviant; now they are finding a constructive way to grow despite the impoverished environment that surrounds them.

In England as in many other countries, policy makers, researchers, and practitioners are joining forces to reexamine child protection services. Their starting point has been the first step in the problem-solving model: identifying what children need. "Many researchers, managers and policy makers have turned to enquiry methods which reveal something about the underlying conditions, for example by asking first what are the needs of a vulnerable child before hanging labels such as 'child protection' or 'family support' on a 'case' " (Dartington Social Research Unit, 1996, p. 4). From that identification of the threshold of need that the community decides it can meet, services to address the need can be developed and evaluated according to how well the need was met. Such services are not likely to be as restricted or categorical as services currently are in the United States—for example, where children in need of mental health services often must be labeled as either "neglected" or "abused" before child welfare agencies can open their doors to help them. And an initial assessment of need must not lead only to further assessments, but rather to services.

Results of this research are provided to practitioners in "Messages from Research" (Her Majesty's Stationery Office, 1995) which has been a critical and broadly applied tool in processes of policy formulation as well as practice development. A Member of Parliament in Bristol has alerted local social service managers to findings from the research regarding permanency and partnership with families (Arthur Keefe, M.P., personal communication, July 2, 1997). Once we have at least a beginning understanding of the social welfare policies of our own lands, we have a basis for comparison or learning from research in other countries. Case Study 6.3 is a summary of a welfare reform experiment in the United States that can be instructive for comparison with other countries' social welfare programs.

MFIP Is Here

JULIE LA POINTE AND ANTHONY BIBUS

PART 1

On April 30, 1997, Governor Arne Carlson signed into law the state of Minnesota's response to welfare reform. This legislation largely focuses on moving families from welfare to work by means of a program known as the Minnesota Family Investment Program (MFIP). Piloted in eight of Minnesota's 87 counties since 1994, this program has been expanded statewide effective January 1998. It has been altered to meet with federal law, setting a five-year lifetime limit on receipt of benefits and increasing the penalties for parents who fail to comply with program requirements. Planning for MFIP began in 1987 when Governor Rudy Perpich requested that an evaluation team propose an alternative means to deliver AFDC services. The team criticized AFDC as a barrier to self-sufficiency and envisioned MFIP as a vehicle to alleviate poverty.

At the time of MFIP's inception, the state recognized that welfare reform should not be driven by cost or numbers of beneficiaries. Rather, reform efforts should promote economic opportunities that contribute to families' well-being. This ideology resulted in the creation of a comprehensive benefit package including a cash grant, health care coverage, day care, food stamps, and employment and training help. Employment was encouraged by allowing a generous earned income disregard; recipients could keep a larger portion of their income than was allowed by AFDC regulations. In addition, case managers coordinated individualized programs for education or employment.

Some of these benefits remain in statewide MFIP. However, there is a reduction in the amount a household can earn without losing their grant as well as limits on the educational component. These reductions and limits result from realization that the MFIP package is costly to implement. The new rules limit a household of three to earning $1311 a month before losing benefits. With the old rules the same household could earn $1544 per month before being cut off.

Although the new version of MFIP should continue to be of more benefit to families than the old AFDC program, its success in alleviating poverty is questionable and remains dependent on the state's willingness to address the fiscal shortcomings brought about by the block granting of federal dollars. Instead, the state has followed the federal government's lead and terminated government responsibility for providing basic needs as an entitlement to families who meet eligibility criteria. It thus appears that the state of Minnesota has retreated from its position of alleviating poverty and providing a safety net for the low-income population. Meanwhile, the federal government has placed economic pressure on the states to move 25 percent of their welfare population to part-time work by fiscal year 1997 or face losing federal dollars. If the budget for MFIP should fall short of money needed for the program, the legislature is not obligated to appropriate more funding to cover the needs of poor families. As a result, recipients possibly face reduction in their benefits in order to stretch the budget to cover all persons applying for MFIP. NASW members should be alert for opportunities to help local programs and communities gear up to support vulnerable families and children as well as to advocate for reinstatement of the entitlement of all Minnesota residents for our welfare.

Other highlights of the new MFIP-statewide include:

1. A parent may stay home to care for a child under age 1. In two-parent households this applies to one person and the law imposes a lifetime 60-month limit on the benefit.

2. Those convicted of a drug felony are eligible for benefits upon completion of their sentence. Those convicted after July 1997 are not eligible to receive General Assistance (GA) for five years after they complete their sentence. Persons who violate parole or are felons on the run are ineligible for GA or MFIP for a lifetime.

3. The state will replace a portion of the SSI benefits (cut by the federal welfare reform) for legal immigrants by offering $290 in case assistance; $85 of this is allotted for food stamps but offered only from July 1997 through June 1998.

4. Legal immigrants remain eligible for Medical Assistance, including coverage for long-term care costs. They are also eligible for MFIP.

5. The new law mandates a residency requirement in which there is a 30-day period upon entering the state when families are not eligible for benefits. After the 30 days, the family receives the lesser amount of the state's benefits for eleven months.

PART 2

In Part 1 of this two-part report, we summarized the statewide Minnesota Family Investment Program (MFIP-S) that is Minnesota's welfare reform program, this state's response to the requirements of the federal Personal Responsibility and Work Opportunity Act of 1996. Although the experiment is not yet completed (it will end one year short of its originally planned five-year time span in June 1998), investigators have drawn some preliminary conclusions. Since MFIP has now become every county's welfare program (with some modifications in the areas of funding, time limits on educational and other supports, and increased punitive sanctions for non-compliance), this article is intended to provide guidance to social workers based on these conclusions. What outcomes might we expect for families participating in MFIP-S in the coming months and what should we be ready to do? Reports from the investigators studying MFIP, the Manpower Demonstration Research Corporation, in November 1995 and December 1996 give useful information.

Preliminary findings for MFIP indicate that its combination of financial supports for families, health and child care, incentives for work, and mandatory employment-related services does help more families remain above the poverty line than traditional AFDC, especially in the urban areas. Analysis of outcomes for 5,289 single parents from urban areas randomly assigned to MFIP or control groups (AFDC) between April of 1994 and December of 1994 found that 27.2 percent more of long-term recipients participating in MFIP moved above the poverty line; total income available to MFIP families increased due to better earnings and more welfare benefits while working. However, in a critically important finding, considering that there is a federally imposed five-year life time limit on MFIP benefits, 43.8 percent of the long-term single-parent families were still below the poverty line. Thus, there is likely to be a large proportion of families needing MFIP-S after five years of assistance. Families using MFIP-S will have a better chance to be employed and to have an income above poverty, but four out of ten families may still need financial and social services to maintain decent living deep into and probably beyond the five-year limit. Even this prediction of continuing need is dependent on continuation of our current prosperous economy and relatively low unemployment rate. When the next recession comes, many more families will need MFIP-S for longer periods of time than five years.

Another important learning from the MFIP experiment is reflected in informal contacts with staff working in the program. Many found their work satisfying and the case management workload fairly manageable and rewarding. They benefited from the high morale that accompanies the program's focus on moving families out of poverty, building on strengths, maintaining child care and other supports while people are working, and helping clients identify and overcome both personal and systemic impediments to gainful employment. There were opportunities for MFIP staff to receive training in understanding involuntary transactions that are to be expected with mandatory programming, applying sanctions in a judicious manner, and working to reduce the negative impact of potentially punitive dynamics.

However, with MFIP-S two key outcome areas are still uncertain. We do not know the effects that increased levels of sanctioning, with cuts of up to 30 percent in a family's benefits now allowed, will have on the children. Previous research would indicate that less income available to families will have profoundly negative impacts on the children's health, education, and welfare. (A "Child Outcomes Study" tracking the effects of MFIP on children is now underway.) And we do not know the effect of increased caseloads for MFIP staff, nearly doubling in size. As a result, case management assumes a more limited scope. In the initial trials, case managers oversaw many aspects of clients' lives and were able to intervene in those areas especially affecting keeping as well as obtaining employment. Now the focus has shifted exclusively to obtaining employment, possibly missing barriers that make sustaining a job difficult.

An unintended consequence of this focus is that staff will still be faced with broader barriers to clients' employment but not be able to address clients' needs adequately. Job satisfaction and service delivery could be compromised because of higher caseloads. In addition, employers could be discouraged by recipients' unmet needs that interfere with job performance. MFIP staff anticipate that employers will be faced with handling these barriers to job performance. The local community is expected to respond by developing programs in nonprofit agencies, religious and neighborhood centers, and businesses to provide the help that case managers in the earlier program provided. With this in mind, the McKnight Foundation has committed up to $20 million over a 2-year period to encourage collaborative responses to the challenges facing MFIP-S participants. The foundation's intent is to move families from welfare to work while at the same time meeting employers' needs. Local partnerships may develop resources such as job coaches, mentors, or nontraditional (24-hour) day care for prospective employees and employers.

IMPLICATIONS FOR SOCIAL WORKERS

This type of collaboration offers opportunities for social workers to use our community organizing skills; there are no doubt several NASW members already involved in these McKnight initiatives, and we would benefit from hearing what you are doing! Please write in to *Newsbytes*. We also need to know what effects the drastic changes in state and federal social welfare programs are having on people. Organizations such as the Children's Defense Fund are monitoring the effects of welfare reform, and we should be part of that effort providing public witness to what is happening to vulnerable people. Again, please send summaries of your experiences to *Newsbytes*.

Those working in MFIP-S at the county and state levels and colleagues elsewhere should join in partnership with families in advocating for extensions of time limits, more support for four-year education to access gainful careers, less reliance on sanctions, manageable caseloads, more transportation help, legitimate exceptions to work requirements, more subsidies for housing, and good use of McKnight funding initiatives. Our professional voices must be raised!

There are many examples of social work scholars providing information on the effects of social policies on a global as well as national scope. The need for social workers to join in international advocacy for social justice is clear. In order to advocate effectively, however, we must be able not only to analyze but also to be knowledgeable. The global perspective expands sources of that knowledge. Comparisons of how countries faced similar or unique issues similarly can be very informative. For example, the role of media exposés in Cleveland, England, and similar tragedies in the United States manifest the importance of social workers learning to use and influence mass media. A local experience of an increase in threats against social workers (Newhill & Wexler, 1997) can be related to worldwide similar increases: in some countries, practicing social work is literally potentially fatal when viewed as a challenge to particular military or political forces.

●●●

FRAMEWORK FOR ANALYSIS FROM A GLOBAL PERSPECTIVE

Most frameworks for description and analysis of social welfare policies would benefit from, and are amenable to, a global perspective. Social work educators have developed frameworks for comparing existing policies in various countries (see, for example, the body of work in cross-national comparisons of family policy and personal social services by Kahn & Kamerman, 1986, 1994). Many scholars have built upon studies that describe policies to create frameworks for analysis and comparison of the processes by which policies are developed and of the forces that influence policy making (Moroney, 1991; Hoshino, 1985; Tracy, 1992). Tracy (1992) states: "Analysis of the reasons for social policies and programs in other countries is facilitated by the use of an analytical framework that asks the same questions about policies in each of the study nations. A framework provides students with a guide to gathering and analyzing information in a methodical and systematic way." The framework is presented and explained by Tracy in the following excerpt.

> The task of analyzing social welfare policies and programs within a cross-national context is concerned with understanding why services and benefits are provided in a certain prescribed way at a specific point in history given all possible alternatives and options. It is a focus on the reasons that explain policy and program service delivery choices that differentiates analysis from description. Most cross-national studies of social welfare policies are focused on descriptions of the basic features of programs and provisions which, while fundamental to analysis, do not necessarily provide insight as to why services are provided and delivered in a specific manner. Knowing what social programs are provided, how they are provided, and who receives them are essential components of analysis, but it is also critical to understand the reasons that explain why policy makers in a given country have rejected all other options and chosen to address an identified social problem or concern with specified goals, objectives, and strategies.
>
> One approach to determining "who gets, what, when, where, how and why" with regard to social programs is to use a process analysis framework. Process analysis is a research model designed to arrive at "a better understanding of the making and implementation of public policy and of its effects" (Antal, Dierkes, & Weiler, 1987, p. 17). There are three basic characteristics: (1) it investigates the processes used in addressing social issues, (2) it examines the conditions under which a given strategy is chosen as an effective and efficient way of addressing the issue, and (3) it examines economic, political, and social determinants of the process.

BOX 6.2

Framework for Analyzing Cross-National Social Policy Processes

MARTIN TRACY

1. Governments' (federal, regional, local) legal authority. Ascertain the governments' role in social policy in terms of legal or constitutional authority.

    Sample questions: *What government agency assumes responsibility for program financing, administration and delivery? At what level of government are decisions made about program rules and regulations? What are the discrepancies between legislation and actual program enforcement? To what extent is the decision making process decentralized? What is the role of nongovernment groups and organizations in decision-making and implementation processes? What public/ private agencies are primarily responsible for program implementation?*

2. Governments' operationalized conceptual orientation to social programs. Explain the governments' role in terms of where a particular policy/program falls along selected conceptual continuum that reflect the governments' operational approach: (a) social insurance/social assistance; (b) preventive/remedial, (c) comprehensive/categorical, (d) integrated/fragmented, and (e) public/private.

    Sample questions: *Where does the program under analysis fall within a continuum? What are the implications of a policy/program's conceptual orientation in the study country in terms of corresponding (socially, politically, economically, culturally) to the country of the analyst?*

3. Governments' level of commitment to the policy/program being analyzed. Amount of financial or in-kind support as proportion of a standard base of expenditures.

    Sample questions: *What proportion of social welfare expenditures are committed to the program under analysis? How has the ratio of expenditures changed over a period of time?*

4. Obstacles and constraints to government policies and programs. Identify the major obstacles to program development and implementation as characterized by policy makers in the study country. Describe the ways in which identified problems appear to have impacted policy a–d program decisions and strategies, including: administrative, financial, geographic, staffing, political and cultural constraints.

    Sample questions: *What are the primary obstacles or barriers as reflected in government documents? How do official documents differ from academic, interest group, or public views?*

5. Catalysts for government policies and programs. Identify the major factors that have contributed to decisions about the policy and program in spite of officially acknowledged obstacles.

Sample questions: *What factors are cited as the major incentives for program development or reform (financial, demographic, social)? Have there been notable changes in demographic, social, political, or economic conditions? What is the apparent source and reliability of data and other forms of evidence of need used to support the rationale for programs?*

6. Specific needs identified by the government as justification for a new or revised policy or program. Determine the definition of the need being addressed by the government. Explain how the response to identified needs has been manifested in terms of legislation, resource commitment, strategic decisions, and implementation.

    Sample questions: *What is the specific need being addressed by the government policy and program? How was the need determined (government studies, interest group pressure, academic research, etc.)?*

7. Goals and strategies contained in policy and program. Ascertain policy and program goals and objectives as articulated by government, including any acknowledgment of risks and limitations.

    Sample questions: *Are the program goals operationally defined? If so, how? What are the short- and long-term goals? What are the major strategies being used to attain the goals? Who is involved in setting goals and strategies (bureaucrats, consumers, administrators, etc.)?*

8. Program description. Describe the program provisions of interest in specific details within the context of steps 1–6.

    Sample questions: *Who gets what, when, where, and how under the provisions of the program?*

9. Evaluation of policy and program. Determine the impact that the policy and program has had in addressing the identified problem and the extent to which the program's outcomes have been achieved based on the country's own assessment.

    Sample questions: *How is the program evaluated in terms of reaching specified goals? What are the major components of the evaluation? Who conducts the evaluation? Has the program been revised based on evaluations?*

10. *Analysis.* Synthesize the information obtained in steps 1–9 focusing on the contrasting implications for policies and programs in one or more nations.

    Sample questions: *Are the social issues that are being addressed among the study counties compatible? In what ways are they similar and dissimilar? How does the information obtained from the various countries compare with regards to each of the first nine steps in the model? What are the limitations in the information base (gaps in information, irrelevant information, unreliable information)? What conclusions can be drawn based on available information? What viable recommendations can be made?*

Framework and excerpt from M. B. Tracy, "Cross-National Social Welfare Policy Analysis in the Graduate Curriculum: A Comparative Process Model." *Journal of Social Work Education* 28 (3): 341–352. Reprinted by permission.

Process analysis in a comparative context first emerged in political science in the early 1970s based on a framework developed by Richard Rose (1973). Rose's model encouraged a view of policy making as a process, rather than a result of disjointed, seemingly unconnected decisions. It examined the stages in decision making and policy formation, including policy initiation, implementation, operation and impact. The comparative policy process framework described below that was developed in 1991 (Tracy) is a synthesis of various aspects of policy models from political science and social work drawn primarily from Chambers (1986), Gilbert and Specht (1986), Gill (1990), Heidenheimer, Heclo & Adams (1975), Heidenheimer (1986), Jones (1984), Morris (1985), Rose (1973), and Teune (1978). Since 1991, the model has been revised, reflecting influences from several sources, including: Gilbert, Specht & Terrell (1993), Ginsberg, (1992), Oyen (1990), and Hofer (1996). An earlier revision appeared in the *Journal of Social Work Education* (Tracy, 1992). As described here, the process model is an applied model primarily concerned with obtaining information that will contribute to developing pragmatic approaches to addressing social issues. While the model allows for recognition of predominant sociological and economic theories that influence government policies, the focus is on the application of knowledge rather than on making a contribution to theory building.

The purpose of the framework is to provide a guide to the methodical and systematic gathering and analyzing of information about the policy processes that shape specific social programs in a given nation. Understanding these processes helps policy makers of one country to make informed decisions as to the applicability of adapting all or part of a particular policy or program of another country. Without this knowledge, the analyst functions at a handicap in determining the practicality and advisability of making a proposed similar change in their own country.

In all countries social welfare policies are in a constant state of flux in a never ending attempt to keep pace with sociological, economic, political and demographic changes. Policy makers and analysts who understand the forces that shape delivery systems are in a better position to offer realistic and viable suggestions that make programs more responsive to meeting identified needs. Understanding the forces that serve to both constrain and propel the process of developing program goals, objectives and strategies is a fundamental aspect of policy analysis. Thus, an examination of why social programs have certain features involves an analysis of the social, economic, political, and demographic factors that are instrumental in determining the intent and the methods of a given social, income, or health care service.

The analytical framework presented in Box 6.2 is a guideline for determining why a specific social policy or program exists in a given nation or nations. It is designed to ascertain who gets what, when, where, how and why in the nation(s) under study. In each component it is necessary to determine how answers compare among the study countries. There are ten basic components of information gathering. While there is some logic to the sequence of components, it is not necessary, nor advisable, that information is obtained sequentially. Despite discernible linear trends in policy and program development, good analysis is essentially non-linear in order to understand the dynamic nature of the complex interaction between the multiple factors that influence policies and program.

Comparisons between countries can also be helpful in demonstrating how the entire framework could be applied. As a class assignment, students can be asked to design a service system to meet children's needs as identified by community members. For example, in a recent graduate-level child welfare class social workers described how they met with families in an inner city neighborhood and discovered that the most critical need was for beds and other furniture for families who were being evicted from their homes or were homeless for other reasons. These practitioners from child protection and community agencies helped establish a warehouse of donated beds and furniture and a system for families to obtain their needed items on short notice. Meanwhile, in a paradox all too typical in social welfare, some managers at the state level are advocating that the child welfare system divide children's cases into two categories: (1) those children suffering extreme physical and sexual abuse and extreme neglect will be responded to with an investigative strategy aimed at bringing their situation to court for remedial action and removal from their homes if necessary; (2) those children in less extremely abusive or neglectful circumstances will be eligible for community and family-based supportive services. Thus it is possible that children who need beds, for example, will have that need addressed only if they fall into the second category, while those who need protection from unsafe neighborhood or family situations will only have that need addressed if they fall into the first category. Students can discuss what practitioners locally should be learning from those in other countries about the potential unintended outcomes of this proposal.

BUILDING COMPETENCIES: CONCLUSION

Social work educators and practitioners worldwide have an obligation to build competencies in understanding social welfare policies, analyzing them, and influencing them to be more responsive to the needs of those most vulnerable and disenfranchised. A global perspective provides the broadest and deepest foundation for these competencies: "The social welfare of the world's peoples can be promoted when effective social policies and programs are implemented at the international level" (Midgley, 1997, p. 34). We must encourage each other in recognizing how international dynamics affect and enrich our practice and join in searching for solutions to global problems. Those of us in the United States, because of its dominant position in the world at the moment, must focus on "monitoring the impact of U.S. policies on other countries' well-being, and increasing our capacity to benefit from and contribute to international dialogue and exchange" (Asamoah et al., 1997, p. 91).

Social work students, educators, and practitioners in the Global North need to stretch to comprehend the reality of economic dislocation and impoverished communities that is gripping daily life in the Global South. Social work has a strong tradition of solving problems by connecting private troubles to public issues (Macht & Ashford, 1991), linking informal helping with formal interventions that can usefully be applied as part of the collective strategy in social welfare policy making on a worldwide basis as well as national, state, local, family and personal levels. Social workers' role in policy practice is to advocate both for specific cases and for general causes (Bull, 1989). Human needs may sporadically and incidentally be met without policies, but to meet needs in a systematic and trustworthy manner we need responsive and just social welfare policies. Social workers must be prepared to understand and develop these policies globally as an integral part of our daily practice.

STUDENT ACTIVITIES

1. Integrating history and policy: The role that social workers played in social welfare history, heroic or mundane, empowering or paternalistic (Simon, 1994), can be brought to

TABLE 6.2

Framework to Assess Engagement in Global Social Work Learning

	Practice and Field
Elements of global social work	
Personal review of global awareness	interested in other countries and world regions
Knowledge of mutual learning country to country	comparing work philosophy, social role, choices across countries
Understanding of cultural competence and respectful language	proactive in exploring culture, aware of own bias and prejudice
Analysis of human rights	applying UN documents to practice
Historical analysis	knowing impact of past on current resources, socioeconomic status
Review of values and ethics	identifying implications of different approaches, country codes
Evaluation of local variations	exploring theories in different nations
Synthesis of professional activity	seeking alternatives, links with other places, building with global awareness

life with assignments such as those in Jansson and Cambra's instructor's manual (1997). One example (Bibus, 1997) is having students choose one of the early leaders in social work, read an article or chapter that focuses on that leader's contributions to social work, and reflect on what social workers today could learn from those contributions. Students could be encouraged to select leaders from a variety of countries; references such as the *Indian Encyclopedia of Social Work* are available in many countries. How might the early social worker practice today? How would she or he organize social work

TOPIC AREAS		
Human Condition and Resulting Behavior	**Social and Economic Policy and Justice**	**Research**
How do I behave in different situations?		
role of class, caste, gender, health		
avoid categories; symbolic interaction as focus; respectful learning		
define, expand, apply to development		
role of colonization in racism		
impact of cloning, euthanasia, organ selling		
widen definition of "normal"		
role of theory in changing human condition		

to meet today's human needs? Then have students prepare a two- or three-sentence statement of the early social work leader's recommendations for the class. For example, if the students chose Jane Addams and read Lundblad's (1995) article, they might imagine Addams recommending: "Beware of depending solely or primarily on the private sector and individual charity to meet human needs. Public government resources at the local and national level must be devoted to serving the most vulnerable and disadvantaged people, even if that means increasing taxes."

2. Complete the column in the framework for social policy in Table 6.2 (developed from the original matrix in Table 1.1 in Chapter 1).

3. Read the text of the Convention on the Rights of the Child (United Nations, 1989) and discuss how far communities of the world have come since the United Nations adopted this declaration in 1959 and passed it into law in 1990 and how far specified countries, including our own place of residence, have to go.

Information Tools for Social Workers: Research in the Global Age

RICHARD ESTES

Technology is a friend. It makes life easier, cleaner, and longer . . . Unforeseen consequences (however) stand in the way of all those who think they see clearly the direction in which a new technology will take us. Not even those who invent a technology can be assumed to be reliable prophets.

—NEIL POSTMAN, *TECHNOPOLY*

An almost dizzying array of informational resources exist to help development-oriented students and faculty understand the complexities of social work practice in a more interdependent world (Glister, 1994; Richards, 1995; Stout, 1996). These resources are especially rich for social workers engaged in international practice but also are of considerable use to social workers whose "domestic" clients are drawn from diverse cultural groups within their own country (Butterfield & Schoech, 1997; Schoech & Smith, 1996). Fortunately, the vast bulk of these resources now are available electronically and can be easily accessed from the global network of computers that make up the World Wide Web (WWW).

This chapter introduces readers to the breadth of international, cross-cultural, and comparative resources available on the WWW. Thus, the chapter is organized in five parts: (1) a brief introduction to the history of the Electronic Revolution (i.e., the various technological innovations that preceded the development of computers and modern information technology); (2) the Information Revolution and its impact on individual privacy in society; (3) social work and the Information Revolution; (4) comparative social research and the Information Age; and (5) the application of modern electronic information technology to comparative social research through a discussion of the international content contained on the author's own home page on the WWW—PRAXIS: Resources for Social and Economic Development. A variety of structured exercises in the Student Activities section make use of Praxis and the WWW to help readers deepen their skill in using the WWW to answer questions of a cross-cultural or cross-national nature.

THE ELECTRONIC REVOLUTION

Geiss and Viswanathan (1986, p. 34–35) identify 1800 as the year in which the first steps in the contemporary Information Revolution were taken. It was in 1800 that Allesandro Volta discovered the chemical battery and direct electric current. Both discoveries initiated a series of developments that, over time, would lead to the creation of the first mechanical calculator by Charles Babbage in 1823; the invention of the telephone by Alexander Graham Bell in 1876; the first vacuum tube by Lee De Forest in 1907; the introduction of the first teletype service in 1931; and, in 1939, the development of the first prototype of a digital computer by Atanasoff and Berry. Only a few years later, in 1945, J. Presper Eckert and John W. Mauchly of the University of Pennsylvania built ENIAC (Electronic Numerical Integrator and Calculator), formerly believed to be the first electronic digital computer. The first nonmilitary computer (UNIVAC I) was delivered to the U.S. Census Bureau in 1951, and the first commercial computer was delivered by the Remington Rand Corporation to General Electric in 1954.

Today, of course, tens of millions of free-standing computers exist all over the world. The computational power of even the most modest of modern computers far exceeds that of earlier generations of computers. And the data-processing power of modern computers continues to expand exponentially, even as the cost of new computers declines sharply each year. The newest generation of electronic computers now are able to perform a billion separate calculations every second! And, of course, computers have become smaller and more portable as a result of the invention of transistorized circuit boards (1958), microchips (1970), and the continuous miniaturization of computers that both inventions have made possible. Thus, the modern computer and the information revolution that followed its development did not just suddenly happen. It required many technological innovations and at least two centuries to accomplish.

THE INFORMATION REVOLUTION

The Information Age and the Information Revolution are the culmination of what futurologists Alvin and Heidi Toffler refer to as the Third Wave—that is, the third major technological revolution that can be expected to forever change the course of humanity (the first two "technological waves" were the Agricultural and Industrial Revolutions) (Toffler, 1970, 1980). The emergence of the Information Age had been heralded by sociologist Daniel Bell in his highly influential *The Coming of Post-Industrial Society: A Venture in Social Forecasting* (1973). Bell, among many others, fully understood the impact that high-speed computers, fax machines, space satellites, and other technological innovations in the flow of information would have on social relations (Coates & Jarratt, 1989). As noted by many other futurologists, the impact was to be nothing less than revolutionary. And, indeed, contemporary information technology is omnipresent and its impact on each of our lives is immediate, profound, and long lasting; over time, it can be expected to force us to reorganize critical social patterns (especially in the areas of work, communications, education, and so on). The Information Revolution will almost certainly make even more of an impact on the lives of future generations as the full potential of this revolution continues to mature.

Many critics of the Information Revolution exist, and justifiably so (Reamer, 1986; Stretch & Kreuger, 1992; Talbott, 1995). High on the list of concerns of these social scientists is the uncanny ability of electronic machines to intrude, almost invisibly, into the private lives of individual citizens (Rothfeder, 1992). By this intrusion, critics of the new technology suggest that computers are destroying the possibility of individual privacy and with it the hard-won freedoms and individual liberties that are enshrined in the central political documents of most Western nations. Critics of information technology are especially concerned about the ability of computers to collect and disseminate large amounts of highly sensitive information on individuals to groups and organizations that harbor little or no respect for the privacy of individuals—without regard to who those individuals may be (Rawlins, 1997).

Concerns about individual privacy in the Information Age are important and must be addressed not only by social workers but by all professionals who collect and disseminate sensitive information concerning individuals (Cwikel & Cnaan, 1991; Reamer, 1986; Stretch & Kreuger, 1992). The issues are especially daunting for the profession given the imperceptible nature of the new technology and its presence in virtually every aspect of our public and private lives (e.g., banking transactions, credit histories, leisure time activities, and even our automobiles).

Social Work and the Information Revolution

Social work's formal entry into the Information Age began with the establishment of the case registry and social survey movements of the late 19th century. Both movements sought to bring together highly detailed information concerning individual clients and the communities in which they lived. In the process, large amounts of socially relevant information were collected and organized in ways that promoted either the establishment of new services or, when already in existence, client access to available services.

The overall thrust of both the case registry and social survey movements was to "rationalize" the human service system through the collection, organization, and sharing of meaningful case- and community-specific information. Over time, of course, telephones would be used to share information among social work professionals and others working in either the same or distant communities. The creation of state and national registries of persons with particular types of needs only amplified the information collection movements that had already begun at the community level.

Today, of course, social workers continue to collect vast amounts of socially relevant information. This information is coded and organized into complex data sets and, as appropriate, is shared with others for purposes of social planning, coordination, cost-setting, research and evaluation. It is shared not only by means of printed documents and the telephone but, more important today, by fax machines, diskettes, computer tapes, electronic transmissions, space satellites, and, of course, the WWW. Advances in information technology, indeed, are adding much to the emergence of innovations in global social work as well.

Though issues of privacy and client confidentiality loom large in all of the profession's information collection and sharing processes, social workers are nonetheless obligated to provide detailed reports on their service activities to the many public and private organizations that finance the delivery of social services. The tensions that currently characterize service providers and funders (e.g., in managed care) are likely to persist well into the future, especially as the informational requirements of all three partners to the service relationship—clients, providers, and funders—continue to expand.

Comparative Social Research and the Information Revolution

Increasingly, social workers and other scholars are creating electronic "home pages" as convenient tools for organizing their most important links to the Internet. These home pages, known as *websites,* usually consist of a large array of textual, statistical, graphical, and other materials related to the scholar's area(s) of research interest. Often, these websites also contain electronic links to the websites of other scholars and to those of scholarly organizations and institutions in whose work the developer of the host website is interested (Butterfield & Schoech, 1997; Richards, 1995).

Electronic websites also serve as inexpensive outlets for the rapid dissemination of scholarly reports, analyses, and other publications. In a matter of minutes, for example, scholars now can "publish" the results of completed analysis on the Internet. In doing so, they are able to make the results of their research instantly available to thousands of scholars scattered everywhere across the planet. In effect, scholars are now able to reduce the length of time required to publish and disseminate a book-length manuscript from two years to two minutes! All the reader needs to access these electronically published reports is an inexpensive computer, a modem, access to the Internet and, when necessary, a printer—equipment that is becoming ubiquitous in even the most modest university and public libraries.

Today, there are more than 10 million electronic websites throughout the world; their number continues to double every year (Stout, 1996). At the same time, some 2,000 scholarly journals covering virtually every area of human inquiry are now published exclusively on the Internet. The number of scholarly books and other publications that are disseminated either entirely or partially over the Internet also numbers in the millions. And their numbers continue to increase exponentially each year—especially as the cost of scholarly publications outstrip the capacity of most students and many scholars to purchase books and monographs.

PRAXIS: RESOURCES FOR SOCIAL AND ECONOMIC DEVELOPMENT

The author's own website on the Internet—Praxis: Resources for Social and Economic Development—will be used to illustrate the variety of informational and other resources that are now available to comparative social researchers over the Internet (the URL address for Praxis is at http://www.ssw.upenn.edu/).

Created in March 1995, the purpose of Praxis is "to promote positive social change through informed action." In pursuit of this goal, Praxis was designed to meet the informational needs of two audiences: (1) social work educators and students with international interests; and (2) other educators and students who require assistance in locating useful

TABLE 7.1 *Directory Structure of Praxis: Resources for Social and Economic Development*

Section 1:   The Social and Economic Development Reference Room

Section 2:   Development Assistance Agencies, Organizations, and Policies

Section 3:   Levels of Social Development Practice

Section 4:   Development Studies Home Pages and News Services

Section 5:   Sectoral Resources for Social and Economic Development

Section 6:   Resources on Historically Disadvantaged Population Groups

Section 7:   Country Resources

Section 8:   Regional Resources

Section 9:   Major Reports of International and Comparative Social Research

Section 10: Funding Resources for Research on Comparative Social Development

Section 11: Internationalizing Social Work Education

Section 12: Careers in Social and Economic Development

Section 13: International Travel

national and international resources on social and economic development. Since its creation, the Praxis website has been "visited" by hundreds of thousands of users from all around the world. A work in progress, the electronic links that form Praxis are being continuously expanded and enriched.

As presently designed, Praxis is divided into 13 major sections or "directories," each of which contains hundreds of electronic links to other websites (Table 7.1). These directories serve as convenient locations for placing websites that contain related information, i.e., in much the same way that chapters of a large reference book conceptually organize and present related materials in discrete chapters.

The remainder of this chapter is devoted to a discussion of the contents of each of the 13 directories that form Praxis. Various exercises are included at the end of the chapter to illustrate the varied electronic resources that are available to investigators engaged in comparative studies. The exercises also should help readers deepen their skills in using the WWW to access other types of electronic data.

Section 1: The Social and Economic Development (SED) Reference Room

The purpose of the SED Reference Room is much like that of the reference room of any university or public library: to assure predictable access to statistical, archival, and other types of information of general interest to a large community of users. Thus, the SED Reference Room links users to a broad range of frequently used electronic reference materials of general interest to students of international development.

More specifically, the SED Reference Room is divided into six areas or "spaces": Views of Planet Earth; Country Flags, Constitutions, and Socio-Political Information; Reference Desks; Social Science WWW Links; Expertise and Address Locators; and WWW Search Engines.

The Reference Desk illustrates the range of electronic resources that may be accessed once the user enters the SED Reference Room. The Reference Desk contains, for example, links to a continuously updated worldwide Yellow Pages, biographies of world leaders (Biography Online), a CyberAtlas, a collection of world maps (MapQuest), a person and address locator (Four11), as well as descriptive and other information concerning nearly all of the world's major cities (CityNet and CitySearch). Both CitySearch and CityNet provide "hot links" to websites located in cities included in their listings—including to major businesses, governmental agencies, tourist sites, and the like. From within these websites users also can send electronic messages to specific local organizations and individuals.

The Reference Desk also links users to more specialized collections of development-related resources. The most valuable of these collections are the CIA World Factbook and the Virtual Library on International Development organized by the Canadian International Development Agency (CIDA). Both resources provide continuously updated, comprehensive information on the social, political, and economic situations of individual countries. Using the CIDA collection, users can also obtain comparable information on major world regions and the world as a whole. The CIDA collection also links users to the electronic libraries of other national and international development assistance organizations, including many hundreds of technical reports prepared by these organizations on a broad range of development-related issues and projects.

The SED Reference Room also contains links to four universities with unusually rich electronic reference collections: the University of Michigan, the University of Pennsylvania, Purdue University, and the University of Texas. In addition to the electronic collections of these universities, the very comprehensive New York University–based collection WWW Resources for Social Workers also can be accessed through the SED Reference Desk.

Section 2: Development Assistance Agencies, Organizations, and Policies

The *Encyclopedia of Associations* (Gale Publishers, 1996) identifies some 22,000 nonprofit organizations worldwide that promote national or international social development. These organizations include *governmental* (e.g., the international development assistance organizations of national governments) and *nongovernmental* (e.g., Save the Children Fund) as well as *quasigovernmental* organizations (e.g., the United Nations, the World Bank, the International Monetary Fund, etc.). All three types of organizations exist in every country of the world and, through a complex network of international organizations, are linked to sister organizations located in other countries and world regions (e.g., local affiliates of the International Red Cross and Red Crescent societies). The vast majority of these organizations maintain websites on the Internet.

Praxis contains linkages to many of the most important national and international development and development assistance organizations. Section 2 of Praxis, for example, groups international development assistance organizations into seven large categories: Directory of International Organizations and Groups; Multinational Aid and Mutual Cooperation Agencies, Organizations, and Policies; Aid Agencies and Organizations of National Governments; Regional Development Banks; Non-Governmental Agencies and Organizations; Social Work and Social Welfare Organizations; and Development-Related Scholarly Societies and Associations.

While not exhaustive, the organizations grouped under the preceding subdirectories do reflect the spectrum of international development organizations. Exercises 2a, 2b, and 2c in

TABLE 7.2 *Levels and Strategies of Development-Oriented Social Work Practice*

Levels of Development-Oriented Social Work Practice	Major Purposes, Outcomes, or Processes Associated With Levels of Development-Oriented Practice
Individual and Group Empowerment	Through "conscientization," the process whereby individuals learn how to perceive and *act upon* the contradictions that exist in the social, political, and economic structures intrinsic to all societies.
Conflict Resolution	Efforts directed at reducing: (1) grievances between persons or groups; or, (2) asymmetric power relationships between members of more powerful and less powerful groups.
Community-Building	Through increased participation and "social animation" of the populace, the process through which communities realize the fullness of their social, political, and economic potential; the process through which communities respond more equitably to the social and material needs of their populations.
Institution-Building	Refers both to the process of "humanizing" existing social institutions and that of establishing new institutions that respond more effectively to new or emerging social needs.
Nation-Building	The process of working toward the integration of a nation's social, economic, and cultural institutions at all levels of political organization.
Region-Building	The process of working toward the integration of a region's social, economic, cultural institutions at all levels of political organization.
World-Building	The process of working toward the establishment of a new system of international social, political, economic, and ecological relationships guided by the quest for world peace, increased social justice, the universal satisfaction of basic human needs, and for the protection of the planet's fragile environmental systems.

Source: Estes, Richard J. (1993; 1997a)

the Student Activities section are designed to familiarize readers with the websites of several international development organizations and with the electronic resources that can be accessed from these sites.

Section 3: Levels of Social Development Practice

The social work profession has a distinguished history of professional service in international development (Estes, 1992, 1995, 1997b; Healy, 1992; Hokenstad, Khinduka, & Midgley, 1992; Lowe, 1995; Lynch, 1989; Mary, 1997; Midgley, 1995, 1997; Sanders, 1982; Van Soest, 1992). Indeed, Estes (1993, 1997a) suggests that after more than 100 years of international practice, development-oriented social work now consists of seven discrete types—more properly, "levels"—of professional intervention. Each of these seven levels of international social work practice is identified in Table 7.2. The table also identifies the unique goals and processes associated with each level of intervention.

The nature of social work practice at each level of development-oriented intervention is illustrated in Section III of the Praxis website under Levels of Social Development Practice.

Section 4: Development Studies Home Pages and News Services

A variety of leading U.S. and foreign universities offer advanced degrees in social and economic development, including in international development. Section 4 of Praxis identifies graduate-level social development programs in Britain. In addition to providing users access to their own archives, the websites of most of these programs also contain links to development studies programs in other countries.

Section 5: Sectoral Resources for Social and Economic Development

Elsewhere I have suggested that development-oriented social work practice occurs in more than 30 "sectors" of organized human activity (Estes, 1993, 1997a). Section 5 of Praxis identifies 25 of the most prominent sectors of social development activity, and, in turn, these sectors contain electronic links to many of each sector's most important websites. Links to various "cross-sectoral" websites also are made in this directory. In all cases, though, the electronic linkages listed in these subdirectories represent only a small fraction of the many thousands of websites and other electronic gateways that could be appropriately linked.

Section 6: Resources on Historically Disadvantaged Population Groups

The United Nations classifies as "historically disadvantaged population groups" all those persons and groups who, for whatever reason, are not able to participate fully in the social, political, or economic life of their nation. In general, these population groups include women, children, the aged, persons with disabilities, the poor, and others who are discriminated against on the basis of age, gender, sexual orientation, religious belief, or national origin. More than two-thirds of the population of many countries qualify as being "historically disadvantaged" under the United Nations' broad definition (i.e., girls and women alone account for at least half the population of most countries).

Praxis contains links to many websites that seek to provide accurate and timely information concerning the causes of social inequality among historically disadvantaged population groups. The majority of these sites are maintained by representatives of "socially excluded" groups and, in the main, their sites are characterized by both a strong community-building and an advocacy orientation. In addition, the vast majority of these sites contain considerable information of great value to students of international development—including copies of treaties, covenants, and declarations (and detailed histories of their abrogation).

Section 6 of Praxis contains the bulk of websites concerned with the special development needs of historically disadvantaged population groups. The directory is organized into nine broad subdirectories, not all of which are mutually exclusive: "first peoples," the aged, children and youth, the poor and poverty, minorities, migrants and refugees, women, and "extraterrestrials" (sic).

Section 7: Country Resources

Almost all of the major directories used to create Praxis contain links to country-specific websites. However, the richest and deepest sources of country-specific information are to be found in Section 7 of Praxis, which provides the most direct links to home pages developed by universities, businesses, and nonprofit organizations located in individual countries. The depth, breadth, and reliability of individual websites varies enormously. Many have been created in languages other than English, but many also have parallel English "pages" for international visitors to their sites. Nearly all of these country-specific websites contain valuable information, including links to other sites that may be of even greater value to individual researchers.

Section 8: Regional Resources

In addition to providing linkages to a rich array of country-specific websites, Praxis also offers links to websites that focus on the development needs of entire world "regions"—that is, countries that either are physically situated close to one another (e.g., Europe) or are "linked by some other characteristic (e.g., religion, ethnic identification, economic development level, etc.)." Section 8 of Praxis contains electronic links to the largest and most resource-rich websites of regional organizations.

Section 9: Major Reports of International and Comparative Social Research

Many of the most important reports of major international organizations are now being published regularly on the Internet. These reports are often rich in both textual analysis and statistical detail. Many contain invaluable charts, tables, and graphs not available from other sources. Virtually all of the content of these reports can now be downloaded onto a user's own computer for future use, including secondary data analysis.

Readers are encouraged to explore the major international social reports listed under Section 9 of Praxis. Other reports will be found on the home pages of major international nongovernmental (e.g., Freedom House and Amnesty International in the human rights sector) and quasigovernmental organizations (including thousands of reports available for the United Nations and its specialized agencies, the World Bank, the OECD, etc.).

Section 10: Funding Resources for Research on Comparative Social Development

Comparative social research, like all other research, requires substantial levels of financial support. Both public and private funding sources are available to assist investigators in financing their studies. Most, though, require considerable skill to access—often in the form of a competitive research proposal.

Section 10 of Praxis identifies dozens of public and private websites that can be of assistance to comparative investigators in helping to identify potential sources of funding for their comparative research projects. Each site must be searched carefully, however, inasmuch as proposals directed to inappropriate funding sources will automatically be rejected. Fortunately, many of the websites listed in Praxis have electronic search mechanisms to help users narrow their potential pool of funding sources to the most appropriate foundations, governmental agencies, and other research funding organizations.

Section 11: Internationalizing Social Work Education

Praxis was initially developed to assist social work faculty members in identifying comparative international teaching materials that could be appropriately included in social work curricula. Thus, Section 11 of Praxis contains a variety of conceptual discussions, teaching modules, bibliographies, and other teaching materials of interest to social work faculty members with international interests. In fact, Section XI of Praxis has served as a valuable resource guide for educators and students in all areas of the social sciences.

Readers are encouraged to explore the extraordinarily rich contents found in each of the six directories that make up Section 11: Internationalizing Social Work Education; Bibliography on Social and Economic Development; Policy Analysis in Social and Economic Development; International Affairs and Curriculum Development Network; Social Work Educational Programs; and Internationalization Efforts of the University of Pennsylvania.

Section 12: Careers in Social and Economic Development

Every development-oriented social work educator is repeatedly asked by students for advice in how to begin a career in international social work or international social development. Section 12 of Praxis was designed to help students and professors alike respond to the most frequently asked questions concerning how one initiates an international social work career.

The three directories that form Section 12 contain links to the following types of websites: Planning a Career in Social and Economic Opportunity; Social and Economic Development Employment Opportunities; and Scholarships, Fellowships, and International Exchanges. The materials contained on these websites are updated continuously and, overall, they provide an excellent starting point for the majority of social work professionals who wish to embark on an international career.

Section 13: International Travel

Certainly one of the most interesting, often enjoyable, aspects of a career in international social work is the opportunity to visit countries and people that one otherwise would not encounter. Such travel, though, tends to be prohibitively expensive, and the various barriers and restraints are discussed fully in Chapter 12 of this book. For students, the cost of international travel alone serves as a disincentive to an international career. Thus, international social workers, like most other groups of professionals with international commitments, must identify a variety of flexible approaches to meeting their international travel needs. Section 13 of Praxis was designed to help users identify safe, reliable, and convenient forms of transportation to international destinations. Section 13 also contains links to hotels, residences, and other forms of housing that may better suit the needs of individual travelers.

Section 13 of Praxis further introduces readers to a broad range of travel and other matters associated with building a career in international social work: Air Transportation and Hotels; Surface Transportation; News, Weather, and Travel Advisories; Scholarly Conferences and Meetings; Money Matters; Communications Information; Museums and Other Tourist Attractions; and World Museums. For further reading see Chapter 10 and also refer to *Resources for Social and Economic Development* by Richard Estes (Philadelphia: University of Pennsylvania School of Social Work, 1998).

ENTERING THE INFORMATION AGE: CONCLUSIONS

Social work has entered the Information Age. The profession took its initial steps into this age early in the century, and since then has embraced the most important advances made in information technology. Today thousands of human service agencies and organizations across the world are linked to one another by the World Wide Web (WWW). These linkages, in turn, are bringing about unparalleled levels of interprofessional and interorganizational cooperation. They also are contributing to international communication and understanding. In virtually every human service agency today, modern information technology now is being used to promote intraorganizational communication and improved service effectiveness and efficiency. Even more benefits are expected to accrue to human service organizations as the Information Revolution continues to unfold.

Advances in information technology also are having a profound impact on the nature of comparative social research, including comparative social work research. Studies that were considered all but impossible a few years ago are now not only possible but can be pursued with excellence across a wide range of research sites. Similarly, much of the isolation social researchers have experienced in the past has been relieved by advances in telecommunications, electronic mail, and the ubiquitous fax machine.

Satellites in space have facilitated communication among scholars, especially through face-to-face teleconferencing across great distances. Some 10,000 electronic discussion groups, covering an almost equal number of topics, can now be found on the Internet and have contributed much to the sense of "public ownership" of the Internet and WWW. Satellites, too, have made possible the almost instantaneous sharing of late-breaking news to people all over the world—all at the same time. And, as illustrated in this chapter, scholarly websites now dominate large areas of the Internet. These sites contain large amounts of valuable new information that was previously unavailable to social researchers.

Thus, recent advances in information technology have created new and important data gathering, analytical and reporting tools. This technology also has made possible the rapid dissemination of the analyses that result from the use of these tools. The impact of these innovations is far reaching and will be long lasting. And the Information Revolution has only just begun! No doubt even more powerful and flexible research tools will emerge as the revolution in information technology continues.

And yet, as further innovations in information technology continue to occur, social workers will need to be remain vigilant to the potential misuses to which such powerful tools may be put (Stretch & Kreuger, 1992; Rothfeder, 1992). In particular, we need to be sensitive to the almost invisible ways in new technologies can intrude into the private lives of individual people, especially into the lives of poor and other marginalized peoples (Geiss & Viswanathan, 1986). History has taught us that new technologies have not always served the needs of the poor well; too often, technological innovations have served as additional instruments of social control rather than liberation. Thus, even as this author and others applaud the possibilities that the new information technologies are contributing toward innovations in global social work practice, we must always be alert to potential social costs that past technological innovations have imposed on others.

• •

STUDENT ACTIVITIES

Orientation: Locate PRAXIS on the WWW at the following address: http://ssw.upenn. edu/

These exercises do require at least a beginning understanding of the structure of the World Wide Web and the various tools that are available for navigating the Web. Readers not familiar with these tools will want to consult the following Internet reference volumes: Butterfield & Schoech (1997); Glister (1994); Richards (1995); Schoech & Smith (1996); and Stout (1996). For an overview of the profession's earliest steps into the Information Age, see Geiss & Viswanathan (1986) and Butterfield & Shoech, 1997.

1. The SED Reference Room:
   a. Basic Reference Sources
      - Open Praxis and point your browser to the SED Reference Room.
      - Explore and become familiar with the contents of each of the major directories that make up the Reference Room: Views of Planet Earth; Country Flags, Constitutions, and Socio-Political Information; Reference Desks; Social Science WWW Links; Expertise and Address Locators; and WWW Search Engines.
      - Enter the SED Reference Desk.
      - Explore the Biography Online website by attempting to locate the biography of a person of historical importance to international development, such as Jane Addams, Martin Luther King, Mahatma Gandhi, Mother Teresa, etc.
      - Point your browser to CityNet and, within CityNet, "travel" to a world city of particular interest to you. Once in the city, try to locate a street map of the city, the city's most important tourist sites, the city's major governmental bodies and agencies, and as possible, information concerning local hotels and local transportation network (e.g., buses, subways, etc).
      - Send an electronic message requesting travel information to the local tourist board.
      - Attempt to locate your regular and electronic mailing addresses from Four11.
      - Explore the range of resources available on the WWW Resources for Social Workers website.
      - Returning back to the PRAXIS home page, explore the many bibliographic and other electronic resources available listed under the Social Science WWW Links directory, especially the Social Science Information Gateway, the Scholarly Electronic Forums, and the Subject-Oriented Internet Resource Guides.
   b. CIA World Factbook
      - Open Praxis and point your browser to the SED Reference Room.
      - Point your browser to the Virtual Library on International Development and fully explore the range of SED resource available at this site.
      - Enter the CIA World Factbook. Explore the contents and general organization of the CIA World Factbook.
      - Identify one country of special interest to you listed in the CIA World Factbook and print out the description pages for that country.
      - Examine your printout so that you can get a fuller appreciation for the historical and contemporary social, political, and economic data contained in the CIA World Factbook for each country.
   c. WWW Search Engines
      - In the Praxis Reference Room, point your browser to the WWW Search Engines directory. (These search engines will enable you to conduct an electronic search of websites that contain highly specialized information of interest to you.)

- Using the Lycos or Yahoo search engines, type in the word "poverty."
- Explore at least 10 of the websites produced by this search.
- Using the same search engine, refine your search by typing in the phrase "poverty in America."
- Again, explore at least 10 of the links produced by this search.
- Repeat the preceding two searches, but this time use either the Alta Vista or InfoSearch or Excite search engines.
- Pursue at least 10 of the links identified in these searches and, where appropriate, make bookmarks to those websites that appear to be of particular value or interest to you.
- Repeat these exercises using another search term or phrase of particular interest to you.

2. Development Assistance Organizations
   a. Development Resources of National Governments
      - Open Praxis and point your browser to the directory entitled Aid Agencies of National Governments.
      - Explore each of the directories contained in this section.
      - Explore the sectoral and other resources listed for the United States Agency for International Development (USAID). Look particularly for recent reports of USAID initiatives in countries or world regions of particular interest to you.
      - Repeat the preceding exercise for the Japanese International Cooperation Agency (JICA).
      - Repeat the preceding exercise for the Danish International Development Agency (DANIDA).
   b. United Nations Resources
      - Open Praxis and point your browser to the Development Assistance Agencies, Organizations and Policies directory.
      - Explore each of the subdirectories contained in this directory.
      - Open the Multinational Aid & Mutual Cooperation Agencies, Organizations, and Policies directory.
      - Briefly explore the electronic resources listed under each of the subdirectory's major headings—that is, those listed under the United Nations, the World Bank, the International Monetary Fund, the Organization for Economic Cooperation and Development, etc.
      - Open the link to the United Nations home page and explore each of the major sections contained in the UN home page.
      - Repeat the exercise for one of the United Nations' specialized agencies, such as the United Nations' Development Programme (UNDP), the World Health Organization (WHO), etc. Note the quantity and richness of the electronic resources available from each of these sites.
      - Return to the United Nations home page, and from there, explore the documentary resources listed under United Nations Documents. Carefully review the types of documents that are available from the Economic and Social Council (ECOSOC).
      - Within the ECOSOC subdirectory, pursue the types of documents that are of particular interest to you (e.g., on issues dealing with women, racial or ethnic minorities, refugees, etc.)

- Repeat this exercise for each of the major sections listed on the UN home page (e.g., Peace and Security, Human Rights, Humanitarian Affairs, and so on).
- Explore the electronic documents available at this site associated with one or more recent world conferences and summits sponsored by the United Nations, including any Declarations, Agreements, and Covenants that have been adopted by these conferences.
- Make bookmarks to those subdirectories and other documents of particular relevance to your research project or term paper.

c. Private and Other Nongovernmental Organizations
- Reopen Praxis, and point your browser to the section entitled Development Assistance Agencies, Organizations and Policies.
- Open the directory entitled Non-Governmental Agencies and Organizations.
- Open the link to The Contact Center.
- Identify a sector of human services or social development in which you have a particular interest (e.g., child welfare, disaster relief, income security, etc.).
- Using the resources of the Contact Center, identify the network of social agencies in the United States and worldwide that engage in work related to your area(s) of interest.
- Using the links to their home pages, identify the unique contributions that each of four organizations listed by The Contact Center makes to local, national, and international development. As possible, using electronic resources that appear on each organization's home page, document the nature of each organization's contribution to international development.
- Repeat the preceding exercise for a group of public interest or advocacy organizations listed under the InterAction subdirectory.
- Repeat the preceding exercise for a group of public interest or advocacy organizations listed under the Public Interest and Advocacy Groups subdirectory.
- Identify how you would use the information and other resources of these organizations to advance your own development-oriented practice at the local, regional, or international levels.

3. Levels of SED Practice
- Within Praxis, explore each of the directories and subdirectories contained under Levels of Social Development Practice.
- Using the links contained in the Community-Building directory, identify Internet and other electronic informational resources that exist in your own community. Make bookmarks to those sites that are of particular interest to you.
- Use the Community-Building directory to identify Internet resources that exist in another community, preferably in another country, of relevance to your class project.
- Using the "send mail" or "e-mail" features of your browser, send a message to one of the persons identified with the Internet resource identified in the other community or country. Be sure to ask them to respond to a particular question of relevance to your project (e.g., descriptive information of the existence of service X or program Y in that community or country).

- Explore the electronic resources linked under the Individual and Group Empowerment and Institution-Building subdirectories. Pursue those links of most relevance to your semester-long project or paper.
- Repeat the preceding exercise with appropriate link(s) listed under the Nation-Building and Region-Building subdirectories.
- Repeat the preceding exercise with links under the World-Building subdirectory. In particular, explore the Global Ideas Bank website for possible solutions to some issue or recurrent social problem of special interest to you.

4. Sectoral Resources

The Sectoral Resources section of Praxis contains hundreds of links to major national and international organizations engaged in specialized development-oriented work.

- Open your browser to the Income Security subdirectory.
- Review the types and range of organizations that are listed in this subdirectory.
- Open one of the sites dealing with welfare reform in the United States.
- Identify reports and other publications listed on the home pages of several welfare reform organizations that are of particular interest to you. As appropriate, make bookmarks to those sites to which you would like to return at a future date.
- Repeat the preceding exercise with one or more sites listed under Corporate Welfare.
- Open the site of Office of International Policy (of the U.S. Social Security Administration) and that of the International Social Security Association. Identify reports and other publications listed on the home pages of these organizations that are of particular interest to you. As appropriate, make bookmarks to those materials which you would like to revisit.
- Repeat the exercise for resources listed under the Communications subdirectory which contains links to more than 5000 national and international newspapers, magazines, wire services, and television and radio networks.
- Repeat the preceding exercise for websites identified in the Health, Housing, Human Rights, and Social Services subdirectories.
- Using your "send mail" or "e-mail" function, send a request to the site's webmaster for additional information of interest to you. Please be as clear as possible concerning the types of materials you would like for the organization to supply (e.g., names of publications, dates, page numbers, etc.).

5. Historically Disadvantaged Population Groups
   a. Open Praxis to the First Peoples subdirectory.
   b. Explore the contents of this directory, and then focus your attention on links to international websites concerned with the status of Australia's and New Zealand's aboriginal people.
   c. Repeat the exercise for websites that focus on social, political, and economic issues of concern to Native Americans.
   - Repeat the exercise for sites that document the social situation of Brazil's Native American populations.
   - Open the Minorities subdirectory and explore the websites linked under Sexual Minorities. Repeat the preceding exercises in your exploration of electronic data sources pertaining to the sociolegal status of sexual minorities in various regions of the world.

- Contrast the types of information relating to gay, lesbian, and bisexual persons available from American, European, and Asian websites.
- Repeat the preceding exercise for websites listed in the Persons With Disabilities subdirectory.
- Repeat the preceding exercise for websites listed in the Women, Migrants and Refugees, and The Poor and Poverty subdirectories.

6. Country-Specific Resources
   - Open Praxis to the Country Resources directory and explore each of the major subdirectories.
   - Point your browser to the World Communities subdirectory. Select two countries of particular interest to you—preferably countries located on different continents.
   - Open the subdirectory for the first country you selected. Explore eight to ten of the electronic links contained on the country page. If possible, try to locate reliable sources for the following types of data/information:

   a country map
   a short political history of the country
   a listing of the country's current leaders
   the country's current demographic trends
   information concerning the country's major economic products
   information concerning the country's racial/ethnic/cultural mix
   information concerning the country's major social challenges
   other information of special interest to you

   - Repeat the preceding exercise for the second country you selected. Contrast the different types of information you find for each country.
   - Using the search engines contained in the Praxis Reference Room, search for even more detailed country-specific information on a topic of special interest to you.

7. Regional Resources
   - Open Praxis to the Regional Resources directory and explore each of the major subdirectories.
   - Point your browser to the EuroLink subdirectory. Select two European countries of particular interest to you—preferably countries with contrasting political and economic histories.
   - Open the subdirectory for the first European country you selected. Explore each of the websites listed on the country page. If possible, try to locate sources for the following types of data/information:

   a country map
   a shortened political history of the country
   a listing of the country's current leaders
   information on the country's major economic products
   information on the country's racial/ethnic/cultural mix
   information on the country's major social challenges
   other information of special interest to you

   - Repeat the preceding exercise for the second country you selected for analysis.

- Point your browser to the European Union website. Search the site for information pertaining to the Treaty of Maastricht and the Treaty of Amsterdam. Familiarize yourself with both the general organization and content of both of these treaties.
- Use the European Union website to link to other sites that deal with Europe as a region. Explore these sites for the types of information that may be obtained for the European continent as a region.
- Repeat all of the preceding exercises for the ASEAN site listed under the Asia and Pacific subdirectory.
- Using the Search Engines contained in the Praxis Reference Room, search for even more detailed region-specific information on a topic of special interest to you.

8. Open the Museums and Other Tourist Attractions subdirectory to identify sights that may be of interest for you to visit when you are not attending conference meetings.

9. International Travel
   - Open Praxis to the International Travel directory. Briefly explore each of the subdirectories located in this directory (e.g., Air Transportation, Surface Transportation, Scholarly Conferences and Meetings, etc.).
   - Within the Scholarly Conferences and Meetings subdirectory, identify an international conference or other meeting that you would like to attend. Make a note of the city in which the meeting will be held, the dates for the meetings, and its venue (e.g., conference center or hotel).
   - Return to the Air Transportation and Hotels subdirectory.
   - Register as a "visitor only" to the Travelocity website and identify the estimated cost and availability of air service to the conference city.
   - Using the Federal Per Diem Rates–International website located under the Money Matters subdirectory, identify the expected per diem (hotel and meals) associated with participating in the conference.
   - Using the Currency Converter website also listed in the Money Matters subdirectory, convert an appropriate amount of your national currency into the local currency of the country in which the conference will be held.
   - Using the Air Transportation and Hotels subdirectory, attempt to locate appropriate hotels, housing, or other accommodations at or near the conference venue.

A Global Model
of Ethnic Diversity
Conflict: Implications
for Social Work with
Populations at Risk

Nazneen Mayadas
Doreen Elliott
Chathapuram S. Ramanathan

From Africa to the Americas, from rural space to urban

life . . . there is no privileged representation of reality,

no single tongue or language in which "truth" can be

confidently asserted.

—Iain Chambers, 1994

Ethnic diversity is a normal human condition. Variety in the human species offers a rich-ness to be celebrated: personalities, physical appearance, languages, religions, art, and achievements in technology are a wonder to behold. Why is it, then, that ethnic diversity in our time at the end of the 20th century causes so much distress and conflict? Wars, neigh-bor fighting neighbor, homelessness, poverty, torture, genocide, hatred, persecution, dis-crimination, and violence continue around the world. This chapter suggests some of the factors that contribute to ethnic conflict across the world, and a model (Figure 8.1) is pre-sented for understanding ethnic diversity conflict, based on a global analysis. The model is applied to social work and its implications for practice with populations at risk are dis-cussed. This chapter serves to illustrate that applying a global analysis allows us to achieve clearer insights into social problems.

Figure 8.1 presents a diagrammatic representation of an analysis of ethnic diversity con-flict from a global perspective. Although diversity is a multidimensional concept covering

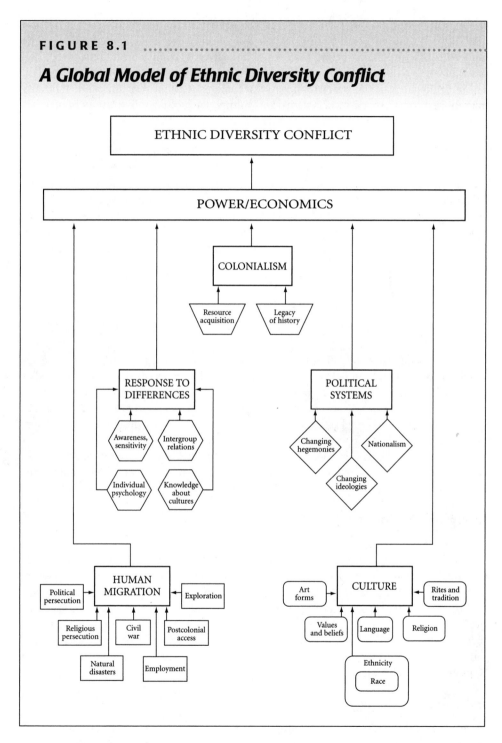

FIGURE 8.1

A Global Model of Ethnic Diversity Conflict

various populations at risk (which include age, gender, sexual orientation, ethnicity, and disability), for the purposes of this chapter only ethnic diversity is under analysis. The model identifies five major factors that cause ethnic diversity conflict around the world. The individual response to difference includes micro explanations of ethnic diversity conflict. The remaining four factors deal with macro explanations of ethnic diversity conflict: human migration, colonialism, political systems, and culture. Each of these five factors in turn has contributing factors, represented by the subgroups presented in the model beneath each of the major factors.

A key issue in this analysis is that these contributing factors are mediated by power and economics, which are seen as central to conflict. In this way, the model departs from more traditional social work analyses that focus on micro, psychological, or intergroup responses. Although no variable indicated in the model is independent of others and there may be overlap in the application of the model, the focus of the chapter is to show the impact of selected salient variables on ethnic diversity conflict. Hence the directional flow in the model is indicated by one-way arrows from the predictor constructs and variables to the main criterion variable under analysis.

RESPONSE TO DIFFERENCE

One of the major factors relating to conflict around diversity is the range of human responses to difference. Both positive and negative attributes are ascribed to groups viewed as different from membership groups or reference groups (Hare, Blumberg, Davies, & Kent, 1996). These perceptions determine the response to groups that are viewed as outsiders. Responses can range from total acceptance to total rejection of diverse groups. In this context, the degree to which ethnic differences deviate from the subjective norm of the dominant group determines the emotional strength of the negative reaction. These reactions are categorized in the model under four subheadings: intergroup relations; knowledge about cultures; individual psychology; awareness and sensitivity.

Intergroup Relations

Examples of incidents where one group uses difference to fan animosity and conflict can be seen in the *dot-buster* attacks of the 1970s and 1980s, in which gangs of young skinheads attacked Hindu women in England, Canada, and the United States, or the attempt in New Jersey by local residents to stop Hindu merchants from celebrating their ethnic religious festival Nauratri (Asamoah, Healy, & Mayadas, 1997). Such intergroup provocations eventually invite retaliation. In 1992, for example, the Los Angeles riots were explained away by then-Vice President Dan Quayle with the phrase "poverty of values" (blaming the victims) rather than a recognition that the interactional nature of diversity conflict is an intergroup response to diversity issues.

Individual Psychology

Prejudice and discrimination are institutionalized in cultures where social stratification is based on discrimination and is internalized by socialization. For example, within the caste system in India, the lowest-stratum people—the *harijans,* who fall below the established four-tier caste order—are treated as outcasts despite the equal opportunity policies of the government. This violation of human rights leads victims of discrimination to suffer psychological, social, and economic abuse in day-to-day transactions. Other examples can be found in daily newspapers and other media reports. Incidents like that of police brutality in the arrest of Rodney King in Los Angeles in the 1990s and the 1997 exposure of prison officer brutality against prisoners of ethnic minority origin in Texas reinforce the use of physical violence instigated through interpersonal discrimination, prejudice, and fear of diversity (Ivins, 1997). Under this response dimension can be listed psychological theories that attribute individual behavioral observations to racial deficits. For example, in the mid 1960s, H. S. Sullivan, using Anglo-European behavioral measures, came to the conclusion of laxity in African-American morals (Watts, 1994). Thus behavioral differences from the dominant culture are regarded as "lack of culture" in ethnic groups rather than as a culture practice unique to the group. This rule of generalization and disparaging stereotype is never applied to the dominant culture.

Knowledge about Cultures

Knowledge about cultures is an important factor affecting response to difference. Ignorance of cultures and traditions highlights differences and accentuates fear and dislike of the unknown. Examples are found in the revulsion embedded in attitudes to various cultural practices relating to food: the eating of horse meat in France, sheep's eyes as a delicacy in the Middle East, dog meat in China, and octopus in Greece may elicit different degrees of distaste in other parts of the world, leading to avoidance rather than expansion of experience to include appreciation of difference. Difference in these instances increases distance between cultures, creating prejudice and discrimination, even though it is based on an irrational distinction. Caviar and escargot are seen as a sophisticated taste, while horse meat, dog meat, and sheep's eyes are seen as distasteful from an ethnocentric Western perspective.

Awareness and Sensitivity

Awareness and sensitivity are seen as variables that mitigate the effects of diversity conflict and negative response to difference. The degree to which the individual is willing to deliberately and openly relate to human differences determines the extent to which difference from self is accepted (Pinderhughes, 1989). Lack of awareness and sensitivity to difference results in myths and stereotypes about various ethnic groups that are detrimental to interpersonal relationships. Stereotypes of Asians as the model minority, Indians as ethnocentric, Middle Easterners as terrorists, or Chinese as lacking emotions are all illustrations of ethnic labels. These perceptions block communication among diverse groups and increase the probability of diversity conflict.

At the same time, an exaggerated cultural awareness and sensitivity can also produce problems. For example, for many years the United Nations failed to speak out on the issue of female circumcision in Africa out of an inordinate respect placed on culture at the expense of broadly accepted global values related to human suffering and human rights. More exposure to, and familiarity with, different cultures may help to distinguish whether commonly accepted values across cultures should take precedence over the right of a culture to impose pain and suffering.

....

HUMAN MIGRATION

Human migration can be traced far back to the prehistoric period. Migration can be viewed as a natural response of humans to ecological, social, political, ideological, and economic change affecting their habitat: in that sense it is a natural human condition (Mayadas & Elliott, 1990). At present, more people migrate than at any other time in history, for a variety of reasons. Migration may be voluntary or involuntary. Voluntary migration patterns may arise out of business needs determined by international corporations or by new patterns of recreational travel—individuals may retire to a place they first visited on vacation, for example. Involuntary migration patterns may be seen in refugee populations. In 1965, the world's refugee population was under 2 million. In 1995, the UNHCR figures for total numbers of refugees is approximately 15 million people. These figures exclude large movements of people, estimated at around 2 million, such as Palestinians and Bosnians who have not been recognized officially as refugees (UNHCR, 1995). If migration is associated with progress rather than with crisis, then it takes on the shape of a desirable condition (Zolberg, Suhrke, & Aguayo, 1989). Many people move around the world not as refugees, but in response to increased opportunities. Seven conditions are categorized in the model in Figure 8.1 under human migration: political persecution; religious persecution; natural disasters; civil war; employment; postcolonial access; and exploration.

Political Persecution

Political persecution has driven many persons out of their country over ideological conflicts or the aftermath of war. In 1993, for example, a massacre of 60 people of Vietnamese origin in the village of Chong Kneas in Cambodia contributed to an exodus of Vietnamese who have lived for generations in Cambodia and whose language is Khmer, the language of Cambodia (UNHCR, 1995). The International Declaration of Human Rights of 1948 states that humans have a right to life, liberty, and security of person. When these conditions are broken, people naturally attempt to migrate.

Religious Persecution

The long-ranging Hindu-Muslim conflicts in India resulted in the partition of the Indian subcontinent at the close of the colonial period in 1947, causing large-scale immigration from India into Pakistan, and vice versa. In 1991–1992, more than a quarter of a million Rohingyas, a Muslim minority group, fled to Bangladesh from the Rakhini state of Myanmar (formerly Burma) as a result of human rights abuses that included forced labor and involuntary relocation (UNHCR, 1996). In Afghanistan, the fundamentalist Taliban have waged the Islamic holy war or jihad on the more moderate group of Muslims led by forces of Ahmed Shah Masood. For a fundamentalist, fighting for Islam is a passport to paradise. As a Taliban warrior reports, "I am not afraid of dying because this would be martyrdom. The Quran teaches us that to die for Islam is a blessing and that God will give me paradise in return" (Burns, 1997). The internal war between the state of Israel and the Arab Hezbollah Muslim militants is a further example of the historical religious conflict between the Israelites and the Ishmiites (Jehl, 1997). Violations of human rights in the name of religion are evident here.

Natural Disasters

Another factor is natural devastation such as floods or earthquakes that cause human kind to leave their homeland for shelter. The 1997 volcanic eruption in Montserrat, the tiny Caribbean island, is a clear example of an evacuation where some of those driven away will never return home (Rohter, 1997).

Civil War

Civil wars displace people within their own country and later may lead them to emigrate to a foreign land. For example, when given the choice of repatriation, 76 percent of Ethiopian refugees who had escaped to Somalia from war-torn Ethiopia preferred to settle in the new country (UNHCR, 1990). Although the examples of displaced persons and refugees suggest involuntary migration and therefore temporary escape from their homeland, prolonged scourges of war make return unlikely and oblige the immigrants to build a new life.

Employment

Another factor in migration is employment, especially as it relates to bordering states. The ongoing flow of migrants from Mexico to the United States despite the perils encountered from the border patrol suggests the economic desperation of individuals who leave their established home and families to improve their economic status by seeking employment in the United States. They have this goal in common with migrants to the United States from many countries, who may seek entry to a country with perceived better living or working conditions. Professionals such as physicians, university professors, and corporate executives are included in this group. Examples of employment-related migration are seen in industrialized countries, where immigrants are allowed into the country via a quota system for various job categories (Miller & Miller, 1996). This is a voluntary form of migration, often referred to as "brain drain" by the emigrants' country of origin. Illustrations can be found in educational, medical, and business institutions in almost all industrialized nations, where foreign immigrants provide skilled and professional labor. Related to the arrival of new immigrants is family reunification, in which immigrants, after settling into the country, gradually help their family members to migrate.

Postcolonial Access

A factor closely associated with employment is postcolonial access. This category of migration is the result of ex-colonial powers relaxing their immigration rules to accommodate immigrants from the former colonies. Examples are the United Kingdom, where many Indians, Pakistanis, and West Indians have settled, and France, where migrants from former North and West African colonies have settled.

Exploration

From age immemorial, exploration of new lands and a sense of adventure have been associated with extensive migratory movements. The continent of North America owes its discovery to just such a pioneering and adventurous spirit. This category of migration also includes fortune hunters and other such groups of speculators who have little to lose and much to gain by migrating to a new country if circumstances allow. However, in recent years, because of a number of factors such as the depletion of unskilled jobs in the labor market and the tightening of the economies of the major industrialized countries, countries all over the globe have tightened their borders and immigration rules to clearly delineate qualifications for entrance. In this context undocumented aliens and those whose visas and permits for stay in the country have expired but who have successfully "disappeared" within the country may fall into the category of the old-time adventurer or pioneer (Marger, 1997).

Whichever road to migration is taken, there are common threads that run through all of them: the arrival of new immigrants brings diversity and sets up xenophobic reactions. In the United States, since most of the recent immigrants are from non-Western countries, their ethnicity, skin color, and physical features are acutely visible, which only widens the chasm between the nationals and immigrants, who are accused of threatening the unity of monocultural populations (Karger & Stoesz, 1998; Mayadas, 1997). Thus, diversity, instead of being treated as a fact of life, becomes a source of conflict between the powerful, dominant group and the relatively powerless newcomers to the country. This effect is clearly evident in growing incidents of xenophobia in Western countries (Mayadas & Elliott, 1992; UNHCR, 1995; Marger, 1997). Immigrants then respond likewise with hostility and retaliation (Cowart & Cowart, 1994).

Colonialism

The model identifies two factors connected with colonialism that have contributed to diversity conflict. One is resource acquisition, a major motivating factor in colonialism, and the other is the legacy of history.

Resource Acquisition

Historically, resource acquisition through conquests and colonization exploited both natural and human resources, which led to land expansion and establishment of strategic positions for military and naval power bases. Gold in West and South Africa, diamonds in South Africa, spices and silk in the East were natural resources that motivated early colonists. Exploitation of human resources was accomplished through capturing indigenous populations in Africa and transporting them via international slave cartels in brutal and inhumane conditions to the New World, where they were enslaved to meet the needs of the labor market.

The Legacy of History

> If there be a fact to which all experience testifies, it is that when a country holds another in subjection, the individuals of the ruling think the people of the country mere dirt under their feet.
> —John Stuart Mill

Because Europeans increasingly captured the land and resources of non-Europeans in Asia, Africa, the Americas, New Zealand, and Australia, they perceived themselves as superior and in the vanguard of world civilizations (Thomas, 1993). Although the first contacts between the native populations and the Europeans were friendly, the colonized countries were viewed as primitive, depraved and hostile, an image that became the accepted and dominant view among Europeans. Along with exploitation of resources, colonial attitudes of superiority led to discriminatory practices in social life, employment, and living conditions generally. This policy set up the cycle of animosity, resentment, and anger that have significantly influenced subsequent ethnic relations.

The legacy of slavery and domination is a powerful factor in ethnic relations around the world today, and especially in the United States, where race relations are influenced by a lack of trust, anger, and guilt, which still influence both interpersonal and intergroup relations.

POLITICAL SYSTEMS

In the context of political systems, three factors contribute to diversity conflict: changing hegemonies, nationalism, and changing ideologies.

Changing Hegemonies

Changing hegemonies, reflecting changes in political power, have historically disrupted communities. Examples include the expulsion of Indians from Kenya and Uganda, population movements in the former Yugoslav Republic, the exodus of the boat people from Vietnam, and the expulsion of Kurds from Iran. A change in government may affect the welfare of a group, who may then select to emigrate or who may be involuntarily deported. These conflicts involve large migrations. One such example is the civil war in Tajikstan 1992–93, where half a million people became homeless and sixty thousand crossed the border into Afghanistan (UNHCR, 1995).

Nationalism

Nationalism has resulted in human migration: the establishment of the state of Israel produced large movements of Jewish people to populate the new country. A recent example is the exodus of Tibetans from their own country as a result of Chinese national expansion.

Changing Ideologies

Changing ideologies may also affect human migration patterns. Fascism in Europe in the 1930s led to the migration of those who could not live under that ideology to other European countries and the United States. Similarly, migration patterns were prompted by the establishment of communism in China, Vietnam, and the former USSR. Many intellectuals fled from Chile after the establishment of the fascist military regime of General Ugarte Pinochet because they had been associated with the previous left-wing government.

In practice, all these aspects of political systems are interwoven, but sometimes one theme emerges as more influential than others. All, however, contribute to population movement around the globe, which in turn contributes to dissension and conflict in the country of arrival. Newcomers may be different in religion, language, physical appearance, and dress. They may be employed in positions that long-term inhabitants of the country think should go to them. Newcomers may bring new skills and start up new industries or trading systems, all of which can be a source of economic resentment to those already there.

CULTURE

The development of the term "culture" has been described in Kroeber and Kluckholn's (1952) seminal work. More recently, Williams (1958, 1981) distinguished a range of meanings, from "a developed state of mind" (as in a cultured person) to the process of this development (as in cultural activities), to the means of these processes as in the arts as well as the anthropological and sociological meaning, indicating "the whole way of life." It is the last meaning that is relevant to this discussion. In this sense, culture may be defined as a "learned system of meaning and behavior that is passed from one generation to the next," usually within specific geographical boundaries (Carter & Qureshi, 1995). It refers to elements such as values, norms, beliefs, attitudes, folkways, behavior styles, and traditions that are linked together to form an integrated whole that functions to preserve the society (Pinderhughes, 1989). Culture may be seen as the signifying system through which a social order is communicated, reproduced, experienced, and explored (Williams, 1981).

Culture, then, is closely associated with socialization, the process by which individuals become identified with their culture. The process of acculturation may be through child-rearing practices in a culture, through assimilation and adaptation to a new culture, or through a conversion process. As such, it develops important though often unarticulated meanings for individuals related closely to individual and group identity and security. The presence of or the need to interact with other cultures may therefore be seen as a threat.

Six categories under culture are identified in the model in Figure 8.1 as contributing to ethnic diversity conflict: race and ethnicity, values and beliefs, art forms, language, rites and traditions, and religion.

Race and Ethnicity

In Figure 8.1 race and ethnicity are presented as overlapping concepts because both denote membership in special groups, show familiarity with particular cultures, and provide affiliation with a common cultural group. The popular conception of race is that it is a biologically defined classification system for dividing humans according to certain hereditary physical traits such as skin color, bone structure, height, and hair texture. This classification of the human species by focusing on biological or genetic differences has long been discredited in scientific circles. As early as 1951, the United Nations issued a statement (revised in 1964) on the biological aspects of race summarizing the arguments against the biological definition of race (United Nations, 1964). Such arguments include, for example, that differences between individuals within a race or within a population are often greater than the average differences between races or populations (United Nations, 1964, art. 5). Other arguments against the biological definition of race state that no race is genetically homogenous (United Nations, 1964, art. 3).

Some controversy has also centered around the extent to which racial characteristics affect less observable differences such as IQ. The assertion that genetics and race play a role in determining IQ has been discredited and race as a biological concept is rejected by some scientists. Instead it is now replaced with the term "ethnicity" (Fraser, 1995; Marger, 1997).

Trickett, Watts, and Birman (1994) conclude that the field of psychology, without explicit acknowledgment, was inextricably linked to a specific sociopolitical agenda supportive of ethnocentrism, racism, and sexism in which psychological IQ tests were used to make a point of discrediting minority groups as genetically inferior. However, the biological concept persists and is a source of ethnic diversity conflict because a biological definition of race is liable to assumptions of genetic inferiority. Once a group is defined by skin color and other physical characteristics, it serves as an ethnic basis for social stratification and leads to discrimination and oppression.

Race, then, is a socially constructed concept, mediated by ethnicity, geography, history, and individual differences. Ethnicity, in contrast, is marked by various distinguishable traits such as territoriality, a unique cultural pattern and a sense of affiliation with persons who belong to that particular region, share the culture and speak a common language (Marger, 1997). Ethnocentricism, or the application of subjective norms to other ethnic groups, is a powerful factor in intensifying diversity conflict, since alternate behaviors, attitudes, and values are seen as deviations from the subjective norm, carrying the stigma of deviance and inferiority. Examples are found in the group consciousness that arose at the breakup of the former USSR and which exists in the regional ethnic divisions of the subcontinent of India. In both instances, despite a common racial and national identity, ethnocentric attitudes form a closed system. Ethnicity influences culture and is in turn shaped by it. The interactive and mutually reinforcing effect of ethnicity and culture draws clear boundaries between ethnic groups that define membership and heighten the potential for diversity conflict.

Culture, therefore, is the focal point around which group differences center and which is illustrated through the variables discussed in this section. Variance between cultures results in social distance and increases the likelihood of diversity conflict.

Values and Beliefs

An often-cited example of value difference is that of coin rubbing in the Vietnamese culture. Mothers or other female figures rub the backs and limbs of children with coins to cure colds and fever. This practice, to the Western view, is abusive and is condemned as child abuse because of the marks and abrasions that remain on the body.

Art Forms

Art is regarded as a means of assessing a country's level of cultural development. Labeling certain art forms as primitive suggests that these types of art lack sophistication and finesse when assessed against some subjective standard. For example, Aboriginal art in Australia or tribal arts in Africa and India are still frequently referred to as "primitive" art.

Language

Lack of language facility is a strong barrier to communication. In certain European countries, for example, individuals may be ignored, despised or mocked if they do not speak the language of the country.

Rites and Traditions

Included under this subcategory are rituals, rules of conduct, dress, food, and social roles. Asian or African national dress is frequently referred to as "costume" by Western cultures. This kind of labeling sets up a barrier to the natural flow of interaction between cultures.

Religion

Difference in religious practice can cause resentment and disgust. For example, Europeans in the East find it distasteful to take off their shoes in mosques and temples before entering since the areas surrounding the entrances to these religious places are often dirty and littered with debris. Non-Christians, similarly, find offensive the notion of eating the body and blood of Christ at the Christian communion or mass, a religious belief that lies at the heart of the Christian religion.

ECONOMICS AND POWER

The model in Figure 8.1 represents the various factors identified with diversity conflict from a global perspective mediated by power and economics. In capitalist technologically based economies, power is directly linked to economics and it might be argued that they are inseparable.

Power and economics influence response to difference at varying levels of phenomena and may contribute to ethnic diversity conflict. The term "economics" is used here to summarize the process by which resources are distributed. Such resource distribution may be viewed at an international level, where we are aware of the inequities in the distribution of world resources between the Global North and the Global South. One measure which may be used to illustrate this effect is per capita gross national product (GNP). In Western industrialized countries, the average GNP per capita is US $20,567; in Asian countries, US $5,021; in Central and South American countries, US $2,456; in former communist countries, US $1,878; and in African countries, US $815 (Midgley, 1997). Similarly, at regional levels, there is unequal distribution of resources.

From 1977 to 1990, the median income for the wealthiest 5 percent of the population grew by $12,819 (in 1990 dollars); for the wealthiest 10 percent it grew by $9,256. By contrast, median income for the poorest 40 percent of the population in the U.S. was actually $1,088 lower (in 1990 dollars) in 1990 than it was in 1977 (Karger and Stoesz, 1998, p. 133). These clear and widely accepted examples of unequal distribution of resource systems are obviously linked to power. What is less widely recognized is that economic factors may influence social issues in more insidious ways that are less often recognized. Chambers (1995) applies an economic analysis to child adoption; Elliott and Mayadas (1996) illustrate how economic issues influence individual and professional responses in family violence and mental health.

In the model in Figure 8.1 economics is linked with response to difference. Discrimination in social policies results in unequal distribution of resources and in turn adds to diversity conflict.

Human migration is linked with economics: the search for survival or improvement of economic standards motivates population changes, which in turn may create diversity conflict (UNHCR, 1995). Economics might be said to be at the basis of colonialism in the sense that the conquest of colonies was motivated by resource acquisition and thus the gaining of power. Economics and political systems are clearly linked because the political organization of a country is central to determining the policies by which resources and wealth are distributed.

Culture and economics are also linked and lead to ethnic conflict because some cultural expressions may be resourced better than others. Examples might be less financial support for Native American cultural enterprises in North America and Aboriginal and Maori cultural enterprises in Australia and New Zealand. Although there are economic considerations attached to colonization, the race or color of the indigenous people also played an important role in determining the extent to which investments were made by conquerors. For example, British investment in Canada alone was larger than that country's combined investments in India and Africa. Similarly, France and Germany did not invest much money in Africa after colonization (Gann & Duignan, 1975). Thus racial domination imposed on millions of non-Europeans by European nations over the centuries still plays a major role in the relationship between whites and people of color (Thomas, 1993).

Economics and power are represented in the model in Figure 8.1 as overlapping concepts because they are inextricably linked. Ultimately, all ethnic diversity conflict is influenced by these two factors. The "race" riots in Liverpool, Bristol, and Los Angeles all had an economic element. The situation in Northern Ireland may be represented as a religious conflict by the labels "Catholic" and "Protestant," but the conflict is essentially economic and cultural. The religious labels are convenient symbols. Geschwinder's (1978) definition of a minority summarizes this view of economics and power in relation to ethnic diversity: a minority group is "any group that is socially defined as different from the dominant group in society, is at a power disadvantage, receives less than its proportionate share of scarce resources due to its power disadvantage, and finds its differential treatment justified in terms of socially defined differences" (1978, p. 17).

In any given society, members of one group attempt to influence the other through the use of power. According to French and Raven (1968), power bases can be created through the use of reward, coercion, expertise, referent identity, and (based on identification) legitimization (based on social sanctions, e.g., United Nations Security Council). For example, if power is seen as the control of resources (reward coercion) then certainly ethnic minority groups are very much at a disadvantage (Gaventa, 1980). Inequitable distribution of wealth can be seen at the international, national, and regional levels—a condition that shapes politics, intercountry dependency relations, and economic imperialism. Furthermore, abuse of this power is seen in industrialized countries, using sweat shop labor in developing countries to stock their own markets with material goods. On a more regional level evidence of coercive power is seen in daily news headlines where police and border patrol troops exercise brutality to implement what is termed as legitimate power in the interest of law enforcement.

In viewing conditions from the referent power perspective (charismatic identification) it would appear that positions of leadership are blocked through prejudice and discrimination toward ethnic minorities so that leadership from among these groups is excluded from earning a referent power status. Exceptional figures such as Martin Luther King in the United States and Mahatma Gandhi in India overcame these oppressive conditions and secured rights for their respective compatriots. However, the exclusion of ethnic minority leaders from national leadership keeps referent power very much within the control of the dominant group.

In cases where ethnic referent power sources succeed in cutting through layers of resistance and prejudice (i.e., civil rights and legitimization of equal opportunities for African Americans in the United States), the backlash to reestablish the previous power imbalance springs into effect. Illustrations of this backlash are the reversal of equal opportunity policies in U.S. universities and strikes against the quota system (the reservationist policy) in India.

Expert power is associated with information technology, and countries that have gained mastery in this area now have a monopoly on information or demonstrate technological imperialism. Japan joins the industrialized West in technological control and influence through dominating information sources. If this dominance is translated to a regional level, ethnic groups are excluded from gaining expert power. An inequitable balance in resources makes access to expertise development virtually out of their reach. Power thus remains with those who exert influence over the distribution of information.

A further source of inequity and power imbalance is the internalized sense of powerlessness and diffidence instilled in ethnic groups through long centuries of white domination (colonization in the East and Africa, slavery in the United States, land exploitation in North America). Even as this cycle breaks, it is overpowered with economic control, blockage of opportunities, and deprivation of equal rights. Thus the balance of power remains heavily weighted on the side of the "haves" and intensifies the conditions for ethnic diversity conflict between the "haves" and the "have nots."

IMPLICATIONS FOR SOCIAL WORK

From its beginnings in the charity organization society and the settlement house movement, social work has been interested in social justice, sustainable gains for humankind, and equal opportunities for all. Based on these goals, social work has consistently endeavored to empower groups and communities to work on their own behalf and, as such, has focused on a developmental model of practice to enable individuals, groups, and communities to become self-sufficient.

The role of social workers has been that of change agents at different levels of practice. In the area of diversity conflict, social workers as change agents attempt to understand and work with factors related to ethnic issues. Consistent with the model presented in this chapter, social work interventions in the areas of response to difference, human migration, colonialism, political systems, and culture, mediated through power and economics, are discussed in the context of ethnic diversity conflict.

As change agents, social workers undertake a range of interventions. For example, they advocate, counsel, mediate, educate and implement programs in collaboration with a range of clients—individuals, groups and communities. Client groups, at whatever level of practice phenomenon, have two interactive conditions in common. As seekers of help, they perceive themselves lacking in resources (material, emotional, psychological, spiritual) and devoid of power to take action on their own behalf to modify the situation. This is more pronounced in ethnic groups who suffer from both economic deprivation and powerlessness (Ekins, 1992).

Thus in planning interventions to dissipate ethnic diversity conflict, a balance of power and economic resources is required to put clients, groups and communities on the road to self-sufficiency (Durst, 1982). In other words, the gains achieved are to be sustained once the intervention is withdrawn (sustainable development). In dealing effectively with response to difference, human migration, colonialism, and political systems, social workers recognize that in times of stress and crisis it is convenient to have a target of blame outside the self that helps to externalize the problem and absolves the self from responsibility (Edelman, 1988). When immigrants and refugees enter the country, especially in times of economic crisis, they are seen as a drain on the economic resources and the social and political institutions of the country. Their cultural practices are resented as bizarre, and there is a concerted negative response at both human and institutional levels. As educators and counselors, social workers have a dual role. One is to demonstrate to the public, through hard data and actual cases, that incoming ethnic groups are an economic asset to the country, once they have achieved a level of sustainable development. At the other end, social workers can take a social development approach, in work with ethnic groups in which they not only achieve a level of self-sufficiency but their productivity benefits the economics of the surrounding community (Elliott, 1993; Midgley, 1995). A good example is that of ethnic restaurants, in which human self-reliance and economic development progress side by side, bringing economic improvement to the area.

Similarly with human migration and political systems, social workers may take the advocate role and question the policies and unfair quota systems that preclude certain classes of persons from entering the country. Social workers can also select to work with regional and national governments to introduce a developmental, as opposed to the current residual, approach to welfare in order to enable refugees and immigrants to reach self-sufficiency within a reasonable time.

Finally, in the mediator role, social workers can intervene in ethnic diversity conflicts, such as race riots, ethnic gangs wars, and intergroup violence in ethnic neighborhoods. While the dominant group oppresses ethnic groups, ethnic groups also oppress each other, based on their perception of where they rate themselves on the socioeconomic power ladder. As mediators and educators, social workers can encourage a united interethnic front among ethnic communities to increase their power base. This would dissipate ethnic diversity conflict and establish a pluralistic society for peaceful coexistence.

RECOGNIZING ETHNIC DIVERSITY PROBLEMS: CONCLUSIONS

The value of an international analysis of a social problem such as ethnic diversity conflict is that it promotes recognition that many issues are shared worldwide, even though the degree to which the problem is experienced may differ from region to region. Not all the factors identified in the model are applicable at all times in all places, but they occur to some degree, at various times. The recognition of shared experiences may lead to greater international understanding and cooperation. In terms of social work practice, we can see more clearly an expanded range of practice for social workers beyond the microsystems interventions so widely practiced.

STUDENT ACTIVITIES

1. Read the case studies and then answer the questions that follow:

CASE STUDY 8.1

Response to Difference

CHATHAPURAM S. RAMANATHAN

Dinesh Chandra Sharma, age 50, was a visitor from India at his brother's home. One day he was talking to a 3-year-old boy who was alone in the backyard next door, where a neighbor provides day care, in Shelby Township, Metropolitan Detroit, Michigan. Sharma brought the boy into the house to give him candy, his relatives said. Within five or ten minutes, police said, the father of another child retrieved the boy. Police said the boy was not harmed, but Sharma was charged with first-degree attempted kidnapping, though his relatives said that the incident was a misunderstanding based on cultural differences. He was held on a $1 million bond for allegedly taking a child from the backyard of a day care provider's home (Jonas, 1997a).

It is interesting that on the same day another story was reported by the same journalist regarding the selection of Jury in the case of a Mt. Clemens man who has been convicted on two misdemeanors while out on bail on charges of assault with attempt to murder and first-degree home invasion, in the same urban area. Percy Daniel, age 30, was charged with a felony stemming from the 1995 attack on a former neighbor. Daniel apparently broke through the ceiling of the 34-year-old woman's apartment in July 1995, stabbed her six times, and escaped. Daniel has been free for two years after posting 10 percent of a $25,000 bond. In the early summer of 1997, he was convicted of fleeing and eluding a police officer and disturbing the peace. Sentencing for those charges was not expected until after the assault trial (Jonas, 1997b).

After being held in high security jail cell for 10 days, Sharma was brought before the 41 A District Court, where the case was adjourned to allow prosecutors to consider the "unique issues" raised in his defense (wherein his supporters insisted that Sharma was innocently displaying his culture's generosity). Kalia, a community college professor, called Sharma's actions well intentioned and explained that it is a tradition throughout India that a neighbor's doors are always open to any children in a village. Also, it is a kind gesture to feed another family's child. The father, who was at the day care when the boy was found missing, dashed over to Sharma's house, retrieved the boy, and returned him to the day care center. The owner of the day care center did not consider the incident serious enough to report to the police. Five hours later, when the owner shared the incident with the mother, she pressed charges.

Witnesses testified that the boy appeared unshaken by the episode, which lasted less than five to ten minutes. Per the hearing, the judge reduced Sharma's bond from $1 million to $25,000 and he was released from Macomb County jail after posting 10 percent of the bond (Lynch, 1997).

Panchayat Raj

CHATHAPURAM S. RAMANATHAN

The word *Panchayat* is derived from *pancha,* which means "five"; it also refers to an assembly of elders who settle disputes. Panchayats are decentralized political institutions, with a tenure of five years. Panchayat raj in modern India is based on equality of status and opportunity. Panchayat raj is a national commitment in India. It is based on the conviction that a three-tier system of panchayat (Gram Panchayat at the village level; Taluk Panchayat at the block level—i.e., a cluster of a few village panchayats; Zilla Panchayat at the district level) will aid in the implementation of development programs with people's participation (Ghorpade, 1991).

In general, few women in proportion to their numbers are in the power structures, or have the level of education and training that men do in the social, economic, and political arenas. This is true in most countries in international bodies and global management. This is also true in India where structural changes and action to facilitate true partnership and full participation are yet to be realized, although "equality" before law is explicitly stated in the constitution (Ramachandran, 1995). In order to empower women through legislative implementation, the 73rd Constitutional Amendment was enacted in the Indian parliament in April 1993; accordingly, all the states in India amended their laws relating to self-government. As a result, for the first time in the political history of India one-third of the total seats in its local government institutions were statutorily reserved for women. This legislation has created a silent revolution in the power structure, which was formerly to a large extent influenced by a patriarchial value system. The 73rd Constitutional Amendment provides opportunities for 1 million women to access national politics through the panchayats and municipalities. Although it has been argued that with the one-third reservation of seats, there may not be enough candidates in the state of Karnataka, about 43.4 percent of the seats were won by women, and more than one-third of the seats were won by women in the state of West Bengal. The legislation requires that one-third of the total panchayats have women members. The act further states that a third of the seats reserved for women are to be represented from the scheduled castes and scheduled tribes—namely, protected groups from lower castes and tribal or aboriginal people (Mohanty, 1995).

· ·

Difference and Real-Life Problems in the Pluralist Workplace

VIVODH ANAND

A manufacturing facility on the outskirts of Chicago has a diverse workforce: machine operators and lower-level workers are West African and Mexican immigrants, first-level supervisors are eastern European Serb immigrants. Personnel in the small front office are native-born white and female. The outside sales force of three and the general manager are native-born white males.

A brief diversity audit at the facility revealed several reasons for concern. Three of the most striking are (1) machines were constantly broke down, indicative of low-level sabotage; (2) there was racist graffiti in a locker room on the factory floor; and (3) poor inventory control caused overages and shortage indicative of poor communication with salespeople who predict production requirements. Two months after the diversity audit, the general manager is fired. The new general manager asks you to assist the organization. What would you do?

· ·

Harassment Issues

VIVODH ANAND

An organization in a mature industry with main corporate offices located in New Jersey has thirty-five hundred employees. A new vice president of human resources from Texas is hired and moves to New Jersey, where she immediately implements legal and consistent human rights practices.

About two months into her tenure in the position, a temporary employee complains to her about sexual harassment by a senior officer. She also notices that the accountant is often referred to as "Jew boy." When asked how he feels, the accountant says that it has been like this for years. One of the senior officers whom she approaches about the sexual harassment tells her not to worry and that she must not be overly sensitive about "the casual way we do things in New Jersey."

Upset, the vice president calls you, her "diversity consultant." What do you do to assist

· the vice president specifically in this difficult situation?

· the corporation that skirmishes with financial disaster from potential litigation?

· ·

Mediating Cultural Differences

VIVODH ANAND

A large laundry that services hospitals, hotels, and other commercial establishments has a largely Latino and Vietnamese factory floor workforce. First-level supervision has been in place for many years and consists of white males who respect the work ethics of the people they supervise. The general manager, who is new to his position, senses that his supervisors need to communicate better with the workers.

An initial conversation with one of the supervisors indicates that he has difficulty understanding some of the unique behavior of the Vietnamese workers, who often request time off from work to meet family and friends coming into the country at the airport. You suspect that this may be just the tip of the iceberg of nonunderstanding. When you report your findings back to the general manager, what are some suggestions you may make?

• •

CASE STUDY 8.6

Difference and Employee Morale

VIVODH ANAND

You are contacted by the human resources manager for a chain of 127 specialty retail stores, each with an employee workforce of under ten people with one or two supervisors. The stores have a history of high employee turnover and theft by employees; to address these problems, there are well-established methods and procedures. Your job is to develop a process to deal with the recent spate of racist/homophobic graffiti that has appeared in some employee washrooms of stores located in New Jersey. How do you proceed?

• •

2. Take a situation involving ethnic diversity conflict with which you are familiar and analyze it according to the model presented in Figure 8.1.
   a. How far do the factors apply to the situation?
   b. Does this form of analysis give any new insights into the situation?
   c. What solutions do you see to the problem?

3. Take current editions of one local and one national newspaper, and identify reports with ethnic diversity content. Analyze these situations according to the model presented.

4. Is race a social or a biological construct? Identify the arguments on each side. Is race an outmoded concept?

5. What role should social work play in improving interethnic group relations?

6. Consider how far your formal education at elementary, secondary, and higher education levels has helped you towards an understanding of ethnic diversity conflict.

7. Review the example of ethnic diversity conflict in Case Study 8.1. If you were a social worker assigned to this case
   a. What would your assessment be?
   b. What interventions would be appropriate?

Global Social and Economic Justice Issues

Arline Prigoff

We just never were able to get the idea of sustainable development taken seriously. And the reason is that the Bank is basically a money pump. It wants to get the money out the door and anything that gets in the way of that—like careful accounting and environmental review—is frowned upon.
—Herman E. Daly (in Caufield, 1996, p. 222)

Social workers in the Global North are equally outraged by and familiar with political platforms that aim to reduce the size of government by cutting taxes, especially capital gains taxes; by drastically shrinking or eliminating public services for poor people and other vulnerable groups; and by privatizing state-funded services. These policy goals are promoted in North America by conservative think tanks such as the Hoover Institute at Stanford University and the well-funded Intercollegiate Student Institute in Bryn Mawr, Pennsylvania, and they are disseminated through mainstream media. Lavishly promoted, these views are apt to be accepted, by persons without access to alternative media, as the conventional wisdom of U.S. society. Voters have been persuaded; public opinion on the role of government has shifted significantly in the last twenty years, as a result both of media impact and of public reaction to involvement in influence peddling by leaders of both major political parties.

The defunding of governmental services is an agenda that is in direct conflict with traditional concepts of social welfare. Based on both value premises and the findings of social research, the international field of social welfare had concluded that the guarantee by government of basic human rights and social entitlements enhances human dignity and the quality of life for all inhabitants of that society. For example, the passage of the Social Security Act of 1935 in the United States indicated that the U.S. public expected government to establish and maintain public services that promote health, education, and the general welfare; that protect public safety and the environment; and that will serve the nation now and in future generations.

Social workers in the United States, Canada, and the United Kingdom have witnessed the dismantling of social welfare entitlements and programs by conservative political forces. How many professional social workers have recognized that the same program for the downsizing of governments and redirection of national resources has been planned and promoted on a global level by officials of international banks and the representatives of transnational corporations? This chapter will address the role of the World Bank and the International Monetary Fund (IMF) in these efforts and their impact on social and economic development. The chapter will provide students with the necessary background to understand policy such as "structural readjustment" and the consequences of these policies for people in poverty. This understanding will help students to recognize the importance of global social justice and their advocacy role in their own community and in the widest context transcending national boundaries.

HISTORY OF ECONOMIC GLOBALIZATION: ROLES OF THE WORLD BANK AND THE IMF

The social environment, which is the context of social work practice, has been profoundly altered in the past fifty years by the globalization of market economies. After the end of World War II, global production and marketing by corporations based in the United States and western Europe, expanded in countries that previously had not been industrialized. To facilitate development, which is defined as increasing industrialization and commerce, the borders and markets of many nations in Africa, Latin America, and Asia that had been protected and preserved for the privileged status of single colonial powers and national elites before the latter part of the twentieth century, were opened to penetration by transnational corporations seeking to exploit the cheaper labor of the Global South. That process was facilitated by two international banking institutions founded by the United States and the United Kingdom at Bretton Woods in 1944.

The World Bank, established to make postwar development loans for infrastructure projects such as roads and utilities that were unlikely to be initiated by private capital because they were not likely to be profitable, and the International Monetary Fund, created to promote world commerce by stabilizing foreign exchange, fostered international trade agreements and served the interests of expanding transnational corporations. The World Bank and the International Monetary Fund were the lending institutions that promoted "developmental" loans that bankrupted nations; later they designed mandatory austerity programs of indebted governments seeking new loans to refinance due interest payments.

It would be difficult to overestimate the central role of those financial institutions in the negative outcomes of international economic development projects undertaken by nations in Africa, Latin America, and Asia during the latter part of the twentieth century. Catherine Caufield writes:

> The Bank is the biggest single lender to the Third World: it holds more than 11 percent of its long-term foreign debt, public and private. But the Bank does much more than lend money; to a great degree it also decides how loans will be spent. It proposes, designs and oversees the

implementation of the projects it funds. It requires its borrowers to adopt the economic and other domestic policies it considers conducive to successful development. Moreover, it has enormous influence over the decisions of other funders to support or abandon a project—or a country. (1996, pp. 1–2)

Caufield notes that while leaders of the World Bank have consistently stated that the reduction of poverty is its primary goal, its projects have achieved very different results:

> The Bank has its own ideology, independent of its members' politics. Its creed is to lend and to be repaid with interest. Acts that appear to be political may merely be an expression of this deep-seated drive. The Bank's stance toward South Africa is an example. Between 1948, when the country officially adopted apartheid, and 1966, South Africa borrowed a quarter of a billion dollars from the Bank, making it one of the Bank's biggest clients. The Bank had doubts about lending to an avowedly racist government, but they were of a financial, not moral nature. It worried that the South African people would overthrow the government and repudiate its debts. (1996, p. 285)

> The Bank is often accused of favoring right-wing governments, whereas what it actually favors are strong governments. . . . The reason for the Bank's enthusiasm for dictators is simple. Autocratic governments are more capable of instituting and seeing through the unpopular reforms the Bank often prescribes for its clients than are democratically elected governments, which rely on the support of the public. (1996, p. 289)

> . . . the Bank's decades-long series of grand experiments in poverty reduction have cost many millions of dollars and millions of disrupted human lives, and required the sacrifice of vast areas of productive forests, soils, rivers, and coastlines. The past half-century of development has not profited the poorest people, nor the poorest countries. Rather, they have paid dearly—and their descendants will continue to pay dearly—for the disproportionately small benefits they have received. On the other hand, there are many who have profited from development. (1996, p. 338)

Structural Adjustment Programs of the World Bank and the IMF

Designed by the World Bank and International Monetary Fund, structural adjustment programs (SAPs) require debtor nations requesting refinancing to foster trade by the elimination of restrictions on imports and exports; to privatize national resources and public utilities; and to cut back public services in health, education, housing and public assistance, often to devalue their currency and to make loan repayment the national priority, all in order to maintain credit and international acceptance of their currency. Significantly, borrowing governments have not been pressured to refrain from purchase of military equipment, an expense item that has often been a major source of national indebtedness and political repression.

The impact of SAPs has also sharply intensified stratification of wealth and income within nations and on a global level. There is ample evidence that the lending policies of these financial institutions significantly contributed to the indebtedness and increasing poverty of developing nations now in crisis, especially in agricultural regions in Africa, Latin America, and Asia. Urban centers and rural districts within technological nations are also showing visible symptoms of social and environmental degradation (MacEwan, 1990). Critical policy studies on SAPs and their outcomes are now in circulation (Bello, 1994; Danaher, 1994, 1996; George, 1990; Greider, 1997; Mander & Goldsmith, 1996; Payer, 1974; Torrie,

1983, and more). SAPs are truly genocidal for indigenous and other subsistence cultures whose identity and way of life are based on relationship with the land. The 1994 uprising in Mexico, led by the Zapatistas in Chiapas, was a historic example of resistance to extermination (Barry, 1995).

Because of the extremely negative impact on women in Africa, Asia and Latin America of the Structural Adjustment Programs, issues of economic development policy have become critical issues for the global women's movement (Braidotti, Charkiewicz, Hausler, & Wieringa, 1994; Enloe, 1990; Grant & Newland, 1991; Jiggins, 1994; Miller, 1991; Momsen, 1991; Mosse, 1993; Peterson & Runyan, 1993; Sen and Grown, 1987; Thomas-Meagwali, 1995; Vickers, 1991; Ward, 1990; Wetzel, 1993; Wignaraja, 1990; Young, Wolkowitz, & McCullagh, 1991).

One of the strongest indictments of the International Monetary Fund was expressed by Davison Budhoo, former senior economist of the IMF from Guyana, who publicly resigned in May 1988:

> Today I resign from the staff of the International Monetary Fund after over 12 years, and after 1,000 days of official Fund work in the field, hawking your medicine and your bag of tricks to governments and to peoples in Latin America and the Caribbean and Africa. To me resignation is a priceless liberation, for with it I have taken the first big step to that place where I may hope to wash my hands of what in my mind's eye is the blood of millions of poor and starving peoples. (Danaher, 1994, pp. 20–23)

In the early 1990s, experts from less industrialized nations testified before the European Parliament on the urgent need to replace SAPs with alternative development models. The testified facts referred to the continuing high mortality rates of children under age 5 (6 million yearly) in Africa, Asia, and Latin America and the failure of the IMF and World Bank SAPs. Further, according to the UNDP, 1.2 billion people in the Global South now live in absolute poverty (almost twice the number in the early 1980s). Also 1.6 billion in the Global South are without potable water and healthy environments in which children can grow (Danaher, 1994).

In Chapter 3 of this book, the case of India's Silent Valley Project was discussed with reference to successful community organizing to prevent the World Bank initiative, which would have disrupted the lives of the indigenous people besides adversely impacting the ecology of the region. In many parts of the world, however, people have not been as successful in resisting the power of the World Bank. As Danaher says, "It is now generally recognized that the environmental impact of the IMF-World Bank on the South has been as devastating as the economic and social impact on peoples and societies" (1994, p. 22).

Herman E. Daly, now professor at the University of Maryland and a senior economist at the World Bank from 1988 until he resigned six years later, suggests that a more accurate term than "free trade" for economic globalization would be "deregulated international commerce." Daly observes that corporations seek to maximize profits and production without consideration for hidden social and environmental costs, which are rising faster than benefits, thereby making the world poorer, not richer. Of his experience at the Bank, Daly comments:

> A lot of what's wrong with the World Bank, in my opinion, can be traced right back to where the Bank's officers got their training. They're mostly economists, and whether they came from Zaire or California, they all went to the same few schools—Harvard, MIT, Stanford, Oxford, Cambridge, Chicago—and they all learned the same thing. . . . They're coming here, trying to apply what they learned, and it's not working. . . .

> We just never were able to get the idea of sustainable development taken seriously. And the reason is that the Bank is basically a money pump. It wants to get the money out the door and anything that gets in the way of that—like careful accounting and environmental review—is frowned upon. (quoted in Caufield, 1996, p. 222)

While the World Bank and IMF have been the promoters of "free trade" in financial circles, elite organizations for the establishment of agreements on international trade have been the means by which transnational corporations have achieved domination of a socially constructed New World Order. The terms "free trade" and "trade liberalization," incorporate descriptions that are echoed by politicians and media, conceal destructive aspects of the North American Free Trade Agreement (NAFTA) or General Agreement on Tariffs and Trade (GATT). Although GATT policies encourage free trade, in reality they legitimize transnational corporations' displacement of local small agricultural producers (Mies & Shiva, 1993). This invasion by transnational corporations affects the local community by usurping people's abilities to produce for subsistence. Students can investigate the effects of GATT policies by comparing the wages paid to banana pickers in Honduras, the price students pay in North American shops for these exported staple crops, and the malnutrition of Honduran children, which goes unnoticed.

Facilitated by trade agreements, penetration of agricultural regions by transnational corporations results in their capture of local markets and the marginalization of local producers. While wealthy national elites may benefit from foreign investment, working-class and peasant families, as well as indigenous and poor communities, lose economic roles and natural resources that are traditional bases of survival (Barnet & Cavanagh, 1994; Mies & Shiva, 1993; Trask, 1993). Ralph Nader, a vocal critic of NAFTA and GATT, anticipated these outcomes in 1993, warning:

> The large global companies have an even more ambitious set of goals for the Third World. They hope to use GATT and NAFTA to capitalize on the poverty of Third World countries and exploit their generally low environmental safety and wage standards. At the same time, these corporations plan to displace locally owned businesses and solidify their control over developing nations; economies and natural resources. . . .
>
> Secrecy, abstruseness, and unaccountability: these are the watchwords of global trade policy-making. Every element of the negotiation, adoption, and implementation of the trade agreements is designed to foreclose citizen participation or even awareness. (Earth Island, 1993, pp. 1–6)

In 1991, under the leadership of Davison Budhoo, the Bretton Woods Reform Organization (BWRO) was formed to launch a global campaign for accountability by the World Bank and IMF. Later, nongovernmental organizations (NGOs), including the American Indian Movement, Greenpeace International, Global Exchange, and Witness for Peace, have united in the "Fifty Years Is Enough!" campaign that calls for dismantling the institutions established at Bretton Woods. That campaign was visible in Denver, Colorado in July 1997, at "The Other Economic Summit" or the TOES Conference, which protested the G-8 Summit's agenda of the further expansion of "free trade."

Meanwhile, in 1996, an international group of economists, researchers, scholars and writers founded the International Forum on Globalization (IFG) to monitor the impact of economic globalization on nations, communities, families, and environments and to educate the public on these issues. David Korten of IFG notes that the system of economic development constructed at Bretton Woods contains flawed concepts: "The first erroneous assumption is that economic growth and enhanced world trade would benefit everyone. The second is that economic growth would not be constrained by the limits of the planet" (Mander & Goldsmith, 1996, p. 21). Edward Goldsmith of IFG examined the objectives of Bretton Woods:

> The massive efforts to develop the [Global South] in the years since World War II were not motivated by purely philanthropic considerations but by the need to bring the [Global South] into the orbit of the Western trading system in order to create an ever-expanding market for our goods and services and a source of cheap labor and raw materials for our industries. This has also been the goal of colonialism especially during its last phase, which started in the 1870s. For that reason, there is a striking continuity between the colonial era and the era of development, both in the methods used to achieve their common goal and in the social and ecological consequences of applying them. (Mander & Goldsmith, 1996, p. 253)

Historic Consolidation of the New World Order under Corporate Rule

The full consolidation of a global, unified market economy essentially owned and managed by transnational corporations and the international financial institutions awaited the demise of the Soviet Union and other state planning systems. The global marketplace is now, in fact, a planned economy. Goals, operations, and structures for distribution of income, goods, and services are now determined by corporate leaders and selected friends in government, finance, education, and the military, a group that does not include nor represent the vast majority of the earth's population.

Tony Clarke, of IFG, describes these recent historic changes and their impact on democratic processes:

> Over the past decade and a half, the number of transnational corporations has increased from 7,000 to more than 40,000. Today, 50 of the top 100 economies in the world are TNCs, 70 percent of global trade is controlled by just 500 corporations, and a mere 1 percent of the TNCs own half the total stock of foreign direct investment. At the same time, the new free trade regimes (e.g. GATT, NAFTA) have created a global environment in which transnational corporations and banks can move capital, technology, goods, and services freely throughout the world, relatively unfettered by the regulations of nation-states or democratically elected governments. Through these processes, transnational corporations have effectively secured a system of rule and domination in the new world order. (1996, p. 5)

As social workers, we need to be very concerned with this new world order. The new world order's aim is not to ensure basic human and democratic rights, but the protection of the rights and freedoms of transnational capital. As Clarke states:

> These realities are further augmented in many countries by corporate financed political strategies designed not only to carry out a massive downsizing of and dismantling of public services, but a fundamental reinvention of the basic roles and responsibilities of governments along with a corresponding redefinition of the rights, freedoms, and responsibilities of citizens in a democratic society. (1996, p. 6)

In its mission statement, IFG presents its analytical framework:

> [IFG] views current international trade and investment agreements, including the GATT, the WTO, Maastricht, and NAFTA, combined with the structural adjustment policies of the

International Monetary Fund and the World Bank, to be direct stimulants to the processes that weaken democracy, create a world order in the control of transnational corporations, and devastate the natural world. (1996, back cover)

Growing Intensification of Economic Stratification

United Nations data indicate that the worlds of rich and poor continue to be ever more polarized:

> Of the $23 trillion global Gross Domestic Product (GDP) in 1993, $18 trillion is in the industrial countries—only $5 trillion in the developing countries, even though they have nearly 80% of the world's people. The poorest 20% of the world's people saw their share of global income decline from 2.3% to 1.4% in the past 30 years. Meanwhile, the share of the richest 20% rose from 70% to 85%. That doubled the ratio of the shares of the richest and the poorest—from 30:1 to 61:1. The assets of the world's 358 billionaires exceed the combined annual incomes of countries with 45% of the world's people. (UNDP, 1996, p. 2)

The *State of the World: 1997* report describes worsening conditions of life for people who are poor:

> Those at the bottom of the economic heap have to contend with meager and unpredictable incomes despite long hours of backbreaking work, insufficient amounts of food and poor diets, lack of access to safe drinking water, susceptibility to preventable diseases, housing that provides few comforts and scant shelter, and the absence of social services that the better-off take for granted. Rich-poor disparities are about much more than just the lack of access to modern conveniences or the inability to accumulate material wealth: they are often a matter of life and death. (Brown et al., 1997, p. 121)

Downsizing and Economic Marginalization

Jeremy Rivkin, president of the Foundation of Economic Trends in Washington, D.C., has become known worldwide as the leading analyst on economic changes that threaten workers. His findings on economic realities that confront communities are relevant for social workers. The social implications of economic insecurity and deprivation are fundamental concerns of the profession. Drawing on economic data from government and corporate sources reported by policy institutes and by the media, Rifkin (1995) reports that millions of workers have been permanently eliminated from the economic process, and whole work categories have largely or totally disappeared. In the United States, *Fortune* magazine (Sept. 20, 1992) found that corporations are eliminating more than 2 million jobs annually. While some new jobs are being created in the U.S. economy, they are in the low-paying sectors and are usually temporary.

Global unemployment has now reached its highest level since the Great Depression of the 1930s. Worldwide, more than 800 million humans are now unemployed or underemployed. That figure is likely to rise sharply between now and the turn of the century. In all three basic sectors of economic activity and employment——agriculture, manufacturing, and services—machines are quickly replacing human labor, leading to predictions of a global economy of increasingly automated production by the mid decades of the 21st century (Rifkin, 1995, pp. 108–109). The social impact, says Rifkin, is brutal:

The death of the global labor force is being internalized by millions of workers who experience their own individual deaths, daily, at the hands of the profit-driven employers and a disinterested government. They are the ones who are waiting for pink slips, being forced to work part-time at reduced pay, or being pushed onto the welfare roles. With each new indignity, their confidence and self-esteem suffer another blow. They become expendable, then irrelevant, and finally invisible in the new high-tech world of global commerce and trade. (1995, p. 197)

The Environmental Impacts of Economic Globalization

The hazardous and toxic wastes that require expensive cleanup operations, left behind by past commercial ventures, continue to erode the quality of life for residents in communities in many regions of the world. The neglect and abuse of the natural environment in commercial production has a basis in the accounting systems used in economics and business accounting. Nature is viewed by the commercial world as a free, available, and inexhaustible resource and sink, from which valuable materials can be extracted by human labor, and into which wastes may be dumped, as if they were thereby eliminated without further consequences. Nature is valued only when it becomes property, a commodity that may be bought and sold. Human impact on nature is viewed as beneficial.

The gross domestic product (GDP), for example, supposedly measures the value of the goods and services produced in a nation. But the most valuable goods and services—the ones provided by nature, on which all else rests—are valued, measured, and protected poorly or not at all. For example, the profit from deforesting land is counted as a plus on a nation's ledger sheet, but the depletions of the timber stock, watershed, and fisheries are not subtracted. The costs of environmental degradation and lost ecosystem services are external to economic calculations: the damage from a massive oil spill is not subtracted from a nation's GDP, but the amounts spent on cleanup and health impacts are counted as additions to the national economy. By this reckoning, it is more profitable to consume a resource today than to save it for tomorrow. This form of accounting disregards the rights of future generations to life-support systems of the planet. Corporate and financial interests favor this exploitative system of accounting and often succeed in avoiding regulatory measures for environmental protection through their corruption of political processes. Economic globalization and technology are now opening up more remote regions, protected in the past by travel barriers, to environmentally abusive economic development.

Haunani-Kay Trask's reflections on environmental issues and sustainability are germane here and reflect the 1854 prophecy of Chief Seattle discussed in Chapter 3 (pp. 40–41):

To me, and to the other Native people who believe as I do, the fate of the earth rests in the fate of the Native people. Because of our genealogy, that is, our familial relationship to the cosmos, the wisdom of our creation is reciprocal obligation. If we husband our lands and waters, they will feed and care for us. In our language, the name for the relationship is malama 'aina; care for the land who will care for all family members in turn. This indigenous knowledge is not unique to Hawaiians, but is shared by most indigenous peoples throughout the world. . . . We are stewards of the earth, our mother, and we offer an ancient, umbilical wisdom about how to protect and ensure her life. This lesson of our cultures has never been more crucial to global survival. In recent years, there has been much talk among those who care about the environment regarding the need for "biodiversity." To put my case in technological terms, biodiversity is guaranteed through human diversity . . . more autonomy, more localized control of resources and the cultures they can maintain. Human diversity ensures biodiversity. The survival of the earth depends on it. (1995, p. 18).

Economies that treat natural resources as limitless degrade their own environments, upon which continuing productivity depends. The ironic fact is that governments in many countries continue to subsidize corporations to engage in activities that result in environmental degradation. For example, the U.S. and British Columbia governments, which manage public range lands, lease land to private firms for logging and grazing at roughly a third of private costs. On a large fraction of public land in the United States and Canada, hard rock mining is still essentially free. These are giveaways to corporations at public expense.

The degree to which corporate rights, established through international trade agreements, now supersede the rights of human communities is perhaps most apparent in the Trade Related Intellectual Property Rights (TRIPS) treaty, incorporated in the final Act of GATT. In *Biopiracy: The Plunder of Nature and Knowledge* (1994), Vandana Shiva exposes the plunder of indigenous peoples, and forest dwellers, in particular, by pharmaceutical corporations that are studying indigenous medicines, are granted patent rights for their manufacture, and thereby gain control over distribution and sources of the product, including land areas essential to indigenous survival.

The Social Impacts of Economic Inequality

In the field of social work, participants in the Violence and Development Project (1994–1997) of the National Association of Social Workers, U.S., learned that the growing incidence of violence in the world is symptomatic of human behavioral, reactive, and chronic responses to traumatization and human victimization produced by violence at these three levels of social organization:

1. *Interpersonal violence:* harmful acts against people or property, visible, easy to condemn, with immediate consequences; perpetrator (and motivations) and victim (and injuries) are easy to identify; considered a punishable crime.

2. *Institutional violence:* harmful actions within institutions that obstruct spontaneous unfolding of human potential; occurs in bureaucracies such as governmental agencies, businesses, prisons, mental institutions, welfare systems, schools, the military, often caused by policies considered necessary for profit or control; usually subtle, indirect, covert, seen as regrettable but not a crime and not important unless it happens to you and/or members of your group.

3. *Structural and cultural violence:* inflicted on populations through poverty, with living conditions that lack resources essential for healthy, productive growth and/or through the way society thinks, which reflects conventional values and everyday practices, customs, and norms; often sinister, difficult to discern; usually accepted as "normal," but destructive in its impact on human development.

The concepts of the Violence and Development Project of the National Association of Social Workers, described in Chapter 3, has relevance to the forms and levels of violence that are imbedded in processes and outcomes of economic globalization as well as in the processes and outcomes of the other abusive, exploitative systems. Research on trauma has shown that the experience of powerlessness and/or victimization, induced by violence on any one of these levels, is likely to set in motion renewed cycles of violence, leading to further violent incidents on any or all levels. With growing penetration by transnational corporations into local markets of vulnerable, less developed nations, economic marginalization and the violence of poverty become endemic.

The growing intensification of corporate control over local and global economic resources and political institutions is a prime example of structural and cultural violence, which already is setting into motion cycles of violence at other levels. Increases in incidence of health and mental health problems, and of social disintegration within families and communities, are anticipated results. As one example of negative consequences of the "free trade" economy, there are now a number of agricultural regions where the marginalization of peasant communities has led to dependency on drug production and drug trafficking for local survival. These situations are likely to multiply and to foster related increases in institutional and interpersonal forms of violence and abuse, based on growing drug involvement and the corruption inherent in the drug business, unless processes of healing and recovery take place on local and global levels that result in basic changes in a global system that is not only unsustainable, but toxic for humanity and planetary life systems.

The dominant model of economic development, which undervalues and fails to preserve the assets of nature, has fatal flaws that doom its operating system. Currently, production of commodities and competition for sales are increasing, while participation in the labor force is downsized and wages decline. Because product demand and sales depend on customer purchases, the extension of credit is promoted. Governments are pressured into services as buyers through government contracts. Governmental subsidies also help to support maximum corporate profitability. National and regional markets have been captured for corporate expansion, which is necessary for survival. But if firms are held liable for damage to environments or local communities they enter and leave in search of new markets and cheap labor, costs will mount and profits and stock prices will drop. These are the fears that now drive secret negotiations by the Organization for Economic Cooperation and Development, comprised of the 29 wealthiest nations, to gain fast-track approval of the Multilateral Agreement on Investments (MAI) and to erase national, regional, and local regulations that hold corporate investors accountable for environmental and social damage.

Alternative Paradigms of Economic Development

Early in the 20th century, conceptual frameworks in the field of physics underwent dramatic changes. Observing those historic changes, Thomas Kuhn began his studies of the paradigm as a set of concepts, values, techniques, and approaches shared by a scientific community and used by that community to define legitimate problems and solutions (Kuhn, 1962). Changes of paradigms, Kuhn concluded, occur in discontinuous, revolutionary breaks with past views and practices. He called these dramatic breaks with past concepts and practices *paradigm shifts*. Fritjof Capra, a theoretical physicist and researcher on ecological systems, defines a paradigm:

> A constellation of concepts, values, perceptions and practices shared by a community, which forms a particular vision of reality that is the basis of the way the community organizes itself. (1996, p. 6)

Two different paradigms now exist simultaneously in the field of economic development. The dominant paradigm stresses investors' rights to capital mobility for the maximization of profit to achieve rising levels of international trade. It is a system of winners and losers that is genocidal for individuals, communities, and cultures that are not competitive, acquisitive, or able to accumulate economic or political power. The other paradigm reflects life-nurturing goals of sustainable human development. The two different systems of thought, values, and action recall the work of archeological historian Riane Eisler, who concluded, after a broad survey of archeological findings, that from the early days of human settlement there have been two basic models of human society:

> The first, which I call the dominator model, is . . . the ranking of one half of humanity over the other. The second, in which social relations are primarily based on the principle of linking rather than ranking, may best be described as a partnership model. In this model beginning with the most fundamental difference in our species, between male and female—diversity is not equated with either inferiority or superiority. (1988, xvii)

The two models of society defined by Eisler may be applied to differentiate the two models of economic development that have occurred within human settlements. The partnership model has survived in many rural and remote areas of the world and still is the practice in some indigenous and cooperative communities. In this model, human labor is directly invested, without wages or individual profit, in production of goods and services consumed by the community. There is no private property, in terms of private ownership of land; natural resources are shared by all.

Eisler and others have noted that in the Bronze Age of the Neolithic period, between five to ten thousand years ago, humans discovered that metals, smelted and forged, could be used to construct lethal weapons. The age of armies, conquest, patriarchy, and the dominator model of society began with that discovery. Throughout the centuries that followed, over and over again the arts and sciences created innovations intended to enhance life and health that were captured and cynically exploited by groups holding power backed by the threat of force.

Today, it is financial institutions that have recolonized Africa, Asia, Latin America and even Eastern Europe, through the threat of economic strangulation. Economic globalization may be seen as a historic culmination of patterns of acquisition set in motion five to ten thousand years ago. Domination by transnational corporations of an increasingly class-stratified world economy, with the related exclusion of large sectors of the world's population from participation in socially useful construction, reflects a paradigm that degrades the natural environment and converts living human beings into disposable commodities.

Social work values of economic justice are incompatible with goals of that system. As described by Capra:

> The more we study the major problems of our time, the more we come to realize that they cannot be understood in isolation. They are systemic problems, which means that they are interconnected and interdependent. . . . There are solutions to the major problems of our time, some of them even simple. But they require a radical shift in our perceptions, our thinking, our values. And, indeed, we are now at the beginning of such a fundamental change of worldview in science and society, a change of paradigms as radical as the Copernican revolution. But this realization has not yet dawned on most of our political leaders. The recognition that a profound change of perception and thinking is needed if we are to survive has not yet reached most of our corporate leaders, either, or the administrators and professors of our large universities. (1996, pp. 3–4)

The importance of social work participation in partnerships with communities is endorsed by Capra's views on a need for systems change, initiated on a local level:

> Not only do our leaders fail to see how different problems are interrelated; they also refuse to recognize how their so-called solutions affect future generations. From the systemic point of view, the only viable solutions are those that are "sustainable." The concept of sustainability has become a key concept in the ecology movement and is indeed crucial. . . . This, in a nutshell, is the great challenge of our time: to create sustainable communities, that is to say, social and cultural environments in which we can satisfy our needs and aspirations without diminishing the chances of future generations. (1996, p. 4)

FOUNDING OF AN INTERNATIONAL MOVEMENT VERSUS "FREE TRADE"

The existence of an international movement of organized opposition to the assumptions, motives, and outcomes of the "free trade" system of economic globalization has been established through international forums and electronic communication. The first international gathering to oppose free trade policies at home and abroad was held in 1996 in Chiapas, Mexico. This event, titled "El Primer Encuentro contra el Neoliberalismo y por la Humanidad," was attended by about 3000 delegates from a variety of countries. A second gathering was held in Spain in July 1997; further sessions are planned to coincide with meetings of the World Trade Organization. In May 1998, those meetings will be held in Geneva, Switzerland. This movement brings together indigenous leaders, including representatives of the Zapatista organization that served as hosts for the initial event, with economists and community activists from Europe, North America, and Asia.

Members of this growing movement tend to be well educated, adept at critical thinking, and committed to sustainable human development in the coming millennium. Many persons who affiliate with activist groups with these perspectives are well versed in Internet telecommunications. A list of current, relevant websites is an asset that confers status among movement activists. Networking for exchange of communication is intense in both local and global circles. A prime example of the effectiveness of electronic networking in action was evident prior to, during, and after the Fourth World Conference on Women, Beijing, China, August–September 1995. Official themes of that historic United Nations Conference were "Equality, Development, and Peace." Forum '95 participants, as representatives of nongovernmental organizations (NGOs), lobbied for approval by the United Nations General Assembly of a strong, united Platform of Action, a policy document in which governments made commitments to address areas of concern that impede the advancement of women worldwide. Both Forum participants and Conference delegates demanded that local, regional, and national economic projects must include investment in human resources, with support for community child care, education, health services, job training, public works, and participation in project governance by women, who will be accountable to ensure that a share of project revenues will benefit local community services.

Goals of the campaign against free trade are to move the point of production from global to local:

1. To regain, for democratic civilian forces, sufficient regulatory power over transnational corporations so they may be held legally accountable to communities for the protection of health, safety, and the environment, and for direct benefit to community residents through employment and/or services.

2. To develop alternative economic ventures at the local and regional level, so that human needs can be met through direct investment of human labor, sometimes defined as "sweat equity," without recourse to money credit from corporate or outside financial institutions.

3. To stimulate agricultural and commercial production in a community, with distribution to local markets, in order to maximize employment in the community and to maximize local economic self-reliance in food production, child care and senior care, health and social services, education, housing, waste management, job training, and other enterprises.

ALTERNATIVE ECONOMIES: COMMUNITY-BASED STRATEGIES AND ACTIONS

Growing numbers of nongovernmental organizations (NGOs) are engaged locally and globally in specific projects to heal the wounds of traumatized populations or groups in conflict through programs for social integration and economic justice. At the local level, community programs that expand opportunities for people who have been excluded from the labor force are healing to members of marginalized and oppressed groups. On a global level, some of the wounds of past inequities are healed when North-South partnerships are established, and the two partners each invest their own uniquely distinct resources to produce shared experiences of mutual benefit.

Democratic Structures Essential for Community Self-Help and Healing

Common features of programs that are empowering for people emphasize mutual self-help and shared participation in decision-making circles. When decisions are made, it is essential that as many representatives and members of community teams as possible have a place at the table. Open and participatory meetings build networks and egalitarian social structure. Exclusion is a form of violence that disempowers and discounts the humanity and worth of individuals and groups. Projects that aim to promote human development are challenged to be self-disciplined in democratic practices, in order to prevent unintended reproduction of past hierarchical social structures. Many movements for social change have defeated their own purposes by establishing a central council that became a new elite through its role and power in decision-making processes.

Social workers are adept at mediation, conflict resolution, community organization, networking, and coalition building. To achieve goals of economic justice, to confront and deconstruct the current system of corporate domination of the world's economy, those are vitally needed skills. Community organization and coalition building are foremost, because until people organize to demand fair compensation, the social, health, and environmental consequences of corporate practices remain invisible and the costs are borne by victimized workers and communities.

Projects of community self-development, initiated by local cultural groups in many regions, are transformational. The social network paradigm, initially a concept, becomes a reality through the construction of alternative economies. Wherever people establish community cooperatives, or replant the forests, or invest their own time, energy, and resources in housing the homeless and feeding the hungry, not for others but for their own joy in sharing (sometimes risking arrest to do so), a life-nurturing system is operating. Examples of local and global solidarity negate the key maxim of the dominant paradigm, which defines "human nature" as a drive for personal gain. There are alternatives to the lean, mean, money-mad society that is advertised in the media and both promoted and celebrated by the global oligarchs of the World Trade Organization. Renewal of spiritual visions of indigenous cultures and of women are vital for preservation of the earth's natural environment and for human health. Vandana Shiva identifies points of connection:

> People, their environment and their society are not separable by rigid and insular boundaries. The boundaries between them are porous and flexible, allowing interchange and influence. The unity here . . . rests on the continuity of life in its interconnectedness; there are subtle and complex connections between diseases of the human body, the decay of ecosystems and the breakdown of civil society, just as there are connections in the search for health at all these levels. . . . The separation between production and reproduction, between innovation and regeneration, has been institutionalised to deny women and nature a productive role in the economic calculus. . . . conservation must happen in the factory or in the city if total destruction is to be avoided. (1994, pp. 3–5)

Promoting the regeneration of nature as a goal for humanity does not imply a wish to return to a world without technology as we approach the advent of the 21st century. The dialectical nature of social reality is full of surprises. Among the ironies of history is that networks of grassroots women's groups and indigenous peoples have discovered that several powerful tools that were formerly produced to achieve conquest of land and labor may now be used to construct a more caring world. Electronic communications, including the Internet and World Wide Web, which were produced initially for military surveillance and which continue to serve as means to control populations, have now also become tools for liberation. People are using the Internet as a tool to send out messages of protest which are being heard around the world, and to organize. It is a tool that, despite its original purpose, is ideally suited for networking by activists.

Because goals of transformation make access urgent, nonelite working people and youth may be empowered by world sources of liberating information. The new millennium has been designated both as the Post-Industrial Age and as the Information Age. "Information resources, which by nature are non-depleting, should be freely shared" (Korten, 1990, p. 176). Class stratification may be extinguished when access is universally available to all children on earth and all can write and share their own views of reality.

STUDENT ACTIVITIES

1. For class discussion and/or essay: expected length 5–6 pages, typewritten, double spaced: Read the following statement by Vivienne Wee and Noelynn Heyzer in *Gender, Poverty and Sustainable Development* (Singapore: Engender). Then answer the questions that follow. These authors note:

Women have become steadily poorer in the context of an increasingly merciless struggle for scarce resources and a denser concentration of wealth at the top of a steep pyramid. In the global estate, women are the workers and the landless squatters. They produce half the world's food, yet constitute 70 percent of the world's 1.3 billion absolute poor. Women work two-thirds of the world's working hours, but own less than 1 percent of the world's property. (1995, p. 36)

a. Why has this happened? Why do women work the hardest and end up as the poorest? Why has women's work—vital as it is—not generated wealth for them?

Prior to formulating their analysis of reasons, Wee and Heyzer examined outcomes of free trade economics and corporate policy perspectives that have been imposed by international financial institutions such as the World Bank and the International Monetary Fund on poor nations needing credit. These policies are similar to those reflected in recent revisions in U.S. social welfare legislation.

Free trade policies call for production for export, with reduction in prices and wages, often also currency devaluation, no restrictions on investors, plus severe cuts in public subsidies for food, education, health care, housing and transport. According to United Nations data, examined by these authors, these policies are resulting in increasing global economic stratification. They conclude that inequality, which in reality is created by historic and legal sanctions which assign property rights, is rationalized by the false assumption that free trade is fair trade:

> . . . the underlying assumption is that without state intervention, a profit-driven market, by itself, can and will supply all needs. Therefore, structural adjustments are put in place to reduce the role of the state and to expand the role of the market. (*Peggy Antrobus at UNIFEM panel, New York, January 16, 1995)

The market is not a level playing field. As noted by Antrobus (1995): "because the market only responds to those who have the capacity to participate in it, it cannot, then, respond to the poor." This is true for individuals, families, communities and countries. Poor people and poor countries end up having to sell all they have. . . . For many poor countries, a chain of consequences is thus set up: (p. 55)

Market driven policies lead to these consequences, according to Wee & Heyzer [p. 56]:

Pressure to generate a monetary income to repay debts and to survive in a market-
dominated economy
↓
Structural adjustments
to cut all activities which do not directly generate income
↓
Marketing of existing resources
the export of natural resources and the supply of labour,
usually at the lowest and most competitive cost
↓
Environmental degradation,
resource depletion, and the destruction of the resource base
of local communities
↓
Widespread impoverishment,
rural-urbanization and international labour migration

In your essay address the questions in Item *a* earlier and the additional questions *b–e* that follow.

b. Based on concepts presented in the chapter, summarize the changing conditions of life for families, communities, and nations around the world as a result of economic globalization, which has led to more concentrated economic wealth and power controlled by transnational corporations and international financial institutions, more violence, poverty, desperation, and global migration.

c. In what ways do your observations on the state of the world reflect an analysis of class stratification that has been presented in this chapter? What sectors of U.S. society do you consider are concerned about social stratification? What might those sectors do to address their concerns?

d. Do you observe contradictions between ethical, religious and spiritual values expressed by prominent sectors of U.S. society and the impact of their acts on vulnerable groups? Cite historical examples when there have been very obvious gaps between words and deeds.

e. What populations may be likely to lose their access to land or other resources as a result of these global changes? How can groups with limited resources make themselves and their issues seen and heard? How can poor groups obtain resources needed for survival and solution of community or global problems? What kind of social changes might reverse current destructive trends, in the direction of sustainable development for human and ecological life systems?

2. Read the following case history and discuss as a group.

CASE STUDY 9.1

Participation in International Social Work for Professional and Personal Growth

For social workers and other persons concerned about social and economic justice, participation in international contacts and exchanges with colleagues in other countries is likely to be a transformational experience, in that it results in a shift in identity and world view. Through a change in the identity of humans, political change in social systems becomes a possibility that may be realized through subsequent united action.

The self-concept and identity of humans are molded by the social context in which people live and perceive themselves to be centered. When dimensions of the context expand or contract, the sense of self may be expanded or diminished. If the center of existence shifts to a different social context in which cultural norms in terms of values, attitudes, and behaviors are different, while identity diffusion and conflict sometimes may occur, there is likely to be active learning about different world views, with rapid growth in awareness of alternative perspectives and more respect for other cultures. Sense of self and estimation of human potentiality expand with expanding horizons.

International experience, when there is person-to-person contact with individuals and groups in other nations, tends to brings a shift in identity, from one focused on national citizenship to that of participant in a global circle of humanity. Scientists, mental health practitioners, and universalist religions teach that children are born with a sense of cosmic and universal connection but are socialized into ethnocentric attitudes by institutions of the state and/or dominant culture. Contact with other cultures makes alternative visions and world views visible. Thought and consciousness are expanded in scope, with a larger mental picture of self in time and space and a vision of the planet as home.

This case study is based on an event and its outcomes. The event, an international gathering of social workers, was the "Human Rights Symposium on Violence Against Women," presented by IASSW, the International Association of Schools of Social Work, at NGO Forum '95, the forum of nongovernmental organizations (NGOs) that was an integral part, along with United Nations sessions, of the Fourth World Conference on Women, in Beijing and Huairou, China. The symposium date was September 2, 1995. The organizer and coordinator of the IASSW Human Rights Symposium, Dr. Janice Wood Wetzel, School of Social Work, Adelphi University, Long Island, New York, opened the session. Dr. Wetzel observed that violence against women within families and communities reflects and reproduces patterns of dominance and subordination, of abuse and victimization, that exist within economic, political and cultural structures. Her message, that "women are the hope of the world," was memorable and empowering.

Panel presentations by social work members of faculty, experts on violence against women in their own national settings, followed. Naveenchandran Bhat, from India, spoke about incidents of wife battering and burning in India. Divna Lakinska-Popovska, of Macedonia, focused on social outcomes of historic periods of political disruption; such as the plight of refugees, who are especially vulnerable to rape, and on social services as a critical need for the elderly. Karen Ling of Hong Kong spoke of the needs of mentally handicapped persons for protection, to prevent overwhelming stress.

These presentations, which documented local concerns about worldwide problems of violence and injustice, became the stimulus for small group workshops that discussed strategies for social action by social workers, in alliance with women's coalitions. Designated participants from small group workshops on these topics reported back to a final plenary on group responses to the symposium introduction, panel presentations, and strategies for action in the following areas:

- prevention/global
- intervention/micro
- refugees/displaced women
- poverty
- women who kill their batterers
- social action/social change
- research/teaching

In small group workshops that included social workers of different national origin, participants from all regions of the world reported that international financial agencies and local businesses have been pressuring governments to cut back on social spending. It was evident to conference participants that governmental priorities in most nations are being set by the business and banking sectors of global and national economies at the expense of women, their families and communities, and the natural environment. Production for export is being promoted, even when that results in loss of land and jobs by other local sectors. Positions for full-time workers with benefits are being replaced by jobs for part-time and temporary employees. Communities with environmental and health and safety regulations or requirements that companies pay local taxes and provide benefits for community residents are losing, in the competition to attract investment, to communities that offer investors subsidies, tax incentives, and tax breaks. Global consolidation of markets is intensifying competition among peoples, thereby adding to existing cycles of violence against women, children, and families.

Symposium participants adopted a resolution and carried it home to educate and to collect signatures among social workers as one of the strategies to achieve social and economic justice through participation in an international social action coalition.

IASSW HUMAN RIGHTS SYMPOSIUM ON VIOLENCE AGAINST WOMEN

Resolution

We submit the following resolution for adoption by this Symposium of the International Association of Schools of Social Work, and by NGO Forum '95:

Whereas the policies and projects of the World Bank and The International Monetary Fund, like those of governments dominated by monied interests that promote free trade agreements and monetarist policies, continue to expand the gap between rich and poor, and to largely benefit consulting, engineering, corporate and financial firms in the industrialized countries; and whereas the World Bank projects displace indigenous populations, evict rural people from their land, thereby swelling the problems of overcrowded cities, while abandoning commitments to human needs in those urban centers, and whereas those projects and policies damage ecological systems which support biodiversity and also fail to maintain a healthy environment for human life and human reproduction; and whereas the IMF and World Bank's economic programs for nations, the so-called Structural Adjustment Programs (SAPs), as well as other monetarist fiscal policies, mandate cuts in government spending that often lead to cuts in social services such as health and education and restricted credit for small producers, with especially impoverishing consequences for women and their children, but they have not mandated cuts in expenditures for armaments or military budgets;

We therefore propose that the Non-Governmental Organizations of women at the NGO Forum of the 1995 United Nations World Conference of Women in Beijing, China, through consensus or by majority vote, join the "Fifty Years Is Enough!" campaign, to pressure the United Nations and its member nations to require fundamental change in the policies and practices of the World Bank and International Monetary Fund, and in related policies and practices by other national and international institutions, in behalf of health, safety, dignity and opportunity for the world's women and their children.

Models of Field Practice in Global Settings

KAREN LYONS
CHATHAPURAM S. RAMANATHAN

What is necessary is to create cultural distance from the student's own experiences so that values and attitudes that have worked before are no longer adequate.

—D. R. GARLAND AND D. ESCOBAR (1988)

Field internships or practice placements have long been recognized as an essential part of social work education, and they are also a universal feature of training programs globally (UN, 1964; Doel & Shardlow, 1996). Despite the early establishment of international networks of social workers (Cannan, Berry, & Lyons, 1992; Hokenstad, Khinduka, & Midgley, 1992), the assumption has been that social work is an essentially local activity for which practice in agencies near the school of social work, or at least in the same state or country are appropriate. The past two decades however, have witnessed an increasing awareness of the relevance of globalization (Axford, 1995), including to the welfare sector. There is a growing body of literature about comparative policies and professional activities as well as the rationale for, and development of, social work educational initiatives that support a global perspective (Healy, 1986; Harris, 1990; Estes, 1992). Today's global economy has accelerated this development (Hokenstad, Khinduka, & Midgley, 1992; Ramanathan, 1991). Within the field of social work there has also been a recognition of the dangers (and legacy) of professional imperialism and the need to recognize and address diversity within and between societies (Midgley, 1991; Rossiter, 1996).

Historically, exchanges between social workers from industrial and developing nations were characterized by a unidirectional flow of methodologies and practice technologies from the West to other nations. Social workers have much to learn from professionals in the Global South, who have developed and implemented innovative strategies for common problems and who struggle with social issues that have a global basis (Midgley, 1991). Assumptions about the practice component of social work education have also been challenged; common goals and issues have been identified; and experience has been gained through international

Former gang members sandbagging in the Hollywood Hills—a service conservation project in Los Angeles

field placements (Rogers, 1995; Horncastle, 1996). The profession's educational practices, however, have lagged behind those of the profession itself; the number of U.S. social work students studying abroad, for example, is relatively small (Healy, 1991). Consequently, international study programs in social work tend to be seen as a marginal adjunct to the regular curriculum, a personal enrichment opportunity (Ramanathan & Kondrat, 1994).

WHY GO ABROAD? A RATIONALE FOR INTERNATIONAL PLACEMENTS

Although individual motivations vary, several scholars have identified a number of reasons for participating in international networks through exchange programs and overseas practicum (Cannan et al., 1990; Coleman, 1996; Hayes et al., 1996; Ramanathan & Kondrat, 1994). For instance, the social work profession has long advocated that students learn about cultures other than their own (Sanders, 1977). Such learning about different cultures is wrongly assumed to define cross-cultural learning. On the contrary, cross-cultural learning lets students transcend some of their original cultural conditioning to view human life and its many possibilities more objectively and sensitively (Ramanathan & Kondrat, 1994).

Classroom experience oriented to cross-cultural issues is not enough to prepare students for cross-cultural practice. Rather, "what is necessary is to create cultural distance from the student's own experiences so that values and attitudes that have worked before are no longer adequate" (Garland & Escobar, 1988). Since the professional orientation of the practicum supervisor has a critical role in the socialization of students (Kadushin, 1991), the practicum supervisor's exposure to and experience of international perspectives may be useful. Therefore, overseas study as a continuing education opportunity may be beneficial to practitioners. A recent study conducted in the United States revealed that even though the majority of respondents had limited exposure to international experiences and reported little awareness of how global issues impact domestic practice, the majority of respondents reported a moderate to strong interest in attending continuing education that focused on international perspectives (Kondrat & Ramanathan, 1996).

For a variety of reasons, population mobility has always been a feature of human activity, and recent population movements require most social workers to have some appreciation of a range of cultures and cross-national influences (Bali, 1997). At a structural level, an appreciation of the interconnectedness of geopolitical, social, and economic policies can be heightened by exposure to other systems and other ways of thinking about welfare and social development. At a professional level, a placement abroad offers very real opportunities to experience alternative approaches to the provision of care and the organization and tasks of social workers. At a personal level, experience elsewhere may increase social workers' capacity to think more creatively about the social work task and to empathize with a diverse range of people in varied situations, whether subsequently practicing at home or abroad (Ramanathan & Kondrat, 1994).

It is very likely that students exposed to other systems will think critically about what they see, both in their home country and the country they visit, and that future practice can be informed by this experience. For example, in a recent overseas program in India, one of the authors and a group of overseas study students had the opportunity to meet for about half a day with social workers and paraprofessionals from a women's grassroots project. After the initial focus on cultural uniqueness and common issues such as feminization of poverty, the discussion focused on related concerns as a result of discrimination caused by gender/caste/color and gender/class/color, respectively. Students carried on a spirited dialogue and exchange with the women from the project, and the learning that resulted included a recognition of similarities and differences in the two cultural situations as well as a more complete appreciation for comparable experiences in each home culture. Students also reflected on the wider applicability of what they had learned as it pertained to empowerment strategies used within the program. This experience was supplemented by a series of lectures on poverty alleviation programs in India, with a special emphasis on programs to alter the status of women (Ramanathan & Kondrat, 1994).

Thus, there is a rationale for social work educators to structure courses in ways that require or enable all or some students to experience placement abroad (Cetingok & Hirayama, 1990). Three fundamental questions relate to the nature of such placements and the rationale for particular types of courses and opportunities:

1. Is the goal of the placement for students to learn more about social work and welfare in a country other than their own (and if so, why that particular country)?

2. Is the placement abroad required to enable comparative research or study of policy and practice?

3. Is the placement intended to be located in an organization engaged in cross-national activities?

These questions relate to how we understand international social work (Hokenstad, Khinduka, & Midgley, 1992), and their answers determine in part the opportunities that might be available and the learning goals which might be appropriate.

At a micro level, the rationale for individual placements will vary according to how programs are structured and the stated purpose of the period abroad, which we will consider further. The motivation of individual students is likely to be influenced both by intellectual curiosity and by more or less overt personal goals. Many, while abroad or on their return, have remarked on the value of the experience at the level of personal development as well as of professional stimulus (Hayes & Jeudi, 1996). Therefore, the personal as well as the professional goals of students need to be explored and established as part of the planning process, and they should be similarly reflected in the assessment and evaluation of the experience.

· ·

SOME MODELS OF INSTITUTIONAL ARRANGEMENTS

Few students can undertake placements abroad without some form of encouragement from educators in schools of social work or, more unusually, field supervisors or agency contacts. In most cases, students wishing to undertake internships or practicum opportunities elsewhere enter programs that promote such opportunities. A range of models have been developed to formalize arrangements.

Periodically, such arrangements are shaped by the policy and funding decisions of international or regional bodies whose goal is to promote internationalization or arrangements between particular countries or continents. A recent influential example is the ERASMUS scheme, initiated by the European Union in 1987 and in operation for a decade (Barr, 1990; Harris & Levan, 1992; Coleman, 1996; Hayes & Jeudi, 1996). The ERASMUS scheme was part of a wider policy of Europeanization at social as well as economic levels, including development of a European consciousness and identity. Funding for curriculum development, staff exchange and multi-lateral seminars, and student mobility is promoted through placements of three months to a year with partner institutions in other EU states (Cannan, Coleman, & Lyons, 1990). In the case of social work this included the opportunity to undertake practice placements, although the period could include college based study and/or project work, as well or instead (Davis, 1995; Horncastle & Brobeck, 1995). National evaluations of the impact of the program, carried out in 1996, identified some imbalance in the flow of students between different countries, but overall the principle of reciprocity operated.

A similar scheme, TEMPUS, has been in operation since the late 1980s to fund arrangements between European Union and former Soviet Union (FSU) countries, although student mobility has been less of a feature of this program. Likewise, U.S. State Department funds were available to organizations involved in social development initiatives to assist Russia in its effort to strengthen social institutes, such as universities, research centers and social service organizations, in a post–Soviet Union era. It is also receiving noticeably less encouragement under the aims and funding arrangements of the SOCRATES scheme, which replaced ERASMUS from Autumn 1997, with a significant diminution in funding and organization on an institutional rather than subject area basis. New arrangements place more responsibility on universities to set up institutional contracts and to establish how funding received should be allocated between subject areas. The social professions are one of about sixteen subject areas to receive funding for operation of a thematic network, but this program does not include any specific provision for student mobility.

A model developed within the European Union has been the establishment of formal networks linking schools of social work and allied professions since the boundaries between occupational groups, job titles and related education and training patterns vary considerably between different European states (Lorenz, 1986; Lorenz, 1994). Within such networks, student mobility has been an explicit and significant activity, with some expectation of a balance between incoming and outgoing students but also some flexibility about student destinations within the network. Thus, within large networks a principle of multi-lateral reciprocity has operated.

There are also examples of variations on this model which have grown out of the ERASMUS scheme. For instance, faculty in two institutions have worked together to design and operate a shared program in which students spend part of their final year of an undergraduate program in the UK and part in Denmark (Horncastle, 1994). Students from other schools in the network can join the program, which includes a practice placement outside the student's own country. A strong comparative dimension is a requirement of some of the assignments.

In another example, a postgraduate course leading to a British qualification is offered in a Dutch school (see Chapter 6). Teaching is arranged in blocks and carried out by a staff team drawn from the participating institutions. The course is open to any student (including from outside the network) who has already completed social work (or equivalent) training, and project work for a master's dissertation can be undertaken in a number of countries, supervised by staff from institutions in the network.

Similarly, U.S. students interested in studying in India or Pakistan may be able to access funding through the American Institute of Indian Studies (AIIS) or the American Institute of Pakistani Studies. There are private U.S. foundations that support both undergraduate and graduate education; students are also able to obtain student loans to undertake overseas study. Like other professionals in the United States, social work practitioners are able to deduct expenses associated with overseas study for continuing education from their federal tax returns as professional advancement expenses.

A more common model assumes the development of bilateral relationships and contracts between individual schools in different countries, although many schools have more than one such arrangement in operation. The advantages of such a model are the continuity and knowledge about each other's conditions and expectations that can be built up, although ensuring a balanced flow of students seeking field practice opportunities under the aegis of partner institutions can be difficult. Although many American universities are promoting institutional linkage arrangements with several overseas universities in various disciplines, only a handful of such linkages exist for social work. Therefore, institutional linkages need to be vigorously pursued, which means that funds have to be earmarked to facilitate this partnership.

An alternative model presumes no availability of funding; provides a framework through the structure of the educational program and assessment offered in one institution; and sees responsibility for arranging placements as an aspect of the students' professional development. An example of this model, based on the principles of adult learning and serial reciprocity, has been developed in a U.K. university, where a one-year program is offered to students who have already completed a professional qualification. Students negotiate placements in a country of their own choosing, with supporting letters from the university as needed. The emphasis is on individual project work that is negotiated before departure and assessed on return, thus placing no formal requirements on colleagues abroad. However, the majority of students (now about 20 a year) undertake voluntary work part time in an agency and have much appreciated spontaneous opportunities for informal learning and support (Lyons, 1996).

At the most informal end of the spectrum, faculty members from schools without international programs sometimes contact colleagues abroad with requests to assist individual students who wish to undertake placements outside their own country. Such requests might be met, but students may lack the infrastructure, either in the home or receiving institution, for preparatory and debriefing periods or even a student cohort with whom to process the experience. They may also find themselves as solitary international students in courses or agencies. The potential disadvantage to students in such situations has been noted by Clarkson (1990) and by Cetingok and Hirayama (1990).

PRACTICUM STRUCTURES

The structure of field practicum varies for both undergraduate and graduate social work students. This variation occurs both for field placement within national boundaries and for overseas placements. The models used include concurrent and block field placement. In the concurrent model, students are simultaneously enrolled in classroom instruction and field practicum courses. In the block field placement, students are simultaneously enrolled in both field seminars and practicum courses, but are not enrolled in any theory classes.

Given the curricular variations among the many social work programs, these variations are also reflected in the area of overseas field placements. Some programs offer overseas placements as an enrichment opportunity, others offer it as an elective, and a few offer it as an integral part of the required content. There are also variations in offering the practicum as a concurrent opportunity or as a block placement. If it is offered as a concurrent placement, then the program administrators and the student will need to assess the number of classroom-based courses the student needs to enroll in. The similarity and difference between the cultures of the home country and the host country need to be used as a yardstick to determine the optimal courseload as well.

For overseas field placement, schools could use a delayed model, in which the first week to ten days after reaching the host country can be used as an opportunity for students to be involved in an on-campus practicum. Curricular content for an on-campus practicum could include basic social work interviewing skills, which include a consideration of the host country's cultural uniqueness. Attention also needs to be paid to safety issues that pertain to expected student behavior while they are studying overseas.

For block placement, in contrast, a practice seminar is usually offered simultaneously. This course usually complements the field experiences and provides an opportunity for students to process their field placement experiences. Thus, the course can be used as an additional opportunity to provide group supervision. Group supervision is not a substitute for individual supervision, however. Further, the mutual consulting activities the instructors engage in with the practicum instructors as they visit all the agencies in which the overseas students are placed must continue.

When to Go?

Debates about the timing (and length) of placements abroad are as varied as those about local internships (Rogers, 1996). While it can be assumed that a degree of maturity, resourcefulness, and resilience are required of students venturing abroad, there is no magic age at which these traits develop—nor are they innately different from the qualities expected of all intending social workers. Thus, decisions about timing relate to the structure of programs and the motivation and personal circumstances of individual students.

In the examples given here, opportunities for placements abroad were provided in the final year of undergraduate degrees or at postgraduate levels. The ERASMUS scheme mentioned earlier specifically excluded students in their first year of higher education. It would seem reasonable that students have first undertaken study and placements in their own country through which they can demonstrate some capacity for critical understanding of the policy context and cultural determinants of the local welfare system and appropriate behavior in a professional setting (Cetingok & Hirayama, 1990).

Where placements abroad are scheduled for undergraduates in the second or third year of courses, some early indication of opportunities enable students to begin thinking about the possibilities and to undertake language classes or other forms of preparation. Where international placements are not a universal feature of the program, issues about selection arise—and about the inclusion of international perspectives for those students remaining at the home institution. Timing within the academic year is also a matter for consideration. Whether students should be away in the first or second half of a year might be partly related to the anticipated input of a host institution, including assessment arrangements, if formal exchange programs operate. Where no contractual arrangements exist, a middle period away allows time for preparatory work with a group of students and for a debriefing and assessment period on their return to the home institution.

Questions also arise about whether students should be in field practice full time while away or whether there should be provision for private study time or attendance at local courses. There are also debates about the appropriate length of such placements, which have generally been designed to coincide with the terms or semesters into which the academic year is divided. Where formal exchange arrangements operate, this may be a focus for negotiation because of the different scheduling of academic calendars, including whether the academic year starts in September or January and the timing and length of vacation periods. The ERASMUS ruling of a minimum period of twelve weeks away in order to qualify for funding has provided a useful baseline, but length of time away is partly related to the purpose and anticipated outcomes of international placements. It is possible to carry out observational placements over a shorter period, and it is certainly necessary to designate much shorter time periods for intensive study visits.

When students are expected to undertake direct work related to practice or research, three months seems to be a viable minimum. Even this short period assumes that students have done some preparatory work and can orientate themselves quickly and engage in tasks in a focused manner. For some purposes, a period of four or five months might be better. However, longer placements also involve students in greater expenditure, with perhaps additional costs if they have family or other commitments back home. An alternative model suggests a year-long placement abroad, where a student might undertake paid part-time work, but many countries have strict rules on such matters and no assumptions can be made about the availability of paid work.

It might be assumed that international placements are only possible for students who are young and single, but experience and some of the literature suggest that such placements can be open to students whose age, experience, and personal circumstances vary considerably (Cetingok & Hirayama, 1990; Moss & Stockman, 1997). As the case studies later illustrate, students have shown initiative and persistence in their placement programs—sometimes aided by personal circumstances, sometimes overcoming apparent obstacles.

Where to Go: Destination Decisions and Implications

As the discussion so far has indicated, decisions about destination are sometimes prescribed by existing institutional arrangements. Arrangements based on a limited number of destinations and on receiving students from the same institutions enables preparatory teaching to be focused; information packs to be assembled; meetings between incoming students and intending outgoing students; relevant language classes to be scheduled; and establishment of other devices to enhance the advantages of this approach. These might include staff exchanges, meetings, and perhaps joint research.

Other approaches assume a greater element of student choice and risk taking. This may be apparent in the choice of an additional program, such as one of the ones described earlier, which requires the student to spend a given period in another country of his or her choice. When students have a choice of destination, a number of factors need consideration. These range from very practical issues to ones concerned with learning goals and more subtle personal motivations, and they can be addressed through a series of questions. Will the student need to work in a language other than their own, and if so, how proficient are they or what support is available? Will accommodation and other living costs be similar to those in the home country or substantially more or less, and are travel costs high or low? Will students be visiting a country about which they already have some general knowledge, perhaps through holidays or family connections, or one completely strange to them? Do their age, race, gender, or other characteristics potentially place them at an advantage or a disadvantage in the intended destination? How realistic are student work plans relative to the likely type of welfare system, social services, and community development activities? Does the student have a particular personal agenda to be addressed in the choice of destination—pursuing a relationship, family reconciliation, or perhaps discovering roots—and how will the placement fare if things do not work out? What expectations are there about local support or continuing conflict with the home institution, and, if the latter, is communication with the home institution by telephone, fax, or e-mail likely to be available?

English speakers have sometimes assumed particular responsibilities in networks, but they have also been challenged if they disregard the tiring and sometimes disempowering effects on colleagues of working in a second (or third) language. While the wish to develop second-language skills in a professional context may be a reason for some students to choose a particular destination, others clearly relate their choice to an ability to operate in their own language, even though this language may show obvious and subtle variations in usage in another country. Others knowingly venture into placements without good knowledge of the national language and can both develop skills—for instance, in nonverbal communication and working through interpreters—and also experience something of the frustration and powerlessness of people who do not share the mother tongue of a majority population.

The prevalence of English as the dominant medium in much professional literature and information technology use suggests certain advantages for English-speaking students, but the dangers of cultural or professional imperialism have already been mentioned and must be consciously addressed, particularly by all English speakers. Similarly, students who have ready access to material resources, including technology, may be at a relative advantage both in seeking placements and in operating in many countries—or may be confronted by unfamiliar difficulties in others. Anticipating such communication constraints might suggest the need both to agree on only exceptional communication with the home institution and to establish more local advice and support networks.

Finally, the opportunity for students who belong to a dominant majority group in their home country to undertake placements where they find themselves part of a minority (for example, for reasons of skin color or language) may afford experiential learning about subtle or more overt forms of curiosity or discrimination toward someone perceived as different. Other students may choose to explore briefly, and from a different perspective, the modern reality of a country from which their parents or grandparents emigrated. However, assumptions that sharing a common ancestry will ensure a welcome by indigenous communities do not always apply, and students need to be prepared for the mixed reactions of those who stayed. The position of being an outsider, under whatever circumstances, can be an enabling experience but can also impact negatively on opportunities for professional development, and is itself part of the learning process.

Study Abroad Liability

The number of American students studying abroad has almost doubled between 1985 and 1995, from 48,483 to 84,403. Of this number, over two-thirds study in countries in the Global North. In the academic year 1997-98, over 100,000 college students are planning to study abroad. Because of incidents of illness and sometimes even death, lawyers are filing lawsuits in state and federal courts to determine who is responsible for taking care of students thousands of miles away from home. Thus, study abroad liability is becoming an important factor both for program developers (i.e., universities) and program participants (i.e., the students) (Buckley, 1997).

Students considering studying abroad should obtain basic information before they enroll in an overseas study program. For example, they should:

1. Ascertain details on crime and accident rates in the intended destination.

2. Find out which staff member on site is responsible for safety, health, and security, and how are emergencies handled.

3. Arrange personal insurance coverage and clarify the program's position on professional indemnity.

In the case of U.S. students, it is possible to invest in a student ID card issued by the Council on International Education Exchange. The $20 charge identifies the bearer as a student and entitles him/her to health and accident insurance of $25,000 toward medical evaluation, inclusive of being transported to treatment elsewhere, and $7,500 toward repatriation of remains in case of death.

PREPARATORY WORK AND PLANNING

Some of the foregoing points suggest that a number of practical and psychological tasks should be undertaken in preparation for placements abroad. Whether a decision about a destination precedes or follows consideration of the placement's purpose and focus varies according to the arrangements and norms of different courses, as does the extent to which preparation is an individual and private matter or a group activity. Language classes or workshops to develop skills in using e-mail and the Internet may be necessary or optional components of courses allowing or requiring placements abroad.

A number of the practical tasks are familiar to anyone used to traveling, irrespective of the purpose. They can be illustrated again by answering a number of questions.

- How far in advance do travel plans need to be made, and are any group bookings or other discounts available?

- How much money will be needed for travel and for expenses while away (and in the case of the latter, in what form—local currency? traveler's checks?) What travel documents are needed—passport? visa? international driving license? certificate of vaccination?

- What health precautions are advised or individually required, and what is the time scale for any necessary vaccinations and medication? To what extent will health facilities and prescription drugs be available, or are any medical supplies needed beyond a basic first aid kit?

- What are the accommodation possibilities and how are they to be arranged? Is there a student union or any other potentially helpful organization in the country to be visited, and what evidence of membership in the home country is required to secure benefits?

- How much travel and health insurance is needed, and where might the best deals be available? Is travel to the country to be visited considered safe or risky by the national government, and what plans are necessary for contact in the case of personal or local emergency?

- What weather conditions might be expected, and are there any local customs or norms that will require appropriate dress or behavior?

Finding the answers and taking action on these questions require individual effort but exchange of information among intending students and/or with those who have returned or are themselves on foreign placements can be useful.

Other aspects of the preparatory stage relate to the purpose of the activity. Who should approach the potential placement, and what information will the receiving institution or agency require? Might there be any chance of grants or loans to help meet expenses, and how do students apply for them? What teaching or learning could be undertaken to orient students to (1) particular places, and/or (2) particular types of work or placement activity, and/or (3) the process of adaptation likely to be experienced on entering a different culture?

How does the proposed placement relate to the student's prior experience, and what are the collective expectations and individual learning goals for it? How and when will work undertaken in placement be assessed (and by whom?), and have relevant guidelines for assignments been circulated and discussed in advance? What materials (literature? writing materials? course handouts? portable computer or typewriter? tape recorder? camera?) might be useful or essential? Are there any contractual, social, or family obligations to be met (a contact list? report to be signed? gifts for hosts or relations?) (Link, 1998).

A number of these issues could be addressed in a group context, and students can assume a level of responsibility for assembling their own teaching and learning materials (including information from the Internet), to be shared in the class—for instance, about the welfare systems of particular countries or about global themes such as poverty or migration. Workshops can also be held with incoming students to share their first impressions about placements abroad, or with outgoing students to discuss their planning and share anxieties and information. Such activities can also be built into the assessment scheme of courses that regularly organize or require placements abroad so that preparatory work does not become a burdensome or neglected addition to existing teaching and assessment commitments. On a practical note, all departing students should submit forms giving destination details and emergency contacts as well as any assignments related to proposals for work to be undertaken and/or contracts about learning goals and assessment. Finally, there might be some contingency planning or discussion about how to proceed in the event of unanticipated problems with the placement.

....

OPPORTUNITIES AND ACTIVITIES ABROAD

The short case studies presented later include some examples of the type of work that students have undertaken in international placements. This work is generally of four types, related partly to the stage at which such a placement occurs in the students' training/career and partly to the overall learning goals of the activity as part of a wider educational or professional development program. The first possibility is that the aims of the placement will be regarded as primarily observational/educational. Students would undertake a planned series of agency visits, perhaps meeting social workers semi-informally and shadowing them in particular aspects of their work. Students might also attend specified classes in the host institution and perhaps meet other home and/or incoming students in seminars or small groups to discuss their observations and raise questions of national policy and practice with faculty.

In this learning context, observations would be recorded and assignments submitted related to the students' perceptions of social work practice and/or organization in the country visited, perhaps drawing direct comparisons between aspects of practice in the home county and in placement. An element of self-evaluation might also be required—for instance, in a log charting students' first impressions and questions and reflecting on the impact of exposure to a different culture and unfamiliar assumptions and ways of doing things. This approach assumes the availability of an agreed input (including arranging agency visits and having a general oversight of the placements) by colleagues in a partner institution and the cooperation of agencies (but without formal practice teaching or supervisory responsibilities).

A second model presumes that the primary aim of the placement is for developing skills and competences in direct practice (case work, family or group work, or community work/development), with the added dimension that this will be in a context in which the legal and policy framework, the resourcing arrangements, the cultural norms, and the societal exceptions influencing social work organization and activity are different. This model obviously requires a more sustained placement with a particular agency, the allocation of a workload, and the provision of supervision or field instruction.

In a third model, an international placement may downplay the development and demonstration of skills and competences that are more conventionally assessed in home placements and instead emphasize the students' ability to organize themselves and to adapt and learn effectively, under probably very different circumstances, as the main goal. Such a placement may include some direct practice, and indeed learning about a different form of practice, or practice under different conditions, may be an important aspect of the placement.

This model, however, might suggest instead or additionally a project approach in which students define in advance an area for inquiry and undertake data gathering on the selected topic during the period away. This may require some input prior to departure about research methods and the role of the researcher, and useful parallels can be drawn between the skills used in direct practice and in research, particularly where more ethnographic methods are encouraged (Powell, 1996). Such a scenario may require a comparative study, but this is not essential, and the availability of advice and guidance by local faculty or practice teachers may be useful.

Before the placement begins, students and participating institutions or agencies should be clear about which of these models most resembles the aims and purpose of their international placement, although there may be variations and ad hoc arrangements negotiated individually. It should also be stressed that any expectations about comparative work, whether formal or incidental, should require students to examine reasons for similarities and differences and do not presume a better or worse dimension. Individual perceptions are inevitably rooted in individual knowledge and experience, but a major purpose of international placements is to promote intercultural learning. The dangers either of idealization of things foreign, or of uncritical acceptance of things at home as right or the norm, limits understanding and, at worst, confirms stereotypes and prejudices, preventing, rather than enhancing learning and professional development (Coleman, 1996).

RETURNING TO BASE

The opportunities that might exist for assessing students who have been abroad, or working further with them in the home institution on return, partly depend on the stage at which the placement occurs. For some students, a placement abroad may be a final stage in their educational program, and subsequent work may relate solely to submission of reports and/or placement assignments. These may be completed on an individual basis without any formal arrangements for reintegration of outgoing students with home students or for the coming together of a group of students who went to different destinations. This is unfortunate, since sharing experiences can be part of a continuing learning process, and there are also issues to be faced on return to the home institution and country.

Less attention has been paid to the adaptation needed to reenter a home situation than to enter an overseas setting. Independent of the experience of the placement, there are likely to be mixed emotions about both leaving and returning. Old conditions or relationships that previously seemed familiar and acceptable may now be questioned; responsibilities or pressures temporarily abandoned may quickly resurface; new demands or changes in personal or professional circumstances may present themselves; old securities may now feel like constraints; and, after perhaps some initial excitement at meeting family and friends again, other people may seem uninterested in or unappreciative of the nature and impact of the student's experience.

Thus, the process of reentry is different from that of adaptation to a new environment, but it may also provoke feelings of uncertainty and isolation associated with further change in personal circumstances and professional role. For instance, students can report back to their colleagues on their impressions or findings in relation to social work elsewhere, and it might be possible to draw out common themes and issues or to better appreciate reasons for differences. The impact of the experience at a personal level and its implications for professional development and future practice can also be explored, perhaps through workshops where students can identify and better appreciate the common stages associated with entry and adaptation to new environments on one hand and the reentry process on the other. Even where these issues had been examined through literature and exercises or discussion before departure, the students' subsequent experiential learning ensures a deeper level of understanding and greater potential for transferability of this knowledge to professional practice.

SOME CASE STUDIES

The following case vignettes are drawn from the experience of one of the authors in facilitating considerable numbers and types of international placements over the past decade. As befits case studies, not all examples illustrate complete, or even partial, success of placement objectives, but they aim to illustrate a number of the points made in the foregoing discussion. While they are largely based on individual cases, many of the situations described have been experienced to varying degrees by a range of students. Names of all students (and sometimes country of origin or destination and focus of the placement) have been changed to preserve confidentiality. Some personal details have been included to indicate some of the likely considerations and advantages or disadvantages individual students are likely to experience.

CASE STUDY 10.1

Carol (black British woman, age 35, married, three children) had to take out a loan and leave her school-age children with her partner to undertake a three-month placement. (She missed them but kept in touch by phone.) Carol chose to return to the Caribbean, where she had (current) family connections, to work in a child welfare agency (a field in which she had previous experience in the United Kingdom) and to explore how the United Nations Declaration on the Rights of the Child had been implemented. Despite preliminary communications about the intentions of the placement, there were suspicions in the local community about her intentions, and so her workload and field of inquiry had to be renegotiated on arrival and periodically throughout. Carol's family connections as well as her own patience and tact proved helpful in negotiating some of the anxieties and obstructions, and she was able to achieve her goals.

This case and many similar ones highlighted the sensitive nature of the relationship between incomers and indigenous workers if there is any suspicion that the incomer may bring superior views or report unfavorably on local policies and practice.

CASE STUDY 10.2

Olga (Greek single woman, age 24) followed other Greek students in taking up an ERASMUS placement in London in a community work project. Previous students had enjoyed the placement, as reflected in evaluation reports, and it had apparently been acceptable to the partner institution. At an early stage, Olga was not enthusiastic about the nature of the work, saying that she could learn little that would be relevant to the sort of work she expected to do on return. Both the supervisor and the placement organizer from the university tried to help Olga draw parallels between the conditions and approaches she was experiencing and the values and skills required, relative to her understanding of national practice, and international perspectives on education for social work. Olga completed the placement and was apparently experienced as pleasant and helpful by other colleagues and service users, but she remained skeptical about the value of the placement to her learning and job opportunities.

This case illustrates the potential for a mismatch between student expectations and what might be offered when placements are negotiated on the student's behalf, and also the extent to which international placements are sometimes viewed as needing to replicate experience available at home or are expected to provide some added dimension that will make students more employable on return.

CASE STUDY 10.3

Diane (white British single woman, age 30) wanted to explore provisions for child care in a completely different culture and arranged a placement with a voluntary agency in an African country. Her initial impressions were overshadowed by accommodation problems and the bad side effects of antimalaria drugs. However, arrangements with a local voluntary agency proceeded smoothly, and Diane was able to develop a different understanding of child development and of the relationship between culture and child rearing practices. She also developed her appreciation of the impact of social attitudes and economic factors on policy and practice in this area of social work.

This and other cases illustrate the practical (including health-related) problems that may confront students and the culture shock that may be experienced even when students have made some academic preparations and hold liberal or nonjudgmental attitudes.

CASE STUDY 10.4

Ben (white Australian man, age 35, with a male partner) had lived and worked in London for the previous decade. He remembered his small home town as narrow minded and his relations with his family as difficult. As well as developing his interest in mental health work, he wanted to use the international placement to revisit his origins, both to reestablish links with his family and to assess the potential for returning to Australia to live and work. The placement was a partial success on both counts. Family attitudes to personal lifestyle, political views (including those on welfare provision), and choice of work were still divergent, but there was some increased mutual acceptance. The proposed work in a mental health team did not materialize, but a chance meeting led to a stimulating involvement in a project addressing experience of poverty and discrimination among aboriginal people. The overall outcome was a decision to return to work in the United Kingdom but enriched by learning about a minority group and community development approaches which would also be relevant in Britain.

This and similar cases illustrate the personal agendas that can be explicitly addressed in the context of international placements as well as the need for flexibility if original plans do not work out.

CASE STUDY 10.5

Stina (single Swedish woman, age 25) was a little uncertain about the costs and benefits of an international placement but was keen to develop her English language skills. Following positive accounts of ERASMUS placements by students returning from England, she decided to request a placement that would include practice and study. Arrangements were made for Stina to have a part-time field placement in a voluntary agency working with refugees and to attend two classes at the university. One was a workshop involving a lot of small group activity; this, combined with accommodation in a hall of residence on campus and her outgoing personality, ensured that she quickly established a social network. Stina also participated enthusiastically in the varied activities of the agency, which sometimes included weekend and evening work. By the end of the semester, she had completed all class assignments to a good standard and received good reports from the agency. Her own evaluation of the placement was also that it had been a very positive experience and that although there were no refugee projects in the area where she was likely to work on her return, she had enjoyed the differences in placement opportunities and classes.

This case, like others, suggests that some cautious questioning before departure can precede an enjoyable and effective experience abroad. A student's active participation in a range of opportunities can ensure a very full placement, professionally and socially, demonstrating that a broad agenda (in this case, to improve language skills) need not detract from more focused professional development.

Hazel (white British woman, age 33, separated, two children) had spent a working holiday in Spain some years before and welcomed the opportunity to take up a placement in a community project arranged through a Spanish partner school with ERASMUS funding. She decided to take her children (age 6 and 8) with her and to make a preliminary visit to set up arrangements. (She had some financial help from her parents and her own part-time earnings.) The preliminary visit included arrangements to exchange accommodation with an incoming student, inquiries about a local school, and a meeting at the agency where she would work.

The placement itself went well although Hazel found that she had to work hard at written and oral communication in Spanish and that she lacked the technical vocabulary needed to make full use of the Spanish professional literature. The children adapted quite well but felt constrained in a small flat in a Spanish winter and without their own friends, making more demands on Hazel's attention than usual. She was also upset on return to find that the student who had occupied her house had not left it in a clean and tidy state. However, having settled down again at home and college (including completing the reflective assessment work), Hazel judged the experience to have been well worth the extra effort involved.

• •

This vignette illustrates varying approaches to family responsibilities and constraints. Every year, some students leave partners and/or have to make special arrangements for dependent relatives. The extent of personal adjustment thus often extends beyond the student who travels; even practical arrangements for care of pets and home can have a bearing on the feasibility and success of the venture.

Maylene (Malaysian single woman, age 35) had been a social worker in Malaysia for many years. The agency she worked in was keen to develop family work and it was agreed that a placement would be sought in England for Maylene to undertake some practical work and attend some courses in this field. Maylene had five months' special leave from her employer and some financial help for this further training/professional development opportunity but in turn was expected to submit reports and lead training sessions as well as contributing to policy and practice developments on her return. In England, after a brief period of orientation, Maylene undertook first cowork with an experienced supervisor and then individual direct work with families in a Family Guidance Unit (three days a week). She also attended courses in family studies and family work at the local university and undertook a series of observation visits to a range of social work agencies. Maylene initially found the climate and living conditions in London inhospitable but soon moved to a room in a YMCA that she found more congenial, if less convenient for traveling, and she felt more settled as her workload developed and classes progressed.

• •

This vignette illustrates some of the practical issues facing incoming students but also the particular role changes and expectations of people undertaking placements outside the usual framework of an initial educational program, particularly if they carry professional obligations on return.

Sita (single British Sikh woman, age 28) wanted to visit the country of her parents' origin, but also wanted to learn about social work practice in very different social conditions, with a view to a possible career in the international social work field. She secured a placement with a project for street children in an Indian city and established good contact with the local school of social work. Besides undertaking voluntary work, she carried out a research project that both met her assessment requirements and was useful to her hosts; she also furthered her learning about her family and cultural origins. Sita considered that the placement had been the most challenging and satisfying aspect of her undergraduate education. On completing her course in the United Kingdom, after a brief period in a temporary post, she gained employment in an international child care agency, initially on a British project concerned with refugee children.

This case illustrates the conjunction of a placement that met personal and educational goals as well as having a direct bearing on subsequent career and professional development opportunities.

Margarita (single Mexican American woman, age 27) went to India for a graduate practicum. She financed her overseas study through scholarships and student loans. Margarita's graduate practicum was in a psychiatric outpatient department. She was enrolled concurrently in an advanced clinical course.

Margarita worked with middle class clients who conversed in English and with other clients through interpreters. She reported the educational value of the power of nonverbal gestures in treatment and the culture's role in negotiating non-verbal communication as it related to assessment and intervention to be very useful. Upon her return to the United States, she shared that the overseas study in India helped her to appreciate diversity based on race, religion, language, color, and culture and helped her to broaden her perspective of diversity beyond color. Since graduation, she works with a multicultural population.

This experience illustrates the role of overseas study in professional growth and development.

FIELD TRAINING RECIPROCITY: CONCLUSIONS

Although field practicum has been universally recognized as an integral part of social work education, until recently it has been viewed as a local activity confined to regional and national boundaries. This has been especially the case for social work education in the Global North. However, students of the profession from the Global South have obtained field training in the North for a long time. Thus, historically, exchanges between social workers have been unidirectional. Similarly, social technology transfer has been unidirectional, from the Global North to the South. Through the use of literature and case examples, this chapter has enumerated the need for and utility of reciprocity in field learning.

The chapter has also addressed the rationale for international placements and models for overseas placements. The educational merits of when and where to go abroad, the logistics of preparation and departure, and reentry issues have been discussed. In a globe that is shrinking, possible challenges because of political instability and contrast in terms of health concerns in living conditions have been mentioned in the context of liability issues. Further, a spectrum of real-life student experiences in overseas placements, and the interactive effects of personal and professional dimensions of adult learning as they pertain to overseas fieldwork, have been examined. Field experiences are a critical element of social work education, and this chapter has demonstrated the ways to ensure that global opportunities are included.

STUDENT ACTIVITIES

1. In small groups, discuss and note the *advantages* and *disadvantages* of undertaking an international placement. What might the opportunities be in your school? If you decide to proceed, how will you do this?

2. In pairs, discuss *where* you will request an international placement and what your *reasons* are for this choice. What information do you already have about the place, and how will you seek more?

3. Individually, draft a curriculum vitae to go with a *letter of application* for an international placement. What do you think another school or agency would like or need to know about you and your previous educational and practice experience to encourage the recipient to give favorable consideration to your application?

4. Write a paper—or, individually or in pairs, make a *class presentation*—about the country you will be going to. What are its main demographic, geographic, historic, economic, and political characteristics? How do these features interact to shape current social policies? Are you aware of any particular social issues that might be of concern to social workers in that country—or how social services are organized, or what forms of social work are most in evidence?

5. Using the questions suggested earlier, draw up your own *checklist* and *action plan* for departure and arrival in a new country. Separately, note some ideas about your *learning objectives* and *the work you want to do* while you are away. Use these notes as the

basis for discussion with someone responsible for international placements before departure and for negotiating a contact with a placement supervisor or confirming a work plan after you have arrived.

6. Discuss with others your *arrangements for departure* and your concerns about travel and arrival. What are the possible problems which might occur? In a worst-case scenario, what *contingency plans* might be helpful?

7. Start a *contact list* before you go and maintain this list while you are away. The list might be kept in an address book, in a card index system, or on a personal computer, depending on your own resources and inclinations. Remember—note fax numbers and e-mail addresses where possible and other useful details like country codes, time differences, titles of important people, or other professional details you may need to know.

8. While you are away, keep a *diary* or *log* for your own personal use. Use it to note down your thoughts and feelings about what you are observing and doing. Separately or at the back, note down specific personal or professional questions that come to mind and generate a list of possible resources to help you find answers, including people or literature to consult. Alternatively, if you have the inclination and a suitable contact, write regular, long, detailed letters to a close friend or relative back home and keep a copy for your own use.

9. Keep a *diary of work engagements*. Use it to schedule in your own study time and deadlines for assignments as well as opportunities for relaxation and informal learning. These devices will help you process and reflect on what you are learning and experiencing as well as enabling you to make best use of the time available. You can use them to recall significant impressions or points of development if you have to write a more formal journal or self-evaluation for assessment.

10. Write an *account* of the organization and practice of social work (or a selected aspect of it) in the country you have visited, noting your sources of information for this (personal observation or work experience? interviews with professionals? agency or government reports? national professional literature?). How does this account differ from what you are familiar with in your own country and/or from what you might have anticipated? What might be the reasons for such differences? Are there any implications for development of future practice and services in your own country or for cross-national initiatives?

11. In pairs or small groups, reflect on the experience of your time abroad. Were there high or low points? In what circumstances or at which stage did they occur? Are any common patterns discernible? How might they be explained? In the case of negative events or feeling, how did you deal with things? What have you learned from this experience that might inform your future professional work and development?

Social Development in Social Work: Learning from Global Dialogue

JAMES MIDGLEY

When there was no drinking water, we carried empty pitchers on our heads and broke them outside the chief engineer's office.

—ALICE GARG
  INDIA'S WOMAN OF THE YEAR, 1997*

Although social development is not a recent innovation, it has been neglected for many years; only since the beginning of this decade has there been a resurgence of interest in the field. The publication of an annual series of "human development" reports by the United Nations Development Program since 1990 and the convening of the United Nations World Summit on Social Development in Copenhagen in 1995 are indicative of a revival of interest in the subject. Social workers are also renewing their involvement in the field. Although they played a major role in conceptualizing the social development approach, interest in the subject waned. However, social workers are now again embracing social development. An indication of their renewed commitment is the inclusion of the first-ever entry on the subject in the *Encyclopedia of Social Work* (Lowe, 1995), the publication of a comprehensive book on social development by a social work professor (Midgley, 1995), and the creation of centers for social development at various social work schools such as Washington University in St. Louis, the City University of Hong Kong, and LaTrobe University in Australia.

---

*She started Bal Rashmi to give slum children of Jaipur a better life. Today hundreds of families in over 300 villages of Rajasthan live with pride and self-respect. The Bal Rashmi Society is a society for community development founded by Alice Garg in 1972; it now has children's homes, schools, health care, women's empowerment groups and an income generation project. Bal Rashmi means "the first rays of a new dawn—the newborn that brings light."

While it is gratifying that social workers are becoming more involved in social development, it is clear that much more needs to be done to promote a developmental perspective in the profession. This is particularly true in the United States, where social development is poorly understood but where it has great potential to transcend the profession's preoccupation with remedial practice and address social needs in a constructive way. However, if social development is to be more widely adopted, instruction in the subject at schools of social work needs to be enhanced and practice opportunities for implementing social development ideas need to be identified. If social development is to augment the profession's conventional concern with remedial and maintenance services, social work educators and practitioners must be properly prepared to engage in the field.

This chapter seeks to encourage the adoption of a social development perspective in social work by seeking to draw on the experiences of countries where social development has been implemented. Attempts to incorporate social development ideas into social work practice have been most successful in countries of the Global South. It is here that social development first emerged as a coherent approach for promoting social welfare. Although social workers in the industrial countries have helped to promote social development and to provide a conceptual basis for social development practice, this model has been most widely adopted in nations of the Global South.

The chapter begins by discussing the need for social development. It shows how recent political events have undermined public support for social work's conventional remedial activities, and it suggests that new approaches that address current realities in constructive ways are badly needed. It contends that social development offers a positive alternative to social work's conventional remedial approach in the Global North. It defines social development, briefly traces the historical evolution of this concept, and describes its main features. Finally, the chapter draws on the experiences of colleagues in different parts of the world to show how a social development approach can be implemented by social workers in the United States.

· ·

THE NEED FOR A SOCIAL DEVELOPMENT PERSPECTIVE IN SOCIAL WORK

The emergence of social work as a profession can be traced back to the latter half of the 19th century, when educated women charity workers in Europe and North America were first employed to investigate applications for poor relief. The Charity Organization Society and similar bodies believed that a "scientific" approach to charity, which was based on a proper investigation of need and a plan to rehabilitate the recipient, was the best way to address the problem of neglect and destitution. These ideas were augmented by the settlements, which focused on poor neighborhoods rather than destitute individuals. However, settlement founders also believed in the importance of trained professional personnel who would possess the knowledge and skills to work with needy people. As governments began to expand social programs in the late 19th and early 20th centuries, the need for professionally trained personnel who could staff the expanding social services was also recognized. The proponents of a statist approach to social welfare believed that a highly trained cadre of social administrators could play a vital role in formulating and implementing public programs to address the pressing social needs of the time.

The founders of social work were able to persuade universities to create training programs in social work. By the early decades of this century, programs of this kind expanded rapidly at leading universities in Europe and North America, as discussed in Chapter 2 of this book. Social workers employed in the charities, settlements, and government agencies concerned with social welfare were increasingly equipped with professional credentials for the task. Professional social work education was perhaps most highly organized in the United States, where efforts to formulate theoretical conceptions for social work practice, standardize the curriculum, and accredit programs were well advanced before World War II.

Although social work in the United States was broadly conceived to address the needs of individuals, groups, and communities through different practice methods, the profession revealed a clear preference for remedial intervention. Most schools of social work stressed courses in therapeutic practice. With the popularization of Freudian psychoanalysis in the 1920s, treatment methods were infused with psychoanalytic ideas; community practice and public sector social work were given secondary status. Despite its intention to deal with the problems of society through diverse forms of professional intervention, social work's remedial activities predominated.

While social work has an obvious role to play in addressing social problems through remedial practice, the excessive emphasis the profession has placed on treatment has created problems. As Specht and Courtney (1994) argue, it has undermined the profession's original mission to promote the welfare of all citizens. By focusing primarily on those who suffer from personal and psychological problems, they contend social work has abandoned its original mission.

The emphasis on remedial intervention has also detracted from the profession's ability to achieve public recognition and respect for its work. In many countries, social work is viewed as a peripheral activity concerned with treating the problems of the most marginal members of society. While its engagement with these clients is perceived by some as a noble, altruistic activity (Lubove, 1965), it has not promoted a positive image of the profession as a mainstream activity that promotes the well-being of society as a whole. Social work's preoccupation with remedial practice has also been criticized for being expensive and ineffective. Some forms of remedial intervention, such as residential care, are very expensive and only serve a small proportion of needy people. In addition, studies of the outcomes of remedial interventions have not been very encouraging.

Concerns about the high costs of remedial social work were first expressed in newly independent developing countries during the 1950s and 1960s, where economic development was given high priority. Although social work was introduced in these countries with government support, the profession soon came under attack from government planners and economists for placing too much emphasis on expensive, remedial programs that detracted from the overriding need for economic development. While social work might be a worthwhile activity, they argued, its emphasis on curative services was unaffordable in societies where the need for economic development was paramount. Low-income countries committed to fostering economic development did not have the resources to build the expensive residential facilities social workers required to house the elderly, the mentally ill, the destitute, and neglected children. Nor could they afford the income maintenance and support programs social workers said were needed to provide for their clients. As Livingston (1969) showed, these arguments were first articulated in the 1960s, but they still have currency today. In a recent publication, Bose (1992) vigorously criticized his Indian social work colleagues for failing to adopt a developmental approach that would refocus the profession's remedial preoccupations to make a significant contribution to the country's economic development.

Social work's remedial activities elicited a different response in the industrial nations. In the 1980s, as attitudes towards the poor and vulnerable hardened, social work came under attack for allegedly encouraging deviance and dependency. As Jones (1992) revealed, Prime Minister Margaret Thatcher in the United Kingdom frequently attacked social workers for encouraging permissiveness and a disrespect for authority. By urging clients to insist on their right to welfare benefits, she alleged that they undermined the work ethic and fostered dependency. The British media supported this attack on the profession by claiming that social workers were generally incompetent and ineffective. This allegation was most frequently made with reference to child abuse cases where social workers had failed to prevent injury to children in their care. It was bad enough that social workers were challenging traditional values; it was unforgivable that they were incapable of protecting children in their care.

Although social work has not been as vociferously attacked in the United States, similar negative sentiments have recently been expressed. Recently, the Council on Social Work Education (1997) reported that an editorial opinion column by James L. Payne of the Heritage Foundation in Washington, D.C. had been widely syndicated in the U.S. press. Payne attacked social workers for allegedly undermining the country's new welfare reform efforts by seeking to find loopholes in the new legislation that would allow clients to continue receiving benefits when they should be seeking employment. Although these allegations are totally unfounded, they project a negative image of social work and undermine the profession's ability to contribute positively to the promotion of the well-being of all citizens in society.

These events suggest that new approaches that redirect social work's conventional commitment to remedial intervention are badly needed. While few would argue that the social work profession should abandon remedial practice, there is an urgent need to transcend these activities and embrace forms of intervention that have a more positive impact on the well-being of all citizens. As suggested earlier, social development is one approach of this kind.

THE NATURE OF SOCIAL DEVELOPMENT

Midgley (1995, p. 25) defines social development as "a process of planned social change designed to promote the well-being of the population as a whole in conjunction with process of economic development." He contrasts social development with other institutionalized approaches to promoting human welfare, such as philanthropy, professional social work, and social service administration, on the premise that social development harnesses the power of economic development for social welfare purposes. Unlike the other approaches, which are concerned with social problems and needs, social development seeks to promote human well-being in association with a dynamic, ongoing process of economic development.

The social development perspective views economic and social processes as two sides of the same coin and equally important components of the development process. Social development cannot take place without economic development, and economic development is meaningless if it fails to bring about significant improvements in the well-being of the population as a whole. Midgley and other proponents of social development have sought to identify various means by which a closer integration of economic and social policies can be promoted. *Three primary mechanisms of this kind have been identified.*

First, the developmental approach seeks to harmonize social and economic policies within an ongoing process of development by creating formal organizational arrangements that integrate economic and social policies. In most industrial countries, the governmental organizations responsible for economic development have no regular contacts with social service agencies. On the other hand, Global South countries that have adopted a social development approach have encouraged economic development and social agencies to work more closely together. These countries usually have a centralized development planning organization that is responsible not only for economic development but for social development as well. These organizations employ economic as well as social development professionals who formulate policies and plans, and work closely with sectoral organizations to coordinate and integrate development effort.

Second, the developmental approach seeks to ensure that economic development has a direct and positive impact on people's welfare. The proponents of social development are critical of societies that experience economic growth but fail to ensure that growth fosters significant improvements in social well-being for all citizens. The disjunction between economic and social prosperity known as *distorted development* (Midgley, 1995) characterizes many countries today. Proponents of the developmental model urge the adoption of economic policies that address this problem directly. Programs that enhance the participation of people in the development process and that raise incomes by creating jobs and self-employment opportunities on a significant scale among all sections of the population are given priority in a developmental approach. Similarly, investments in human and social capital, along with the provision of credit and other forms of economic assistance that facilitate maximum participation in the economy among all citizens, are also emphasized.

Third, social development encourages the introduction of social service programs that contribute directly to economic development. While there will always be a need for remedial social services, proponents of the developmental model favor programs that foster economic growth. This goal can be furthered by adopting policies that promote the mobilization of human capital, enhance social capital formation, and increase opportunities for productive employment and self-employment among low-income and special needs groups. Because social development emphasizes the participation of traditional social service clients in the economy, it is also known as the *productivist approach* to social welfare.

There are at least three ways that the social welfare programs can promote the participation of the poor and other traditional client groups in the economy. These include the adoption of human capital programs, the promotion of social capital formation and the introduction of programs that enhance productive employment and self-employment. With regard to human capital development, numerous economists (Becker, 1964; Psacharopoulos, 1973, 1992; Psacharopoulos & Woodhall, 1986; Schultz, 1981) have demonstrated that investments in education, childhood nutrition, health care, skills training, housing stock, and similar programs generate a return on investment and contributes positively to economic development. Studies by sociologists such as Coleman (1988) and Putnam (1995; Putnam et al., 1993) have shown that strong community networks and solidaristic relationships create social capital that enhances economic development efforts. These studies strongly suggest that investments in community building are not an altruistic activity but a sound investment in economic development. Finally, it is now more widely recognized that programs that provide vocational training, skills development and job placement for clients with special needs are an effective alternative to conventional remedial and maintenance oriented interventions. By assisting previously dependent clients to engage in productive employment or self-employment, their self-esteem and sense of self-worth rises, their participation in the economy is enhanced and society as a whole benefits (Else & Raheim, 1992; Livermore, 1996).

As has been shown, social development seeks to enhance the well-being of the population as a whole through harnessing the power of economic development for social ends. This does not mean that social development ignores poor people or clients with special needs. However, in catering for needy people, it emphasizes social interventions that augment established remedial and maintenance-oriented approaches by implementing programs that draw previously marginalized people into the mainstream of the economy. In this way, social programs make a positive contribution to economic growth. This productivist emphasis is a unique feature of social development's attempt to reformulate conventional social services. However, to ensure that needy people are brought into the productive economy instead of relying indefinitely on social welfare benefits, investments that provide the skills and opportunities they need to become productive are required. Although the social development approach has been criticized for insisting that those in need can solve their problems by finding a job, this is a gross oversimplification of the argument. Social development requires substantial resource allocations by governments to invest in those who need to acquire the skills that will insure their integration into the economy. They also require supports to ensure that they are able to use the opportunities available to them to achieve economic integration. For this reason, social development is also known as the *social investment* approach to social welfare.

THE HISTORY OF SOCIAL DEVELOPMENT

The history of the social development approach has been sketched out previously by Midgley (1994, 1995), who has emphasized the colonial origins of this approach. He shows how dissatisfaction with conventional remedial interventions in the colonial and newly independent developing countries in the years immediately following World War II fostered a search for alternative forms of intervention that would address social needs and, at the same time, contribute positively to economic growth. However, as was noted earlier, the importation of remedial social work into these countries was soon recognized to be an expensive way of responding to the needs of only a small proportion of the population. While remedial social work dealt with the most conspicuous manifestation of social need, such as delinquency, destitution, begging, and homelessness in the urban areas, it neglected the pressing problems of poverty and deprivation that afflicted the majority of the population in the rural areas.

Midgley points out that British colonial social welfare administrators in West Africa first implemented social programs that sought to enhance people's welfare in ways that promoted economic development. One such program was mass education, which was introduced by colonial social workers in the Gold Coast, as Ghana was then known (Brokensha & Hodge, 1969). Mass education not only involved literacy education in the narrow sense of the term, but sought to enhance the standards of living of ordinary people, particularly in rural areas. This goal was achieved through the development of crafts and the technologies; the promotion of small-scale agriculture; the construction of economic and social infrastructure such as feeder roads, community water supplies, sanitary facilities, bridges, and local irrigation systems; the establishment of small family enterprises; and the creation of health centers, schools, and other community facilities. Mass education clearly transcended the welfare department's limited remedial interventions. It not only shifted social welfare away from remedial programs that consumed scarce revenues on unproductive services but promoted social welfare within an economic development context. The British Colonial Office in London encouraged the adoption of this approach throughout the Empire. However, the term "mass education" seemed inappropriate, and it was soon replaced by the term "community development." This new term explicitly connoted a concern with development and a focus on communities rather than individuals.

Community development did not replace the conventional remedial services of the welfare departments but instead linked them to the new developmental programs. In many countries, urban remedial services and rural development programs were administered by the same government department. In 1954, the term "social development" was formally adopted by the British government to connote the combination of remedial social welfare and community development. The new term also suggested that both approaches be linked to wider efforts to promote the overall development of societies.

While social development has played a major role in social welfare in the developing countries, it should be noted that it has not completely replaced conventional remedial services. Nevertheless, it is in the context of development in the Global South that social development ideas have been most widely implemented. The British government played a decisive role in the formulation of the social development approach, but its contribution was subsequently augmented by the United Nations and other international agencies, such as the International Labor Office and the World Bank, especially during the administration of Robert McNamara in the 1970s. The United Nations adopted the term "social development" in the 1950s and began to promote its spread throughout what was then called the Third World. However, the United Nation's viewed social development somewhat differently from the British. While the British approach emphasized community level activities, the United Nations stressed the role of national interventions by governments through central planning. At the time development planning was being widely adopted in the developing countries, but it focused almost entirely on economic matters. Central planning agencies were staffed by economists who were exclusively concerned with mobilizing investments, promoting economic growth and fostering rapid industrialization.

Some officials in the United Nations were critical of the emphasis placed on economic planning, which they believed had resulted in the neglect of the social dimensions of development (Hardiman & Midgley, 1982). By the end of the 1960s, these officials were promoting an integrated or "unified" approach that sought to balance the economic and social aspects of development (United Nations, 1971a). They recommended that government economic planning agencies be more concerned with social issues and introduce policies that directly addressed the problems of poverty, inequality, and other human needs. They also proposed that social planning divisions be created in the development planning agencies and that social planners be trained to implement policies that raised levels of living, increased human capital, and expanded the social services.

Although the United Nations originally conceived of social development as the responsibility of central government, the statism of the social planning approach was criticized both by advocates of community-based development strategies and by proponents of laissez-faire economics. Community activists reproached the United Nations for promoting a top-down style of development that relied excessively on government intervention, claiming that this approach failed to involve local people in the development process. Those on the political right attacked the social development approach for its reliance on government-directed development, which, they claimed, was doomed to failure. It was generally recognized that the United Nations approach to social development had neglected community-level social development programs, and efforts were made to redress the imbalance. During the 1970s, the organization reformulated older approaches to community development, such as grassroots activism and community participation (United Nations, 1971b, 1975). Other international agencies such as UNICEF and the WHO also gave priority to community-based social development programs (United Nations Children's Fund, 1982; World Health Organization, 1982). As a result of these developments, community-based interventions are now regarded as a vital part of social development (Midgley, 1995).

It was more difficult to contest the attack from the political right. As criticisms from the right gained momentum in the 1980s, social development lost momentum. Other events also contributed to the declining influence of social development. Inflation and economic stagnation in the industrial countries had caused labor unrest and widespread discontent and this fostered electoral support for radical right-wing political movements. Many developing countries had borrowed extensively on international financial markets, and when the global recession caused by the two oil shocks occurred, they found that they could not repay their debts. By the early 1980s, right-wing governments in the United Kingdom and the United States sought to retrench the extensive state welfare programs that had been introduced by their predecessors. Similar retrenchments occurred in the developing countries as a result of the imposition of structural adjustment programs. As national development planning agencies lost authority, social programs were curtailed. By the mid-1980s, social development all but disappeared from international discussions on social welfare.

The recent revival of interest in social development resulting from the United Nations World Summit in 1995 offers a hope that a developmental perspective that effectively addresses the pressing problems of poverty and deprivation that characterize the lives of hundreds of millions of people throughout the world will gain international support. It is also hoped that it may form the basis for a new approach in social welfare in which social programs that are productivist and focus on social investment rather than remedial and maintenance consumption services are emphasized.

· ·

SOCIAL DEVELOPMENT AND SOCIAL WORK

The definition of social development by Midgley (1995) given earlier in this chapter contends that social development is a distinctive social intervention that can be distinguished from other institutionalized approaches to enhancing people's well-being such as philanthropy and social service administration. Midgley's definition makes clear that social work and social development are not synonymous but interlinked. Both are concerned with the promotion of human well-being, and both rely on human agency to achieve this goal. In addition, as was shown earlier, colonial social workers played a formative role in identifying the social development approach during colonial times. Social workers in the United States have also been involved in the promotion of social development. In the 1970s and early 1980s, they sought to formulate a conceptual basis for social development in several books and leading journal articles (Paiva, 1977; Sanders, 1980; Jones & Pandey, 1981).

While social work and social development are distinctive interventions, it is argued in this chapter that social work can embrace a developmental perspective that will facilitate its engagement in activities that transcend its conventional remedial and maintenance roles. As will be shown, a social development perspective can be integrated within the profession's current practice philosophies and commitments and can harness its established practice methods.

Although social workers have been involved in promoting social development for many years, their impact on the profession has been limited. One reason for this effect is the failure to articulate a set of tangible prescriptions for implementing a social development approach. Many social work advocates of a developmental approach have engaged in excessive rhetorical idealism, defining the developmental perspective in hortatory terms and emphasizing its commitment to abstract ideals. These include the promotion of social justice; progressive social change; peace; social integration; and the attainment of a humanistic, caring society. However, they have not explained how these abstract albeit commendable ideals can be attained through social work practice. Several commentators have criticized proponents of social development for failing to specify in precise, practical terms what professional roles social workers should adopt if these abstract ideals are to be attained through professional practice (Lloyd, 1982; Lowe, 1995; Midgley, 1996).

The failure to articulate a clear set of practice prescriptions for implementing a developmental approach in social work has confused the issue. One example of this confusion has been the tendency to relabel nontherapeutic forms of social work practice as social development. While some social work authors such as Spergel (1982) have equated community organization, administration, and planning with social development, they have failed to show how these forms of macro practice foster development goals. Other writers such as Maas (1984) and Paiva (1977) have claimed that the use of direct practice methods to help clients enhance their interactive skills, fosters their personal growth, and thus enhances the development of the well-being of society as a whole. But again, it is not clear why the concept of social development needs to be employed to connote these forms of social work practice.

If social workers are to identify and adopt developmental forms of practice, they need to indulge less frequently in idealized rhetoric and focus instead on the practical ways in which the profession can promote material improvements in people's welfare. They need to show how social work practice can create and harness economic opportunities for social welfare. Social work's established practice methods need to be directed toward this end to cater not only to the profession's traditional clients but to the wider community as well. However, this requires a materialist perspective that emphasizes the role of economic development in social welfare. While some social workers will be skeptical of an emphasis of this kind, it will be shown that a materialist approach to social development can be effectively implemented to refocus the profession's traditional preoccupation with remedial welfare. In addition, the adoption of a materialist perspective does not negate social work's commitment to cherished values and ideals but instead provides an opportunity to realize them.

The three forms of intervention identified earlier in this chapter offer a framework for identifying and implementing a social development approach in social work. Social work interventions that stress human capital, social capital, and productive employment and self-employment are needed. To show how this can be done, the experience of other countries where these ideas have already been implemented can be instructive.

SOCIAL DEVELOPMENT THROUGH GLOBAL EXCHANGES

Social workers have long exchanged ideas and experiences internationally. Indeed, professional developments in many different parts of the world have been shaped by influences from other nations. In the early years of social work's evolution, ideas emanating from the United Kingdom were widely adopted in the United States and other countries. The Charity Organization Society's belief in the virtues of "scientific philanthropy" and the use of women caseworkers to investigate applicants for relief was enthusiastically adopted in the United States. The settlements were a British invention that, like social casework, was also emulated in the United States. In the early decades of the 20th century, the flow of ideas from the United Kingdom to the United States was reversed as psychoanalytic casework, which had initially emerged in social work educational circles in the United States, spread to Britain and other countries. Diffusionary tendencies in social work accelerated onto a global level in the decades following World War II, when both U.S. and British approaches to social work were widely exported to the newly independent developing countries of the so-called "Third World." Many of the countries of the Global South introduced Western-style social work, believing it to be a "modern" approach to dealing with social problems. As Midgley (1981, 1984) suggests, the replication of Western approaches may have been misguided, but it was entirely compatible with the then-prevalent belief that the newly independent countries needed to modernize their economies and social institutions in order to accelerate the processes that would ensure that they themselves became modern, industrial states.

While the adoption of U.S. and British social work was initially applauded, in the 1970s several critics from the Global South began to question the unidirectional flow of social work theories and practice methods that placed excessive emphasis on remedial intervention (Almanzor, 1967; Khinduka, 1971; Midgley, 1981; Shawkey, 1972). They argued that the problems facing Third World nations required different interventions that were more inclusive and preferably developmental in focus. Social development was widely promoted as one approach suited to the "indigenization" of the profession in the Third World. While social development was indeed often advocated as a suitable approach to social work practice, it has not been universally adopted in the developing countries. Nevertheless, their experience has been vital not only for the formulation of a developmental perspective in social work but for the identification of tangible practice opportunities by which these ideas can be implemented. As in other fields where it is possible to learn from the Global South, their experiences are highly relevant and instructive in fostering the adoption of social development in the industrial nations.

Several countries of the Global South have successfully implemented developmental social work programs that are materialist in nature and that focus on the three productivist intervention approaches described earlier. These are human capital, social capital, and productive employment and self-employment programs. In some cases, one of these approaches has been used to provide a rationale for a developmental program; in others, they have been combined. In many cases, developmental programs have been implemented in a community setting, but in others they have focused on individuals or groups of clients. Social workers in many countries of the Global South have recognized the role of human capital investments in dealing with their clients, particularly in the field of child welfare.

Transcending traditional child protective services models that are primarily remedial in nature and directed at the most neglected or abused children, these approaches seek to cater to the needs of larger groups of children whose needs for health care, adequate nutrition, and education are equally pressing. Many Asian countries have now transformed their child welfare systems by adopting on a developmental approach in which social workers mobilize whole communities to establish day care centers to educate and improve the health and nutritional standards of their children. One of the most extensive of these programs is the Indian Integrated Child Welfare Services Scheme, but similar programs have been introduced in Thailand, Indonesia, and the Philippines. Using conventional community organization techniques, social workers motivate parents and local leaders to establish day care centers which are operated through a combination of local and public resources.

The centers also offer opportunities for maternal health education, family planning information, and other programs that enhance the status of women. In addition to implementing a developmental approach to social work, these human capital programs also promote preventive and remedial forms of practice. Malnutrition, which is a major cause of death of young children, is effectively combatted, and children participating in community-owned day care programs are provided with both preventive and remedial health care. Similarly interventions to deal with child abuse and neglect services are more effective because they do not respond reactively to reports of abuse or neglect but instead involve the whole community in prevention and remediation.

Social workers in countries of the Global South have also been involved in programs that promote the formation of social capital. Like human capital programs, social capital also enhances the profession's involvement in social development. The concept of social capital and its relevance for social work has been examined by Midgley and Livermore (1998), who note that it has been used in several ways. The term has been used to refer to social work programs that create cooperative and solidaristic social relationships conducive to productive economic activities. It has also been used to refer to social programs that foster the development of physical infrastructure and encourage asset accumulation. Social workers in many countries have wide experience in community organizing activities designed to strengthen local social networks. In some parts of the world, such as Africa, they have been involved for many decades in community development projects that mobilize local people to engage in small-scale agriculture, the construction of schools and clinics, the development of networks of rural feeder roads, the creation of clean drinking water supplies and many other community assets. These projects create the physical infrastructure needed for economic development, and involve social workers directly in developmental activities. They also strengthen community networks that, as Putnam (Putnam et al., 1993; Putnam, 1995) suggests, have positive implications for economic development.

Social workers in the industrial nations would benefit from adopting social capital programs of this kind. While community social work practice in these countries has been traditionally concerned with local organizing for social and political purposes, the materialist emphasis on economic projects in African community development can be applied to address the pressing social problems facing many poor communities, and particularly in the United States (Midgley & Simbi, 1993).

For many years social workers in countries of the Global South have contributed positively to economic development by assisting low-income and special-needs clients to engage in productive employment or self-employment. They have accumulated a good deal of experience in helping special-needs clients to participate in vocational educational programs and to find work. They have also helped to create micro-enterprises among their clients. Self-employment ventures include both small-scale individual and family-owned businesses as well as larger cooperative enterprises. Social workers are extensively used in micro-enterprise development in Asian countries such as the Philippines, where the government abolished its traditional social assistance program in the mid-1970s and replaced it with a reasonably successful micro-enterprise program for special-needs populations (Reidy, 1981). In the Philippines and other low-income countries where the formal employment sector is small, micro-enterprise development offers an innovative opportunity for clients to participate in the productive economy. While micro-enterprise development among clients can take the form of single proprietor or family-owned businesses or cooperative activities, evidence suggests that family participation and the creation of neighborhood cooperatives are more successful in the long term.

Cooperative ventures are particularly well suited to special-needs clients such as the mentally ill or physically disabled, who derive strength from working in a mutually supportive environment. Although social work in the industrial nations has long been engaged in vocational rehabilitation and job placement, their involvement has often been limited to referring clients to agencies that specialize in these services. With the enactment of the 1996 Personal Responsibility and Work Opportunity Reconciliation Act, social workers will have to become much more involved in employment and self-employment related services. The experience of colleagues in the Global South can be very helpful in facilitating a closer engagement of this kind. Indeed, as Livermore (1996) reveals, the experience of developing countries has already informed efforts to promote micro-enterprise and micro-credit programs among low-income groups in the United States. These examples reveal that social workers in the United States can usefully learn from the experience of other countries as they seek to identify developmental forms of practice that transcend the profession's conventional remedial interventions. Many have expressed an interest in pursuing developmental forms of social work but lack practical guidelines. The experience of the developing nations in implementing a developmental perspective that promotes economic development and enhances the material welfare of individuals should be carefully studied and, if appropriate, adapted to fit local conditions. In this way, the profession can benefit from international exchanges and, at the same time, offer new directions for social welfare at a time when new ideas are urgently needed.

STUDENT ACTIVITIES

1. Write a short essay describing the way social development differs from remedial social welfare. In your essay, give your *own* opinion on whether social development is preferable to remedial social welfare.

2. In your own community, find an example of a social agency that does *one* of the following:
   a. Develop the human capital of needy people.
   b. Create and/or enhance social capital in poor communities.
   c. Help social welfare clients move into employment.

   Describe this agency and identify how it achieves its objectives. The agency may be government or nonprofit.

3. In the past, the developing countries copied social policies and programs from the Western industrial nations. Social development is an example of an approach that reverses this trend. Write a short essay discussing the advantages and disadvantages of adopting the social development approach in a Western industrial country such as the United States.

Professional Growth
in the Global Context

John F. Jones
Asfaw Kumssa

As the social work community expands and develops
throughout the world, we . . . must strive to be involved,
meaningful citizens of that greater community—not in
the sense of exporting our 'technologies' to others, but as
learners, as partners and, where appropriate, as
resources.

—Stanley L. Witkin (1998)

A frequent question that practitioners, educators, and students ask is: "How do I get a job in the international field?" It's a hard question to answer, partly because there is no single entry point, no list of openings readily available, no formula for breaking into this challenging arena. But there is another underlying reason that makes a response difficult, and that is the issue of qualifications, triggering in turn a different set of questions that must first be dealt with: What do you bring to the table? What relevant experience do you have? What are your credentials?

Most professionals working in the human services would like to believe, with some justification, that their education and degrees qualify them in a unique way for work overseas. After all, they have not only acquired at considerable expense the expertise of their profession but also possess training in cultural sensitivity as well as in human relations, giving them a disciplined and self-conscious approach to helping others in contrasting circumstances. These claims cannot be dismissed lightly, since such knowledge and skills do indeed open possibilities for careers in widely different fields.

That said, however, there still remains an obstacle that people elsewhere and outside a particular profession may perceive, and that in fact is more than a matter of perception. Working in another country requires an intellectual and emotional framework that professional or technical training does not provide in and of itself. And even if the intention is to stay at home and acquire an expertise in global affairs, the road to this goal passes through unfamiliar territory. In other words, an overseas assignment requires a match between person and place in addition to the precise knowledge and skills which the job demands. All this presupposes preparation of a particular kind and a person geared up for a wholly different world.

This chapter addresses issues of professional development in a global environment. It deals with learning strategies for both faculty and students along with the opportunities that academic institutions offer (or should be nudged into offering) to promote an international culture.

··

FACULTY: THE PLACE TO START

Faculty, no less than students, are learners. An academic institution is always a community of learners, and this is certainly true for international understanding. If faculty strive to create their own global vision, they act as models for students and in so doing foster an atmosphere for student learning. For this kind of atmosphere to flourish, there must be some thinking on the "what" of learning as well as strategies to bring about the desired goal—the "how" of learning.

The What of Learning

International social work is a broad field, as wide as the world and diverse as social work itself. To make knowledge manageable, it is usually desirable to target areas of concentration. Faculty development goals will vary from college to college, from department to department, and will depend in no small measure on expertise currently available on campus, faculty interest, institutions abroad, and area studies already in place as well as funding opportunities. The array of inquiry is vast, and just as curriculum development demands the discipline of goals and objectives, an outline of topics, and a learning schedule, so too does faculty development in international social work. Some degree of consensus is essential to prevent a purely piecemeal approach and the temptation for every faculty member to go his or her way, thus losing the benefits of mutual help and a common direction.

Settling on a theme for faculty development, whether this is to extend over a series of meetings or is organized as a single workshop or brown-bag lunch, is not easy. In the international arena, the topic choices are many, but they usually fit into one or two of the following categories. The themes each have advantages and disadvantages when it comes to delivering a faculty development program. Their degree of abstraction or concreteness, time available, and audience readiness must be considered before starting out. International social work themes, allowing a little room for overlap, can be divided as follows:

- Comparative social policy analysis
- Social development, including locality-based development
- Selected socioeconomic problems and issues
- Area studies, with a focus on country-specific social welfare programs
- Social work practice modalities in different regions or countries
- Social work education around the world

Comparative social policy analysis has the advantage of starting where most faculty are—with an understanding of U.S. legislative initiatives and federal/state programs. From there it is possible to branch out to Europe, Africa, Latin America or Asia, utilizing the common tools of policy analysis cited by Bibus in Chapter 3. Few presenters can carry off this sort of comparative analysis in a single session, but the topic lends itself to a brown-bag discussion or a series of meetings. A tool currently being developed by Kumssa (1998) is the framework for assessing sustainable human development, which provides the basis for dialogue on our ways of assessing sustainable development among all nations.

Social development is another, somewhat different, method of gaining or disseminating an understanding of ways to assist communities, regions, and nations deal with social problems such as poverty, war or hunger and is discussed in depth in Chapter 11 (Jones & Pandey, 1981; Sanders & Matsuoka, 1989; Midgley, 1995). Note that here we put communities ahead of regions and nations to get away from the generalities of global development that, at least for some faculty, seem too vague and overarching, too remote from intervention, to be immediately engrossing, making the full sweep of social development less appealing as a theme for a faculty development program. If, on the other hand, the focus is narrowed to locality-based development, faculty unfamiliar with the subject can more easily get their arms around it. Local social development fits into that category, that conceptual box, where practice predominates. Its stress is on operationalizing the idea of development at the community level and implementing plans that further the welfare of people in their neighborhoods and households. While it relates to national policy and global trends, local social development is essentially programmatic. Its focus is on the local community, whether urban or rural; its objectives are pragmatic and geared to specific improvements in health, housing or income; and its method of inquiry relies heavily on case research. Local development attempts to promote people's welfare at the household level and, in so doing, to foster the stability, group cohesion, and self-reliance of communities.

The How of Learning

In faculty development programs, it is very important not only to latch onto what interests faculty, but to create learning opportunities where faculty feel they have a reasonable chance of using what they learn—in the field supervising their own or exchange students, designing training programs, or helping communities in a practical way. In organized programs of self-enrichment and growth, faculty paralysis occurs when global realities are juxtaposed to the mandates of social justice without any plan to do something. Robert Reich put it another way when he complained that cosmopolitanism can engender resignation if dilemmas "seem so intractable and overpowering in their global dimension that any attempt to remedy them appears futile" (1991, p. 310). Social development, as enunciated by its most prestigious booster, the United Nations, as well as in scholarly publications and university classrooms, is not entirely guiltless of the grandiose. In one way, an insistence on principle and a moral stance are to the credit of visionaries, especially in this new era of globalization, when sociopolitical ideology has by and large given way to economic imperatives in national planning. At the same time, the philosophic tendency of traditional social development can too easily leave out of consideration the practical problems facing rural townships, villages, settlements, and small urban communities. The emergence of local social development (which is, incidentally, closely allied to community social work and reliant on its methods, though with perhaps a stronger economic and local government bent) marks a significant shift in thinking (Jones and Yogo, 1994). For these reasons, we are inclined to favor faculty development programs that emphasize locality-based development over trying to present a complete overview of development.

Selected socioeconomic problems and issues offer another means of narrowing the focus of international social work in crafting a faculty development program. One of the dangers everyone faces when teaching international social work is the risk of being out of date. Because global affairs are so complicated, quick to change, and uncertain, it is almost impossible for one person to master the total environment. As a result, it may make more sense in organizing faculty development to concentrate on particular problems and issues of social and economic importance. We group the social and economic together, since to understand social work at the international level it is crucial to study the economic infrastructure, dealing with such things as transitional economies, structural adjustment programs, the World Bank, and the International Monetary Fund. (Prigoff expands this learning for students and faculty in Chapter 9 of this book.)

In today's interdependent world, economic and technological factors are at the forefront in determining the dynamics of global change as well as the behavior of nation states. They are the centrifugal forces creating a borderless society. The revolution in computer technology, telecommunications, and transport has dramatically changed the way goods and services are produced as well as the way individuals and businesses interact (Boisier, 1997). One consequence is that multinational corporations faced with growing production costs in the North are relocating their production plants in developing countries.

Globalization, while integrating the world economy and increasing the flow of resources, is imposing the rules of the global market on national governments and limiting the effectiveness of their policies (Ohmae, 1995). Another issue that calls for analysis is the emergence of transitional economies that followed the collapse of the Soviet system and an almost worldwide rejection of the central planning model in favor of a liberal market economy. While this has enhanced the spread of democracy, its less positive consequences have included the weakening of previously existing social safety nets. While integrating national economies into a global economy, and increasing the flow of goods and services as well as the factors of production, globalization has also increased income disparity and has marginalized many vulnerable groups and nations (Falk, 1997).

Area studies can offer an entry point for the study of global issues from a social work perspective. Where universities and colleges have links with other institutions abroad, or where they concentrate in their educational programs on special regions of the world, a social work unit does well to piggyback on these ongoing relationships. It happens, for example, that the University of Denver has close ties with China and has an office in Beijing at the People's University. This link allows the Graduate School of Social Work to pursue its own agenda of faculty exchange with China. It is not that the networking must be precisely the same as the university administration's, but the predisposition of top administrators to the China connection smoothes the way for academic units to map out their own fields of interest. In this case, the Graduate School of Social Work, through well-established and independent relations with the All-China Youth Federation, is free and actively encouraged to arrange joint conferences, exchange visits, and teaching in the Social Work Department of Beijing's Youth College of Politics.

While taking advantage of area studies both as an academic discipline and a jumping off point for faculty and student exchange, it is imperative to keep the social work perspective in mind. In other words, a social work faculty development program would fall short if it only covered the general aspects of a country's culture without giving attention to the social aspects of its development and specific programs that tackle problems of malnutrition, housing, or poverty.

Returning to the case of China, we have here a transitional economy where a gradualist approach has had considerable impact on the country's social development. Since the reform policy was launched in 1978, China has improved some of its social conditions. For instance, between 1978 and 1995, infant mortality rate has declined by 11.1 percent while the life expectancy rate improved by 2.1 percent (World Bank, 1996, p. 18). Also, although the exact figures are in dispute, some Chinese scholars claim that the government, through an active Poverty Alleviation Program, has managed to reduce the number of people in absolute poverty from 200 million in 1978 to 80.8 million in 1992 (Wang, 1997, p. 56). According to Wang (1997), this Poverty Alleviation Program is designed to eventually solve the basic needs of the remaining 80.8 million people and transform China into an affluent society. In this regard, international social workers have a lot to learn from the experience of China. Establishing faculty as well as exchange programs similar to the University of Denver's promotes international understanding and individual enrichment.

Social work practice modalities in different regions or countries are usually of interest to all faculty, and discussion of the different ways practitioners go about their work can catch the attention of colleagues who are less drawn to global policy issues. Here the focus of study or discussion is not so much on program administration as practice itself, such as social work intervention with religious Jewish families in Israel or among the traveling people in Ireland. But it is possible to utilize a wider framework to study social work practice, such as conscientization as a technique of intervention favored by many practitioners in Latin America. The reconceptualization of social work that has emerged in Brazil, Argentina, Chile, Colombia, Peru, and Uruguay offers a point of comparison to practice in the United States. There is considerable interest nowadays within continents, subcontinents, and countries in developing their own approaches to social work practice—in China, social workers talk about the need for a Chinese type of social work; the same quest occurs in postcolonial Africa. While one cannot expect consensus in all these matters, if only because of the multiple roots of the discipline or what Lorenz (1994) calls, in the European context, "intellectual homelessness," there are some universal tenets in social work as discussed in Chapters 7 and 13 of this book.

A faculty development program initiated by the University of Denver Library has been very successful in using international students, visiting faculty, and "armchair experts" to introduce faculty and staff to other places and peoples. Called "Postcards from . . . ," the program consists of a series of monthly meetings (with refreshments) in which, for example, someone who comes from or has just visited Morocco, Poland, or Afghanistan gives a short talk, possibly illustrated, on that country (Jones et al., 1998). This type of program could easily be adapted by a social work faculty and student body interested in learning more about social work in different settings. Because social work education around the world is a topic that interests educators, it should require a minimum of circus barking to gather an audience. This, too, allows either a narrow or broad focus, along the lines of "Postcards from . . ." on one hand or area studies on the other. A social work program such as that of the University of Papua New Guinea, with its emphasis on social development, offers an intriguing illustration of how a small department in a developing country educates students and practitioners alike to address diverse nationwide issues like youth policy, social aspects of the produce industry, women's councils, street children, peer education on AIDS, assistance for the deaf-blind, micro-credit, and village-based businesses. Few schools of social work in the United States or other industrial countries can claim such a challenging agenda and the University of Papua New Guinea, which works closely with sectoral agencies to train their personnel, provides a model for this (*PNG Social Development Newsletter,* 1997).

To take an area studies orientation, social work in Europe (or any other continent, for that matter) can offer contrasting theoretical approaches to social work education (Healy, 1997). Animation and social pedagogy, to name but two movements and conceptualizations of practice, have heavily influenced European social work education—the first in France, as well as in French-speaking parts of Belgium and Switzerland, and in Italy and Spain; the latter principally in Germany but not confined to that country. There is considerable cross-fertilization in European schools and departments of social work, transcending language barriers. For instance, an Austrian social work school has started training its students in Sozio-Animation for statutory social work positions. Here is a deliberate attempt to introduce a methodology that stimulates creativity and partnership in statutory work, with the aim of bridging the gap between casework methods and social activism as well as inhibiting a split between social control and animation thinking (Lorenz, 1994). The diversity of thought that European social work educators can offer American colleagues, especially in approaches to social policy and community activity characteristic of both animation and social pedagogy, is potentially rich. Faculty who possess a broad view of social work education have much to gain by studying other educational systems and novel conceptualizations of learning.

· ·

STUDENTS: THE FUTURE COSMOPOLITANS

Students as a rule are open to international issues, and not a few come to professional education with some experience of working or traveling abroad. The challenge facing globally minded faculty is to nourish incipient interest and to supply opportunities for those who are already committed to giving their lives or careers an international dimension. This cannot be done through a single course, although curriculum development must play an important role in international social work education. The curriculum is certainly a starting point, but it should not be seen as the total solution. Similarly, no one course should be the final goal or the end of endeavor.

Reinforcing other chapters in this volume, we will briefly mention here five important ways and means of imparting an international perspective in social work education, whether at the undergraduate or professional practitioner level:

· Curriculum development

· Dual or joint degrees

· Doctoral education

· Fieldwork abroad

· Extramural studies

Curriculum development's final goal is lifelong—that is, to graduate students and educate practitioners who are, consistently and throughout their careers, dedicated to the needs of their neighbors worldwide. The endeavor to achieve this goal should be carried on throughout their professional education and permeate all aspects of the learning process.

It is thus a mistake to compartmentalize international education excessively. While we strive for structured faculty development and an ordered student curriculum, teaching is more extensive than any course or section. The fact is that for international learning to occur, it is necessary that cosmopolitan issues be considered in regular social policy classes, that child welfare include some mention of child labor and the rights of the child, that human growth and the social environment make reference to other cultures (those close to our borders and further afield), that direct and indirect practice courses routinely consider immigrants and refugees, and so on. Similarly, it is crucial to create an atmosphere in which students feel free to discuss global concerns and in which faculty are prepared to advise and instruct in these matters. In this respect, faculty development is almost always a prerequisite for student development.

With these broad assumptions, the task of creating a course of study begins. Ideally, conceptualization should be in terms of the school's or department's full educational offerings so that all courses impart international content. While daunting at first, this goal is attainable, particularly if undertaken in conjunction with a periodic curriculum review—in preparation for reaccreditation, for instance. Failing that, it is still possible in a course exclusively covering international social work to refer to sections of the regular curriculum with the aim of broadening the students' perspective. The actual design of a course will depend on some of the factors discussed earlier in relation to faculty development. The content area, too, can cover similar themes—comparative social policy analysis, social development, international social work issues, and country-specific programs and practice. The Council on Social Work Education, through its International Commission, has a wide range of curriculum models, principally course outlines, for teaching in this area (Healy & Asamoah, 1997).

Dual and joint degrees offer another means of educating students in both social work and international studies. (A dual-degree program confers two diplomas in diverse disciplines; a joint degree is a single credential.) A graduate student at the University of Denver, for instance, can earn an MSW and an MA in International Studies through a dual-degree program. The advantages are obvious, since the dual degree provides expertise in both fields and the time needed for completion is less than the individual degrees pursued separately would require. However, even in such a program, it is necessary to ensure that the two disciplines are not indeed pursued in isolation from each other, a charge occasionally levied at dual-degree programs. For that reason, an integrated seminar in which faculty of the two disciplines participates is certainly desirable, and sometimes necessary to keep communications open. The joint dual-degree model has many applications and is especially appropriate in area studies.

Doctoral education, arguably the best road to professional growth for educators, can be given a cosmopolitan orientation, either for individuals seeking this or for a cohort of students. To dedicate an entire PhD social work program exclusively to the international is probably unrealistic, given the competing interests of faculty and student preferences, but to offer a concentration in the field is feasible. Easier still is gearing the doctoral education of individual students to international social work or social development, and this can be done for a number of such students. At a time when many social work doctoral programs are competing for students, the possibility of attracting foreign students should not be overlooked. Overseas students are not only a source of revenue (appealing to financial officers), they also enrich the student body, their presence supplying a international dimension to a program. In order to meet the needs of overseas and internationally minded students, however, preparation and planning are necessary. Since social work departments seldom possess a full range of international courses, doctoral students should be allowed and encouraged to take these classes outside their unit—in international and area studies, economics, business, or wherever suitable courses can be found. Besides coursework, the dissertation is a superb means—very often the chief means—that students possess for merging their international interests with doctoral research. Unfortunately, it is not unknown for students to meet opposition when they put forward social development proposals or suggest topics on global socioeconomic issues, on the grounds of their irrelevance to social work. Here is where education of colleagues is so crucial.

Fieldwork abroad invariably appeals to students; its very possibility excites them. While no one who has tried to arrange field placements overseas can have any illusions about the obstacles encountered, notably the expense, the goal remains a worthy one, and there are ways of lessening the difficulty. One way is to link field placements to the regular "semester abroad" program that many colleges offer their undergraduate students. There is generally an academic infrastructure already in place that can be utilized for social work block placements, either during the summer or in the regular school year. Student advisement and support are essential both in preparation for the placement and, more important, during the fieldwork itself, as discussed in Chapter 10. While supervision may be easy to arrange— done for recompense or in reciprocity—supervision alone falls short of the full support students need, especially where the stress of cultural differences are unforeseen by students or their hosts. That is why a resident advisor from the home institution is invaluable for facilitating the transition. There are alternatives to, and adaptations of, block placements that give students social work experience in other countries. A study tour, preferably led by a social worker familiar with the host country, is a very good way of introducing students or practitioners to social work in different settings.

Other arrangements, generally made individually rather than in groups, include short-term assignments. Faculty who do research or consultation abroad should be mindful of their own students and, where possible, include them as research assistants or the like. Besides the immediate benefit of research assistance, including students in projects familiarizes colleagues abroad with the students' potential, sometimes opening the way for internships or even job placements. Extramural studies are especially suitable for the working practitioner who is keen to learn more about international social work. Since learning is a lifelong process, the practitioner who pursues knowledge in this or any other field can truly claim to be an adult learner. Extension courses with a global perspective are mechanisms for supplying an understanding of other countries and cultures. Coupled with a study tour, an extension course is an exciting opportunity for broadening horizons.

Distance learning, though still novel in social development training and education, is beginning to be discussed, planned, and slowly implemented (Jones & Kumssa, 1996). Websites of all sorts, dedicated to specific countries or covering global concerns, are online; electronic journals or newsletters offer yet another means of keeping current with events on the other side of the world. Although quality and accessibility of information varies, the emerging technologies can link practitioners in one country with the social work scene in another. At home on the computer, a practitioner can zoom in on local situations far away or, taking a wider angle, cover the globe. To an extent not previously possible, an enterprising learner can design and follow her or his individual curriculum on international development.

THE ROLE OF ADMINISTRATION: INSTITUTIONAL SUPPORT

Educating students and preparing them for a global labor market is both expensive and labor intensive. The same is true of faculty recruitment and development in an international context. It is important for administrators to recognize this fact of life.

Some of the means necessary to achieve these ends are:

- Well-organized financial support
- Internationalization of programs
- Appropriate and adequate teaching and learning resources
- Effective and efficient career placement services
- Internships and study abroad

Financial support programs include assistance with grants, work-study, and loans for needy and academically qualified students from abroad. Funding is required not only for student aid, but also to support faculty research, conference attendance, and those other endeavors aimed at preparing faculty for a global mission. In this regard, universities and colleges must include internationalization in their fundraising agenda, actively seeking financial assistance from corporations, foundations, government agencies, NGOs, and private donors.

Internationalization of programs at the college or university level is no less necessary than at the school or departmental level. Farsighted colleges are incorporating this goal into their strategic plans and are even changing the administrative structure to reflect a global orientation by appointing vice presidents or vice provosts of internationalization, creating units that cater to their foreign students, but more importantly signaling to their departments on campus the need to focus on global concerns. In today's highly competitive and worldwide market, providing students with technical skills and knowledge, while necessary, is not sufficient. Students should acquire expertise in global affairs and be familiar with international issues. This requires infusing curricula with international content, arranging faculty as well as student exchange programs and study abroad, and fostering collaboration with educational institutions in countries across the globe. There is also room, indeed need, for diversification of teaching staff, recruiting overseas faculty members either on a contract or tenure-track basis.

When the School of Social Development of the University of Minnesota–Duluth was founded, a conscious effort was made to recruit current and former United Nations personnel, in particular, to assist in building a program devoted to social development. The effort paid off, and the addition of superbly experienced and scholarly faculty from (in this case) the Indian subcontinent promoted social development not only in Minnesota but in the country at large (Midgley, 1995, pp. 30–32, 63–64).

Teaching and learning resources, whether through library facilities, campus-wide computer services, or instructional and media programs, should be sufficient to allow faculty and students access to the international arena. Earlier remarks on distance learning are relevant in this context. The new electronic technologies are very suitable for delivering distance education in international studies and social development. Distance learning is an established tradition in many applied and academic disciplines, both in a wide range of regions of the North and South. It is important for academic administrators to realize that distance education is not just a question of reaching out to recruit students, but is also a means of providing on-campus students with a world vision, supplying them with the tools to learn about other places and people.

The utilization of television, video, online communication, and computers in distance education has been introduced in many universities and colleges. Surprisingly, however, not enough utilization of these resources is occurring in the field of internationalization, either at the general undergraduate level or in graduate and professional programs. Colleges stand in need not only of standard textbooks on international affairs in their libraries, but of popular magazines and journals dealing with global concerns, made readily available in faculty lounges and student gathering places. Library holdings in serials, monographs, and ephemera should be sufficient to allow faculty to develop up-to-date expertise in area studies, and teaching materials with an international focus—both print and multimedia—should be of such quality and design to attract and hold the attention of students.

Career placement programs should play a greater role than they generally do in international job searching. Traditionally, career placement fairs and the like have catered to students and employers looking to the home market, with international placement treated as a game of hide-and-seek. Campus career offices and departmental placement services likewise have fallen down in making serious attempts to help students find overseas positions or jobs in government agencies, corporations, and international organizations that might lead to overseas posting. In part, the problem is circular. Academic administrators and career counseling staff are not confident that the education their institutions offer has the breadth and depth to qualify students for overseas assignments or to interest employers in such recruitment—a state of affairs that in turn leads to a distribution of resources that ignores global priorities. The solution lies in having central administrations and faculty senates take a bold stand on the importance of internationalization so that students are qualified to take up international positions and are assisted to do so.

Internship programs and semesters abroad can serve as a bridge between academe and the labor market. Since prior experience plays a crucial role in overseas placement, students who have studied or lived in a foreign environment, or worked in agencies with a global mission, have an advantage. In the business field, an internship with an overseas company or with a corporation geared to global marketing gives the intern an edge in seeking employment in today's international labor market. This is partly a matter of networking—companies are inclined to hire from current or past pools of interns. Thus, for a college to establish and actively push international internships is simultaneously to confer a benefit on students and to strengthen its institutional standing in the academic world.

Professional Collaboration and Social Development

For a number of years, the University of Denver has been involved with the United Nations Center for Regional Development (UNCRD) in Nagoya, Japan, first in assisting the Center's social development research and training program, and later in the study of the social dimensions of transitional economies. The collaboration started in the design of a training curriculum for front-line workers in Asia principally, then in Africa, and somewhat tentatively in Latin America. UNCRD's training in regional development has three dimensions: economic development in the global context; planning in technical fields such as regional environment; and, last, improvement of people's welfare and stability by strengthening their capacity for development at the local level.

It is in this last training initiative that the University of Denver (DU) Graduate School of Social Work first became involved. The Center has a practice of taking the initiative in inviting experts from developing and, though to a lesser extent, developed countries to assist in its various projects. The scope of the University-Center collaboration—which was originally limited to local social development training in Papua New Guinea, the Philippines, Sri Lanka, and Thailand—broadened over the years to extend to a number of the UNCRD's ongoing research projects in related fields, such as the study of transitional economies.

A tangible result of the local social development training program was UNCRD's publication of a two-volume manual, *New Training Design for Local Social Development* (Jones & Yogo, 1995), which lays the ground for country-specific training in different regions. One of the incidental outcomes of the collaboration was an exchange of personnel whereby a United Nations national expert joined the DU Graduate School of Social Work's doctoral program with Fulbright support; DU doctoral students participated in U.N. missions in Asia, Africa and Latin America; and DU graduates were hired by UNCRD.

•••

The broader significance of the international partnerships among universities being promoted by UNCRD is the wealth of expertise that a global exchange can bring to our shores. A crucial component in social development has been the contribution of experts and leaders from developing countries who in different guises offered the earliest models of South-South and South-North development assistance. Not only have these leaders and front-line workers formed the workforce of the NGOs and the backbone of national and local administrations in their own countries, their influence on the international scene is considerable through world bodies such as the United Nations and its member organizations. Scholars from the developing world draw on a diversity of cultural and ethnic backgrounds to enrich the concept of development, formulating and then interpreting for a global audience national strategies, regional problems, and new approaches to social change, in journals such as *Social Development in Africa* and *Regional Development Studies*.

Much of the early impetus for a social development curriculum came from scholars, educators, and practitioners (many with U.N. experience) from Asia in particular. As mentioned in Case Study 12.1, Asian scholars were prominent in the University of Minnesota–Duluth School of Social Development and have continued their involvement through the Interuniversity Consortium for International Social Development. Where the tradition of scholarly enrichment from the developing world is alive and well, U.S. higher education, including social work education, is the beneficiary.

INTERNATIONAL SOCIAL WORK: CONCLUSIONS

Professional growth in a global context is a complex and challenging task, in part because it requires the cooperation and partnership of educational institutions, academic departments, and government agencies as well as international organizations. Furthermore, as internationalization and globalization unfold, new themes, subjects, and areas of study come to the forefront. In the field of international social work, themes such as comparative social policy analysis, local social development, structural adjustment in developing countries, and reform in transitional economies emerge, for some at least, as novel and perhaps unfamiliar areas of teaching and research. But this relatively uncharted territory also offers an opportunity for professional development. The comparative social policy analysis of different countries and continents enables students, practitioners, and educators to increase their understanding of other societies and the steps their governments have taken to address national problems. At the other end of the spectrum, the study of locality-based development, both in urban and rural areas, illustrates how front-line workers and local planners deal with health, education, housing, or income at the community level.

Emerging socioeconomic problems and issues require proper attention in designing student curricula and faculty development programs. It is likely that within the next decade international social work education will be paying far more attention than at present to transitional economies, globalization (including its causes: advances in telecommunications, transport, computerization and miniaturization), growth triangles, regionalization, and to the major actors in the new order—the multinationals, the World Bank, the International Monetary Fund, the United Nations, and its member organizations. If this happens, a reorientation of educational goals and strategies, including those of social work education, should begin now. The new global prospect may seem threatening, given the loss of community control implied by such a scenario, but this is where a combination of realism and idealism is needed, if only to counter the worst effects of the emerging future. For faculty and student growth that encompasses a world vision to occur, academic administration has a central role to play. In truth, universities and colleges if they are to survive in a global environment and if they are to prepare their students for a worldwide labor market, have little choice in the matter: they must internationalize their programs. Expenditure in time, money, or resources is unavoidable, but the ultimate benefits to education far outweigh the costs.

STUDENT ACTIVITY

Taking your cue from Case Study 12.1, plan a collaborative arrangement between a college and any international agency of your choice. Use your imagination, but base your design on a real environment (a college you know and an agency with which, from experience or perhaps from a distance, you are reasonably familiar).

In your plan, incorporate the following items:

1. Your overall vision of collaboration and the goals you hope to achieve.
2. The personal and institutional linkages you would establish or utilize to promote your idea.
3. The entry point or first step in the process, such as a miniproject.
4. Options for future directions of the collaboration, described in outline.
5. A proposal for evaluation of the joint endeavor.

Future Visions
for Global Studies
in Social Work

CHATHAPURAM S. RAMANATHAN
ROSEMARY J. LINK

Om Sahanaavavatu

Saha Nav Bhunaktu

Saha Veeryam Karavaavahai.

Tejasvi naava dheetamastu

Maa Vidvishaavahai

Om Shaantih Shaantih Shaantih . . .*

—THE UPANISHADS

This chapter provides a capstone for our book by advancing issues for the social work profession to deliberate and act upon as we move into the millennium. Here we will revisit the reasons that the global perspective remains so elusive and will summarize ways in which chapters in this text have identified innovations that integrate global perspectives. This is followed by a section on the steps that faculty, students, and practitioners may take to become more globally oriented. Following the practical steps of review, we turn to a discussion of current reality: the globe is us. This reality is addressed in terms of economics and environment, migration, international law, and health. Finally, the chapter draws together the threads of the book in a statement concerning future commitment and realities. Completing the framework to engage in global social work learning presented in Table 1.1 in Chapter 1, we add futuristic considerations and common professional principles in international social work education (see Table 13.1). Further, we connect global issues to current and anticipated action. Thus, the enormity of the challenge ahead for our profession inspires instead of intimidates us. At this time, when social work students, practitioners, and

*See p. 236 for an English translation.

TABLE 13.1

Framework to Assess Engagement in Global Social Work Learning

	Practice and Field
Elements of global social work	
Personal review of global awareness	interested in other countries and world regions
Knowledge of mutual learning country to country	comparing work philosophy, social role, choices across countries
Understanding of cultural competence and respectful language	proactive in exploring culture, aware of own bias and prejudice
Analysis of human rights	applying UN documents to practice
Historical analysis	knowing impact of past on current resources, socioeconomic status
Review of values and ethics	identifying implications of different approaches, country codes
Evaluation of local variations	exploring theories in different nations
Synthesis of professional activity	seeking alternatives, links with other places, building with global awareness

educators stand at a crossroads, our ending inspiration comes from a young Indian woman in her poem "The Edge."

As we move into the millennium, the social work profession will be drawn further into global issues of human condition. This means that social work educators, practitioners, and students, through developing their knowledge and applying their social work skills, will address the global aspects of the human condition and actively take part

TOPIC AREAS		
Human Condition and Resulting Behavior	**Social and Economic Policy and Justice**	**Research**
how do I behave in different situations?	view of absolute poverty, experience attitude to Global North and South	process records, personal observation
role of class, caste, gender, health	child labor, wages impact structural readjustment	sustainable development program evaluation
avoid categories; symbolic interaction as focus; respectful learning	being alert to prejudice in language; alternate ways to organize community	ethnomethodology
define, expand, apply to development	identifying basic rights to survive	human rights, injustice
role of colonization and racism	having access to power, equal distribution of wealth	sustainable development indicators
impact of cloning, euthanasia, organ selling	reviewing own and others' access to power	variety of codes
widen definition of "normal"	respecting a variety of consumer rights	global case studies
role of theory in changing human condition	social workers committing to global learning	expanding reciprocal research

in the improvement of the quality of life between interdependent countries. Despite economic categories, the Global North and Global South are not two separate entities, but two parts of the same entity. It seems meaningless to dichotomize the human condition as problems between rich and poor nations. Problems labeled as issues of the South are also seen in the North, the most obvious being the environmental conditions of air and water pollution.

• •

WHY THE GLOBAL PERSPECTIVE IS SO ELUSIVE

We believe that the recognition that a global perspective is elusive is a first step in confronting our geocentrism. During a classroom discussion (Link, 1998), students from countries including Colombia, Somalia, Cambodia, and the United States commented on the paradox that they all value their country of origin and also want to learn about and understand other cultures, but are alienated by the language of some politicians who claim that one country may be freer or better than others—for example, "the best educators in the world," as U.S. President Bill Clinton said of American teachers in his State of the Union address in February 1998. Language that makes claims to superiority enters our minds by stealth and undermines our ability to freely reach out, despite our best intentions. From our review of the literature and in dialogue with colleagues, it seems that in international issues we do tend to put our own experience first, so that the comparative process leads to "us" and "them," nation-to-nation parallels that may seem to preserve identity but militate against the collective notion of "we." The task is to respect identity and unique experience while simultaneously embracing universal bonds.

In collaborating to write this text, it has been apparent to the authors that all of us habitually respond based on our own experiences and thereby are locked into our own definition of history and reality. It thus becomes difficult to entertain different interpretations, let alone look at the relevance or efficacy of these different perspectives. In this text, for example, it has been a constant struggle to write in terms that do not put our country of origin first; only some of the time are we aware of the subtle biases that we carry. This endeavor to become more global has heightened recognition of the way we connect identity to our immediate national universe and citizenship, and, depending on our power and status, before cultural membership.

As we emphasized in Chapter 1, language is power, and it is action packed, not passive. It is critical that we rethink our tendency to categorize nations in value-laden terms that devalue whole groups of people. This is true when we refer to certain groups of people living in human conditions that we label "underdeveloped" or "Third World." Obviously, these classifications are based on certain indicators. It is important to question how these indicators are selected and why certain other indicators are not selected. For example, how is it that we look at gross national product (GNP) without including per capita deaths that result from domestic violence or death by handgun as indicators for classifying the globe (Prothrow-Stith, 1997)? When GNP is used as the indicator, furthermore, it ignores the unpaid contributions of millions of women all over the world who are working in the informal labor market (including the home, village, market, and farming environment), devaluing their labor disproportionately to that of men.

The majority of countries classified as "Third World" were historically colonized, leading to economic stagnation caused by decision making of colonial powers in the interests of their own nations. Ignorance of such an historical context may lead to blaming rather than understanding—that is, holding the people of the Global South completely responsible for their current economic deficits. In a classroom dialogue where students were expressing views relating to poverty in the Global South, a first reaction was to criticize family size, saying that families are poor because they have so many children. On reflection and through readings, such as Trainer's *Developed to Death* (1997) and review of the NASW Violence Prevention video, students came to realize that families are large in the Global South because infants die of preventable diseases at a faster rate than in the North and also because children are a source of income. Similarly, with reference to classification and poverty, "There is the challenge of understanding of poverty, while some researchers are not poor, and of understanding of the South's challenge to the global dispensation, while researchers are mostly from the North. The North-South divide is deep and cannot be dismissed as due to differences in economic acumen" (Kannappan, 1995, p. 874).

Our position is consistent with a Gandhian view of development, which emphasizes that development is not merely economics or technology or social issues, but a moral force that accepts neither the widening disparities between the rich and poor nor overexploitation of natural resources. This is true for nations both in the North and the South. Rich nations, too, need to be conscious of the overexploitation of natural resources and the widening gap between rich and poor within and between nations (Chowdhry, 1989). Recently, mounting scrutiny of social well-being (the European Social Charter, for example, addresses more equal distribution of income and recognition of work in the home) and "welfare reform" (terminology used in the United States and Britain) in several countries of the Global North has come, along with increased awareness of the socially damaging and "spectacular rise in the wealth of the few"—a trend the Global South has long been conscious of and has raised as an issue of distributive justice.

Paradoxically, according to Kannappan (1995), Paul Streeten's appeals for a universalist and integrative system—wherein the world economic order would be open to processed exports and immigration from the nations of the Global South, which would give them a voice in the world councils—is bleak. It is bleak because the economic summits of the G-7 nations (Canada, France, Germany, Japan, Italy, the U.K., and the U.S., with Russia holding observer status) did not make a commitment to this system even when their economies were preeminent. Kannappan (1995) borrows a medical metaphor of a healer, the radical cardiologist Dean Ornish (1990), who works with patients to mobilize inner resources to achieve reversal of heart diseases rather than using invasive procedures, whereby economically successful countries can be healers of others. Kannappan further asserts that economically poor nations need experts who are compassionate, with a sense of reciprocity and a healing touch. Just as the economic discipline is urged to undertake a paradigmatic shift, we as social workers need to view the globe in its entirety.

As an example of shifting identities, in recent years the European Union has been extending the identity of what it means to be "European." During 1996–97, all new passports issued in EU countries were uniform; for example, the blue British passport became a smaller red one stamped "Citizen of Europe." This change came without personal warning (certainly it had been debated long and hard in the media and at the polls) and people adjusted with intriguing differences in acceptance. Among members of an older generation who had waged World War II there was consternation at the loss of British identity; for younger generations, in contrast, there is more optimism about the economic and social benefits of the new citizenship (Rev. Donald and Mrs. Gwendoline Flatt, personal communication, 12 July 1997). This example illustrates the need to assume new identities within larger geopolitical groups and also shows that national identity is less important than cultural identity. As we let go our preoccupation with national sovereignty and engage in greater cooperation and mutual recognition of finite resources and the destructiveness of poverty, we move toward social justice without denying our cultural roots.

Filo watches hungrily as his cousin Paz rushes to get her share.

As another illustration of the challenge in communicating effectively about common bonds across uniqueness, one of the authors was admiring the intricacy and beauty of lace made in Idrija, Slovenia and commented to a Slovenian colleague that it reminded her of the lace she had seen in Cuernavaca, Mexico. The colleague immediately commented that this lace is unique and could not be the same. The author realized that while she had intended to refer to the sharp juxtaposition of acute poverty and maintained loveliness, demonstrated in the ability of women in impoverished circumstances to transcend their deprivations, to cherish and maintain their artistic skills, her intended compliment had sounded as though the comparison was speaking to sameness and therefore undermining the uniqueness of the lace itself. The identity of the women in Idrija is invested in their lace, as it is for the domestic workers in Cuernavaca discussed in Chapter 4; the resilience displayed in their work and art is the common human condition while the details of the art are spectacularly unique.

This example also reminds us that absolute poverty is a misleading policy concept, since it misses the issue of social exclusion from community (Oppenheim & Harker, 1996). In a community experiencing poverty, resilience is maintained where there is a sense of inclusion and self-esteem. However, in a wealthy community that contains but excludes or denigrates people experiencing poverty, the self-esteem of these people is continually attacked. The effect of this onslaught on self-esteem is that such people may be physically better off than their counterparts in more extreme poverty conditions, but their resilience is lower. This is the paradox that leads us to the irony that a fabulously well-resourced country such as the United States contains both the richest and the poorest people of the world.

Scholars recommend that we move beyond identity politics to achieve parity through coalition building (Anner, 1996). Although the literature refers to current national boundary-based issues, we believe this notion of coalition building and coexistence has relevance globally. The shift from nation-to-nation concepts toward a true world view helps to reinforce the need to focus on the human condition in general, as opposed to communication based on the perspective of a specific hemisphere or nation state or interest group. This shift does not mean a diminishing of cultural bonds as a foundation to identity, but it does mean a suspending of the attachment to nation state as defining who we are. Refugees, migrant workers and illegal immigrants tackle these issues early in their journey towards places of safety and co-existence; for others it is a longer road (Gulaati, 1994).

As detailed in Chapter 2, embracing international and global issues in social work has been an uneven path during the 20th century. Although schools of social work were involved in peace initiatives in the 1930s, there was a direct turning inward after the wounds of World War II and, for the United States, after the Vietnam War (Sullivan, 1993). It seems as though the focus on developing theory and a body of research for social work led to an overemphasis on domestic issues and a resulting sense that international elements are just "more" items in a packed curriculum rather than a natural part of what we currently study and practice. As discussed in Chapter 8, becoming more globally aware includes the process of becoming ethnically competent practitioners, with parallel recognition of issues of economics and power imbalance. This discussion of the socioeconomic aspects of our global interdependence was continued in Chapter 9, where we were reminded of the extraordinarily concentrated groupings of power in the economic and banking worlds that have an impact on all of us, every day of our lives. This fact was dramatically played out in the 1998–1999 Southeast Asian economic crisis.

Another feature that reinforces the elusive quality of internationalizing practice and curriculum is the sense that it is exotic or too complex to think about and something that easily can overwhelm us, as discussed in Chapter 12. In Chapter 4, barriers to global reach were discussed in terms of the impact of the media, the different approaches to education, and the difficulty of "operationalizing" or making concepts transferable. Perhaps the slogan "Think globally, act locally" has become too familiar, but the basic principle at issue here is to find ways to live intentionally in a way that urges us to understand our worldwide interdependence. Let us now identify seven steps for colleagues in the process of becoming actively "global" that, without underestimating the barriers, focus on the opportunities.

SEVEN STEPS TO GLOBAL ORIENTATION

Faculty, students, and practice colleagues can follow these steps to become more globally oriented.

Making a Personal Review of Global Awareness

How may we be reflective towards fostering a wider view? An important starting point is reflective questioning, such as: How often do I focus on international issues pertaining to social conditions beyond my country or union of citizenship? On a more personal yet pragmatic view, how often do I stop and look and then think about where my clothes were made, by whom and under what conditions (Nurske & Castello, 1990; UNICEF, 1997)? How often do I read international news or papers from other countries and track my knowledge of changing country boundaries? How well do I know the globe? Where is Surinam, or Sri Lanka or Myanmar? How often do I stop to appreciate that, as Martin Luther King once commented, "before I finish breakfast I have depended on half the world"?

Finally, reflecting Cross's idea that acts of cultural destructiveness in the past have perpetuated forms of communication that promote one group's power over another, when do we think about the language we use to refer to various parts of the world? For example, why is "Third World" an unacceptable term to many? What are the conceptual problems raised by debt restructuring, "welfare reform," and the language of the International Monetary Fund discussed in Chapter 9? If we can acknowledge the power imbalances and destructiveness of ignoring the equal worth of humans across the globe, we can understand and gain insight from the anger of Trainer's work *Developed to Death* (1994), in which he identifies the rampant hunger of millions of the world's children as ethically unacceptable.

Expanding Knowledge of Practice in a Range of Countries

How far do we expect to build information about practice in other countries in order to critically reflect and expand our own practice expertise? Ideally, we would never anticipate innovation without seeking and paying credence to similar experiences elsewhere in our world. As Midgley states in Chapter 11, social workers repeat costly mistakes by not looking more widely to parallel experience in other countries. For example, homelessness and refugee resettlement is a common human need; in Slovenia, refugees from Bosnia are currently housed in the empty former Yugoslavian army barracks. In Minneapolis, the homeless shelter for women and children overflows while the empty barracks at Fort Snelling a few miles south stand empty. Cross refers to cultural blindness—or, for these authors, neutrality—when we remain complacent about our domestic knowledge because we assume that people are the same and we treat people with respect whoever they are.

It is impossible, however, to achieve genuine respect for people unless we recognize the gaps in our domestic knowledge and extend ourselves into new inquiry and understanding of the concepts "universal" and "different." While looking for similarities among humankind globally, we need to be sensitive to the nation state's cultural, sociopolitical, and religious uniqueness. Sensitivity to the various nation states' uniqueness according to historical experience in a regional and global context will help prevent social work educators and practitioners from the Global North being perceived as "infiltrating," imposing and attempting to achieve professional imperialism.

Another crucial element here is the emphasis on reciprocal learning. Rather than exporting "consultants" or anticipating "giving" knowledge, the approach congruent with an interdependent world is one of mutual learning. In a current project in the U.S. Midwest a nursing home has developed a nonmedical "Service House" for seniors based on the Swedish model. Practitioners, including social workers, nurses, and administrators, have visited Sweden and Swedish colleagues have visited St. Paul. While the Midwesterners are interested in how to set up a respectful, home-atmosphere, integrated service unit with minimum intrusion into personal privacy, their Swedish colleagues have been interested to learn about volunteer recruitment and training (Lyngblomsten, 1997).

Understanding "Cultural Competence" and Respect for Language

By "cultural competence," we often refer to our local populations and the need for sensitive practice, but we also look at the recency factor or event—for example, who moved here most recently, who is indigenous, who is migrant, who is pilgrim. For the U.S. scenario, Gould has said: "Do not look at culture as white people versus people of color, established immigrant versus new immigrant, American minorities versus Global South cultures; rather, reach for thinking at a transcultural level rather than a model that merely provides specific strategies for ethnic sensitive practice." This does not mean that ethnic sensitive practice is not useful, but it has its limits in its inability to address structural concerns of access to power and resources to improve human conditions. Thus, in terms of cultural competence, we ask ourselves: How far have we advanced on Cross's continuum? Are we reviewing culturally destructive history, questioning cultural neutrality, recognizing our precompetence when we begin to know other cultures well, moving toward nondefensive and curious competence followed by advanced competence as we scrutinize our activism both personally and in our practice domain. Thus, in this text, we expand Cross's (1986) continuum by seeking the meaning of transcultural communication worldwide.

By "transcultural," we mean the ability to transcend the dictates of our own culture, by going outside our own circle to truly see the multiple points that make up the circle of global life: "For lasting changes to occur in race relations, people belonging to different racial groups must navigate the issues of power, justice, and equality" (Dyson, 1996). Ramanathan and Kondrat (1994) have drawn upon an analogy from symbolic interaction theory of the puzzle in which nine dots, three in each of three rows, are configured into a square. The task is to connect all the dots using only four connecting lines. So the task can be accomplished only by going outside the square configuration. What makes the task a challenge is that one is conditioned to perceive only the square gestalt and not opportunities outside the customary configuration.

Furthermore, as discussed in Chapters 1 and 3, language is constantly underestimated as a factor in power relations. While it is critical to rethink our categorization of nations in value-laden terms such as "underdeveloped" or "Third World" that devalue whole groups of people, it is similarly crucial to be aware of terms that indicate our geocentric approach to the world, such as "East Indian," used in the United States to refer to colleagues from the Indian continent.

Analyzing Global Policy Instruments Built upon Consensus

As discussed in Chapter 3, it is vital in achieving a global perspective for students to include in all their topical studies a review of the relevant global policy instruments, such as the U.N. Declaration of Human Rights, that are based on consensus—for example, for child welfare, to review the Convention on the Rights of the Child; for women's issues, to read the record of the U.N. Beijing Conference; for issues of violence, to read the Declaration of Human Rights. On April 24, 1997 there was a protest at Alliant Technical Systems in Hopkins,

Minnesota, against this company's manufacture of landmines. Many human service practitioners, educators and students participated. Following their arrest at the court hearing in October 1997, the MacDonald sisters, two Catholic nuns, well known as peace veterans, claimed articles from international law for their defense and their right to protest the manufacture of weapons of human destruction. The judge lectured them on their incomplete knowledge and the dangers of referring to international law as a way to avoid local jurisdiction. The irony lies in his indignation that issues of international law should be brought to his doorstep. Since then, the landmine protesters have gained their own reward in the shared recognition of the 1997 Nobel Peace Prize.

Becoming Historically Aware

We know from our history that when we do not think globally, our omission has repercussions on large numbers of people. The social work profession exists because of societal sanctions, but we have viewed sanctions in a parochial way, according to national boundaries. For example, in the images of gang life portrayed by DeCesare (1993), we see marginalized youth becoming involved in gang violence and drugs, lacking opportunities for employment, and crossing borders illegally. The police and human service professionals in the countries concerned are just beginning to cooperate and seek knowledge from one another concerning the needs and ways to work with these young people (DeCesare, 1997).

Historically, it is always difficult to find the way to recognize and atone for pain inflicted by one culture on another. Take, for example, the oppressive history of British colonialization of India: perhaps in small part toward healing, the relationship of Gandhi and Louis Mountbatten is a role model in the obvious mutual respect of these leaders as India gained independence, but it was complicated by the "old" attitudes of superiority held by those in the Global North unwilling to let go of this legacy of power over the South. For the United States, the history of the treatment of Native American people continues to be a wound that is slow to heal in the obvious economic deprivations that tribes still struggle with. Cognitive steps in addressing our ancestral and contemporary part in maintaining power and unequal distribution of resources can play a significant part in addressing human service issues such as those of violence. Violence erupts when there is a scarcity of needed goods and supplies. Jean-Paul Sartre addressed this idea vividly in the 1960s; in the 1990s, the National Association of Social Workers find the same structural connections through the Violence and Development Project funded by USAID. Thus, when there are not enough goods, supplies, or resources for everyone, each individual perceives others as unwanted competition and hence as a danger.

As we move into the millennium, we need to continue to understand and research the nature of extensive violence at personal, collective, and structural levels. At structural levels, the employment of child labor discussed in Chapter 3 is a major demonstration of ways the Global North initiates and legitimizes violence against the Global South. The imposition of structural readjustment on communities that sell their best coffee beans or bananas at modest prices to fulfill export requirements and then go hungry also represents the exploitation of the North and is well documented in Chapter 9. This information is available to social workers and helps us to understand some of the tensions in our current practice with migrant workers or victims of poverty.

In the 21st century, violence will not only occur as domestic violence at the personal level or as isolated instances of bombing by lone terrorists. There is enough technology available all over the globe to create havoc from a distance of thousands of miles with no more than a button and a remote image. Human services commitment to social justice is a key instrument for peace; as discussed throughout this text, a central role for social work can be in furthering human rights. In this context, a Gandhian view of social development that is based on the philosophy of *Sarvodaya*—that is, the welfare of all—through a structural/institutional change initiative is germane. A Gandhian perspective of equality is a critical and crucial element in global efforts to establish a nonviolent and free world society. Pandey, a contemporary student of Gandhi, urges us to understand the significance of addressing a leveling down of the few richest people and nations of the globe and a leveling up of the striving millions (Pandey, 1996).

In Chapter 7, the entry of social work into the Information Age was recognized as a force to be harnessed. The chapter traced steps the profession has taken historically from the early 1900s into the Information Age. Also discussed were the most recent developments in information technology. In this context, we believe it is imperative not to equate technology with knowledge. Nations of the Global South are still struggling with the indigenizing of their social work knowledge base. Equally important is to acknowledge and value all forms of knowledge, whether qualitative or quantitative, technically or humanly transferred (we have in mind the contrast between an e-mail, a web page, and a tract).

The struggles of the Global South in indigenizing their social work knowledge base partly result from the fact that in the past they have been mostly placed in the position of silent consumers whose voices and issues have not been systematically pursued in the advancement of knowledge. Therefore, it is very important, as we develop and disseminate knowledge, that we acknowledge the limited resources available to professional social workers of the Global South; be inclusive in the generation of knowledge (increasing reciprocity between professionals from the North and South); and collaboratively pursue research topics such as distributive justice, viability of energy resources, and universality of issues surrounding technology and ethics. This mutuality is critical in order to use technology proactively and prevent another wave of professional imperialism provoked by uneven access to all technologies, including the Internet.

Reviewing Values and Ethics

Although this text recognizes the relative nature of values, it is important that we consider the universal values of human dignity, worth of the individual, and sanctity of life. Values relating to the accumulation of wealth give us a vivid example for reflection: thus, "the pursuit of excessive wealth and higher consumption risks human happiness and is detrimental to the community at large. Buddhist teachings would dismiss the premise of modern economics on the grounds that more wealth neither increases human wellbeing nor community welfare" (Mendis, 1994). The settlement house leader Jane Addams sounded this theme in the early part of the 20th century when she reminded us that "the good we secure for ourselves is precarious and uncertain . . . until it is secured for all of us and incorporated into our common life" (Addams, 1910). As we enter the 21st century, social workers' commitment to social justice can be one way to live out these teachings.

The paradox for students in the Global North, however, is that they are constantly surrounded by the ubiquitous search for more material goods, even though we now know our global resources are finite. Social workers are confronted more directly as a profession than perhaps other professions to articulate the meaning of poverty and the importance of sharing our scarce resources as part of their ethical and responsible practice. Whereas poverty for many in the United States or United Kingdom may mean life without a television or car, for children in Bangladesh or the sweatshops of Hong Kong poverty is the need for food, clothing, safety, and shelter. This does not mean that there are no hungry and homeless people in the North, just as there are wealthy people in the South, but the general experience of wealth and poverty in these two global regions is profoundly different.

Evaluating Local Variations and Uniqueness

The tension between establishing global or "unitary" principles of social work while respecting indigenization has been a theme throughout this book and for much of the history of internationalizing social work curriculum, as discussed in Chapter 2. Finding a synthesis that asserts universal principles that strengthen the profession while respecting individual or local uniqueness is an ongoing dialogue, as illustrated in the example of the lacemakers in Slovenia and Mexico cited earlier in this chapter. Our goal is not "sameness," which restrains creativity, but "unified purpose," which demonstrates our collective vision and supports courageous action in challenging social and economic injustice. The authors believe that by establishing and supporting global principles of social work we will:

1. Confirm our collective vision and mission for the next millennium.

2. Strengthen the goals of the profession.

3. Be heard and understood more clearly by other professions, politicians, and community groups.

4. Move forward in joint work across borders, to gather our experience in achieving social and economic justice.

5. Role-model ways to simultaneously respect indigenous approaches, which address unique needs, and embrace global cooperation, which improves the universals of the human condition.

Following the practical steps of review just presented, we now return to the discussion of current reality, addressed in terms of geography, migration, economics, environment, international law, and health.

•••••••••••••••••••••••••••••••••••••••

THE GLOBE IS US

In Chapter 11 Midgley refers to nation state changes (illustrations are the new pioneers of people without documentation) as a scenario of the future, and the more we look the more we see these changes happening.

Geography and Citizenship

No map of the globe is current today. Changes in national boundaries and wars disputing territory abound, making geography and citizenship inextricably entwined issues. In the former Yugoslavia, the tensions among Bosnians, Serbians, and Croatians are ever further from resolution. The Hong Kong territories have now returned to China, with resulting tensions for people who had no choice of citizenship, while Taiwan claims its independence but is simultaneously claimed by China. The peace initiatives toward creating a sovereign nation state for the people of Palestine are currently in violent disarray. Also, as discussed earlier in this chapter, the European Union is working toward cooperation above national citizenship in many aspects of daily life, including its proposed common currency, the euro.

Migration

Another pressing issue is the need to accept the concerns of women and children as a common human condition everywhere in the world, because of developmental issues that affect them, such as women in migration, unpaid work, and interpersonal violence. Leela Gulaati (1994) cites vivid statistics of the thousands of women who moved in the last twenty years from southern India to Kuwait to fill the needs of this wealthy oil nation for domestic service. Very similarly to the women of Cuernavaca, Mexico discussed in Chapter 4, domestic workers in Kuwait are underpaid and have few rights in terms of benefits, paid leave, or hours worked (Gulaati, 1994). Further in regard to international migration of migrant workers in the Middle East, in the mid-1980s figures refer to about 3.5 million people on the move; of this, two-thirds were women aged 25–39 years and about half of all women migrant workers were domestic workers or maids. Many of the female workers were sexually exploited and abused (Huguet, 1989).

After the end of the Vietnam War in 1975, about 1 million Southeast Asian refugees have been resettled in the United States, including about 35,000 Amerasians, offspring of U.S. military men and Vietnamese women, and about 50,000 family members (American Council for Nationalities Service, 1993). The Amerasian children, with fathers whose race was different from traditional Vietnamese, were considered outcast and were marginalized in Vietnam. After arriving in the United States, they seemed also to be isolated from the mainstream, and about a fourth of them suffered from reactive depression (Hirayama, Hirayama, & Cetingok, 1992).

Victims of migration and ethnic diversity conflict belong to minority groups who are often despised, sometimes unwanted, and often discriminated against. Given the predicament of this marginalized or socially excluded group of people, social workers need to seek social justice through group work, community organization and social action, and work with governments to alert them regarding these realities, and require them to protect rights and pursue bilateral and multilateral conventions (Cox, 1991).

Economics and Environment

A global perspective immediately provides us with a realization of the domination of "haves" over "have nots" as well as raising questions of social justice as a means of achieving economic well-being, illustrated in Chapter 9. The resources and goods that affect functioning (Hansen's disease breeds in tropical climates where refrigeration is scarce; only 5 percent of the world's population live in areas such as Alaska, Siberia, Alberta, North Dakota, South Dakota, and Minnesota because of the subzero temperatures and needs for energy sources in order to survive) have bearing on existence and our identity as effective humans. This is true at the individual, group, family, community, national, and global level, as demonstrated by the Silent Valley Project (Chapter 4). In this instance, the role of the

Global North as dominator in relation to the Global South is critical in our understanding of various policies currently in place for the convenience of nations in the Global North (see Chapter 9). For example, the nations of the Global South tend to be energy starved, but the Global North in the name of nuclear nonproliferation makes restrictive policies on accessing and using nuclear power. Lack of the needed power/energy has a direct bearing on the industrial sector of the economy of these nations and thus a direct impact on employment opportunities.

An illustration of the impact of economics on an environment with no viable alternative energy sources, is the use of coal as an energy source by people in the Global South. Such use of coal causes the nations of the Global North to criticize its impact on the environment while they fail to acknowledge the pollution caused by industrial and household emissions in the Global North. There is a preponderance of energy and other basic resource shortages in the Global South. For instance, according to the United Nations, 2.4 million people in Africa, Asia, and Latin America will experience cooking fuel shortages by the year 2000. Consequently, the use of solar cookers is becoming popular, and the governments of India and China have been promoting solar cookers for over 12 years. More than 500,000 cookers have been manufactured by one company, Suurya Jyothi Devices in India; 100,000 of these cookers are in use in China. While the numbers of solar cookers in use is much smaller in Africa and Latin America, the idea is catching on. The popularity of solar cookers is increasing as people recognize the need for fuel conservation, maintenance of air quality, and sustainable development (*WIN News,* 1995).

A related issue is access to nuclear technology. Although some nations of the Global South have developed nuclear technology for power generation, a significant number do not have access. While we do not advocate the proliferation of nuclear technology, the need for a steady supply of power is critical. For instance, India, a nation in the South, despite being the ninth most highly industrialized country in the world, still experiences power shortages. The power shortage impacts both industrial output and residential consumption, with economic consequences. As stated earlier, the nations of the South are experimenting with alternative sources of energy, including solar energy. Because these energy sources are not fully developed, it may be unethical to insist that these nations delay their active participation in the industrial sector of the global economy because of these power shortages.

Thus, oppressed people worldwide struggle to meet basic needs for food, clothing, and shelter and for emotional and economic security; that is, they struggle to transact with their environment. According to Rappaport and colleagues (1975) people experience educational, political, and economic exclusion because of their demographic characteristics, not their individual characteristics. Paradoxically, in the context of the Ladahk region in northwestern India, Norberg-Hodge asserts: "When one-third of the world's population consumes two thirds of the world's resources and then exhorts others to do as they, it is little short of a hoax. Development, it turns out, is all too often a euphemism for exploitation, another form of colonialism" (1992). On the other hand, V.K. Rao brings the insights of Gandhi to bear today: "If I could produce all my country's wants by means of 30,000 people instead of 30 million, I should not mind it provided that the 30 million are not rendered idle and unemployed" (1982). Gandhi emphasized bottom-up planning to address the realities of development. To Gandhi, development planning meant focusing on the poorest of the poor. In Gandhi's thinking, development success did not lie in the growth of the gross national product, but in the removal of poverty and inequality, and the productive use of manpower

TABLE 13.2   *How They Compare: Percent Immunization in the U.S. and the "Developing World," 1992*[a]

Developing Nations		United States (by city)	
Poland	96	Boston	58
China	94	Washington, D.C.	45
Honduras	92	New York	43
Malaysia	90	Los Angeles	34
Kazakhstan	88	Detroit	28
Tanzania	87	Houston	11

[a]Children under two fully immunized against TB, DPT, polio, and measles.

Source: Alliance for a Global Community: Inter Action, 1717 Massachusetts Ave. NW, Suite 801, Washington, D.C. 20036.

(Chowdhry, 1989). He was ahead of his time in identifying for us the concept of "sustainable human development" now connecting social with economic change and part of the United Nations' *Human Development Report* (1994).

International Law

The United Nations Declaration of the Rights of the Child, discussed both in this chapter and in Chapter 3, is a key example of the significant dialogue and attention to children's rights that result from intentional international policy instruments. The student lobby to gather signatures to persuade the U.S. President to sign the declaration in 1989 brought to light this country's reasons for not signing—including the reluctance to give up the nation's rights to incarcerate minors with adults, even on death row. The declaration helps us to consolidate our concerns for child labor and gives us the language and collective power to challenge those who perpetuate economic exploitation for corporate gain. The definition of children's rights and human rights also supports our actions as social workers and reminds us that individual countries can be held accountable.

Health

Case Study 3.5 in Chapter 3 addresses the tragic reality that we have health solutions to diseases such as Hansen's disease, measles, or death through dehydration, but not the capacity to distribute our resources effectively enough. Hansen's disease still exists in tropical parts of the world, and measles recently led to the deaths of Hmong babies in the U.S. Midwest because of lack of a health immunization policy and low resistance to the disease among immigrants. We know from the research on oral rehydration that infant death statistics could be drastically reduced if information and resources were spread through impoverished areas. These health issues do not belong to one region of the world alone; urban environments worldwide suffer from unnecessary disease because of unresolved poverty. Statistics on rates of immunization comparing U.S. cities with areas of the world often shock readers (see Table 13.2).

Health is a matter both of economics and social well-being. Old diseases such as TB, malaria, and measles are coming back; new diseases such as cancers and HIV and AIDS are evading solutions. The movement of people means the urgent need to find ways to see health not as a commodity to trade, but as a common human need affecting the well-being of all.

Let us turn to another health related issue. Although it was conducted in the name of advancing medical science, the infamous Tuskegee experiment was a U.S. study that began in 1932, in which 300 African-American men were used as guinea pigs and injected with a live virus to test the long-term effects of untreated syphilis (Dyson, 1996). Despite the fact that this kind of test has been condemned recently by the U.S. government, a study financed by the Center for Disease Control and Prevention currently in operation is investigating a placebo test in contrast to AZT in the treatment of AIDS. Pregnant women in the Ivory Coast are offered an opportunity to participate in the study several minutes after learning that they carry the AIDS virus. Many of these women are from impoverished backgrounds who do not understand what a placebo is or why they have been given this treatment instead of real medicine. Once the test showed that AZT regimen 076 reduced the transmission of the virus sharply from mothers to their baby, tests were ended. It would be impossible, according to experts, to receive approval for a placebo study of AIDS-infected mothers in the Global North, specifically in the United States, but such tests are funded by the North and carried out in Southern nations, such as the Ivory Coast, Thailand, and the Dominican Republic (French, 1997).

Following this stark illustration of ways the course of human lives are in great part determined according to the environment we are born into, we turn now to the framework begun in Chapter 1 to see how innovatively we, as students of the social work profession, can integrate the various dimensions of social work in a global context (see Table 13.1). Traditionally, writers in many parts of the world have looked at social welfare and social work from an institutional (society has a responsibility to set up welfare structures) and residual (offer services to targeted groups rather than all in fear of creating dependence) perspective. In this book we draw on the United Nations' concept and goal of sustainable human development, which can only be built on a definition of social development that considers a combination of social, economic, and cultural conditions that gather and recognize community assets. Our own professional organizations can work against progress if they do not transcend national boundaries in their deliberations with regard to practice implications. For example, the current discussion of a focus on community organization domestically is somehow separate from social development issues and therefore mutually exclusive, rather than an integral part.

It is a paradox, however, that when poverty is a global phenomenon, our initiatives have been confined to national boundaries (Link, 1998). When there are violations of human rights, furthermore, nation states are held accountable by the United Nations, whereas in terms of domestic violence and the deaths of women, children, and men they are not. When deaths that result from domestic violence are not viewed as a consequence of human rights violations, nation states are not held accountable by the United Nations. Additionally, the media in the North does not give equal attention either to isolated yet unfortunate dowry-related deaths of women in a Southern nation like India or to the hapless death of women as a result of domestic violence in the nations of the Global North. There is a dissonance in terms of Global North and Global South; death by handgun has become epidemic in parts of the Global North as discussed by Prothrow-Stith (1997) but this outbreak does not receive the attention it should as a life-and-death, health-related epidemic, in contrast to a 1995 bubonic plague outbreak in a nation in the South. We seek here linkages rather than competition. When we have a global understanding of social work and social development, it will lend itself to recognizing social development activities wherever we are.

Advancing technology has already taken us ahead of ourselves in terms of practice. Social workers are confronted daily with situations which have implications for the future condition of the human race, including the prolonging of life, assisted suicide, contaminated blood, genetic engineering, and surrogate motherhood. How pressing these issues seem to be depends on where the practitioner is placed on the planet. However, it is a false security to assume that situations occurring in economically challenged countries, such as organ and body fluid sale, do not affect people living in economically advantaged countries. Just as El Niño knows no national boundaries, germs, air, water, and the stuff of life are all flowing back and forth across our globe. We are beginning to learn more about interdependence from examples of empowered communities, especially from women's organizations in economically challenged countries, which have organized effectively, for example the cooperatives in Bolivia, the Self Employed Workers' Association in India, and the Bal Rashmi Society in Rajasthan, but this learning, especially in the Global North, is too slow.

Thus, during the 20th century the focus was often residual policy—selective, bandaid service. Now, as we recognize our interdependence and the realities of human development in concert with economic and social development, we may be able to use the paradigm of social development for a more universal approach in the 21st century. What we do in reaching for a global perspective and commitment for actions and what we do not do, in remaining passively geocentric in education and practice, will determine our relative success in reaching professional goals. It is a period of extraordinary opportunity and scientific discovery and simultaneously a period of immense pain and carnage. As social workers we can take leadership in issues of social and economic justice in concert with colleagues worldwide. As our profession is at the crossroads to reclaim its history, and at the edge of challenge and opportunity, we close with the winning poem of 15-year-old Indian student Lavanya Krishnan in the Inter Schools on the spot poetry composition and recitation competition of June 1997:

The Edge

Strolling along the stream of Today,
I came upon the Edge . . .
The Edge of now,
The start of tomorrow,
The golden boat of possibility
Beckoning to follow

What lies beyond . . .
. . . beyond the Edge . . .
What does the future hold?
Alluring but evasive
It dances before me
Unfolding hopes of dreams untold.

I look over . . . over the edge
Is it a steep fall
Or a gentle guiding slope?

Is there a room of darkness
With not a glimpse of hope?
Or . . . is there a room
With rainbow coloured triumphs
Waiting . . . to be explored?

I stand at the Edge of Today
Wondering whether I will
Dare to cross it;
For will I like what
Tomorrow has to show
I stand at the Edge
Waiting . . . to know.*

This text has taken us on a journey towards identifying, discussing and analyzing global principles and resources in the practice of social work in a global era. We believe this perspective helps us to reclaim the history of the profession and embrace, now and in the future, the variety of ways to enhance human experience and implement social justice.

Oh, May the Supreme protect us
May the Supreme cause to enjoy
May we exert together.
May our studies be thorough and faithful
May we never quarrel with each other
Peace Peace Peace.

*Quoted with permission: Lavanya Krishnan, 1997.

References

Accident Facts. (1996) Itasca, IL: National Safety Council.

Adams, P., & K. Nelson. (1992) *Reinventing Human Services: Community and Family-Centered Practice.* Hawthorne, NY: Aldine de Gruyter–Bloom.

Addams, J. (1910) *Twenty Years at Hull House.* Chicago.

Agarwal, A. & S. Narain (Eds.). (1985) *The State of India's Environment 1984–1985: The Second Citizen's Report.* New Delhi: Centre for Science and Environment.

Agostinelli, M. (1979) *The United Nations Declaration on the Rights of the Child: On Wings of Love.* New York: Collins.

Almanzor, A. (1967) "The Profession of Social Work in the Philippines." In Council on Social Work Education, *An Intercultural Exploration: Universals and Differentials in Social Work Values, Fictions and Practice,* pp. 123–137. New York: Council on Social Work Education.

American Council for Nationalities Service. (1993) *Refugee Reports.* Brentwood, TN: A News Service of the U.S. Committee for Refugees.

American Council for Nationalities Service. (1993) *Refugee Reports.* Brentwood, TN: Author.

Anner, J. (1996) *Beyond Identity Politics: Emerging Social Justice Movements in Communities of Color.* Boston: South End Press.

Anon. (1981) *Flora and Fauna of Silent Valley, Attappadi and Sabarigiri Forests.* Report of the Study Team appointed by the Government of Kerala. Trivandrum: Kerala State Electricity Board.

Anon. (1982) Ecological aspects of the Silent Valley. Report of the Joint Committee. New Delhi: Department of the Environment, Government of India.

Antal, A. B., M. Dierkes, & H. N. Weiler. (1987) "Cross-National Policy Research: Traditions, Achievements and Challenges." In M. Dierkes, H. N. Weiler, & A. B. Antal (eds.), *Comparative Policy Research: Learning from Experience,* pp. 13–30. Brookfield, VT: Gower Publishing Company.

Asamoah, Y., L. M. Healy, & N. Mayadas. (1997) "Ending the International-Domestic Dichotomy: New Approaches to a Global Curriculum for the Millennium." *Journal of Social Work Education* 33(2): 389–401.

Ashby, M., Gilchrist, L., & A. Miramontez. (1987) "Group Treatment for Sexually Abused American Indian Adolescents." *Social Work with Groups* 1(10): 21–32.

Athanasiou, T. (1996) *Divided Planet: The Ecology of Rich and Poor.* Boston: Little, Brown.

Axford, B. (1995) *The Global System: Economics, Politics and Culture.* Cambridge: Polity Press.

Balakrishnan, M. (1984) "The Larger Mammals and Their Endangered Habitats in the Silent Valley Forests of South India." *Biological Conservation* 29: 277–286.

Balgopal, P. R. (1995) "Asian Americans Overviews." In R. Edwards (ed.), *Encyclopedia of Social Work,* 19th ed. Washington, DC: National Association of Social Workers Press.

Balgopal, P. R. (1995) "Asian Indians." In R. Edwards (ed.), *Encyclopedia of Social Work,* 19th ed. Washington, DC: National Association of Social Workers Press.

Bali, S. (1997) "Migration and Refugees." In B. White, R. Little, and M. Smith (eds.), *Issues in World Politics.* London: Macmillan.

Barnet, R. J., & J. Cavanagh. (1994) *Global Dreams: Imperial Corporations and the New World Order.* New York: Touchstone.

Barnet, R. J., & R. E. Muller. (1974) *Global Reach: The Power of the Multinational Corporations.* New York: Simon & Schuster.

Barr, H. (1990) In *Europe,* vol. 1, *Social Work Education.* London: Central Council for Education and Training in Social Work.

Barry, T. (1995) *Zapata's Revenge: Free Trade and the Farm Crisis in Mexico.* Boston: South End Press.

Basha, S. (1987) "Studies on the Ecology of Evergreen Forests of Kerala with Special Reference to Silent Valley and Attappady (South India)." Ph.D. thesis, University of Kerala, Trivandrum.

Bass, E., & L. Davis. (1988) *The Courage to Heal.* New York: Harper & Row.

Becerra, R. M. (1997). "Can Valid Research on Ethnic Minority Populations Only Be Conducted By Researchers from the Same Ethnic Group?" In D. de Anda (ed.), *Controversial Issues in Multiculturalism,* pp. 110–118. Boston: Allyn & Bacon.

Becker, G. (1964) *Human Capital: A Theoretical and Empirical Analysis with Special Reference to Education.* New York: Columbia University Press.

Bédoui, M., & R. Gouia. (1995) "Patterns and Processes of Social Exclusion in Tunisia." In G. Rodgers, C. Gore, & J. B. Figueiredo. *Social Exclusion: Rhetoric, Reality, Responses.* Geneva: International Institute for Labor Studies, International Labor Organization (ILO) Publications.

Beliappa, J. (1991) *Illness or Distress: Alternative Models of Mental Health.* London: Confederation of Indian Organizations (UK).

Bell, D. (1973) *The Coming of Post-Industrial Society.* New York: Basic Books.

Bello, W. (1994) *Dark Victory: The United States, Structural Adjustment and Global Poverty.* Oakland, CA: Food First.

Beverly, C. (1989) "Treatment Issues for Black Alcoholic Clients." *Social Case Work: The Journal of Contemporary Social Work,* 70(6): 370–377.

Bibus, A. A. (1995) "Reflections on Social Work from Cuernavaca, Mexico." *International Social Work* 38(3): 243–252.

Bibus, A. A. (1997) "Connecting the Classroom to Clients: Involving a Group of Service Users in Teaching an Introductory Social Work Course." *Journal of Baccalaureate Social Work* 2(2): 71–86.

Bibus, A. A., & R. Link. "In Partnership with Families: A Global View." National Family Based Services Conference Proceedings, November 1997.

Billingsley, A. (1993) *Climbing Jacob's Ladder.* New York: Simon & Schuster.

Billups, J. O. (1994) "The Social Development Model as an Organizing Framework for Social Work Practice." In R. G. Meinert, J. T. Pardeck, & W. P. Sullivan (eds.), *Issues in Social Work: A Critical Analysis.* Westport, CT: Auburn House.

Bloom, B., et al. (1956) *Taxonomy of Educational Objectives: The Classification of Educational Goals.* New York: Longman.

Boisier, S. (1997) *The Elusive Goal of Regional Development: Between the Black Box and Political Agenda.* Santiago, Chile: Latin American and Caribbean Institute for Economic and Social Planning.

Bonilla, C. S. (1993) "Historia del trabajo social en México." Unpublished dissertation, Universidad National Autonóma de México, Mexico City.

Bose, A. B. (1987) "Development of Social Welfare Services." In *Encyclopaedia of Social Work in India,* 2nd ed. New Delhi: Government of India, Ministry of Welfare.

Bose, A. B. (1992) "Social Work in India: Developmental Roles for a Helping Profession." In M. C. Hokenstad, S. K. Khinduka, & J. Midgley (eds.), *Profiles in International Social Work,* pp. 71–84. Washington, DC: National Association of Social Workers.

Boushel, M., & M. Farley. (1992) "Towards Empowerment in Child Protection." *Children and Society* 6(1): 38–50.

Boutros-Ghali, B. (1995) *An Agenda for Development, 1995.* New York: United Nations Public Information Office.

Braidotti, R., E. Charkiewicz, S. Hausler, & S. Wieringa. (1994) *Women, the Environment and Sustainable Development.* London: Zed.

Braun, D. (1994) *The Rich Get Richer: The Rise of Income Inequality in the United States and the World*. Chicago: Nelson-Hall.

Brecher, J., J. B. Childs, & J. Cutler (eds.) (1993) *Global Visions: Beyond the New World Order*. Boston: South End Press.

Brecher, J., & T. Costello. (1995) *Global Village or Global Pillage: Economic Reconstruction from the Bottom Up*. Boston: South End Press.

Bricker-Jenkins, M. (1993) "Building a Strengths Model of Practice in the Public Social Services." In Saleebey, *Strengths Perspective in Social Work Practice*, pp. 122–135. New York: Longman.

Brigham, T. M. (1984) "Social Work Education in Five Developing Countries." In C. Guzetta, A. Katz, & R. English (eds.), *Education for Social Work Practice: Selected International Models*. Vienna: International Association of Schools of Social Work.

British Association of Social Workers. (1996) *The Code of Ethics for Social Work*. Birmingham, UK: BASW.

Brokensha, D., & P. Hodge. (1969) *Community Development: An Interpretation*. San Francisco: Chandler.

Bronfenbrenner, U. (1970) *Two Worlds of Childhood: US and USSR*. New York: Russell Sage.

Brown, K. A., & M. K. Oliveri. (1997). "Do Therapeutic Methods, Techniques and Modalities Need to Be Tailored to Specific Ethnic/Cultural Populations?" In D. de Anda (ed.), *Controversial Issues in Multiculturalism*, pp. 166–180. Boston: Allyn & Bacon.

Brown, L., et al. (1997) *State of the World: A Worldwatch Institute Report: Progress Toward a Sustainable Society*. New York: W. W. Norton.

Brundtland Commission (1987). *Our Common Future*, pp. 43–44. Prepared for the 1992 World Conference on Environment and Development, Rio de Janeiro.

Buckley, T. J. (September 12, 1997) "Studying Abroad: Who Is to Blame When U.S. Students Become Ill or Even Die." *USA Today*, p. 1, 1A.

Bull, D. (1989) "The Social Worker's Advocacy Role: A British Quest for a Canadian Perspective." *Canadian Social Work Review* 6(1): 49–68.

Bull, D. (1997) Orientation lecture to the BICEP (Bristol International Credit Earning Programme). Bristol, UK: University of Bristol.

Burbach, R., O. Nunez, & B. Kagarlitsky (1997). *Globalization and Its Discontents: The Rise of Postmodern Socialisms*. Chicago: Pluto Press.

Burgest, D. (1973) "Racism in Everyday Speech and Social Work Jargon." *Social Work* 18 (July 20–26).

Burns, J. E. (1997) "In a Statement, Afghan Foe Reload." (August 24, 1997) *New York Times*, international section, p. 10.

Butterfield, W. H., & D. Schoech. (1997) "The Internet: Accessing the World of Information." In Richard Edwards (ed.), *Social Work*, supplement to the 19th ed, pp. 151–168. Washington, DC: National Association of Social Workers.

Cacinovic Vogrincic, G. (1997) *Constructionist Concepts in Social Work Education: A Framework for Professional Ethics*. Ljubljana, Slovenia: University of Ljubljana Plaidoyer.

Cannan, C. (1992) *Changing Families, Changing Welfare*. Hemel Hempstead, UK: Harvester Wheatsheaf.

Cannan, G., R. Coleman, & K. Lyons. (1990) In *Europe*, vol. 2, *Links and Exchanges*. London: Central Council for Education and Training in Social Work.

Cannan, G., L. Berry, & K. Lyons. (1992) *Social Work and Europe*. London: Macmillan.

Capra, Frutjof (1996). *The Web of Life*. New York: Doubleday.

Carter, R. T., & A. Qureshi. (1995) "A Typology of Philosophical Assumptions in Multicultural Counseling and Training." In J. G. Pontevotta, L. A. Suzuki, & C. M. Alexander (eds.), *Handbook of Multicultural Counseling*. Thousand Oaks, CA: Sage.

Caufield, C. (1996). *Masters of Illusion: The World Bank and the Poverty Nations*. New York: Henry Holt.

Cavanagh, John (ed.). (1992) *Trading Freedom: How Free Trade Affects Our Lives, Work and Environment*. San Francisco: Institute for Food and Development Policy.

Cetingok, M., & H. Hirayama. (1990) "Foreign Studies in Social Work Schools: Their Characteristics, and Assessment of Programs in the U.S." *International Social Work* 33(3): 243–253.

Chambers, C. A. (1967) *Seedtime of Reform: American Social Service and Social Action: 1918–1933.* Ann Arbor, MI: University of Michigan Press.

Chambers, C. A. (1971) *Paul Kellogg and the Survey.* Minneapolis: University of Minnesota Press.

Chambers, D. E. (1986) *Social Policy and Social Programs: A Method for the Practical Public Policy Analyst.* New York: Macmillan.

Chambers, D. E. (1995) "Economic Analysis." In *Encyclopedia of Social Work,* pp. 824–833. Washington, DC: National Association of Social Workers.

Chambers, I. (1994) *Migrancy Culture Identity.* London: Routledge.

Chestang, L. W. (1972) *Character Development in a Hostile Society.* Occasional Paper 3. Chicago: University of Chicago.

Chilman, C. (1978) *Adolescent Sexuality in Changing American Society: Social and Psychological Perspectives.* Washington, DC: U.S. Department Health Education and Welfare.

Chomsky, Noam (1994). *World Orders Old and New.* New York: Columbia University Press.

Chowdhry, K. (1989) "Poverty, Environment, Development." *Daedalus* 118(1): 141–154.

Churchill, W. (1993). *Struggle for the Land: Indigenous Resistance to Genocide, Ecocide and Expropriation in Contemporary North America.* Monroe, Maine: Common Courage.

Clark, R. (1988) "Social Justice and Issues of Human Rights in the International Context." In D. S. Sanders & J. Fischer, *Visions for the Future: Social Work and the Pacific-Asian Perspective,* pp. 3–10. Honolulu: University of Hawaii Press.

Clarke, T. (1996) *The Emergence of Cooperative Rule and What to Do About It: A Set of Working Instruments for Social Movements.* White Papers No. 1. San Francisco: International Forum on Globalization.

Clarkson, E. (1990) "Teaching Overseas Students in Great Britain." *International Social Work* 33(3): 353–364.

Coates, Joseph F., & Jennifer Jarratt. (1989) *What Futurists Believe.* Bethesda, MD: World Futurist Society.

Coleman, J. (1988) "Social Capital in the Creation of Human Capital." *American Journal of Sociology* 94: 95–120.

Coleman, R. (1996) "Exchanges Between Britain and Overseas Social Work and Social Work Education." In S. Jackson & S. M. Preston-Shoot (eds.), *Educating Social Workers in a Changing Policy Context.* London: Whiting and Birch.

Collier, George. (1994) *Basta! Land and the Zapatista Rebellion in Chiapas.* Oakland, CA: Institute for Food and Development Policy.

Conference on International Social Welfare Manpower. (1965) *The Time Is Now.* Conference proceedings. Washington, DC: U.S. Government Printing Office.

Cooney, R., & H. Michalowski. (1987) *The Power of the People.* Philadelphia: New Society.

Cornely, S. A., & D. D. Bruno. (1997) "Brazil." In N. S. Mayadas, T. D. Watts, & D. Elliott (eds.), *International Handbook on Social Work Theory and Practice.* Westport, CT: Greenwood Press.

Coulton, C. J. (1995) "Riding the Pendulum of the 1990s: Building a Community Context for Social Work Research." *Social Work* 40(4): 437–439.

Council on Social Work Education. (1952) *Curriculum Policy.* New York: Author.

Council on Social Work Education. (1962). *Official Statement of Curriculum Policy for the Master's Degree Program in Graduate Professional Schools of Social Work.* New York: Author.

Council on Social Work Education. (1971) "Curriculum Policy for the Master's Degree Program in Graduate Schools of Social Work." In *Manual of Accrediting Standards for Graduate Professional Schools of Social Work,* pp. 55–60. New York: Author.

Council on Social Work Education. (1984) "Curriculum Policy for the Master's Degree and the Baccalaureate Degree Programs in Social Work Education." In *Handbook of Accreditation Standards and Procedures.* New York: Author.

Council on Social Work Education. (1994) "Curriculum Policy Statement for Master's Degree Programs in Social Work Education." In *Handbook of Accreditation Standards and Procedures*, pp. 134–144. Alexandria, VA: Author.

Council on Social Work Education. (1995) *Standards for Accreditation.* New York: Author.

Council on Social Work Education. (1997) *Social Work Education Reporter.* New York: Author.

Counts, A. (1996) *Give Us Credit.* New York: Random House.

Cowart, M. T., & R. E. Cowart. (1994) "Breaking the Cycle of Violence of Southeast Asian Refugees." *NASSP Bulletin* 77 (December 1993): 41–45.

Cox, D. (1991) *Patterns of Migration in the Asia South Pacific Region.* In S. Swell & A. Kelly (eds.), *Social Problems in the Asia Pacific Region.* Brisbane, Queensland: Boolarong Publications.

Crosby, J., & D. Van Soest. (1997) "Challenges of Violence Worldwide: An Educational Resource." Washington, DC: National Association of Social Workers.

Crosby, J., & D. Van Soest. (1997) *Challenges of Violence Worldwide: A Curriculum Module.* Washington, DC: National Association of Social Workers Press.

Cross, T. (1986) *Cultural Competence Continuum.* Seattle: University of Washington Press.

Crowdog, M. (1991) *Lakota Woman.* New York: Harper Perennial.

Curiel, H. (1991) "Strengthening Family and School Bonds." In M. Sotomayer, *Promoting Hispanic Children's School in Empowering Hispanic Families: A Critical Issue for the 90s.* Milwaukee, WI: Family Service America.

Cwikel, J., & R. Cnaan. (1991) "Ethical Dilemmas in Applying Second-Wave Information Technology to Social Work Practice." *Social Work* 36(2): 114–120.

Danaher, Kevin (ed.). (1994) *Fifty Years Is Enough: The Case Against the World Bank and the International Monetary Fund.* Boston: South End Press.

Danaher, Kevin (ed.). (1996) *Corporations Are Gonna Get Your Mama: Globalization and the Downsizing of the American Dream.* Monroe, ME: Common Courage Press.

Davis, A. (1995) "British Social Work Education and Europe: Views from an Erasmus Network." *Social Work in Europe* 2(1): 50–55.

Davis, L. V., & J. L. Hagan. (1992) "The Problem with Wife Abuse: The Interrelationship of Social Policy and Social Work Practice." *Social Work* 37(1): 15–20.

DeCesare, D. (1997) "Photographic Narrative: Gangs across Borders." Presentation to the Minnesota Chapter of the NASW International Committee, June.

DeCesare, D. (1993) "El Salvador: War, Poverty and Migration: A Photo Essay." *Fellowship* 59, 3 (March).

Desai, A. (1987) "Development of Social Work Education." In *Encyclopaedia of Social Work in India,* New Delhi: Government of India, Ministry of Welfare.

DiNitto, D. M. (1991). *Social Welfare: Politics and Public Policy,* 3rd ed. Englewood Cliffs, NJ: Prentice-Hall.

Doel, M., & S. Shardlow (eds.). (1996) *Social Work in a Changing World.* Ashgate, VT: Arena, Aldershot.

Doling, J., & B. Stafford. (1989) *Home Ownership: The Diversity of Experience.* Aldershot, UK: Gower.

Dubois, W. E. B. (1979) *The Souls of Black Folk.* New York: Dodd, Mead.

Dunn, L. C. (1975) *Race, Science, and Society.* Paris: UNESCO Press. New York: Columbia University Press.

Durst, D. (1982) "The Road to Poverty Is Paved with Good Intentions: Social Interventions and Indigenous Peoples." *International Social Works* 35: 191–202.

Dyson, M. E. (1996) *Race Rules.* Reading, MA: Addison-Wesley.

Earth Island Press (ed). (1993) *The Case Against Free Trade: GATT, NAFTA and the Globalization of Corporate Power.* San Francisco and Berkeley: Earth Island Press and North American Books.

Edelman, M. (1988) *Constructing the Political Obstacle.* Chicago: University of Chicago Press.

Editorial. (1972) *International Social Work* 15(4): 1–3.

Edwards, K. (1997) *Individual Development Accounts: Creative Savings for Families and Communities.* Policy Report, Center for Social Development. St. Louis: Washington University, George Warren Brown School of Social Work.

Eisler, R. (1988) *The Chalice and the Blade.* San Francisco: Harper & Row.

Eisler, R., & D. Loye. (1990) *The Partnership Way: Healing Our Families, Our Communities, and Our World.* New York: HarperCollins.

Ekins, P. (1992) *A New World Order: Grassroots Movements for Global Change.* London: Routledge.

El Nasr, M. (1997). "Egypt." In N. S. Mayadas, T. D. Watts, & D. Elliott (eds.), *International Handbook of Social Work Theory and Practice.* Westport, CT: Greenwood Press.

El-Gawhary, K. (1995) "Delta Blues: The Nile." *New Internationalist* 273 (November): 21.

Elkind, D. (1981) *The Hurried Child.* Addison-Wesley.

Elliott, D. (1993) "Social Work and Social Development: Towards an Integrated Model for Social Work Practice." *International Social Work* 36: 31–36.

Elliott, D., & N. S. Mayadas. (1996) "Social Development and Clinical Practice in Social Work." *Journal of Applied Social Sciences* 21(1): 61–68.

Elliott, D., & R. Walton. (1995) "United Kingdom." In N. S. Mayadas, T. D. Watts, & D. Elliott (eds.), *International Handbook on Social Work Education.* Westport, CT: Greenwood Press.

Else, J. F., & S. Raheim. (1992) "AFDC Clients as Entrepreneurs: Self-Employment Offers an Important Option." *Public Welfare* 50(4): 36–41.

Encyclopedia of Associations. 1996. Detroit, MI: Gale Publishers.

Encyclopedia of Social Work, 19th ed. (1995) Washington, DC: National Association of Social Workers.

Encyclopaedia of Social Work in India, 2nd ed. (1987) New Delhi: Ministry of Welfare, Government of India.

Enloe, C. (1990). *Bananas, Beaches and Bases: Making Feminist Sense of International Politics.* Berkeley: University of California Press.

Envall, E. (1997) "President's Message: International Federation of Social Workers." Oslo, Norway: IFSW, secr.gen@ifsw.org

Estes, Ralph (1996). *Tyranny of the Bottom Line: Why Corporations Make Good People Do Bad Things.* San Francisco: Berrett-Koehler.

Estes, R. J. (1992) *Internationalizing Social Work Education: A Guide to Resources for a New Century.* Philadelphia: University of Pennsylvania School of Social Work.

Estes, R. J. (1993) "Toward Sustainable Development: From Theory to Praxis." *Social Development Issues* 15(3): 1–29.

Estes, R. J. (1995) "Education for Social Development: Curricular Issues and Models." *Social Development Issues* 16(3): 68–90.

Estes, R. J. (1997a) "Social Work, Social Development and Community Welfare Centers in International Perspective." *International Social Work* 40(1): 43–55.

Estes, R. J. (1997b) "The World Social Situation: Social Work's Contribution to International Development." In R. Edwards (ed.), *Encyclopedia of Social Work,* supplement to the 19th ed., pp. 343–359. Washington, DC: National Association of Social Workers.

Estes, R. J. (ed.). (1992) *Internationalizing Social Work Education: A Guide to Resources for a New Century.* Philadelphia: University of Pennsylvania, Social Work.

Faber, E., & A. Mazlish. (1988) *How to Talk So Kids Will Listen and Listen So Kids Will Talk.* New York: Avon Books.

Falk, R. (1997) "Resisting Globalisation from Above Through Globalisation from Below." *New Political Economy* 2(1): 17–24.

Figuera, A., T. Altamirano, & D. Sulmont. (1995) "Social Exclusion and Social Inequality in Peru." In G. Rodgers, C. Gore, & J. B. Figueiredo, *Social Exclusion: Rhetoric, Reality, Responses.* Geneva: International Institute for Labor Studies, International Labor Organization (ILO) Publications.

First International Conference of Social Work. (1929) *Proceedings of the First International Conference of Social Work*, Paris, July 8–13, 1928.

Fisher, R., & H. J. Karger. (1997) *Social Work and Community in a Private World: Getting Out in Public*. White Plains, NY: Longman.

Foucault, M. (1980) *Power/Knowledge*. New York: Pantheon Books.

Francis, Sybil. (1997) Founder, Social Welfare Training Center, University of the West Indies, Kingston, Jamaica. Personal interview conducted April 24.

Fraser, S. (ed.). (1995) *The Bell Curve Wars: Race, Intelligence, and the Future of America*. New York: Basic Books.

Freiberg, S. (1974) "Blind Infants and Their Mothers: An Examination of the Sign System." In M. Lewis & Roseblum, *The Effects of the Infant on Its Caregiver*. New York: John Wiley.

Freire, P. (1989) *Pedagogy of the Oppressed*. New York: Continuum.

French, H. W. (1997) "AIDS research in Africa: Juggling Risks and Hopes." *New York Times*, October 8, 1997, A1, A8.

French, J. R. P., & B. Raven. (1968) "The Bases of Power." In D. Cartwright & A. Zander (eds.), *Group Dynamics: Research and Theory*, 3rd ed., pp. 259–269. New York: Harper & Row.

Freud, S. (1946) *The Ego and the Mechanisms of Defense*. New York: International Universities Press.

Friedlander, Walter A. (1949) "Some International Aspects of Social Work Education." *Social Service Review* 23(2): 204–210.

Gambrill, E. (1990) *Critical Thinking in Clinical Practice*. San Francisco, CA: Jossey-Bass.

Gandhi, M. K. (1940) *An Autobiography: The Story of My Experiments with Truth*. Ahmedabad: Navajivan.

Gangrade, K. D. (1962). "The India Project Seen Through the Eyes of a Delhi Participant." *Social Work Education* 10(2): 7–10.

Gangrade, K. D. (1970) "Western Social Work and the Indian World." *International Social Work* 13(3): 4–12.

Gangrade, K. D. (1987) "Development of Voluntary Action." In *Encyclopaedia of Social Work in India*, 2nd ed. New Delhi: Government of India, Ministry of Welfare.

Gann, L. H., & P. Duignan. (1975) *The Economics of Colonialism*. Cambridge: Cambridge University Press.

Garland, D. R., & D. Escobar. (1988) "Education for Cross Culture Social Work Practice." *Journal of Social Work Education* 24(3): 229–241.

Gaudier, M. (1993) *Poverty, Inequality, Exclusion: New Approaches to Theory and Practice*. In G. Rodgers, C. Gore, & J. B. Figueiredo, *Social Exclusion: Rhetoric, Reality, Responses*. Geneva: International Institute for Labor Studies, International Labor Organization (ILO) Publications.

Gaventa, J. (1980) *Power and Powerlessness: Quiescence and Rebellion in an Appalachian Valley*. Urbana: University of Illinois Press.

Geiss, G. R., & N. Viswanathan (eds.). (1986) *The Human Edge: Information Technology and Helping People*. New York: Haworth Press.

George, S. (1990) *A Fate Worse than Debt: The World Financial Crisis and the Poor*. New York: Grove Weidenfeld.

Germain, C. (1993) *Human Behavior in the Social Environment*. New York: Columbia University Press.

Germain, J. (1995) "To Reduce U.S. Domestic Abuse, Outlaw Spanking, as in Sweden." *Minneapolis Star Tribune*, April 1.

Geschwender, J. A. (1978) *Racial Stratification in America*. Dubuque, IA: W. C. Brown.

Ghorpade, M. Y. (1991) *Developmental Ethos and Experience*. Bangalore, Karnataka: Southern Economist.

Gilbert, N., & H. Specht. (1974) *Dimensions of Social Welfare Policy*, 1st ed. Englewood Cliffs, NJ: Prentice-Hall.

Gilbert, N., & H. Specht. (1986) *Dimensions of Social Welfare Policy,* 2nd ed. Englewood Cliffs, NJ: Prentice-Hall.

Gilbert, N., H. Specht, & P. Terrell. (1993) *Dimensions of Social Welfare Policy,* 3rd ed. Englewood Cliffs, NJ: Prentice-Hall.

Gilgun, J., & S. Gordon. (1985) "Sex Education and the Prevention of Child Sexual Abuse." *Journal of Sex Education and Therapy,* pp. 46–52.

Gill, D. G. (1981) *Unraveling Social Policy.* Boston: Schenkman.

Gill, D. G. (1990) *Unraveling Social Policy: Theory, Analysis, and Political Action towards Social Equity,* rev. 4th ed. Cambridge, MA: Schenkman.

Gilligan, C. (1982) *In a Different Voice.* Cambridge: Harvard University Press.

Ginsberg, N. (1992) *Divisions of Welfare: A Critical Introduction to Comparative Social Policy.* London: Sage.

Glennister, H., & J. Midgley. (1991)*The Radical Right and the Welfare State: An International Assessment.* Hemel Hempstead, UK: Harvester/Wheatsheaf.

Glister, O. (1994) *The Internet Navigator,* 2nd ed. New York: John Wiley.

Gore, C. (1995a) "Markets, Citizenship and Social Exclusion." In G. Rodgers, C. Gore, & J. B. Figueiredo, *Social Exclusion: Rhetoric, Reality, Responses.* Geneva, International Institute for Labor Studies, International Labor Organization (ILO) Publications.

Gore, C. (1995b) "Social Exclusion and Social Change: Insights in the African Literature." In G. Rodgers, C. Gore, & J. B. Figueiredo, *Social Exclusion: Rhetoric, Reality, Responses.* Geneva: International Institute for Labor Studies, International Labor Organization (ILO) Publications.

Gould, K. H. (1995) "The Misconstruing of Multiculturalism: The Stanford Debate and Social Work." *Social Work* 40(2): 198–205.

Grant, Rebecca and Newland, Kathleen (eds.). (1991) *Gender and International Relations.* Bloomington, Indiana: Indiana University Press.

Green, R., & M. White. (1994) *Measuring the Effects of Home Owning: Effects on Children.* Chicago: Center for the Study of the Economy and the State.

Greider, W. (1997). *One World, Ready or Not: The Manic Logic of Global Capitalism.* New York: Simon & Schuster.

Gross, H. (1992) *Wasted Resources, Diminished Lives.* St. Paul: Upper Midwest Women's History Center, Hamline University.

Gudykunst, W. B., & M. R. Hammer (1987) "Strangers and Hosts: An Uncertainty Reduction Based Theory of Intercultural Adaptation." In Y. Y. Kim & W. B. Gudykunst (eds.), *Cross-Cultural Adaptation: Current Approaches.* International and Intercultural Communication Annual, vol. 11. Newbury Park, CA: Sage.

Gulaati, L. (1994) "Women and International Migration." *Social Development Issues* 16(1).

Gutiérrez, L. M., K. A. DeLois, & L. GlenMaye. (1995) "Understanding Empowerment Practice: Building on Practitioner-Based Knowledge." *Families in Society* 76: 534–542.

Guzzetta, C. (1996) Presentation to annual program meeting, Council on Social Work Education, Washington, DC.

Harcourt, W. (ed.) (1994) *Feminist Perspectives on Sustainable Development.* London: Zed.

Hardiman, M., & J. Midgley. (1982) *The Social Dimensions of Development: Social Policy and Planning in the Third World.* Chichester, UK: John Wiley & Sons.

Hare, A. P., H. H. Blumberg, M. F. Davies, & P. Kent. (1996) *Small Groups: An Introduction.* Westport: Praeger.

Harris, R. (1990) "Beyond Rhetoric: A Challenge for International Social Work." *International Social Work* 33(3): 203–212.

Harris, R. (1997) "Internationalizing Social Work: Some Themes and Issues." In N. S. Mayadas, T. P. Watts, & D. Elliott (eds.), *International Handbook of Social Work Theory and Practice.* Westport, CT: Greenwood Press.

Harris, R., & A. Lavan. (1992) "Professional Mobility and the New Europe: The Case of Social Work." *Journal of European Social Policy* 2(1): 1–15.

Hartman, A. (1991) "Words Create Worlds." *Social Work* 36(4): 275–276.

Hashem, M. (1995). "Patterns and Processes of Social Exclusion in the Republic of Yemen." In G. Rodgers, C. Gore, & J. B. Figueiredo, *Social Exclusion: Rhetoric, Reality, Responses.* Geneva: International Institute for Labor Studies, International Labor Organization (ILO) Publications.

Hawkins, M. (1986) *Achieving Educational Excellence for Children at Risk.* Washington, DC: National Association of Social Workers.

Hayes, P. T., & P. Jeudi. (1996) "The European Agenda: Social Work and Social Work Education." In P. Ford & P. Hayes (eds.), *Education for Social Work: Arguments for Optimism.* Ashgate, VT: Avebury, Aldershot.

Healy, L. M. (1985) "The Role of the International Dimension in Graduate Social Work Education in the United States." PhD dissertation, Rutgers University.

Healy, L. M. (1986) "The International Dimension in Social Work Education: Current Efforts, Future Challenges." *International Social Work* 29: 135–147.

Healy, L. M. (1988) "Curriculum Building in International Social Work: Toward Preparing Professionals for the Global Age." *Journal of Social Work Education* 24(3): 221–228.

Healy, L. M. (1990) "International Content in Social Work Educational Programs Worldwide." Unpublished raw data.

Healy, L. M. (1992) *Introducing International Development Content in the Social Work Curriculum.* Washington, DC: National Association of Social Workers.

Healy, L. M. (1994) "The Global-Local Link: International Challenges to Social Work Practice." Inaugural Conference, Center for International Social Work Studies. University of Connecticut School of Social Work, West Hartford.

Healy, L. M. (1995) "Comparative and International Overview." In T. Watts, D. Elliott, & N. S. Mayadas, *International Handbook on Social Work Education.* Westport, CT: Greenwood Press.

Healy, L. M. (1995) "International Social Welfare: Organizations and Activities." In *Encyclopedia of Social Work,* 19th ed., pp. 1499–1510. Washington, DC: National Association of Social Workers.

Healy, L. M. (1997) "Baccalaureate Survey Reveals Growing Internationalization," in *Inter-Ed,* Newsletter of the CSWE International Commission, April.

Healy, L. M., & Y. A. Asamoah (eds.). (1997) *Global Perspectives in Social Work Education: A Collection of Course Outlines on International Aspects of Social Work.* Alexandria, VA: Council on Social Work Education.

Healy, L. M., & Y. Kojima. (1991) "Perspectives on International Content for Social Workers: A Comparison of Schools of Social Work in Japan and the USA." *Journal of the Korean Social Policy Institute* 3:297–313.

Healy, Lynne. (1992) *Introducing International Development Content in the Social Work Curriculum.* Washington, DC: National Association of Social Workers.

Heidenheimer, A. J. (1986) "Comparative Public Policy Studies Examined: An Odyssey in Four Parts." *International Social Science Journal* 108(2): 159–177.

Heidenheimer, A. J., H. Heclo, & C. T. Adams. (1975) *Comparative Public Policy: The Politics of Social Choice in Europe and America.* New York: St. Martin's Press.

Henderson, H. (1994) "Development Imperatives for the Future." In *Development 1994* (4), Special Edition on "A New Ethic for Global Human Security."

Henderson, H. (1995) *Paradigms in Progress: Life Beyond Economics.* San Francisco: Berrett-Koehler.

Henderson, H. (1996). *Building a Win-Win World: Life Beyond Global-Economic Warfare.* San Francisco: Berrett-Koehler.

Hentoff, N. "A Footnote to 'Baby Doe.'" *Atlantic Monthly,* January, 1985.

Her Majesty's Stationery Office. (1995) *Child Protection: Messages from Research.* London: Author.

Hilliard, J. F. (1965) "AID and International Social Welfare Manpower." In *Conference on International Social Welfare Manpower, The Time Is Now,* pp. 13–17. Washington, DC: U.S. Government Printing Office.

Hirayama, K. K., H. Hirayama, & M. Cetignok. (1992) "Mental Health Promotion for Southeast Asian Refugees in the USA." *International Social Work* 36(2): 119–129.

Hirshberg, C., & M. Barasch. (1995) *Remarkable Recovery: What Extraordinary Healings Tell Us about Getting Well and Staying Well.* New York: Riverhead.

Hockenstadt, M. C. (1984) "Curriculum Directions for the 1980's: Implications of the New Curriculum Policy Statement." *Journal of Education for Social Work* 20(1): 15–22.

Hofer, R. (1996) "A Conceptual Model for Studying Social Welfare Policy Comparatively." *Journal of Social Work Education* 32(1): 101–114.

Hoff, M. D., & J. G. McNutt (eds.). (1994) *The Global Environmental Crisis: Implications for Social Welfare and Social Work.* Aldershot, UK: Avebury.

Hokenstad, M. C. (1984) "Teaching Social Policy and Social Work Practice in an International Context." In D. S. Sanders & P. Pedersen (eds.), *Education for International Social Welfare,* pp. 39–55. Honolulu: University of Hawaii Press.

Hokenstad, M. C., S. K. Khinduka, & J. Midgley. (1992) "The World of International Social Work." In M. C. Hokenstad, S. K. Khinduka, & J. Midgley (eds.), *Profiles in International Social Work.* Washington, DC: National Association of Social Workers.

Hokenstad, M. C., S. K. Khinduka, & J. Midgley. (1992) *Profiles in International Social Work.* Washington, DC: National Association of Social Workers.

Hope, A., & S. Timmel. (1984) *Five Responses to Poverty in Training for Transformation.* Harere and Gweru: Mambo Press.

Horncastle, J. & H. Brobeck. (1995) "An International Perspective on Practice for References for Teaching." Foreign Students *Social Work in Europe* 2(3): 48:52.

Horncastle, J. (1994) "Training for International Social Work: Initial Experiences." *International Social Work* 37(4): 309–318.

Horncastle, J. (1996) "The Experience of Social Work Students in Foreign Placement." In P. Ford & P. Hayes (eds.), *Educating for Social Work.* Brookfield, VT: Avebury.

Hoshino, G. (1985) "The 'Fiscal-Occupational-Social,' 'Institutional-Residual,' and 'Universal-Selective' Conceptualizations of Social Welfare: A synthesis." Unpublished ms, University of Minnesota School of Social Work.

Huguet, J. W. (1989) "International Migration from the ESCAP Region." In R. T. Appleyard (ed.), *The Impact of International Migration in Developing Countries.* OECD: Paris.

Iatridis, D. S. (1995) "Policy Practice." In *Encyclopedia of Social Work,* 19th ed., pp. 1855–1866. Washington, DC: National Association of Social Workers.

Ihonvbere, J. O. (1995) "Economic Crisis, Structural Adjustment and Africa's Future." In Gloria Thomas-Meagwali (ed.), *Women Pay the Price: Structural Adjustment in Africa and the Caribbean.* Trenton, NJ: Africa World.

Irish, D., K. Lundquist, & V. Nelsen. (1993) *Ethnic Variations in Dying, Death and Grief: Diversity in Universality.* Washington, DC: Taylor & Francis.

Irvine, E. (1978) "Psychiatric Social Work: Training for Psychiatric Social Work." In E. Younghusband (ed.), *Social Work in Britain 1950–1979,* pp. 176–203. London: Allen & Unwin.

Ivins, M. (August 24, 1997) "Private Prisons: In Texas We Test your Bad Ideas for You." *Star Telegram,* section D: 1.

Jackson, S., & R. Link. (1992) "Comparative Case Studies in International Social Work." A presentation to the Annual Program Meeting of the Council on Social Work Education, Atlanta, GA, USA.

Jackson, S., & M. Preston-Shoot. (1996) *Educating Social Workers in a Changing Policy Context.* London: Whiting & Birch.

Jacobi, J. (1951) *The Psychology of C. G. Jung,* p. 178. New Haven, CT: Yale University Press.

Jansson, B. S. (1994) *Social Policy: From Theory to Practice,* 2nd ed. Pacific Grove, CA: Brooks/Cole.

Jansson, B., & J. Cambra. (1997) *Instructor's Manual to Accompany: The Reluctant Welfare State,* 3rd ed. Pacific Grove, CA: Brooks/Cole.

Jayson, E. A. (1990) "Community Ecology of Birds in Silent Valley." In *Ecological Studies and Long-Term Monitoring of Biological Processes in Silent Valley National Park.* Kerala Forest Research Institute Research Report, pp. 55–107.

Jebb, Eglantyne. (1929) "International Social Service." In *First International Conference of Social Work Proceedings,* pp. 637–655. Paris, July 8–13, 1928.

Jehl, D. (August 14, 1997) "Palestinians Accuse Israel of Raid Plans." *New York Times,* international section, p. 4.

Jiggins, J. (1994) *Changing the Boundaries: Women-Centered Perspectives on Population and the Environment.* Washington, DC: Island Press.

Johnson, A. (1983) *The Black Experience.* Chapel Hill: International Dialogue Press.

Johnson, H. Wayne. (1996) "International Activity in Undergraduate Social Work Education in the United States." *International Social Work* 39(2): 189–199.

Joint Working Group on Development Education. (1984) *A Framework for Development Education in the United States.* New York: InterAction.

Jonas, I. (September 4, 1997) "Kidnapping Case in Court." *Detroit Free Press.*

Jonas, I. (September 4, 1997) "Trial Begins in Assault Case." *Detroit Free Press.*

Jones, C. (1984) *An Introduction to the Study of Public Policy,* 3rd ed. Monterey, CA: Brooks/Cole.

Jones, C. (1992) "Social Work in Great Britain: Surviving the Challenge of Conservative Ideology." In M. C. Hokenstad, S. K. Khinduka, & J. Midgley (eds.), *Profiles in International Social Work,* pp. 43–58. Washington, DC: National Association of Social Workers.

Jones, J. F. (1981) *Hard Times and the Search for a Frugal Utopia: Social Development in Times of Economic Uncertainty.* New York: International Council for Social Welfare.

Jones, J. F. & T. Yogo. (1994) *New Training Design in Local Social Development.* Nagoya, Japan: United Nations Center for Regional Development.

Jones, J. F., & A. Kumssa. (1996) "Distance Training in Local Social Development and the Emerging Technologies." *Social Development Issues* 18(3): 1–13.

Jones, J. F., & R. S. Pandey (eds.). (1981) *Social Development: Conceptual, Methodological and Policy Issues.* New York: Macmillan.

Jones, L. M., P. Clark, K. Messas, & A. Cowhill. (1998) "Building Community Through Staff Development Initiatives." *Technical Services Quarterly* 15(4).

Jordan, B. (1984) *Invitation to Social Work.* Oxford: Blackwell.

Kagle, J. D., & C. D. Cowger. (1984) "Blaming the Client: Implicit Agenda in Practice Research?" *Social Work* 29, 4: 34–351.

Kahn, A. J., & S. B. Kamerman. (1980) *Social Services in International Perspective: The Emergence of the Sixth System.* New Brunswick, NJ: Transaction Books.

Kahn, A. J., & S. B. Kamerman. (1994) *Social Policy and the Under 3's: Six Country Studies.* New York: Columbia University Press.

Kannappan, S. (1995) "The Economics of Development: The Procrustean Bed of Mainstream Economics." *Economic Development and Cultural Change* 43(4): 863–888.

Karger, H. J., & D. Stoesz. (1994) *American Social Welfare Policy: A Pluralist Approach,* 2nd ed. New York: Longman.

Karger, H. J., & D. Stoesz. (1998) *American Social Welfare Policy: A Pluralistic Approach.* White Plains, NY: Longman.

Karl, M. (1995) *Women and Empowerment: Participation & Decision Making.* London: Zed.

Keigher, S. (1997) Personal communication with Anthony Bibus.

Kendall, K. A. (1967a) "Highlights of the New CSWE Program of International Cooperation in Social Work Education." *Social Work Education Reporter* 15(2): 20–23, 37, 42.

Kendall, K. A. (1967b) "Social Service." In *Encyclopedia Britannica*, pp. 769–772.

Kendall, K. A. (1969) *Teaching of Comparative Social Welfare*. New York: Council on Social Work Education.

Kendall, K. A. (1978). "The IASSW 1928–1978: A Journey of Remembrance." In K. Kendall, *Reflections on Social Work Education 1950–1978*. Vienna: International Association of Schools of Social Work.

Kerala Forest Research Institute. (1990) *Ecological Studies and Long-Term Monitoring of Biological Processes in Silent Valley National Park*. Kerala Forest Research Institute Research Report.

Khinduka, S. K. (1971) "Social Work in the Third World." *Social Service Review* 45(1): 62–73.

Kohlberg, L. (1978) "Revisions in the Theory and Practice of Moral Development." *New Directions for Child Development*, vol. 2.

Kojima, Yoko. (1988) "Japan's National Report on International Content in Social Work Curricula." In *Yearbook of Social Work Education*, vol. 9. Japan Association of Schools of Social Work.

Kondrat, M. E., & C. S. Ramanathan. (1992) "International Perspectives and the Local Practitioner: An Exploratory Study of Practitioner Perception of Attitudes Toward Globalization." *Social Development Issues* 18(2): 1–17.

Kondrat, M. E. (1992) "Reclaiming the Practical: Formal and Substantive Rationality in Social Work Practice." *Social Service Review* 66(2): 237–255.

Konopka, G. (1969) "Introduction to Workshop on Teaching of Comparative Social Welfare." In K. Kendall (ed.), *Teaching of Comparative Social Welfare: A Workshop Report*. New York: Council on Social Work Education.

Korten, D. C. (1990) *Getting to the 21st Century: Voluntary Action and the Global Agenda*. West Hartford, CT: Kumarian Press.

Korten, D. C. (1995) *When Corporations Rule the World*. West Hartford: Kumarian Press and Berrett-Koehler.

Krishnamurthy, K. G. (1987) "Development of Social Services." In *Encyclopaedia of Social Work in India*, 2nd ed. New Delhi: Government of India, Ministry of Welfare.

Kroeber, A. L., & C. Kluckholn. (1952) "Culture: A Critical Review of Concepts and Definitions." *Papers of the Peabody Museum of American Archeology and Ethnology* 48.

Kübler-Ross, E. (1974) *Questions and Answers on Death and Dying*. New York: Macmillan.

Kübler-Ross, E. (1985) *Children and Death*. New York: Macmillan.

Kuhn, T. S. (1962) *The Structure of Scientific Revolutions*. Chicago: University of Chicago Press.

Kumssa, A., & C. Gates. (1998) *Transition of Asian, African and European Economies to the Market, and Socioeconomic Dislocations*. New York: UNCRD.

Kunjufu, J. (1984) *Developing Positive Self-Images and Discipline in Black Children*. Chicago: African American Images.

Kupp, M., & G. Wirtow. (1996) "Social Care Markets in England: Early Postreform Experiences." *Social Service Review* 70(3): 355–377.

Law, P. (1995) *The Politics of Power and Empowerment*. Portola Valley, CA: Share.

Leiby, J. (1978) "A History of Social Welfare and Social Work in the United States." New York: Columbia University Press.

Leung, V., B. Lay, A. Ketchell, C. Clark, & R. Harris. (1995) "Hong Kong Social Work Students at the University of Hull." *Social Work Education* 14(3): 44–60.

Lewis, M. B. (1986) "Duty to Warn versus Duty to Maintain Confidentiality: Conflicting Demands on Mental Health Professionals." *Suffolk Law Review* 20(3).

Link, R. (1995) "Parent Participation in British Family Centres." *Community Alternatives International Journal of Family Care* 7 (Spring).

Link, R. (1998) *Syllabus: Exploring Child and Family Services in Slovenia.* Minneapolis, MN: Augsburg College.

Link, R., & A. A. Bibus. (1998) "In Partnership with Families: An International View." Proceedings, 11th National Association Family Based Services Conference, Minneapolis, MN, November 1997.

Livermore, M. (1996) "Social Work, Social Development and Micro-Enterprises: Techniques and Issues for Implementation." *Journal of Applied Social Sciences* 21(1): 37–44.

Livingston, A. (1969) *Social Policy in Developing Countries.* London: Routledge & Kegan Paul.

Lloyd, G. (1982) "Social Development as a Political Philosophy." In D. S. Sanders (ed.), *The Development Perspective in Social Work.* Honolulu: University of Hawaii Press, pp. 43–50.

Loewenberg, F. M., & R. Dolgoff. (1992) *Ethical Decisions for Social Work Practice.* Itasca, IL: Peacock.

Long, J., & S. Caudill. (1992) "Racial Differences in Homeownership and Housing Wealth, 1970–1986." *Economic Inquiry* 30: 83–100.

Lorenz, W. (1986). "Social Work Education in Western Europe: Themes and Opportunities." *Issues in Social Work Education* 6(2): 89–100.

Lorenz, W. (1994) *Social Work in a Changing Europe.* New York: Routledge & Kegan Paul.

Lowe, G. R. (1995) "Social Development." In R. Edwards. (ed.), *Encyclopedia of Social Work,* 19th ed., pp. 2168–2172. Washington, DC: National Association of Social Workers.

Lubove, R. (1965). *The Professional Altruist: The Emergence of Social Work as a Career.* Cambridge, MA: Harvard University Press.

Lundblad, K. S. (1995) "Jane Addams and Social Reform: A Role Model for the 1990s." *Social Work* 40: 661–669.

Lynch, J. (1989) *Multicultural Education in Global Society.* London: Palmer.

Lynch, K. (September 5, 1997) "Kidnap Charge Against Tourist from India May Be Dropped." *Detroit News.*

Lyngblomsten Service House. (1997) *Orientation.* St Paul, MN: Author.

Lyons, K. (1996) "Education for International Social Work." In International Federation of Social Workers and International Association of Schools of Social Work, *Proceedings: Joint World Congress,* pp. 189–191. Hong Kong: Authors, July 24–27.

Maas, H. (1984) *People and Contexts: Social Development from Birth to Old Age.* Englewood Cliffs, NJ: Prentice-Hall.

Maastricht. (1997) *European Institute of Social Studies Catalog.* The Netherlands.

MacEwan, A. (1990) *Debt and Disorder: International Economic Instability & U.S. Imperial Decline.* New York: Monthly Review.

Macht, M. W., & J. B. Ashford. (1991) *Introduction to Social Work and Social Welfare,* 2nd ed. New York: Macmillan.

Macy, H. J., Flax, M., Sommer, V. L., & R. L. Swaine. (1995) *Direct the Baccalaureate Social Work Program.* Jefferson City, MO: Association of Baccalaureate Social Work Program Directors.

Mander, J. (1991) *In the Absence of the Sacred: the Failure of Technology and the Survival of the Indian Nations.* San Francisco: Sierra Club.

Mander, J., & E. Goldsmith (eds.). (1996) *The Case Against the Global Economy: And for a Turn Toward the Local.* San Francisco: Sierra Club.

Manilal, K. S. (1988) *Flora of Silent Valley Tropical Rainforests of India.* Calicut: The Mathrubhumi (MM) Press.

Marger, M. N. (1997) *Race and Ethnic Relations: American and Global Perspectives,* 4th ed. Belmont, CA: Wadsworth.

Marmor, T. R. (1990) *America's Misunderstood Welfare State: Persistent Myths, Enduring Realities.* New York: Basic Books.

Mary, N. L. (1997) "Linking Social Welfare Policy and Global Problems: Lessons Learned from an Advanced Seminar." *Journal of Social Work Education* 33(3): 587–597.

Maslow, A. H. (1968) *Toward a Psychology of Being*. Princeton, NJ: Van Nostrand.

Mathen, G. (1990) "Studies on the Lepidopteran Fauna of Silent Valley." In *Ecological Studies and Long-Term Monitoring of Biological Processes in Silent Valley National Park*. Kerala Forest Research Institute Research Report, pp. 13–53.

Mayadas, N. S. (1997) "Should Social Workers Celebrate Unity or Diversity?" *Journal of Social Work Education* 33(2): 230–234.

Mayadas, N. S., & D. Elliott. (1990) "Refugees: An Introductory Case-Study in International Social Welfare." In D. Elliott, N. S. Mayadas, & T. D. Watts (eds.), *The World of Social Welfare*. Springfield: Charles C Thomas.

Mayadas, N. S., & D. Elliott. (1992) "Integration and Xenophobia: An Inherent Conflict in International Migration." *Journal of Multicultural Social Work* 2(1): 47–62.

Mayadas, N. S., & D. Elliott. (1995) "Developing Professional Identity Through Social Groupwork: A Social Development Model for Education." In M. D. Feit, J. H. Ramey, J. S. Wodarski, & A. R. Mann (eds.), *Capturing the Power of Diversity*. New York: Haworth.

Mayadas, N. S., & D. Elliott. "Lessons from International Social Work: Policies and Practices." In M. Reisch & E. Gambrill (eds.), *Social Work in the 21st Century*. Thousand Oaks, CA: Pine Forge Press.

McCubbin, H., & M. McCubbin. (1988) "Typologies of Resilient Families: Emerging Roles of Social Class and Ethnicity." *Family Relations* (July).

Media Network Guide. (1994) *In Her Own Image*. Video. New York: Media Network.

Meinert, R., & E. Kohn. (1987) "Towards Operationalization of Social Development Concepts." *Social Development Issues* 10(3): 4–18.

Mendis, P. (1994) "Buddhist Economics and Community Development Strategies." *Community Development Journal* 29(3): 195–202.

Meyer, C. H. (1987) "Content and Process in Social Work Practice: A New Look at Old Issues." *Social Work* 36(3): 253–258.

Midgley, J. (1981a) "International Social Work: Learning from the Third World." *International Social Work* 32: 171–182.

Midgley, J. (1981b) *Professional Imperialism: Social Work in the Third World*. London: Heinemann.

Midgley, J. (1984) "Diffusion and the Development of Social Policy." *Journal of Social Policy* 13(2): 167–184.

Midgley, J. (1990) "International Social Work: Learning from the Third World." *Social Work* 35(4): 295–301.

Midgley, J. (1991) "Social Development and Multicultural Social Work." *Multicultural Social Work* 1(1): 85–100.

Midgley, J. (1994) "Defining Social Development: Historical Trends and Conceptual Formulations." *Social Development Issues* 16(3): 3–19.

Midgley, J. (1995a) "International and Comparative Social Welfare." In *Encyclopedia of Social Work*, 19th ed., pp. 1490–1499. Washington, DC: National Association of Social Workers.

Midgley, J. (1995b) *Social Development: The Developmental Perspective in Social Welfare*. Thousand Oaks, CA: Sage Publications.

Midgley, J. (1996) "Social Work and Social Development: Challenge to the Profession." *Journal of Applied Social Sciences* 21(1): 7–14.

Midgley, J. (1997a) "From Social Casework to Social Development: Reflections on an International Intellectual Journey." *Reflections* (Summer).

Midgley, J. (1997b) *Social Welfare in Global Context*. Thousand Oaks, CA: Sage.

Midgley, J. (1997c) "Toward a Developmental Model of Social Policy: Relevance of the Third World Experience." *Journal of Sociology and Social Welfare* 23(1): 59–74.

Midgley, J., & M. Livermore. (in press) "Social Capital and Local Economic Development: Implications for Community Social Work Practice." *Journal of Community Practice*.

Midgley, J., & P. Simbi. (1993) "Promoting a Development Focus in the Community Organization Curriculum: Relevance of the African Experience." *Journal of Social Work Education* 29(3): 269–278.

Mies, M. (1986) *Patriarchy and Accumulation on a World Scale*. London: New Internationalist.

Mies, M., & V. Shiva. (1993) *Ecofeminism*. London: Zed.

Mill, J. S. (1977) "Considerations of Representative Government." *Collected Works of John Stuart Mill*, vol. 19. In J. M. Robson (ed.), *Essays on Politics and Society*, p. 571. Toronto: University of Toronto Press.

Miller, D. (1981) "The Sandwich Generation: Adult Children of the Aging." *Social Work* (September 1981): 419–423.

Miller, E. W., & R. M. Miller. (1996) *United States Immigration: A Reference Handbook*. Santa Barbara, CA: ABC-CLIO Series: Contemporary World Issues.

Miller, F. (1991) *Latin American Women: and the Search for Social Justice*. Hanover, NH: University Press of New England.

Miller, P. (1968) "Social Work Education and the International Education Act." *Social Work Education Reporter* 16(2): 34–37.

Minneapolis Star Tribune. (1995) Editorial, Judge Stanoch. "Stop the Shooting Before It Starts."

Minneapolis Star Tribune. (1996) "UN Agency Finds 250 Million Kids Working Worldwide." November 12, p. A7.

Mohanty, B. (1995) "Seventy-Third Constitutional Amendment and Its Implications: What Is Personal Is Political." Women's Political Participation, Coordination Unit Report–India, World Conference on Women–Beijing.

Momsen, J. (1991) *Women and Development in the Third World*. London: Routledge.

Mori, Kyoko. (1996) "Changes in International Social Welfare Education in Japan." In International Federation of Social Workers and International Association of Schools of Social Work, *Proceedings: Joint World Congress*, pp. 217–219. Hong Kong: Authors, July 24–27.

Moroney, R. M. (1991) *Social Policy and Social Work: Critical Essays on the Welfare State*. New York: Aldine de Gruyter.

Morris, R. (1985) *Social Policy of the American Welfare State: An Introductory to Policy Analysis*, 2nd ed. New York: Longman.

Moss, M. J., & S. Stockman. (1997) *Disability Issues in Social Work Education: Maximizing Potential*. Wrexham, UK.

Mosse, J. C. (1993) *Half the World, Half a Chance: An Introduction to Gender and Development*. Oxford: Oxfam.

Mulenga, D. (1994) "Participatory Research for a Radical Community Development." *Australian Journal of Adult and Community Education* 34(3): 253–261.

Murdock, S. H., & M. Michael. (1996) "Future Demographic Change: The Demand for Social Welfare Services in the Twenty-First Century." In P. R. Raffoul & C. A. McNeece (eds.), *Future Issues for Social Work Practice*, pp. 3–18. Needham Heights, MA: Allyn & Bacon.

Nagpaul, H. (1972) "The Diffusion of American Social Work Education in India." *International Social Work* 15: 3–17.

Nagy, G. & D. Falk. (1996) "Teaching International and Cross-Cultural Social Work." Paper presented at the International Congress of Schools of Social Work, Hong Kong, July.

Nair, P. V. & K. Balasubramanyan. (1984). "Long-Term Environmental and Ecological Impacts of Multipurpose River Valley Projects." *Wildlife Studies in Idukki, Periyar and Silent Valley*. Kerala Forest Research Institute Report.

Nanavatty, M. C. (1997) "India." In N. S. Mayadas, T. D. Watts, & D. Elliott (eds.), *International Handbook of Social Work Theory and Practice*. Westport, CT: Greenwood Press.

National Association of Social Workers, (US). (1997a) Privacy of Ethics Procedures Upheld. *NASW News* 42(2). Washington, DC: National Association of Social Workers.

National Association of Social Workers. (1997b) "Social Workers and the Challenges of Violence Worldwide." Video conference hosted by Charles Kuralt. Washington, DC: National Association of Social Workers.

National Association of Social Workers. (1997c) *Code of Ethics.* Washington, DC: Author.

National Council on Foreign Language and International Studies. (undated). Brochure. [This organization has disbanded and has been replaced by the American Forum for Global Education, New York.]

National Safety Council. (1994) *Accident Facts.* Itasca, IL: Congress Catalogue 91-606 48.

Newhill, C. E., & S. Wexler. (1997) "Client Violence Toward Children and Youth Services Social Workers." *Children and Youth Services Review* 19, 3: 195–212.

Newhill, C. E., & S. Wexler. (1997) "Client Violence Toward Children and Youth Services Social Workers." *Children and Youth Services Review* 19, 3: 195–212.

Norberg-Hodge, H. (1992) "Learning from Ladakh: A Passionate Appeal for 'Counter-Development.'" *Earth Island Journal:* 27–28.

Norton, D. (1992) *The Dual Perspective.* Washington, DC: National Association of Social Workers.

Nurske, D., & K. Castelle. (1990) *Children's Rights: Crisis and Challenge.* New York: Defense for Children International USA.

Ohmae, K. (1995) *The End of the Nation State.* London: HarperCollins.

Oliver, M., & T. Shapiro. (1995) *Black Wealth/White Wealth.* New York: Routledge.

Oppenheim, C., & L. Harker. (1996) *Poverty: The Facts.* London: Child Poverty Action Group.

Orwell, G. (1971) *1984.* London: Penguin.

Oxfam America (1995). *The Impact of Structural Adjustment on Community Life: Undoing Development.* Washington, DC: Oxfam America.

Oyen, E. (1990) *Comparative Methodology: Theory and Practice in International Social Research.* London: Sage.

Page-Adams, D. (1995) "Home Ownership and Marital Violence." Unpublished manuscript.

Page-Adams, D., & M. Sherraden. (1996) "What We Know about Effects of Asset-Holding: Implications for Research on Asset Based, Anti-Poverty Initiatives." Working paper no. 96-1. St. Louis: Washington University, GWB Center for Social Development.

Page-Adams, D., & N. Vosler. (1995) "Effects of Home Ownership on Well-Being Among Blue Collar Workers." Unpublished manuscript.

Paiva, F. J. X. (1977) "A Conception of Social Development." *Social Service Review* 51(2): 327–336.

Pandey, R. (1996) "Gandhian Perspectives on Personal Empowerment." *Social Development Issues* 18(2).

Parcel, T. (1982) "Wealth Accumulation of Black and White Men: The Case of Housing Equity." *Social Problems* 30(2): 199–211.

Parry, J. K., & A. S. Ryan. (1995) *A Cross-Cultural Look at Death, Dying and Religion.* Chicago: Nelson Hall.

Payer, C. (1974) *The Debt Trap: The International Monetary Fund and the Third World.* New York: Monthly Review.

Pecora, P. J., J. K. Whittaker, & A. N. Maluccio. (1992) *The Child Welfare Challenge: Policy, Practice and Research.* New York: Aldine de Gruyter.

Peters, V., & R. Link. (1997) "Expanding Ideas about Social Work Through Experience in Mexico." In K. Van Wormer, *Social Welfare: A World View.* Chicago: Nelson Hall.

Peterson, V., & A. S. Runyan. (1993) *Global Gender Issues.* Boulder: Westview.

Pinderhughes, E. (1989) *Understanding Race, Ethnicity, and Power.* New York: Free Press.

Pipher, M. (1994) *Reviving Ophelia.* New York: Ballantine.

Plant, J. (ed.). (1989) *Healing the Wounds: The Promise of Ecofeminism.* Philadelphia: New Society.

PNG Social Development Newsletter. (1997) University of Papua New Guinea Department of Anthropology and Sociology.

Postman, N. (1992) *Technopoly: The Surrender of Culture to Technology.* New York: Alfred A. Knopf.

Postman, N. (1992) *Technopoly.* New York: Vintage Books.

Powell, W. E. (1988) "The Ties that Bind: Relationships in Transitions." *Social Casework* 11: 556–562.

Prigmore, C. (1968) "Special Report: A Brief Overview of International Activities Sponsored by Schools of Social Work." *Social Work Education Reporter* 16(3): 23, 48.

Prigoff, A. (1995) "Violence, Trauma, Loss and Deprivation: Psychological Wounds and Processes of Healing." Paper presented at the 10th Annual North America–Nicaragua Health Colloquium, Managua.

Prothrow-Stith, D. (1997) *Deadly Consequences.* New York: HarperCollins.

Psacharopoulos, G. (1973) *Returns to Education: An International Comparison.* Amsterdam: Elsevier.

Psacharopoulos, G. (1992) *Returns to Investment in Education: A Global Update.* Washington, DC: World Bank.

Psacharopoulos, G., & M. Woodhall. (1986) *Education for Development: An Analysis of Investment Choices.* New York: Oxford University Press.

Pumphrey, R. E., & M. W. Pumphrey. (1961) *The Heritage of American Social Work: Readings in Its Philosophical and Institutional Development.* New York: Columbia University Press.

Pushkarna, V. (1997) "Alice's Wonderland." *The Week,* pp. 62–71. Kerala, India.

Putnam, R. (1995) "Bowling Alone: America's Declining Social Capital." *Journal of Democracy* 6: 65–78.

Putnam, R. D., with R. Leonardi & R. Y. Nanetti. (1993) *Making Democracy Work: Civic Traditions in Modern Italy.* Princeton: Princeton University Press.

Queiro-Tajalli, I. (1997) "Latin America." In N. S. Mayadas, T. D. Watts, & D. Elliott (eds.), *International Handbook of Social Work Theory and Practice.* Westport, CT: Greenwood Press.

Raffoul, P. R., & C. A. McNeece (eds.). (1996) *Future Issues for Social Work Practice.* Needham Heights, MA: Allyn & Bacon.

Raheim, S. (1995) "Self-Employment Training and Family Development: An Integrated Strategy for Family Empowerment."

Rahmani, A. R. (1980) "Silent Valley: India's Last Tropical Rainforest." *Tigerpaper* 7, 1: 17–19.

Ramachandran, P. (1995) "Women in Decision Making." *What Is Personal Is Political.* Women's Political Participation, Coordination Unit Report–India, World Conference on Women–Beijing.

Ramakrishnan, P. S., & J. S. Singh. (1981) "The Silent Valley Forest Ecosystem and Possible Impact of Proposed Hydroelectric Project." *Ms.*

Ramanathan, C. S. (1991) "Occupational Social Work and Multinational Corporations." *Journal of Sociology and Social Welfare:* 135–142.

Ramanathan, C. S. (1992) "EAP's Response to Personal Stress and Productivity: Challenges for Occupational Social Work." *Social Work* 37(3): 234–239.

Ramanathan, C. S. (1994) "Health and Wellness at the Workplace in Developing Nations: Issues Confronting Occupational Social Work." *Employee Assistance Quarterly* 10(1): 79–90.

Ramanathan, C. S., & M. Kondrat. (1994) "Conceptualizing and Implementing a Social Work Overseas Study in Developing Nations: Politics, Realities, and Strategies." *Social Development Issues* 16(2): 69–75.

Rao, V. K. (1982) *Indian Socialism, Retrospect and Prospect.* New Delhi: Concept.

Rappaport, J., W. Davidson, M. Wilson, & A. Mitchell. (1975) "Alternatives to Blaming the Victim or the Environment: Our Places to Stand Have Not Moved the Earth." *American Psychologist* 30: 525–528.

Rawlins, G. (1997) *Slaves of the Machine: The Quickening of Computer Technology.* Cambridge, MA: MIT Press.

Reamer, F. G. (1986) "The Use of Technology in Social Work: Ethical Dilemmas." *Social Work* 31(6): 469–472.

Reamer, F. G. (1995) *Social Work Values and Ethics.* New York: Columbia University Press.

Red Horse, J. (1980) "Family Structure and Value Orientation in American Indians." *Social Casework* (October 1980): 462–467.

Reich, R. B. (1991). *The Work of Nations: Preparing Ourselves for 21st Century Capitalism.* New York: Knopf.

Reidy, A. (1981) "Welfarists in the Market." *International Social Work* 24(2): 36–46.

Resnick, R. P. (1995) "South America." In T. D. Watts, D. Elliott, & N. S. Mayadas (eds.), *International Handbook on Social Work Education.* Westport, CT: Greenwood Press.

Rich, B. (1994) *Mortgaging the Earth: The World Bank, Environmental Impoverishment and the Crisis of Development.* Boston: Beacon Press.

Richards, L. (1995) *Using the Internet.* Toronto: Self Counsel Press.

Rifkin, J. (1995) *The End of Work.* New York: G. P. Putnam's Sons.

Rodgers, G. (1995) "What Is Special about a 'Social Exclusion' Approach?" In G. Rodgers, C. Gore, & J. B. Figueiredo, *Social Exclusions: Rhetoric, Reality, Responses.* Geneva: International Institute for Labor Studies, International Labor Organization (ILO) Publications.

Rodgers, G., C. Gore, & J. B. Figueiredo. (1995) *Social Exclusion: Rhetoric, Reality, Responses.* Geneva: International Institute for Labor Studies, International Labor Organization (ILO) Publications.

Rogers, C. (1965). *Client-Centered Therapy.* Boston: Houghton-Mifflin.

Rogers, G. (1995) "Practice Teaching Guidelines for Learning Ethnically Sensitive Anti-Discriminating Practice: Canadian Example." *British Journal of Social Work* 25(4): 441–457.

Rogers, G. (1996) "Comparative Approaches to Practice Learning." In M. Doel & S. Shardlow (eds.), *Social Work in a Changing World: An International Perspective on Practice Learning.* Ashgate, VT: Arena, Aldershot.

Rohter, W. (September 4, 1997) "In the Mirror, a Ghostly Replica of Pompeii." *New York Times,* p. E4.

Rooney, R., & A. Bibus. (1996) "Multiple Lenses: Ethnically Sensitive Practice with Involuntary Clients Who Are Having Difficulties with Drugs or Alcohol." *Journal of Multicultural Social Work* (2):59–73.

Rose, R. (1973) "Comparing Public Policy: An Overview." *European Journal of Political Research,* 1: 67–94.

Rossiter, A. (1996) "Finding Meaning for Social Work in Transitional Times: Reflections on Change." In N. Gould & L. Taylor (eds.), *Reflective Learning for Social Work.* Ashgate, VT: Aldershot, Ashgate.

Rothfeder, J. (1992) *Privacy for Sale: How Computerization Has Made Everyone's Private Life an Open Secret.* New York: Simon & Shuster.

Ryan, W. (1976) *Blaming the Victim.* New York: Vintage.

Saleebey, D. (ed.). (1993) *The Strengths Perspective in Social Work Practice.* New York: Longman.

Sanders, D. S. (1977) "Developing a Graduate Social Work Curriculum with an International–Cross-Cultural Perspective." *Journal of Education for Social Work* 13(3): 76–83.

Sanders, D. S. (1980) "Multiculturalism: Implications for Social Work." *International Social Work,* 23, 2: 9–16.

Sanders, D. S. (ed.) (1982) *The Development Perspective in Social Work.* Honolulu: University of Hawaii Press.

Sanders, D. S., & J. Fischer. (1988) *Visions for the Future: Social Work and Pacific-Asian Perspective.* Honolulu: University of Hawaii Press.

Sanders, D. S., & J. K. Matsuoka. (1989) *Peace and Development: An Interdisciplinary Perspective.* Honolulu: University of Hawaii Press.

Sanders, D., & P. Pederson (eds.), *Education for International Social Welfare.* Honolulu: University of Hawaii School of Social Work.

Santer, J. (1995) *Institutional Reform in the European Union.* Brussels: Eur-op News.

Satir, V. (1976) *Making Contact.* Millbrae: Celestial Arts.

Scanlon, E. (1996) *Home Ownership and Its Impacts: Implications for Housing Policy for Low-Income Families.* Working paper no. 96-2. St. Louis: Center for Social Development, George Warren Brown School of Social Work, Washington University.

Schoech, D., & K. K. Smith. (1996) "How to Use the Internet and Electronic Bulletin Boards." In T. Trabin (ed.), *The Computerization of Behavioral Health Care.* San Francisco: Jossey-Bass.

Schultz, T. W. (1981) *Investing in People.* Berkeley, CA: University of California Press.

Seedhouse, D. (1989) *Ethics: The Heart of Health Care.* New York: Liss.

Seidman, E. (1983) *A Handbook of Social Intervention.* Beverly Hills, CA: Sage.

Sen, G., & C. Grown. (1987) *Development, Crises and Alternative Visions: Third World Women's Perspectives.* New York: Monthly Review.

Shaw, A. "Defining the Quality of Life." *Hastings Center Report* 7, 5 (1977): 149.

Shawkey, A. (1972) "Social Work Education in Africa." *International Social Work* 15(1): 8–16.

Sherraden, M. (1991) *Assets and the Poor: A New American Welfare Policy.* New York: M.E. Sharpe.

Shiva, V. (1997) *Biopiracy: The Plunder of Nature and Knowledge.* Boston: South End.

Shiva, V. (ed.). (1994) *Close to Home: Women Reconnect Ecology, Health and Development Worldwide.* Philadelphia: New Society Publishers.

Simon, B. L. (1994) *The Empowerment Tradition in American Social Work.* New York: Columbia University Press.

Sklar, H. (1995) *Chaos or Community? Seeking Solutions, Not Scapegoats, for Bad Economics.* Boston: South End Press.

Smith, A. (1986) "The Burden of Bearing Arms." *Esquire* (July), pp. 55–56.

Smith, M. (1962) *Professional Education for Social Work in Britain: An Historic Account of Social Work Education.* London: Allen and Unwin.

Smuckler, R. H., R. J. Berg, & D. F. Gordon. (1988) *New Challenges New Opportunities.* East Lansing, MI: Center for the Advanced Study of International Development, Michigan State University.

Smyke, P. (1993) *Women & Health.* London: Zed.

Social Services Inspectorate, Dept. of Health. (1995) *The Challenge of Partnership in Child Protection: Practice Guide.* London: HMSO.

Solomon, B. B. (1976) *Black Empowerment.* New York: Columbia University Press.

Sommers, M., & O. M. Ruiz. (1995) *The Many Faces of Mexico.* Minneapolis, MN: Resource Center of the Americas.

Sontheimer, S. (ed.). (1991) *Women and the Environment: A Reader—Crisis and Development in the Third World.* New York: Monthly Review.

Specht, H., & M. E. Courtney. (1994) *Fallen Angels: How Social Work Has Abandoned Its Mission.* New York: Free Press.

Spergel, I. (1982) "The Role of the Social Developer." In D. S. Sanders (ed.), *The Developmental Perspective in Social Work.* Honolulu: University of Hawaii Press.

Srivastava, K. D. (1988) *Commentaries on the Factories Act, 1948.* Delhi: Eastern Book Company.

Stapelvoort, I. (1997) *Hogeshool Maastricht—University of North London.* European Institute of Comparative Social Studies. Maastricht: EICSS Maastricht.

Stein, H. (1957) "An International Perspective in the Social Work Curriculum." Paper presented at the annual meeting of the Council on Social Work Education, Los Angeles, January.

Steiner, J., & T. Briggs. (1984) "Social Work Traditions and Professional Solidarity." In C. Guzzettaa, A. Katz, & R. English, *Education for Social Work Practice: Selected International Models.* Washington, DC: CSWE.

Stoesz, F., & H. J. Karger. (1993) "Deconstructing Welfare: The Reagan Legacy and the Welfare State." *Social Work* 38: 619–628.

Stone, C. (1994) *Focus on Families: Family Centres in Action.* London: MacMillan. *Studies in Child Protection.* (Series). London: HMSO.

Stout, R. (1996) *The World Wide Web Complete Reference.* New York: McGraw-Hill.

Stretch, J., & L. Kreuger. (1992) "New Challenges of Technology for Social Work Administrators." In Lynne Healy (ed.), *Managers' Choices: Compelling Issues in the New Decision Environment.* Washington: National Association of Social Workers.

Streeten, P. (1991) "Global Prospects in an Interdependent World." *World Development* 19(1): 123–133.

Studies in Child Protection. (Series). (1995) London: HMSO.

Sullivan, M. (1993) "Social Work's Legacy of Peace: Echoes from the Early 20th Century." *Social Work* 38: 513–520.

Suppes, M. A., & C. C. Wells. (1996) *The Social Work Experience: An Introduction to the Profession and Its Relationship to Social Welfare Policy.* New York: McGraw-Hill.

Swensen, M. K. (1994). "Guatemalan Families: Cultural Attributes and Biculturation." Unpublished thesis, Augsburg College, Minneapolis, MN.

Swift, R. (1995) "Flood of Protest." *New Internationalist,* (November): 7.

Talbott, S. (1995) *The Future Does Not Compute: Transcending the Machines in Our Midst.* Sebastopol, CA: O'Reilly and Associates.

Tannen, D. (1990) *You Just Don't Understand: Women and Men in Conversation.* New York: William Morrow.

Teare, R. J., & B. W. Sheafor. (1995) *Practice-Sensitive Social Work Education: An Empirical Analysis of Social Work Practice and Practitioners.* Alexandria, VA: Council on Social Work Education.

Teune, H. (1978) "A Logic of Comparative Policy Analysis." In D. F. Ashford (Ed.), *Comparing Public Policies: New Concepts and Methods,* pp. 43–55. Beverly Hills, CA: Sage.

Thomas, M., & J. Pierson (eds.). (1995) *Dictionary of Social Work.* London: Collins Educational.

Thomas, R. W. (1993) *Racial Unity: An Imperative for Social Progress.* Salem, MA: Association for Bahai studies.

Thomas-Meagwali, G. (ed.) (1995) *Women Who Pay the Price: Structural Adjustment in Africa and the Caribbean.* Trenton, New Jersey: Africa World.

Thurow, L. C. (1996) *The Future of Capitalism: How Today's Economic Forces Shape Tomorrow's World.* New York: Penguin Books.

Tibaijuka, A., & F. Kaijage. (1995) "Patterns and Processes of Social Exclusion in Tanzania." In G. Rodgers, C. Gore, & J. B. Figueiredo, *Social Exclusion: Rhetoric, Reality, Responses.* Geneva: International Institute for Labor Studies, International Labor Organization (ILO) Publications.

Titmuss, R. (1968) *Commitment to Welfare.* New York: Pantheon.

Titmuss, R. (1974) *Social Policy: An Introduction.* London: Allen & Unwin.

Titmuss, R. M. (1962) *Income Distribution and Social Change.* Toronto: University of Toronto Press.

Toffler, A. 1970. *Future Shock.* New York: Random House.

Toffler, A., & H. Toffler. (1980) *The Third Wave.* New York: William Morrow.

Torrie, J. (ed.). (1983) *Banking on Poverty: The Global Impact of the IMF & World Bank.* Toronto: Between the Lines.

Tower, C. (1993) *Understanding Child Abuse and Neglect.* Needham Heights, MA: Allyn & Bacon.

Towle, C. (1945) *Common Human Needs.* Washington: National Association of Social Workers.

Townsend, P. (1990). *The Future of the National Health Service.* Bristol University Papers.

Tracy, M. B. (1991) *Social Policies for the Elderly in the Third World.* Westport, CT: Greenwood Press.

Tracy, M. B. (1992) "Cross-National Social Welfare Policy Analysis in the Graduate Curriculum: A Comparative Process Model." *Journal of Social Work Education* 28(3): 341–352.

Trainer, T. (1994) *Developed to Death.* London: Green.

Trask, H.-K. (1993) *From a Native Daughter: Colonialism and Sovereignty in Hawaii.* Monroe, ME: Common Courage Press.

Trask, H.-K. (1995) "Environmental Racism in the Pacific Basin." *Lei o Ka Lanakila* (Spring): 14–18.

Trattner, W. I. (1994) *From Poor Law to Welfare State: A History of Social Welfare in America,* 5th ed. New York: Free Press.

Trickett, E. J., R. J. Watts, & D. Birman. (1994) "Towards an Overarching Framework for Diversity." In E. J. Trickett, R. J. Watts, & D. Birman (eds.), *Human Diversity: Perspectives on People in Context.* San Francisco: Jossey-Bass.

Uba, L. (1994) *Asian Americans: Personality Patterns, Identity, and Mental Health.* New York: Guildford Press.

United Nations. (1964) *Proposals on the Biological Aspects of Race.* Quoted in *Race, Science, and Society,* pp. 355–359.

United Nations. (1964) *Training for Social Work: Fourth International Survey.* New York: Dept. of Social and Economic Affairs. U.N.

United Nations. (1971a) "Social Policy and Planning in National Development." *International Social Development Review* 3: 4–15.

United Nations. (1971b) *Popular Participation in Development.* New York: Author.

United Nations. (1975) *Popular Participation in Decision Making for Development.* New York: Author.

United Nations. (1989) *United Nations Convention on the Rights of the Child.* New York: Author.

United Nations. (1994) *Human Rights and Social Work.* Geneva: Centre for Human Rights.

United Nations. (1996) *The United Nations and the Advancement of Women 1945–1996.* United Nations Blue Books Series, vol. 6, rev. ed. Department of Public Information, 60–73. New York: Author.

United Nations. (1997) *The World Conferences: Developing Priorities for the Twenty-first Century.* U.N. Briefing Papers, Dept. of Public Information. New York: Author.

UNICEF. (1989) *The Rights of the Child:* Video by Sir Richard Attenborough. New York: United States Committee of the U.N. Children's Fund.

UNICEF. (1997) *The State of the World's Children.* New York: Oxford University Press.

UNICEF. (1982) "Popular Participation in Basic Services: Lessons Learned through UNICEF's Experience," *Assignment Children* 59/60(1): 121–132.

United Nations Development Programme. (1994) *Human Development Report 1994.* New York: Oxford University Press.

United Nations Development Programme. (1995) *Human Development Report 1995.* New York: Oxford University Press.

United Nations Development Programme. (1996) *Human Development Report 1996.* New York: Oxford University Press.

United Nations High Commissioner for Refugees. (1990) *Asylum in Europe: Refugees,* vol. 73 (March): 19–42.

United Nations High Commissioner for Refugees. (1995) *The State of the World's Refugees in Search of Solutions.* New York: Oxford University Press.

United Nations High Commissioner for Refugees. (1996) *The Internally Displaced: Refugees,* vol. 1(103).

United Nations Children's Fund. (1997) *The State of the World's Children, 1997.* Oxford: Oxford University Press, UNICEF.

Unnikrishnan, P. N. (1989) *Silent Valley National Park Management Plan 1990.91–99.2000.* Mannarghat: Silent Valley National Park Division.

Van Soest, D. (1992) *Incorporating Peace and Social Justice into the Social Work Curriculum.* Washington, DC: National Association of Social Workers, Office of Peace and International Affairs.

Van Soest, D. (1992) *Incorporating Peace and Social Justice into the Social Work Curriculum: Curriculum Materials and Suggestions for Faculty and Students.* Washington, DC: National Association of Social Workers.

Van Soest, D. (1997) *The Global Crisis of Violence: Common Problems, Universal Causes, Shared Solutions.* Washington, DC: National Association of Social Workers.

Van Soest, D. (1997) *The Global Crisis of Violence: Common Problems, Universal Consequences, Shared Solutions.* Washington, DC: National Association of Social Workers Press.

Van Soest, D., & J. Crosby. (1997) *Challenges of Violence Worldwide: A Curriculum Module.* Washington, DC: National Association of Social Workers Press.

Van Soest, D., & S. Bryant. (1995) "Violence Reconceptualized for Social Work: The Urban Dilemma." *Social Work,* 40, pp. 549–577.

Van Soest, D. (1992) *Incorporating Peace and Social Justice into the Social Work Curriculum: Curriculum Materials and Suggestions for Faculty and Students.* Washington, DC: National Association of Social Workers.

Vickers, J. (1991) *Women and the World Economic Crisis.* London: Zed.

Vijayan, V. S., & M. Balakrishnan. (1977) *Impact of Hydroelectric Project on Wildlife. Report of the First Phase of Study.* Peechi: Kerala Forest Research Institute.

Walker, A., & C. Walker (eds.). (1997) *Britain Divided: The Growth of Social Exclusion in the 1980s and 1990s.* London: Child Poverty Action Group.

Wang, H. (1997) "Regional Development for Developing Countries: The Chinese Experience." In A. Kumssa & J. F. Jones (eds.), *Current Issues in Regional Economic Development and International Cooperation.* Nagoya, Japan.

Ward, K. (ed.). (1990) *Women Workers and Global Restructuring.* Ithaca, NY: Cornell University, School of Industrial and Labor Relations Press.

Watts, R. J. (1994) "Paradigms of Diversity." In Trickett, E. J., Watts, R. J., & Birman, D. (eds.), *Human Diversity.* San Francisco: Jossey-Bass.

Watts, T. D., D. Elliot, & N. S. Mayadas (eds.). (1995) *International Handbook on Social Work Education.* Westport, CT: Greenwood Press.

Wearne, P. (1996) *Return of the Indian: Conquest and Revival in the Americas.* Philadelphia: Temple University Press.

Wee, V., & N. Heyzer. (1995) *Gender, Poverty and Sustainable Development.* Singapore: Engender.

Weston, K. (1991) *Families We Choose, Lesbians, Gays Kinship.* New York: Columbia University Press.

Wetzel, J. W. (1993) *The World of Women: In Pursuit of Human Rights.* London: Macmillan.

Whitaker, W. H., & R. C. Federico. (1997) *Social Welfare in Today's World,* 2nd ed. New York: McGraw-Hill.

Wignaraja, P. (1990) *Women, Poverty and Resources.* New Delhi: Sage.

Williams, R. (1958) *Culture and Society.* London: Chatto and Windus.

Williams, R. (1981) *Culture.* Glasgow: William Collins.

WIN News. (1995) "Solar Cooking Spreads to Fifty Countries." *Women and Development* 21(1): 15.

Wolfe, M. (1995) "Globalization and Social Exclusion: Some Paradoxes." In G. Rodgers, C. Gore, & J. B. Figueiredo, *Social Exclusion: Rhetoric, Reality, Responses.* Geneva: International Institute for Labor Studies, International Labor Organization (ILO) Publications.

World Bank. (1996) *World Development Report 1996: From Plan to Market.* Oxford and New York: Oxford University Press.

World Health Organization. (1982) *Activities of the World Health Organization in Promoting Community Involvement for Health Development.* Geneva: Author.

Yandrick, R. (1986) "Considerations for Implementing U.S.-Based EAPS at Overseas Locations." *The Almacan* 16(10): 20–24.

Yépez, I. (1994) *Review of the French and Belgian Literature on Social Exclusion: A Latin American Perspective.* Discussion paper series No. 71. Geneva, International Institute for Labor Studies.

Young, K., C. Wolkowitz, & R. McCullagh (eds.). (1991) *Of Marriage and the Market: Women's Subordination Internationally and Its Lessons.* London: Routledge.

Zavirsek, D. (1997) *Empowerment in Mental Health Networking.* Slovenia, Ljubljana: University of Ljubljana.

Zolberg, A. R., A. Suhrke, & S. Aguayo. (1989) *Escape from Violence: Conflict and the Refugee Crisis in the Developing World.* New York: Oxford University Press.

Zoological Society of India. (1986) *Records of the Zoological Survey of India* 84, 1–4.

Name Index

Subject Index